Deviant
Globalization

Deviant Globalization

Black Market Economy in the 21st Century

Edited by

**Nils Gilman
Jesse Goldhammer
Steven Weber**

continuum

2011

The Continuum International Publishing Group
80 Maiden Lane   The Tower Building
New York   11 York Road
NY 10038   London SE1 7NX

www.continuumbooks.com

Library of Congress Cataloging-in-Publication Data
Deviant globalization: black market economy in the 21st century / edited by Nils Gilman, Jesse Goldhammer, Steven Weber.
    p. cm.
  Includes bibliographical references and index.
  ISBN-13: 978-1-4411-9312-4 (hbk.: alk. paper)
  ISBN-10: 1-4411-9312-X (hbk.: alk. paper)
  ISBN-13: 978-1-4411-7810-7 (pbk.: alk. paper)
  ISBN-10: 1-4411-7810-4 (pbk.: alk. paper) 1. Black market. I. Gilman, Nils, 1971-
II. Goldhammer, Jesse, 1967- III. Weber, Steve, 1961- IV. Title.
  HF5482.6.D48 2011
  330—dc22   2010033005

ISBN: 978-1-4411-7810-7 (PB)
        978-1-4411-9312-4 (HB)

Typeset by Pindar NZ, Auckland, New Zealand

Contents

"To A, G, and J"

Essay Sources

Ambagtsheer, Frederike. *The Black Market in Human Organs*. Previously unpublished.

Baker, Raymond. "Illicit Money: Can it be Stopped?" Reprinted with permission from *The New York Review of Books*. Copyright © 2009 NYREV, Inc.

Berinato, Scott. "Inside the Global Hacker Service Economy." *CSO Security and Risk*. 1 Sept. 2007. Web. <csoonline.com>. Copyright CXO Media and CSOonline.com, a website for security and risk management; used by permission.

Black, Andrew. "Weapons for Warlords: Arms Trafficking in the Gulf of Aden." Originally published on June 18, 2009 in the Jamestown *Terrorism Monitor*. Volume: 7 Issue: 17.

Clapp, Jennifer. "Seeping Through the Cracks." *SAIS review* 22:1 (2002), 141–155. © 2002. The Johns Hopkins University Press. Reprinted with permission of the Johns Hopkins University Press.

Ellis, Stephen. "West Africa's International Drug Trade." *African Affairs*. (*Lond*) April 2009. 108:171–196. By Permission of Oxford University Press.

Flynn, Sean. "The Sex Trade, Part 1: Pleasure, At Any Price." Originally published in *Gentleman's Quarterly* in August 2005 and online at http://www.gq.com/news-politics/big-issues/200703/phillipine-sex-clubs-global-sex-trade-part-1

Flynn, Sean. "The Sex Trade, Part 2: The Great Sex Migration." Originally published in *Gentleman's Quarterly* in September 2005 and online at http://www.gq.com/news-politics/big-issues/200703/phillipine-sex-clubs-global-sex-trade-part-2

Guevara, Marina Walker, Mabel Reinfeldt, and Marcelo Soares. *Smuggling Made Easy. Landlocked Paraguay Emerges as a Top Producer of Contraband Tobacco*. Publication. Washington, DC: Center for Public Integrity, 2009. http://www.publicintegrity.org/investigations/tobacco/articles/entry/1439

Hari, Johann. "The Dark Side of Dubai." *The Independent* 7 Apr. 2009.

Junger, Sebastian. "Blood Oil." Copyright © 2007 by Sebastian Junger. Reprinted by permission of the Stuart Krichevsky Literary Agency, Inc. This article originally appeared in *Vanity Fair*, February 2007 issue.

Keefe, Patrick Radden. "Snakeheads and Smuggling: The Dynamics of Illegal Chinese Immigration." *World Policy Journal* 26.1 (2009).

Khatchadourian, Raffi. "The Stolen Forests: Inside the Covert War on Illegal Logging" *The New Yorker* 6 Oct. 2008 and online at http://www.newyorker.com/reporting/2008/10/06/081006fa_fact_khatchadourian

Reding, Nick. *Methland: The Death and Life of an American Small Town*. Chapter 3. New York: Bloomsbury, 2009. Reprinted by permission of International Creative Management, Inc. Copyright © 2009, by Nick Reding.

Robb, John. *Brave New War: The Next Stage of Terrorism and the End of Globalization*. Hoboken, N.J.: John Wiley & Sons, 2007. The first three pages of chapter 1 and Pages 142–151. Reproduced with Permission of John Wiley & Sons, Inc.

Seager, Joni. "The Global Sex Trade," from *The State of Women in the World Atlas* by Joni Seager, copyright © 1997, by Joni Seager, text. © 1997 by Myriad Editions, Ltd, maps & graphics. Used by Permission of Viking Penguin, a division of Penguin Group (USA) Inc.

Steinberg, Jonny. *The Illicit Abalone Trade in South Africa*. Rep. no. 105. Pretoria, South Africa: Institute for Security Studies, 2005. http://www.issafrica.org/index.php?link_id=3&slink_id=426&link_type=12&slink_type=12&tmpl_id=3

Sullivan, John P. "Future Conflict: Criminal Insurgencies, Gangs and Intelligence." Originally published on May 31, 2009 in *Small Wars Journal* (2009). http://smallwarsjournal.com/blog/journal.docs-temp/248-sullivan.pdf. Small Wars Foundation.

Acknowledgements

This book began with an undergraduate seminar the three of us taught together at UC Berkeley in 2007, where a wonderfully creative and interdisciplinary group of students convinced us that the topic was not just a curiosity, but in fact theoretically and politically important. Marie Claire Antoine at Continuum first approached us with the idea of turning it into a book specifically designed for undergraduates.

Along the way, we've had plenty of help, notably from Benedicte Gilman and Jennifer Brass, who provided valuable editorial assistance; from Amy Nelson, who assisted with web design; from Andrea Cohen, who helped compile the bibliography and assembled the manuscript; and from Byron Tapley at the University of Texas Center for Space Research, who provided us with the cover image. The ideas themselves have developed though many conversations, both formal and informal, above all with our colleagues at Monitor 360 and Global Business Network. Alberto Vespaziani of the University of Molise, George Roos of the European Futures Conference, and Stewart Brand of the Long Now Foundation deserve thanks for helping us to refine our thoughts via speaking engagements. And the Carnegie Corporation of New York provided funding that helped make possible much of the above.

The meat of the book belongs of course to our authors, who have engaged in heroic and often dangerous investigations to help uncover unpleasant underside of today's global political economy. This book really belongs to them.

Finally, our deepest gratitude goes to Ariel, Gina, and Jennifer, who have put up with way too much deviance over the years.

Introduction

The black market was a way of getting around government controls. It was a way of enabling the free market to work. It was a way of opening up, enabling people.[1]

—*Milton Friedman*

All fixed, fast frozen relations, with their train of ancient and venerable prejudices and opinions, are swept away, all new-formed ones become antiquated before they can ossify. All that is solid melts into air, all that is holy is profaned, and man is at last compelled to face with sober senses his real condition of life.

—*Karl Marx*

This book introduces and examines the phenomenon of *deviant globalization*. The unpleasant underside of transnational integration, deviant globalization describes the cross-border economic networks that produce, move, and consume things as various as narcotics and rare wildlife, looted antiquities and counterfeit goods, dirty money and toxic waste, as well as human beings in search of undocumented work and unorthodox sexual activities. This wide and thriving range of illicit and informal services and industries takes place in the shadows of the formal, licit global economy, and its rapid growth is challenging traditional notions of wealth, development, and power. The goals of this book are, first, to describe the concept of deviant globalization; second, to identify its shared characteristics and structures across a range of seemingly disparate "deviant" activities; and, third, to interpret what deviant globalization means for the future of the global political economy.

Consider the following anecdotes:

Sex Trafficking: In the early 1990s, after the fall of Communism, sex trafficking took root in Albania. Lured by fake engagements, real marriages, and false job offers, thousands of men, women, and children were taken to Greece, Italy, and other countries for sexual exploitation and forced labor. In some cases victims were sold by their own families, who believed that any life on the other end of the circuit was bound to be an improvement over the one in Albania. This deviant globalization industry thrived in Albania because poverty, an absence of trafficking laws, and robust demand in richer European countries created the perfect environment for the business to grow.[2] And it's not just Albanians: According to the United Nations, more than 12 million people work in sexual servitude or forced labor, many of them having been trafficked across borders — a massive industry enabled equally by state complicity and the persistent business-seeking energy of deviant entrepreneurs.

Organ Trade: Deviant entrepreneurs know how to seize a sudden business opportunity. For example, in 2005, an earthquake and subsequent catastrophic tsunami in the eastern Indian Ocean killed a quarter million people and devastated coastal communities. In the immediate aftermath, brokers entered refugee camps in India and Sri Lanka, offering individuals hundreds of dollars to help get their families back on their feet. In exchange, they asked only that the villagers offer to help save the life of a desperately sick person — by donating a kidney to a transplant center in Chennai or Mumbai, where American, Middle Eastern, and Israeli dialysis patients were waiting desperately for an organ transplant.[3]

Terror Financing: The Taliban have taken to heart the mantra of economic diversification. Since it would be bad business to rely solely on opium, whose price can fluctuate,[4] the Taliban have substantially broadened their financing sources: They tax wheat farmers and other small businesses, they run extortion rackets, charge road transit fees, and sponsor fund-raising events throughout the Middle East.[5] It's a strategy of diversified revenue streams that would be familiar to the Chief Financial Officer of any medium-sized international business.

These stories are unsavory, but unexceptional. They describe economic activities that are present everywhere in today's globally interconnected world and that are as direct a byproduct of the contemporary global political economy as the trade in shoes and aircraft parts, the outsourcing of data entry from Greenwich to Bangalore, or the dealing of foreign exchange between the dollar and the yen. What distinguishes these deviant economic transactions is the simple fact that they are an affront to mainstream Western morality.

The first and core argument of this book, sustained across a range of examples drawn from the work of authors with diverse perspectives and methodologies, is that *deviant globalization is inextricably linked to and bound up with mainstream globalization*. Both are market-driven economic activities. Both are enabled by the same globally integrated financial, communication, and transportation systems. Both break down boundaries — political, economic, cultural, social, and environmental — in a dynamic process of creative destruction. And both are present in virtually every globalizing platform: American sex workers advertising on Craigslist may offend some of us, but their exploitation of today's hyperefficient online classified advertising is no different from that of local house painters; a Chinese shipping company delivering a container of illegally harvested Burmese hardwood to a furniture manufacturer in Italy may be engaged in something illicit, but that makes it no less a part of the synchronized global intermodal shipping system; and the burgeoning cell phone networks of Pakistan are just as useful to Afghan heroin wholesalers as they are to members of the Pakistani diaspora sending remittances to their families back home. The infrastructure of the global economy is dual use and value neutral. As these systems become increasingly efficient, interconnected and indispensable, they help not only the formal global economy to grow but also its conjoined, deviant twin.

What makes deviant globalization unique is its ability to satisfy demand for goods and services that are otherwise illegal or unavailable in the formal, licit economy. What creates this market opportunity? We do! When we codify and institutionalize our moral outrage at selling sex by making prostitution illegal, for example, we create a market opportunity for those who would kidnap women and smuggle them into sexual slavery. When we decide that methamphetamine is a danger to public health and prohibit it, we create opportunity for drug dealers who delight in the high profit margins as they fill the illicit orders. When we assemble lists of endangered species in an effort to protect global biodiversity, we create *à la carte* menus for daring global gastronomes and collectors. Every time a community or nation, acting on the basis of their good faith and clear moral values, decides to "just say no," it creates an opportunity for arbitrage.

Deviant globalization is the ultimate arbitrage activity, growing at the intersection of ethical difference and regulatory inefficiency. Wherever there is a fundamental disagreement about what is right as well as a connection to the global market, deviant entrepreneurs are there to meet the unfulfilled demand. In meeting our collective desires, they see the differences in notions of public good, morality, and health as bankable market opportunities. Neoliberalism's wide-open, market-oriented rules may govern globalization, but the game gets played on a morally lumpy field.

That moral unevenness exists for both the global rich and the poor and helps to explain why deviant globalization affects different groups of people in inconsistent and divergent ways. For the global rich, deviant globalization meets a range of otherwise unfulfilled individual demands. Some of these demands, such as replacement organs, represent life and death needs; others, such as illegal drugs, are more complex. For the most part, however, the global rich are not engaged in deviant globalization to increase their wealth. They have ample above-board opportunities to make money.

By contrast, the global poor have a different relationship to deviant globalization. For them, it is both a powerful engine of wealth creation and a symbol of their exclusion and abjection. On the one hand, participating in deviant globalization is often an individual's fastest ticket out of poverty and a way for the entire community to experience economic development. On the other hand, deviant globalization not only often entails harrowing individual suffering, but it can also provide money and power to self-dealing government officials, brutal warlords, and fanatical terrorists.

Mexico illustrates this dynamic well. Meeting Western appetites for illicit drugs has generated vast fortunes south of the American border. This money pays for an army of employees that, by some estimates, numbers upward of half a million people, larger than the entire Mexican oil and gas industry.[6] It pays for the development of rural Mexican towns and villages that, thanks to generous drugs lords, now have everything from running water to computers and broadband Internet access. At the same time, however, the drug money also pays for the daily violence, assassinations, and mayhem that are crippling the Mexican state.[7]

The example of Mexico highlights the second major point of this book, namely that *it would be a grave mistake to view deviant globalization as a mere sideshow* to what "really matters" in the global political economy. There are lots of reasons why some observers want to believe this (and want others to believe it), even though the numbers suggest that this view is wrong.[8] At the end of the day, to make a sober judgment about what really matters requires a comprehensive and honest assessment of the entire globalizing landscape.

To make such an honest assessment requires first putting aside moral outrage. Deviant globalization includes abhorrent activities, to be sure. But when people allow moral repulsion to come first in their thinking, it clouds their ability to understand the complexity and implications of deviant globalization. We get bogged down in insolvable debates about "legitimate" market activities; blinded by the apparent moral deficiencies of those involved in supplying or consuming deviant services; and fixated on the good intentions behind our failed regulations and public policies. Only when we suspend moral judgment can we begin to understand the ways in which moral outrage enables deviant globalization — by creating opportunities for entrepreneurs to profit at the margins of the market where the "normal" norms don't seem to apply.

If these claims about deviant globalization hold up under scrutiny, it will be fair to put forward a third and bolder claim: *Deviant globalization is in the process of changing the landscape and distribution of power in the world economy* in ways nearly as profound as any openly visible political-economic trend or event has done since the end of the Cold War. Nobody disputes that the regulatory reactions to the global financial crisis of 2008–09, the institutional configuration of global economic governance, or the future of climate change negotiations (to name a few obvious candidates) are crucial to our shared political-economic future. We believe deviant globalization should be added to this list. In fact, none of these other big drivers of change make much sense without understanding how deviant globalization connects to, modifies, and influences them.[9]

Just as the recent financial crisis upended cherished views of market efficiency and consequent economic growth, a clear-eyed evaluation of deviant globalization shatters cherished beliefs about what actually drives the global market. It disrupts mainstream views of power, undermines the certainty of claims about what is do-able in economic life, and puts at the forefront of debate a set of unfamiliar competitors for leadership and legitimacy. All of this should cause intellectual and cognitive discomfort. But breaking down old categories is the cost of building new ones that can make better sense of the real conditions of life in the global economy.

The final point of this book, and its central normative claim, is that *we have to abandon the assumption that deviant globalization is a removable cancer* in an otherwise healthy global economy. Many proponents of mainstream globalization are seduced into the mistaken belief that the right mix of policy, regulation, and law enforcement could curtail all of this deviant stuff, letting us get back to our "acceptable" business practices. The truth of the matter is that deviant globalization is a massive, permanent phenomenon that is central to the lives of hundreds of millions of people. On balance, it has improved their material lot more than the mainstream development and philanthropic projects in which Westerners invest hopes, dollars, time, and good intentions.

We will conclude with a discussion of the practical options available for dealing with deviant globalization. We don't believe that engaging the idea of deviant globalization has to mean policy despair. But to understand this point, we need to understand how a large set of seemingly unrelated deviant activities around the world comprise a unified phenomenon propelled by common forces. To drive home this point, we will explore the impact of deviant globalization along three critical dimensions:

1. From a policy perspective, deviant globalization changes the problems of governing a global economy. The formal organizations — both national and transnational — that try to regulate this complex system are at present not prepared to deal systematically with deviant globalization, in large part because their decision makers don't fully recognize how integrated, innovative, and influential deviant entrepreneurs have become.

2. From a welfare perspective, any effort to improve aggregate global welfare, and/or the distributional landscape of the global economy must take into account the consequences of deviant globalization. Like it or not, deviant globalization supplies much needed welfare to a significant slice of the world's population. If well-wishers ignore hide from that fact, they should be prepared for massive unintended consequences, not all of which will on balance be good for the human condition.

3. And, finally, from a moral and ethical perspective, deviant globalization mixes and muddles extant judgments about what is "good," "just," or "fair." Many of those judgments, we believe, have become encrusted in time, shaped by the power structures and belief systems of so-called winners and irrelevant to the daily reality of the so-called losers. A recalibration of these judgments is required of anyone who wishes to intervene effectively in the domain of deviant globalization.

The rest of this introduction features five short sections. First, we examine some mainstream perspectives on what globalization is and means. This sets up a counterpoint to our own definition of deviant globalization, in which we get more specific about the boundaries between them. Next we lay out two conventional lenses on deviant globalization, which effectively become null hypotheses for the rest of the book. We then put forward two alternative lenses, that make up what we believe are more powerful analytics for the cases that follow. We end by describing the plan for the rest of the book.

What is Globalization?

Because it is rare that an economic buzzword survives for more than a single decade, the word *globalization* stands out: Coined in the 1980s, it survived through the 1990s into the 2000s and seems certain to remain a focus of debate and discussion in the coming decade. Yet there is still no consensus on how to define globalization. People argue a great deal about what it means, what caused it, and what its consequences are supposed to be. Sometimes they argue about all three without realizing which agenda and disagreement is on the table. This leads to a lot of confusion.

It is always best to start with simple definitions. We define globalization as the *cross-border integration of value-added economic activity*. This integration happens because the core ingredients of economic activity — goods, services, money, people, and ideas, in no particular order — have become increasingly mobile across space, time, and political boundaries.[10]

It seems obvious today that economic activity will always strain to expand beyond the boundaries of physical and political space, but it wasn't that way for most of human history. It's not just that not much value-added economic activity was taking place, but what value was being created usually stayed close to home — for reasons of technology (it was hard and expensive to move things over mountains and across rivers), reasons of information (if people on the other side of that mountain didn't speak your language, how would you get to know the quality of what they might offer to trade?), and reasons of mind-sets and beliefs (for example, items with religious significance).

Physical mobility, broadly understood, has been increasing for several hundred years, and with that trend economic activity has expanded in scope. That's a reminder that globalization did not begin in 1989 or even in 1889. By some calculations, capital moved across political borders nearly as freely at the end of the nineteenth century as it did at the end of the twentieth. For many countries, trade as a percent of gross domestic product (GDP) only recently surpassed the levels achieved a hundred years ago. And for the most part, people moved across borders *more* freely then than they do today (about a hundred million people left Europe for the New World in the last half of the 1800s).

At important moments during the past hundred years, mobility has experienced dramatic accelerations. In the last sixty years, two stand out. First, the end of the Cold War opened up vast new territories to capitalism, and permitted more complete global economic integration than had ever been achieved before. Indeed, the popularity of the term globalization during the 1990s came in part because it served as effective shorthand to describe the rapid integration of former communist states into the existing US-centric liberal-capitalist global economic order, via versions of the "shock-therapy" privatization programs in the former Communist bloc that put state assets into the hands of private entrepreneurs, precisely so that these assets could gain mobility and tradeability as quickly and as painlessly as possible.[11]

The second key accelerator of globalization in the late twentieth century was information technology. The natural barriers of time and space that used to separate markets collapsed before the relentless march of Moore's Law.[12] In 1930 a telephone call from New York to London cost over $300 per minute (inflation-adjusted) *if* you could get through; today it costs a few cents for a circuit switched call — or it is free if you use Skype, which routes calls over the Internet. Similarly, the cost of shipping goods from southern Chinese factories to consumers in the American Midwest has dropped to a rounding error on the final retail price. A price on a stock market trade that takes place in a NASDAQ computer located in suburban Connecticut travels at literally the speed of light to equity markets all over the world. A simple web application called eBay has taken an iconic localized marketplace (what used to be called a flea market) and made it nearly global. It's not an exaggeration to say that the technological determinants of mobility have never fallen so fast, across so many dimensions, and for so many people on the planet in such a short period of time.

But politics and institutions, norms and rules, move at slower clips. That the late nineteenth century phase of rapid globalization came to a crushing end in a world war and a great depression underscores that integration is anything but inevitable. It took thirty years, another world war, and the emergence of a new liberal global hegemon to put the world back on a path toward economic integration. And it has been anything but a smooth path since. Crises in trade negotiations, capital markets, and immigration policies are the rule, not the exception. Politics is a stubborn business; and it responds not so much to what technology pundits say "must happen," as to the fears, hopes, and prejudices of the people on whose lives that technology acts.

Despite the bumpy road toward global economic integration, despite even the great financial crisis of the 2008–09, a powerful and romantic utopianism continues to hew to globalization. This optimism comes in a variety of flavors: Academic, especially economics and political science departments in wealthy countries; corporate, including the Chief Executive Officers (CEOs) and boards of major multinational corporations in just about every sector; media, which saturate airwaves and fiber optics with reporting on the march of globalism; and government, where even leftist governments in rich countries have con-figured state institutions to embrace the global marketplace. Ironically, some left-leaning governments claim they are better suited than their right-leaning competitors to configure their country for a successful globalization play. Much of this romantic utopianism was concentrated in some popular contemporary analyses that appeared in the 1990s and soon became hackneyed buzzwords: "The End of Geography," "The Death of Distance," "The End of History," "The Network Society," and above all, Tom Friedman's cliché-of-the-decade, "The World is Flat," — all of which painted a world in which the compression of space and time meant that everyone could be everywhere and have everything at once, and mostly "for free" in an unstoppable march toward a benign free market capitalism.[13]

To others, of course, this romantic vision of global economic integration seemed the very opposite of utopia. Although Marxism as a practical politi-cal program did not meaningfully survive after 1989, the vast and growing disparities of wealth both inside and between countries continue to create fundamental political cleavages of the sort that Marx understood. Moreover, as increasingly open markets demand standardization, uniformity, normaliza-tion, and efficiency, the fear remains that capitalism will crush the autonomy of individuals and societies to make decisions and chart their own futures. As long ago as 1944, Karl Polanyi in *The Great Transformation* argued that unfet-tered capitalism inevitably undermines the social and political foundations necessary to sustain markets.[14] More recently, Naomi Klein has contended that free market capitalism feeds on disasters, transforming human misery into corporate-friendly policies and big profits.[15] Today, there is a chorus of voices hostile to globalization, claiming that it will destroy political bargains, devastate the natural environment, displace populations, undermine human health, erode the state's ability to provide safety nets to citizens, and generally wreak havoc with almost everything that matters to human beings other than economic productivity.[16]

From the perspective of this book, however, what is most important is how both the enthusiasts and critics of mainstream globalization have largely ignored the phenomenon of deviant globalization. On the one hand, insofar as the cheerleaders even mention the subterranean world of the deviant, it is generally depicted as a mere annoyance, one that can be addressed via better policing. On the other hand, deviant globalization is also ignored at the dystopic end of the globalization debate: Because mainstream critics of globalization see the crucial issue as exploitation and consider that globalized capital produces it continuously, they are not much interested in the different sorts of exploitation produced by mainstream and deviant globalization, nor much concerned with the political implications of the different sorts of capitalists that are being empowered.

There is one thing on which both the enthusiasts and critics of mainstream globalization agree: Globalization enhances the power of nonstate actors, above all corporations. Enthusiasts celebrate this outcome because it means that profit-seeking corporations can replace inefficient state enterprises, bringing Western levels of productivity and prosperity to the developing world. Critics decry the growth of corporations because they transfer activity out of the sphere of democratically accountable institutions and over to organizations dedicated not to the public good, but to the maximization of shareholder profit. What both sides tend to ignore is that the businesses that drive global integration are not just the ones whose CEOs show up as talking heads on CNBC (that is, the heroes in Tom Friedman's books and the villains in Naomi Klein's), but just as often the sketchy figures from the deviant-globalization world bootstrapping their way to prosperity. Heard of Gregorio Sauceda Gamboa? Viktor Bout? How about "Flyman"? Simply put, here is a third category of nonstate actor, the deviant entrepreneur, who is acting on the same stage as the CEOs and anti-World Trade Organization activists, and whose wealth is increasing thanks to the miracle of the global market, but who continues to play a mostly invisible part in this ongoing drama.

What is Deviant Globalization?

Our goal is to add the concept of deviant globalization to the center of the ongoing debate about the dynamics and implications of global economic activity. In contrast to how deviant globalization practices and activities have been framed in the mainstream globalization debates, we consider deviant globalization more than just an annoyance or just another form of exploitation. Rather, it is a different category of economic action. What makes these value-additive processes deviant and distinctive is that they violate noneconomic, conventional, "Western" norms expressed in terms of human rights, modalities of violence and health, and even notions of the sacred.[17]

Deviant globalization is an economic concept, and also a legal and moral one. It cannot, however, be reduced merely to economic activities that violate the law, however the law is codified. On the one hand, some expressions of deviant globalization are perfectly legal, such as the journeys of American pedophiles to Canada, where the legal age of consent was fourteen (until 2008, when it was raised to 16, in order to "harmonize" with US laws).[18] On the other hand, some illegal economic activities, such as monopolistic pricing, are not deviant in the sense of offending conventional moral sensibilities. Even some of the damaging, but perfectly legal, effects of globalization are not deviant per se. The loss of unskilled jobs in Lincoln, Nebraska, to off-shore call-centers in Bangalore, India, is a distributional problem of globalization that helps some and hurts others, but it is not an example of moral arbitrage, regardless of the debate over its impact on aggregate wealth.

In contrast, here's something deviant, by our definition: Exporting toxic waste from junked European cell-phones and burying that waste in African landfills next to populated urban slums where the next generation of children will ingest high levels of mercury from landfill runoff water.[19] This example is not just a redistribution of the cost of a waste stream from one part of the world to another; it is a deviant globalization flow, for it violates what the waste-exporting players would conventionally claim are their own norms about human health. And here's another: Americans who fly to Southeast Asia to have paid sex with local young women. This transaction is not just about the exploitation of labor, but specifically about *the knowing economic exploitation of the differences in morality between the two cultures*; if those men could get the same services back home, most of them probably wouldn't pay to join the global flow of sex tourists.

Because deviant globalization operates on globalization's infrastructural backbone, we find it useful to think of it in terms of global flows of goods, services, information, people, animals, and microbes around the world.[20] What determines the pathways of deviant flows is not just border security and state authority but also the particular factor endowments that generate comparative advantage for deviant globalization processes. For instance, Romania is a hotbed of hacker activity focused on economic scams thanks to the availability of technical education, good broadband connectivity, and the relative paucity of information technology jobs that might otherwise absorb young, gifted coders into the mainstream economy.[21] Deviant flows also move through and to places that have robust demand and/or supply of particular goods and services that make up these flows — drugs, antiquities, some minerals and stones, exotic wildlife, human organs, sex, oil, highly enriched uranium, toxic wastes, and so on.

In contrast to some mainstream theories of globalization, which depict it as a process that annihilates differences across space,[22] the concept of deviant globalization highlights the continued importance of spatial differences in the structure of the global economy. Appreciating the geographic particularities of deviant flows is therefore crucial. Deviant flows move through cities — in a de facto archipelago that runs from the inner metropolitan cities of the United States to the *favelas* of Rio de Janeiro to the *banlieues* of Paris to the almost continuous urban slum belt that girds the Gulf of Guinea from Abidjan to Lagos. They move through towns and villages — along the cocaine supply route that links the mountains of Columbia to São Paulo and the waterways of West Africa to noses in the Netherlands. And they move through the "global nodes" that make up the world's financial infrastructure — from Wall Street to the City of London to Tokyo's Nihombashi District. In sum, it is possible to find manifestations of deviant globalization in almost every city, every household, every shipping lane and port, as well as almost every IP address connected to the global economy.

This broad scope is also not new. Like mainstream globalization, deviant globalization has a long historical record of geographic scope. Consider piracy, a phenomenon as old as sea-based navigation and commerce itself. Consider the eighteenth-century transatlantic slave trade, with its interconnected system of trade in human beings as well as addictive substances: Sugar, alcohol, and tobacco. Consider the Victorian-era drug trade and the British East India Company's war with the Qing Dynasty in China over trade in opium, which the company produced mainly on its colonial plantations in India.[23]

Globalization, then, has always had a deviant component. But here's where an element of conventional wisdom is actually quite correct: The scale, speed, scope, and impacts of deviant globalization have increased dramatically in the past twenty years. The articles in this book demonstrate four reasons for this acceleration, whose significance varies depending on the particular activity.

The first two reasons for this acceleration we have already discussed, because they are also the principal drivers of early twenty-first century mainstream globalization. That is, technology has compressed space and time in ways that were previously unimaginable, and the end of the Cold War opened up massive new geographies and populations, which — although not entirely discon-nected from deviant globalization flows in the previous era — were suddenly liberated from structural constraints that complicated their ability to engage. The third reason is new: Ascendant neoliberal ideology allowed the disciples of privatization and marketization to spread eastward and southward — most visibly to China — and in doing so set up conditions for the disruption of traditional moral economies and the formation of radically new ones. With all these changes came an explosion of opportunities for initiative, innovation, and entrepreneurship, not all of which rest in mainstream and licit economic action.

These three drivers of change are exactly what one would find in almost any mainstream political-economy analysis of globalization. There's a fourth dimension that sits apart from and modulates the relationships between the first three. And that is simply "power," in all its own dimensions, including most importantly the ability to define the principles and norms that make some things sanctioned and others not. In this respect, globalization and deviant globalization are no different from other socially embedded human processes, which always depend on some source of power to separate acceptable from aberrant, normal from deviant, legitimate from illegitimate behavior and action.[24]

Let's put it plainly: What enables globalization, enables deviant globalization as well. But, whereas globalization reinforces the power structures that enable it, deviant globalization works against those very sources of power. Our collective fascination with globalization's wonders can blind us to the ways in which this "good news" story is itself generating an important and powerful counternarrative. Here are some obvious but poignant examples of how deviant processes connect to, are enabled by, intersect with, or synergize around globalization:

Mainstream Globalization	Deviant Globalization
Companies like Walmart are using extraordinary supply-chain technologies to revolutionize logistics; this generates jobs for workers in developing countries and brings much cheaper mass-consumption goods to the global middle classes.	The same supply chain technologies are used to tune up the efficiency of the global supply chain for counterfeit goods. Many of the inputs for the factories that make counterfeits are competitively sourced on global markets at minimum price, and the products are transported with new efficiency to consumers.
The Internet facilitates the global distribution of information, collective production of knowledge goods, and enhances freedom to speak and to listen.	The Internet has become the easiest entry point to global systems for hostile and exploitative technologies (malware); social exploits (scams and spam); the identification of remote targets for pederasts; and the dissemination of radical ideologies that oppose or negate freedoms.
Capital mobility across national borders improves the efficiency with which the global economy allocates investment and should thereby enhance productivity immediately and, in particular, over the long term.	Capital mobility makes all kinds of finance for illegal activities, including crime and terrorism, as well as the laundering of money from other illicit activities for criminal far easier, and much more challenging for political authorities to address.
The spreading ideology of privatization and market allocation released an historic burst of entrepreneurial energy, and raised on the order of a billion people out of abject poverty in less than a generation.	The same ideologies have lent legitimacy to the concept of "everything for sale" including human beings (both whole and in pieces). Privatization ideologies in particular have led to the collapse in public goods provision — for example, by dumping waste and garbage "elsewhere."

Although this chart draws a firm line between mainstream and deviant globalization, in practice deviant globalization operates without clear boundaries. Rather, it stretches and integrates: From the licit to the illicit, from the visible to the hidden, and from the conventional to the rogue. As the stories in this book show, the transplant doctors who arrange dubiously brokered organs for clients are also doing perfectly aboveboard transplant surgeries; the Mafiosi who traffic drugs and counterfeit goods into Europe are also running perfectly legitimate bakeries, laundromats, and farms; the companies that dump toxic waste in the Global South are listed on stock exchanges in London and New York and receive investment from pension funds that pay the healthcare benefits for retired American workers.

Seen from another perspective, it's also apparent that virtually every mainstream industry is shadowed by a deviant doppelgänger. Prescription painkillers and psychotropic medicines have their deviant counterpart in illegal narcotics; recreational travel includes sex tourism; collecting antiques fuels archaeological theft and grave-robbing; military procurement supply chains also furnish weapons to warlords; software finds its counterpart in malware; financial services mirrors money laundering; and so on. All of which is simply to say that the deviant and the mainstream are inseparable. Which is precisely why enabling mainstream globalization inevitably also enables deviant globalization.

Conventional Lenses and Alternative Starting Points

Most stories that depict what we are calling deviant globalization include some subset of the following words: *Dignity, autonomy, agency, choice and justice* — usually conspicuous for their absence in the cases described. Deviant globalization stories typically show the loss of human dignity, the subversion of individual autonomy, and the abrogation of any reasonable standard of justice. While in many cases deviant globalization produces "bads," it is also important to recognize that deviant globalization often involves a more positive set of outcomes. To understand this ambiguity requires us to examine two conventional lenses, one affective and the other analytic, and to recognize their limitations.

The first we'll call revulsion or, more simply, "the yuck factor." Yuck is an *emotional* phrase that connotes disgust, an instinctive judgment that is more about experience than cognition, that's felt more in the gut than thought in the brain. Here we should be especially clear: The point is not that one shouldn't levy a moral judgment on deviant globalization; rather, it is to observe that one way to know that you've identified a quintessential modality of deviant globalization is when the bile rises in your throat. Furthermore, this emotional basis is not by itself a reason to take the yuck factor less seriously. There *is* something disgusting to so-called modern sensibilities, or at least off-color, about, say, removing kidneys from poor brown people in fetid slums and transplanting them to rich white bankers in pristine stainless-steel, sterilized surgical suites.

But it is just as important not to let the yuck factor foreclose a deeper understanding of what deviant globalization is all about. That kind of emotion can be a starting point for an analytic process by which we try to understand what it is about the phenomenon in question that has led us to feel that queasiness. What's the difference, exactly, between selling one organ and renting others, such as a womb? Is transferring the property rights on an organ once and for all any worse than selling a per-use license on organs over and over again — as in prostitution for example? Why is selling a kidney more emotionally disturbing to us than the daily experience of migrant laborers in oil fields and construction projects in most parts of the world? Is selling labor or selling kidneys more ruinous to a life? And, for all of these questions, what does it mean for the seller or the buyer, for that matter, to choose freely? Aren't all of our choices bounded and constrained, sometimes painfully so, as we are reminded every time the poor slum dweller with a healthy kidney and the rich banker with damaged ones engage in this deviant transaction?

Emotional reactions and comparisons like these can't really be ignored, but they rarely serve as a good basis for making economic, legal, or even moral judgments. There's just too much variance in what sets off those reactions between people and between cultures. And the lines between what is acceptable and unacceptable just move too unpredictably over time. It's also the case that many nonyucky things profoundly undermine dignity, autonomy, choice, and so on — at least as much as the yucky things do. Ask a Chinese coalminer about dignity and choice.[25]

A second conventional lens is more *analytic* than emotional, more explicitly political than affective or psychological. Call this "the coercion factor." The coercion factor distinguishes between voluntary exchanges among informed, willing players and exchanges that occur thanks to compulsion, intimidation, or in reaction to power operating without consent. There's an inherent neoliberal logic to this lens that draws from American contract law: As long as we are talking about individuals' entering into a contract for exchange through a "meeting of the minds" — as in, independent minds that get to express their preferences and search for common ground or a contract zone — why label any transaction as "deviant"? That could only represent a value judgment by a third party standing outside the contractual relationship. And what business is it of hers?

Unlike mainstream globalization, whose actors are bounded by and usually respect a dense global patchwork of laws, regulations, treaties, and agreements, deviant globalization is basically unfettered; law enforcement amounts to a cost of doing business, not an impediment to engaging in business itself. Uneven and inconsistent legal, institutional, and regulatory regimes make — even encourage — these kinds of deviant activities, illustrating how deviant globalization floats between the legal and illegal, appearing in different guises wherever there are meaningful divergences in the values that people impose on market transactions. One reasonable way to view deviant globalization, in other words, is as the purest expression of free-market capitalism. Put it this way: Every time someone buys sex with a child, sells heroin to a junkie, or brokers a kidney sale, Atlas Shrugs.[26]

Such stark libertarianism has some obvious analytic virtues. In this abstract world of contract law and autonomous human beings, the contract for exchange is ever expandable to new forms of transactions, so long as the community in which the exchange takes place considers those transactions legitimate. The problem is that this is not the world that most of humanity inhabits — even in America. It's not just that the prerequisites for a noncoercive meeting of the minds are rarely present in most of human life. It's also that almost everyone believes that there are certain kinds of transactions that simply should not be freely entered into — although no two people draw the lines in the same places.

In other words, coercion is both too broad and too narrow an analytic lens. It's too broad because deviant globalization often involves trade and exchanges that are made voluntarily, with full awareness and freedom to choose. (At least in the preaddiction phase, nobody forces anyone in New York or Rome to buy a gram of cocaine.) It's too narrow because the suggestion that all "licit" globalization processes take place in a noncoercive environment is to succumb to hyperliberal wishful thinking. To recycle an old cliché: No little kid ever dreams that when he grows up he'll be selling his kidney to make a living.

In contrast to these two conventional lenses, an important goal of this book is to spell out and demonstrate the analytic potency of two alternative perspectives that portray deviant globalization in a different light.

The first of these alternative perspectives on deviant globalization is a *psychodynamic* interpretation of demand, which is captured by the phrase "the return of the repressed." Here is how this perspective operates: Once upon a time, Western Europe and then the United States and then parts of Asia built a global market that supported a stunningly vast range of transactions; they got rich; and the rest of the world remained more or less poor. The underdogs (underprivileged, underresourced), who were innovative as a function of necessity, recognized that the rich actually had a range of demands that were not being met. Moreover, these demands were generated by repressed desires for things that the rich communities themselves either marginalized or forbade. So often perceived as victims, especially by those who take a dystopic view of globalization, the poor transformed themselves into wily innovators, capable of rapid adaptation in the service of their own modality of development. Some got rich and powerful, in many cases lending much-needed economic support to their compatriots.

Isn't this essentially what the developed world always claimed it wanted for the underdeveloped? The "problem," however, is that these "downtrodden" found a set of deviant market opportunities and cunningly learned how to use the rules, infrastructures, and systems of globalization to meet them. And, as a result, all of the goods and services that the rich tried to expel from their communities have returned.

The return of the repressed adds analytic ballast to the debate about deviant globalization. It helps us to understand and discuss how deviant supply is driven by deviant demand. It helps us to make a connection — even if only analogous — between the contradictions and complexities of our individual psychologies and the ways in which they are projected onto and reflected by the societies in which we live. Seen in this light, deviant globalization is nothing more than a highly efficient, adaptive, and systematic mechanism for meeting repressed desires without moral constraint. It is, in short, human, all-too-human, and as such, it's not going away.

The second lens through which to view deviant globalization is *regulatory economics*, which proceeds from the realization that deviant globalization isn't going away.[27] After all, if illicit activities are here to stay (indeed, by all measures they seem to be growing), then what are we to make of the prohibitions that enable deviant globalization? We need to stop thinking of surveillance, intelligence, law enforcement, and punishment as implements of a war that is winnable (or for that matter losable). Instead, these are simply control systems whose role is to *define the shape of illicit marketplaces*.

Regulatory economics spotlights crucial dimensions of the deviant globalization 'control' dynamic. For example, it helps us understand how and why governments are often subject to "regulatory capture" by illicit industries — that is, governments become more or less witting tools of the industries they are regulating. (Does the US Drug Enforcement Agency *really* want to win the war on drugs? How about Hamid Karzai?) Regulatory economics also helps us understand that the essence of deviant globalization is "regulatory arbitrage" — that is, taking advantage of the differences in rules and enforcement practices across jurisdictions in order to make a profit. Deviant entrepreneurs relish those differences because they can easily convert them into profit opportunities, ensuring that even the most sordid commodities get brought to market.

In sum, the regulatory-economics lens pushes us to reevaluate the rules by which mainstream globalization has been governed. If we want to retain globalization in any meaningful form, while minimizing the bads associated with deviant globalization, our best hope is to manage the rules of the game, for *both* deviant *and* mainstream globalization. Just as we have learned to talk about optimum unemployment or crime rates, we can learn to talk about optimal levels of drug trafficking, prostitution, toxic-waste dumping, money laundering, and so on. In short, regulation and management are our best options.

To summarize: A lens is not quite a theory, but any particular lens does magnify some things and drive others into the background, which forces a particular set of questions and dilemmas to be seen with greater clarity. We'll assess the results of that experiment in the concluding chapter. But a simple reflection stands out as a starting point across the different lenses: Just as globalization is not entirely good news, deviant globalization is not all bad news. Along with its downsides, deviant globalization has brought significant benefits to vast swaths of humanity and is certain to bring more of this to more people in the future. As we shall see in the articles that comprise this book, deviant globalization often offers more immediate benefits to participants than do most instantiations of Western concepts of development — from the abstract, such as modernization theory and the Washington Consensus, to the concrete, such as nongovernmental organizations (NGOs) providing direct assistance.

The unavoidable truth is that both mainstream globalization and its deviant twin present difficult choices and trade-offs for everyone who engages in, analyzes, or experiences their processes. And that is now almost everyone. To see these choices and trade-offs for what they are, not what we wish they might be, is a prerequisite for governments, businesses, transnational organizations, and anyone else to construct policies that will ensure that the benefits of globalization, broadly understood, get maximized and its horrors minimized.

Plan of the Book

Because deviant globalization takes place in the shadows of the global economic system, hidden by design from the formal scrutiny of governments, it is not a topic that is (or perhaps even can be) formally and systematically measured and tracked. Wrapping one's head around deviant globalization requires, therefore, not just perusing the differences between the formal economies and politics of different societies, as captured in the statistics and measurements of governments and NGOs like the World Bank or Transparency International, but also a more earthy and experiential form of learning and reporting — one that gets up close to the phenomena of deviant globalization, that understands the intimate social and economic contexts in which the moral arbitrage that defines the phenomenon takes place. To put it in academic terms, understanding deviant globalization requires an ethnographic rather than strictly quantitative approach.

The structure of this book reflects this methodological constraint. In our introduction, here, we have attempted to define the general nature of the deviant globalization — that is, to show how a series of seemingly disparate and shadowy phenomena in fact conform to an underlying structure and logic. In the conclusion, we will lay out what, in our view, it all adds up to from the point of view of international relations and policymaking. In between, we present a series of articles and essays by other authors, each of which uncovers a different and particular aspect of deviant globalization.

These essays have been picked to provide a sense of the global breadth of the deviant globalization phenomenon, as well as its geographic particularity. (It's no coincidence that certain places, such as the United States, Africa, China, and Russia appear and reappear in chapter after chapter.) It's important to note that none of these articles was written with this book, or even the concept of the deviant globalization, in mind. Because it is so multifarious, and so inherently slippery, the topic of deviant globalization demands a sundry accounting. A diversity of sources and styles is thus not a bug but a differentiating feature of this book: The essays vary from academic research, to policy analysis, to investigative journalism. Despite this variety of investigative methodologies and writing styles, however, these essays share a common intuition that their individual topics are somehow intimately connected to and inseparable from the process of globalization. We hope that collectively they make apparent how the seemingly disparate phenomena of deviant globalization in fact share structural commonalities rooted in the universal conditions of contemporary globalism.

To provide some structure to these diverse essays, we've divided them into four sections. The first section addresses *the human flows* associated with deviant globalization. Patrick Radden Keefe's essay focuses on human trafficking — "deviant immigration." Patrick Flynn exposes the sordid world of the international sex work — "deviant sex." Frederike Ambagtsheer documents the global flow of human organs — "deviant health care." And Johann Hari picks up the rock that is the official state image of Dubai to reveal the transnational social rot that festers under its glittering surface — "deviant urbanism." Hari's oblique references to the drug-fueled lifestyles of the expatriate community in Dubai also connect us to the next topic, drugs.

One of the central lessons of deviant globalization is that the vast global demand for psychotropic substances, and the vain and uneven attempts by governments to control the supply of these, is intertwined with virtually every other form of illicit commodity flow. The next section therefore addresses the question of *drugs* head-on, from a variety of angles. Marina Walker Guevara, Mabel Rehnfeldt, and Marcelo Soares investigate cigarette smuggling in South America, which turns out to be the central commodity around which numerous other illegal supply chains in counterfeit and stolen goods have been built. Stephen Ellis reveals the way that West Africa has recently emerged as a key transshipment zone, and possibly future production zone, for cocaine and other narcotics being produced in South America for the European market.

And Nick Reding offers an intimate account of the development and impact of the methamphetamine trade in small-town "Middle America."

The next section homes in on some of the particular resource flows associated with deviant globalization, many of them legal in principle but illicit in common practice. Jonny Steinberg discusses how amphetamine-pushing gangsters have taken over the illicit harvesting of shellfish in South Africa that is feeding demand in China — "deviant dining." Next comes Jennifer Clapp's essay on the global flow of toxic waste, which focuses in particular on dumping in Africa and South Asia — "deviant recycling." Raffi Khatchdourian describes illicit logging in the Russian Far East, which feeds the insatiable demand of Chinese manufacturers and western consumers of paper, furniture, and countless other goods — "deviant forestry." Moving beyond the cliché of "blood diamonds," we conclude this section with Sebastian Junger's essay on the violent insurgency unfolding in southeastern Nigeria — "deviant oil."

Junger's essay also provides a natural bridge to the last section, on the new organizational forms that deviant entrepreneurs are creating to support their endeavors. This last section begins with Scott Berinato's description of the growth, professionalization and transnationalization of financially motivated networks of computer hackers. Raymond Baker and Eva Joly discuss how the vast sums of money generated in deviant markets get reintegrated into the licit financial system — that is "laundered" — via the system of "offshore" financial gray zones that have been built by and for the benefit of formal global financial capital. Andrew Black analyzes the way that gray markets in light weapons supports warlords in East Africa. John Sullivan argues that Central American gangs, originally formed in the crucible of Cold War–era civil wars, have become transnationally networked criminal enterprises with definite proto-political self-conceptions. Last of all, John Robb takes us to the heart of deviant globalization's darkness, showing how global guerrilla groups have learned how to leverage global information flows to increase their innovation rates, thus accelerating their ability to challenge incumbent state actors.

To repeat: Our claim is not that this book provides a scientific sample of deviant globalization's diverse manifestations — a task that is anyway impossible given deviant globalization's inherently shadowy nature. Nor do we claim to have been comprehensive in our selection of topics. (For additional readings on all these topics, we include a bibliography at the end of the book.) Instead, we simply hope that these essays collectively reveal enough about the depth and breadth of the deviant globalization to support the synthesized claims we have made here in this introduction and that we will end with in our conclusion.

Notes

1. PBS Interview with Milton Friedman (1 October 2000): http://www.pbs.org/wgbh/commanding heights/shared/minitext/int_miltonfriedman.html.

2. Dan Bilefsky, "On Speedboats, Albania's Sex Trade Could Flare," *The New York Times* (16 July 2009).

3. Dan McDougall, "Wives fall prey to kidney trade: An Observer investigation into India's cash-for-organs trade reveals that transplants are making fortunes for brokers as desperate victims of the tsunami undergo dangerous surgery," *The Observer* (18 February 2007).

4. The Taliban reportedly charge a 10% "flat tax" to poppy farmers, an additional tax on heroin refiners, and finally a tariff for trafficking the heroin through to Quetta, Pakistan. See Gretchen Peters, *Seeds of Terror: How Heroin Is Bankrolling the Taliban and al Qaeda* (New York: Thomas Dunne Books, 2009), p. 14.

5. Jacob Townsend, "Taliban shape an opium economy," *Asia Times* (27 January 2009).

6. Philip Caputo, "The Fall of Mexico," *The Atlantic Monthly* (December 2009).

7. William Finnegan, "Silver or Lead: A drug cartel's reign of terror," *The New Yorker* (31 May 2010).

8. Estimates of the total size of the global illicit economy vary tremendously, depending on definition. According to the World Bank, as much as a third of the total global GDP may take place in the informal, grey, or untaxed economy, making it worth upwards of US$20 trillion. Of course, not all of this economic activity is necessarily illegal, nor does most of it cross borders. In *Illicit*, Moisés Naím estimates the value of the illicit trade at between $2 trillion and $3 trillion a year, and claims that it is expanding at seven times the rate of legitimate world trade. For more scholarly attempts to measure the size of the underground economy (along with discussion of the difficulties of doing so), see Matthew H. Fleming, John Roman, and Graham Farrell, "The Shadow Economy," *Journal of International Affairs* 53:2 (2000): 387–409; and Christopher Bajada and Friedrich Schneider, eds., *The Size, Causes and Consequences of the Underground Economy* (Burlington: Ashgate Publishers, 2005).

9. Phil Williams, "From the New Middle Ages to a New Dark Age: The Decline of the State and U.S. Strategy," Strategic Studies Institute (3 June 2008).

10. Our view of mainstream globalization is particularly indebted to David Harvey's seminal *The Condition of Postmodernity: An Enquiry into the Origins of Cultural Change* (London: Wiley-Blackwell, 1991). The literature on globalization is vast, ranging from popular bestsellers such as Thomas Friedman's *The World is Flat: A Brief History of the 21st Century* (New York: Picador, 2007) and Martin Wolf's *Why Globalization Works* (New Haven: Yale University Press, 2005) to more specialized books about the economic and technological foundations of globalization — particularly excellent here are George Gilder, *Telecosm: How Infinite Bandwidth will Revolutionize Our World* (New York: The Free Press, 2000), Kevin O'Rourke and Jeffrey Williamson's *Globalization and History: The Evolution of a Nineteenth-Century Atlantic Economy* (Cambridge: MIT Press, 2001), and Marc Levinson's *The Box: How the Shipping Container Made the World Smaller and the World Economy Bigger* (Princeton: Princeton University Press, 2006) — and the cultural impact of globalization, for which Mike Featherstone, ed., *Global Culture: Nationalism, Globalization, and Modernity* (London: Sage Publications Ltd, 1990) is the classic, standard work. As important as these books are, none of them systematically address the deviant dimensions of globalization, much less put them at the center of the story of globalization. Among the standard works, Manuel Castells's *The Rise of Network Society* comes closest to acknowledging that the sordid elements of globalization

are inseparable from the aboveboard elements, and that the facilitators of black markets are, in their structural essentials, little different from the arbitrageurs of Wall Street or the Chicago Board of Trade; see *The Rise of Network Society* (Malden: Blackwell Press, 1996), v. 3, ch. 3, "The Perverse Connection: The Global Criminal Economy." But even for Castells, globalized criminality, extralegality, and informality is primarily a sideshow to the main story of globalization. Only two monographic works place what we call deviant globalization at the center of the story of globalization: Moisés Naím's *Illicit: How Smugglers, Traffickers and Copycats are Hijacking the Global Economy* (New York: Doubleday, 2005) and Misha Glenny's *McMafia: A Journey Through the Global Criminal Underworld* (New York: Knopf, 2008). While both books are excellent in their own ways, they share not only a sensationalist quality that purports to be shocked, shocked at the things they report, but also a sense that incremental enforcement of existing policy approaches could significantly reduce the phenomena they describe. Neither book treats deviant globalization as essential to contemporary mechanisms of global integration and legitimation, nor fully appreciates the radical challenge that deviant globalization poses to the current geopolitical order.

11. Though the "theft of the state" was widely lamented on moral grounds, what was more significant from the perspective of this book was that the so-called oligarchs who emerged from this book were prototypical deviant globalizers. In the seedy late phases of the centrally planned economies, getting anything done economically required a willingness to flout official rules and to operate decisively in a situation of fundamental uncertainty. (See Steven L. Solnick, *Stealing the State: Control and Collapse in Soviet Institutions* [Cambridge: Harvard University Press, 1999].) Those who had acquired these skills were perfectly positioned, both economically and psychologically, to take advantage of the post-perestroika chaos in the former Soviet bloc. As Misha Glenny carefully documents in *McMafia*, many former mid-level apparatchiks quickly retooled themselves into deviant entrepreneurs, providing new opportunities to under-employed populations (i.e., cigarette smuggling and sex trade) and, as a result, generated tremendous wealth. Interestingly, Odd Arne Westad has observed a similar pattern in China, a bit earlier: According to Westad, the ability of those engaged in (illicit) foreign procurement to keep their factories operating even at the height of the Cultural Revolution (1966–1976) was one of the inspirations to economic reforms of 1979. See Westad, "The Great Transformation: China in the Long 1970s," in Niall Ferguson, Charles Maier, Erez Manela and Daniel Sargent, eds., *The Shock of the Global: The International History of the 1970s* (Cambridge: Harvard University Press, 2010).

12. Named after Intel cofounder Gordon Moore, Moore's Law describes a long-term trend in the history of computing hardware, in which the number of transistors that can be placed inexpensively on an integrated circuit has doubled approximately every two years. The result has been inexorable exponential growth in many critical computing capabilities, including processing speed, memory capacity, sensing capabilities, and even the number and size of pixels in digital cameras. For Moore's original statement of the case, see Gordon E. Moore, "Cramming more components onto integrated circuits," *Electronics* 38:8 (19 April 1965).

13. Richard O'Brien, *Global Financial Integration: The End of Geography* (New York: Council on Foreign Relations Press, 1992); Frances Cairncross, *The Death of Distance: How the Communications Revolution Is Changing our Lives* (Cambridge: Harvard Business Press, 2001); Francis Fukuyama, *The End of History and the Last Man* (New York: Free Press, 1992); Manuel Castells, op cit.; Thomas Friedman, op cit.

14. Karl Polanyi, *The Great Transformation* (Boston: Beacon Press, 2001 [1944]).

15. Naomi Klein, *Shock Doctrine: The Rise of Disaster Capitalism* (New York: Metropolitan Books, 2007).

16. Important titles in this vein include Joseph E. Stiglitz, *Globalization and Its Discontents* (New York: W.W. Norton, 2003); John McMurtry, *The Cancer Stage of Capitalism* (London: Pluto Books, 1999); Andrew Nikiforuk, *Pandemonium: How Globalization and Trade Are Putting the World At Risk* (St Lucia: University of Queensland Press, 2006); Noam Chomsky, *Profit Over People: Neoliberalism and the Global Order* (New York: Seven Stories Press, 1999); Arundhati Roy, *Power Politics* (New York: South End Press, 2002).

17. Our concept of "deviance" is partly a serious nod to classic sociological theories of social deviance (which derive from the seminal work of Emile Durkheim and Sigmund Freud), which stress that social deviance is, as Kai Erikson put it, "a normal product of stable institutions, a vital resource which guarded and preserved by forces found in all human organizations"; and partly an ironic nod to the fact that it is the uncritical social construction of deviance — that is, of socially unacceptable behavior — which makes possible both the opportunities and the horrors described in this volume. See Kai Erikson, "Notes on the Sociology of Deviance," *Social Problems* 9:4 (1962).

18. "Low age of consent luring pedophiles to Canada," *CBC News* (19 December 2006).

19. "Europe's e-waste in Africa," *Ghana Business News* (5 September 2009); Jon Mooallem, "The Afterlife of Cellphones," *New York Times* (13 January 2008).

20. Alternately, deviant commodities can also be thought of as "hopping" rather than "flowing" from place to place — in the sense that they skip certain locales and distribute themselves unevenly. See James Ferguson, *Global Shadows: Africa in the Neoliberal World Order* (Durham: Duke University Press, 2006).

21. Christopher Condon and Scott Morrison, "Phishing, pharming and fraud: How hackers' prying eyes threaten confidence in online commerce," *Financial Times* (9 March 2005); Nils Gilman, "Hacking Goes Pro," *Engineering and Technology* 4:3 (2009).

22. Cultural analyses of mainstream globalization tend to highlight this "deterritorializing" aspect of globalization; see for example John Tomlinson, *Globalization and Culture* (Chicago: University of Chicago Press, 1999); Nikos Papastergiadis, *The Turbulence of Migration: Globalization, Deterritorialization and Hybridity* (New York: Wiley, 2000).

23. David Courtwright, *Forces of Habit: Drugs and the Making of the Modern World* (Cambridge: Harvard University Press, 2004); Alan Karras, *Smuggling: Contraband and Corruption in World History* (London: Rowman & Littlefield, 2009).

24. In other words, we are asking the same questions of deviant globalization that Foucaultians ask of mainstream markets: How does the regulation of customs, norms and values give rise to deviant globalization and how, in turn, do deviant flows and processes impact and undermine the more traditional notions of power associated with sovereignty? See Michel Foucault, *Discipline and Punish: The Birth of the Prison* (New York: Vintage Books, 1995) and *"Society Must Be Defended": Lectures at the College de France, 1975-1976* (New York: Picador, 2003).

25. China produces 35 percent of the world's coal, but 80 percent of its coalmining fatalities, usually north of 5000 a year. See this report in the Chinese official daily newspaper: Zhao Xiaohui & Jiang Xueli, "Coal mining: Most deadly job in China," *China Daily* (*Xinhua*), (13 November 2004).

26. Referring, of course, to Ayn Rand's libertarian jeremiad *Atlas Shrugged* (New York: Random House, 1957).

27. For a brief intellectual history of regulatory economics and regulatory rollback, see Michael A. Bernstein, "Regulatory Economics and its Discontents: Some Theoretical and Historical

Observations," *Info: The journal of policy, regulation and strategy for telecommunications* 9:2–3 (2007). For the original statement in favor of deregulation on the grounds that regulatory unevenness empowers criminals, see Bruce Yandle, "Bootleggers and Baptists: The Education of a Regulatory Economist," *Regulation* 7:3 (1983).

PEOPLE

Snakeheads and Smuggling: The Dynamics of Illegal Chinese Immigration

Patrick Radden Keefe

At first glance, the city of Changle seems like any other bustling boomtown on the southern coast of China. Cranes punctuate the horizon, signaling the construction of shopping centers, office towers, and luxury hotels. The local population has given up bicycles for cars, and old roads are widened, while new roads paved every day. Sleek textile plants line the highway on the outskirts of town, churning out bales of nylon and other industrial fabrics around the clock.

But Changle is unusual. Along with a handful of neighboring cities and towns in Fujian Province, a mountainous sliver of coast north of Hong Kong and across the strait from Taiwan, Changle owes its economic prosperity not just to the rising tide of China's economy, but to hundreds of thousands of native sons and daughters who have been smuggled out of the country in recent years to make their fortunes overseas.

For the past three decades, residents of Changle and other Fujianese villages and towns have left China and migrated to Japan, Europe, Australia, Canada — but most of all, to the United States — where they live, often as illegal immigrants, and work to save money and send it home. Dishwashers in Los Angeles, delivery men in Washington, and seamstresses in New York, all send their savings back to Fujian Province, and the money has helped fuel the local economy in towns like Changle. These emigrants provide funds for schools and community centers, underwrite wedding banquets and new business ventures, and allow for the construction in their ancestral villages of impressive mansions of tile and brick. By the 1990s, remittances to Changle from this expatriate population amounted to hundreds of millions of dollars each year. One of the major intersections in town is dominated by a soaring steel sculpture of a sail flanked by a pair of angular wings. When I visited recently, my host, a local entrepreneur named Lin Li, explained that the monument was erected to acknowledge that the region owes its prosperity to those who left the country by boat and plane.

Magnet for the Undocumented

As the United States confronts a dire economic crisis and soaring unemployment, illegal immigration and the role that undocumented laborers play in the American economy will inevitably become a source of controversy and debate. During the past few decades of sustained economic growth, the United States has been a magnet for undocumented migrants from China and dozens of other nations, to a point where by some estimates as many as 12 million people without legal status live in the country today. There are real questions, however, about whether the hard times ushered in by the financial crisis in the past year will diminish the attractiveness of the United States as a destination for migrants, and the risks that paperless laborers are prepared to undertake in order to get here. One possibility is that a contraction of economic opportunities will discourage further illegal immigration, and even persuade some undocumented sojourners already living in American cities to return to their native countries. But the prospect of a widespread global recession could also mean a dramatic uptick in irregular migration, as hard times hit the developing world with increasing fury, pushing ever greater numbers of migrants to leave their home countries in search of any economic environment that is even marginally more promising than their own.

The Chinese labor force is astonishingly mobile. Enterprising Chinese have proven willing, even eager, to pursue better opportunities not just outside their villages or on the other side of the country but at the farthest reaches of the earth. Chinese traders have laid down roots in Lima, Havana, Singapore, and Sydney. Today, Chinese companies are building roads and power networks throughout Africa, and Chinese farmers are cooperating with local counterparts to grow crops for export in Kenya, Uganda, Ghana, and Senegal. Through the darkest years of the war in Iraq, the Chinese restaurant was a durable feature in Baghdad. So how Chinese laborers respond to the global economic crisis may provide a sort of bellwether for the broader trends in irregular migration that we are likely to witness in the future. As China's economy has boomed in recent years, the number of people who chose to emigrate illegally has leveled off. But China has not been immune to the grim economic troubles of recent months, and it could very well be that as Fujian and other manufacturing centers along the coast begin to suffer, dramatic numbers of under-employed laborers will again pay to be smuggled abroad.

The Largest Diaspora

No one knows precisely how many ethnic Chinese live outside of China, but estimates tend to range from 40–50 million or more. After the descendents of African slaves, the Overseas Chinese, as they are often called, represent the largest diaspora on the planet. But the Chinese who have emigrated in recent decades are anything but representative of the country at large. In fact, the overwhelming majority originate from Changle and other parts of northern Fujian Province — an area smaller than the state of Connecticut. Most of the migrants who have left the region and made their way to Europe or North America undertook the journey illegally.

The demand for illicit passage out of one country and into another has given rise to a distinctive breed of well-connected immigration brokers. In China (and in Chinatowns around the planet), these underworld entrepreneurs are known as snakeheads. No one knows the precise origins of the term "snakehead," but in a recent criminal trial in New York, one snakehead suggested that the expression derives from the manner in which undocumented migrants slide under the fences separating sovereign countries, their bodies slithering "like a snake." The snakeheads reap considerable profits and operate in a transnational black market that is as shadowy as it is extensive. But for the migrants who they usher out of China, the service that the snakeheads provide is often perceived as a fundamental social good, and these smugglers are widely regarded not as criminals but as resourceful and enterprising tour-guides in a world of clandestine migration flows. If the global economic crisis creates a surge in illegal migration from developing countries to developed ones, and from the third world to the first, the process will likely be facilitated by precisely these sorts of brokers.

In an effort to understand the massive flows of undocumented migrants that currently circulate the planet and may very well intensify in the event of a deepening global recession, it is instructive to consider the mechanics of the dramatic population displacement from the villages of Fujian Province to the streets of cities like New York. And any effort to grasp that displacement must begin with an exploration of the snakehead trade.

Origins of the Out-Migration

Bounded by mountains on three sides and the South China Sea on the fourth, Fujian Province has always been an unusually outward-looking corner of China. In the fifteenth century, the famous Chinese Admiral Zheng He set sail from Fuzhou with an armada of white-hulled junks and ventured into the South Seas and as far away as Africa, giving rise to the legend of Sinbad the Sailor. Adventurous Fujianese merchants established seed communities throughout Southeast Asia, and today vast numbers of ethnic Fujianese are scattered around the region. Eighty percent of the Chinese in the Philippines can trace their roots to Fujian, as can 55 percent of the Chinese in Indonesia. Taiwan is a mere hundred miles across the strait; the Fujianese settled there as well. So many made the crossing in the seventeenth and eighteenth centuries that modern day Taiwanese speak a dialect similar to that spoken in the southern Fujianese port of Xiamen. Well over one million Chinese in Hong Kong, Macau, and Taiwan have roots in a single northern Fujianese commune, Tingjiang, which, like Changle, is located just outside the provincial capital of Fuzhou.

Because migrating even internally, much less leaving China altogether, was heavily restricted during the Mao years, very few Chinese succeeded in emigrating during the 1950s and 1960s. Those who did make it to the United States during this period were generally "ship jumpers" who served as crews on merchant vessels and abandoned ship when they called at ports in New York or California. Because of the seafaring culture in Fujian and the busy ports at Xiamen and Mawei, a historic maritime hub just outside Fuzhou, many of the ship jumpers who arrived in the United States were Fujianese. These first pioneers saw themselves as sojourners — men who left their families behind on the crossing to America, working in restaurants and laundries with an eye to sending money to their families back home. Most of them planned to return eventually.

During the 1970s, many Fujianese sought to leave their villages and migrate to Hong Kong, and it was during these years that the earliest snakeheads went into business, charging a fee to ferry customers from Changle or Fuzhou overland to the mainland city of Shenzhen, and from there into the British colony. After establishing residence in Hong Kong, it was often possible to continue the journey to Taiwan, Japan, Europe, or the United States, and during the 1980s snakeheads began charging a steeper price to coordinate these more ambitious trips. Because of the small seed community of Fujianese ship jumpers, New York became a destination of choice. Before long, the fee for passage to New York had reached $18,000. As more Fujianese arrived on the streets of New York's Chinatown, the traditional Cantonese community, which had dominated the neighborhood since its origins a century earlier, looked down on these undocumented newcomers who spoke a northern Fujianese dialect incomprehensible even to Mandarin speakers. They called them "Eighteen-thousand dollar men."

For the next two decades, the overwhelming majority of Chinese immigrants to the United States originated from Fujian Province, and they arrived in truly epic numbers. Because irregular migration is by its very nature an undocumented activity which leaves no reliable paper trail, and because estimates by immigration authorities are generally based on a crude extrapolation from the number of individuals law enforcement actually succeeds in apprehending at the border, there are no solid figures on how many Fujianese entered the United States illegally during this period. Conservative estimates tend to put the number in the tens of thousands each year. By the early 1990s, the Central Intelligence Agency estimated the figure was closer to 100,000. According to Peter Kwong, a leading scholar of American Chinatowns and the history of the Chinese in America, the largest number of illegal Chinese in history entered the United States between 1988 and 1993.

One particular irony of this situation was that these migrants were coming from Fujian at a time when the economy in the province was experiencing double-digit growth. After Mao's death in 1976, Deng Xiaoping initiated a series of sweeping economic reforms designed to experiment with a more market-based economy. In 1980, Beijing established a number of Special Economic Zones, more open to international trade and with certain tax incentives to lure foreign investment. The southern Fujianese city of Xiamen was selected. In 1984, 14 other coastal cities were designated Special Economic Zones, and Fuzhou made the list.

As a result, the fortunes of the province improved dramatically during precisely the period when so many Fujianese were struggling to leave. One explanation for this apparent anomaly was that many Fujianese farmers and fishermen who had traditionally enjoyed a lifestyle that, while meager, was also stable and predictable, were suddenly dislocated in the new market economy. Unmoored from these more traditional professions, many found it difficult to find work. But another explanation is that, as a rule, out-migration is not driven by absolute poverty. It is seldom the poorest sectors of a country that generate migrants.

Indeed, China's poorest provinces, in the country's interior, have never been a source of significant emigration. Rather, demographers have found that people are driven to leave home and venture abroad by "relative deprivation" — an uneven distribution of material comforts, or put simply, the experience of watching your neighbor do better than you. Prior to the economic reforms, the people of Fujian Province had been fairly homogenous when it came to social class and spending capacity. But as the region became a center for manufacturing and trade, some did better than others, and suddenly certain material amenities, from refrigerators to televisions to automobiles, began to distinguish those who had prospered in the new climate from those who had not.

Thus, in something of a paradox, economic development actually drove people to leave, rather than stay put. And the process fed upon itself. A construction worker in Changle could move to New York, find a job washing dishes or chopping vegetables, and make in a year what he would have made in a decade back home. These migrants lived thriftily and sent the bulk of their earnings back to China. The funds they sent were used to engage in hitherto unimaginable forms of conspicuous consumption. Local families erected garish multi-story mansions which rose, incongruously, from the rice paddies. These spectacular buildings only served further to underline the income stratification in the region, and soon a sense took hold in even the most remote villages of northern Fujian Province that a family which didn't have at least one able-bodied member living abroad and sending US dollars home must suffer from some embarrassing deficit of pride or pluck. As this cycle perpetuated itself, a fever to migrate gripped the region.

"Everybody went crazy," a *Sing Tao Daily* journalist reported from Fuzhou in the mid-1990s. "The area was in a frenzy. Farmers put down their tools, students discarded their books, workers quit their jobs, and everybody was talking about nothing but going to America."

The Mechanics of Human Smuggling

The sophisticated, planet-spanning industry that arose to accommodate this frenzy and transplant those farmers and students from the Fujianese countryside to American cities has received little rigorous scrutiny. Black markets enjoy an astonishingly extensive global reach, but because the activities in question are generally illegal, often paperless, and always secretive, they tend to confound the techniques of inquiry traditionally employed by journalists or academics. The customers of human smuggling organizations are undocumented migrants who are often fearful about discussing their experiences. While smugglers operate with relative impunity in some countries, in others they can face stiff penalties for transporting illegal aliens across borders, and as such they tend also to be reluctant to detail their operations. In addition to these constraints on the available sources of information, the human smuggling business is often misunderstood and mischaracterized in the media and in scholarly literature due to a common semantic slippage: Commentators conflate human smuggling with the related — but separate — crime of human trafficking. As a rule, human trafficking involves transporting individuals from one place to another either against their will, or under some false pretense. Human smuggling, while arguably also exploitive in some ways, is based on a contract and a corresponding meeting of the minds between smuggler and customer. The smuggler is not duping the customer into making the journey, and whereas many trafficked individuals end up in forced sexual or manual labor, instances of human smuggling customers ending up as sex workers, while not unheard of, are exceedingly rare.

Another prevalent misconception about Chinese human smuggling in particular is that the activity is monopolized by centralized criminal rackets, in the manner of the Sicilian mafia. While there have been some instances of established Chinese Triads taking an interest in the snakehead trade — and the revenues generated are sufficiently lucrative that other criminal elements, such as Chinatown gangs, have occasionally dabbled in the business — most Chinese human smuggling is carried out by more diffuse international networks of individual entrepreneurs and middlemen. They may come together on an ad hoc basis to smuggle a load of immigrants, or three, or five, and then go their separate ways. No central nerve center or criminal hierarchy governs the activity, and no blood oaths or bonds of loyalty bind the perpetrators. The snakehead business is more decentralized, even atomized. Individuals collaborate when it is convenient to do so, then move on to work with others. In this manner, each assembles an extensive roster of contacts in other countries with whom he or she may work again in the future.

Payment in Full

For most prospective Fujianese migrants, the first step in going to America involves assembling the down payment. Because the journey is circuitous and often involves passing in and out of multiple transit countries before reaching the ultimate destination, snakeheads have not traditionally demanded the entirety of their fees up front. Instead, they allow customers to make an initial down payment of several thousand dollars, with the balance due upon the successful completion of the journey. (In recent years, this practice has begun to shift, with some snakeheads requiring payment in full before commencing the trip.)

While the down payment may represent only a small fraction of the total cost of the service, it was nevertheless a considerable sum of money in China during the 1980s and 1990s. This is another explanation why it was often the working and middle class, not the poorest, who left the country illegally. The very poorest Chinese would not have been able to assemble even the initial payment to embark on the trip.

Over the years, an intricate taxonomy of brokers, couriers, and middlemen has evolved to facilitate the complex international logistics associated with smuggling migrants from China to Chinatown. The logistical masterminds, who also pocket the lion's share of the profits, are known as "big snakeheads." They are often Overseas Chinese, based in Taiwan, Europe, or North America. These individuals tend to think of themselves as entrepreneurs rather than criminals, and they usually run multiple other licit enterprises in addition to their smuggling operations. They provide the capital and contacts, and use their connections in China to drum up business. The local recruiters in the villages and towns of southeastern China are known as "little snakeheads." They are generally the first point of contact for aspiring migrants. If you were living in Changle and wanted to be smuggled to the United States, you would seek out a little snakehead who could make you a proposal, stating a total price, the sum that was due up front, the route, and mode of transport. Because of understandable concern that customers might reach their destination only to abscond without paying the balance of their fees, little snakeheads often require the assurances of some friend or relative who is already in the United States and can serve as a guarantor.

From the earliest days of the industry, snakeheads have exploited a dizzyingly ingenious array of routes to ferry their passengers abroad. Initially, the snakeheads would bribe local officials to secure exit visas to Hong Kong, then employ further well-placed bribes to obtain visas to various Latin American countries. These visas could be used to board flights bound for Latin America that had layovers in Toronto or New York, where customers were instructed to disembark and demand asylum at the airport. (In New York in particular, the backlog of pending asylum cases was so extensive that it often took over a year to process claims, during which time Chinese applicants were released into the city, where they could find work.) "Photo-sub" passports were another popular device; snakeheads would purchase genuine passports belonging to Asian men and women and replace the photographs of the actual passport holders with pictures of their customers. These passports could be recycled multiple times, with the snakeheads arranging for successful arrivals to mail the passport back to China for use by the next customer.

In 1991, just as demand in Fujian Province for passage to America was beginning to exceed the logistical ability of the snakeheads to furnish phony documents and plane tickets, Taiwan announced a ban on drift-net fishing, which left a fleet of ocean-going vessels suddenly unable to perform their traditional function, and ripe for reassignment. Soon dozens of Taiwanese fishing boats were crisscrossing the oceans with hundreds of passengers in their holds. In the minds of the snakeheads, human cargo was ultimately a form of cargo like any other — subject to the economies of scale. Sending passengers on planes meant paying for expensive tickets and for legitimate or fraudulent passports and visas. In some cases, a snakehead who charged tens of thousands of dollars to send a customer by plane ended up netting only $5,000 after covering all the relevant expenses. The snakeheads realized that Fujianese demand for passage to America was so insatiable that they could oblige their customers to forego the comforts of economy class for conditions that better resembled freight, and shift the business from a retail model to a wholesale one, without making any allowances on the price that they charged.

$35,000 Ticket

Ships delivered passengers to Japan, Taiwan, and Thailand; to Guatemala and Mexico; to Hawaii, San Francisco, New Bedford, and New York. By the mid-1990s the cost of passage had reached $35,000 and snakeheads were diversifying, crafting new routes to take customers to new places. In order to evade detection and take advantage of logistical loopholes in international travel networks, they often sent their customers on a circuitous path. Even a partial listing of the routes that law enforcement discovered during these years reads like the bizarre itinerary for some madcap world tour: "Fuzhou–Hong Kong–Bangkok–Moscow–Havana–Managua–Tucson," or "Fuzhou–Hong Kong–Bangkok–Kuala Lumpur–Singapore–Dubai–Frankfurt–Washington."

In the early years of the trade, during the 1980s, snakeheads would actually accompany their passengers at each stage of the trip. But as the business grew, the big snakeheads began subcontracting to a series of local guides and fixers who operated in a kind of relay through the duration of the route. After customers had traveled overland from Changle to the western city of Kunming, near China's border with Burma, local guides in Kunming would accompany the passengers over the border, and hand them off to Burmese guides, who would usher them over the jungle-covered mountains and malarial swamps to the Golden Triangle, where a group of Thai guides would be waiting to bring them over the border into Thailand, then all the way to Bangkok. There, the customers would stay in safe houses operated by middlemen who would then escort them either to the airport, where they could board a plane with phony documents, or south to the Gulf of Thailand, where Taiwanese ships sat at anchor, their holds retrofitted with plywood planks and mattresses, ready to ferry their illicit cargo to the United States.

Many of the passengers never made it to their destinations. They were apprehended at one border or another and jailed or sent back to China, or they perished when their guides led them astray in the mountains of Burma or their ship overturned in a storm.

Those who did manage to survive the journey were met by armed enforcers who would transport them to a safe house. One common misconception about the snakehead business is that new arrivals who owe the balance of a $35,000 fee are obliged to spend years working as indentured servants until they can pay off their snakeheads. As a practical matter, such an arrangement would make little sense for the snakeheads. They do not want to spend months or years keeping track of various debtors and insuring that no one skips town without fulfilling his end of the transaction. Instead, the snakeheads generally allow a grace period of 48–72 hours after the customer has arrived for the friends and family of the customer to produce the balance of the fee. (American authorities have occasionally charged Fujianese snakeheads with hostage taking, because new arrivals are sometimes held at gunpoint until relatives pay the snakeheads thousands of dollars. To the Fujianese customers, however, this process, while unpleasant and sometimes violent, is generally perceived not as a ransom situation, but as the fulfillment of a contract.)

In this manner, the snakeheads can generally collect their fee in full within days of successfully smuggling a passenger to the United States, and the big snakeheads can then use those funds to pay off the various subcontractors along the stages of the route. Having been released from the safe house, meanwhile, the customers may not be indentured to the snakeheads, but they have borrowed heavily in order to satisfy their debts, so they do become indentured in some sense to the family and friends who helped pay the balance of their fees.

A Global Enterprise

It is no accident that the explosion of the snakehead trade during the 1990s coincided with the broader globalization of international commerce. One seldom-remarked irony of globalization is that — while the increased interconnection undoubtedly facilitated a host of useful new innovations for consumers, corporations, and governments — the unfettered flow of goods, people, capital, and ideas that so characterized the 1990s also presented major opportunities for the enterprising cross-border criminal. The snakeheads exploited the volume and variety of international transportation and trade to facilitate their business. They drew on modern communications technologies to establish far-flung networks of contacts and fixers at transshipment points around the planet and modeled their distribution networks on the efficient global supply chains of licit multinational corporations. They took advantage of what Microsoft's Bill Gates once referred to, approvingly, as "friction-free" capital flows to remit their passengers' fees and their payments to subcontractors from one country to another, and to launder their profits and keep them beyond the reach of authorities.

Cheng Chui Ping, known as "Sister Ping," was one of the most famous and prolific snakeheads. Active for two decades until her arrest in Hong Kong in 2000, Sister Ping had contacts in two-dozen countries and used her own underground banking network to wire funds to associates in New York, Fuzhou, Hong Kong, Thailand, Guatemala, and South Africa. According to the Federal Bureau of Investigation, she accumulated some $40 million, tax-free.

Snakeheads like Sister Ping rely above all on global corruption. Any international effort to regulate clandestine trade — whether of drugs, guns, or people — will only be as good as the least vigilant nation in the system. If the community of nations relies on official documents issued by sovereign countries to denote who is entitled to travel where, it only takes one spoiler principality to undo the whole endeavor. What's more, the better the rest of the system works — the more harmonized and efficient the international regulatory architecture — the higher the rewards will be for the one country willing to cheat, offering an illicit back door into the licit international system.

These "geopolitical black holes," as one observer refers to them, have become durable hubs in the international networks of the snakeheads in the same manner that the international airport in Houston, Texas is a hub for Continental Airlines. In Bangkok, corrupt officials at the airport would overlook obvious improprieties in the papers of Fujianese passengers and allow them to board flights to the United States. American officials who visited the airport during the 1990s recall an almost comic tableau: In a relatively empty departures lounge, short lines would form at each of the first eight ticket windows, and a very long line at the ninth — where the snakeheads had told their passengers to queue, because the official there was on the take.

In addition to Thailand, Latin America became an indispensable staging post for the snakeheads. If Chinese passengers reached Guatemala, Honduras, Panama, or Belize, they could make their way overland to Mexico, where their snakeheads subcontracted with local "coyotes," or Mexican human smugglers, to accompany them on the final leg of the journey over the border into Texas, Arizona, or California. Given the extent of local corruption in Central America, and the widespread feeling that Chinese human smuggling was a victimless crime, the snakeheads soon found eager partners in the region.

In 1991, the Honduran National Assembly passed a law that was nominally designed to attract foreign investment, but actually amounted to a cash-for-citizenship scheme. A sophisticated ring of corrupt officials made nearly $20 million selling Honduran passports to Chinese customers. In 1995 alone, the immigration directors of Panama, Belize, and Guatemala were all fired for accepting bribes from smugglers.

Nor was the United States immune to corruption within its own ranks. In 1997, Jerry Stuchiner — who had been the top US immigration official posted to Hong Kong and then to Honduras, and who had been responsible in both locations for taking the lead in combating the snakehead trade — was arrested in Hong Kong for attempting to sell blank Honduran passports to Chinese customers. Corruption has continued to be an endemic problem for American immigration authorities at even the most senior levels. In June 2008, the assistant chief counsel of US Immigration and Customs Enforcement, was arrested at a casino in Highland, California, and charged with accepting thousands of dollars in bribes.

Above all, the snakehead business has been adaptable and well suited to a globalized age. Because of loose-knit organizational structures and the diversity of international contacts, smugglers can take advantage of shifts in the regulatory or geopolitical landscape and exploit them in innovative ways. When snakeheads discovered that it was relatively easy to obtain visas for Chinese passengers to visit Russia, a new route soon developed, with passengers flying into Moscow, then trekking over the loosely patrolled border into Ukraine and then Slovakia. From there, a minivan would ferry them to Prague, and from Prague to points west — the Netherlands, Belgium, Italy, France, and Britain. New Chinatowns have popped up in cities from São Paulo to Dubai. After sanctions were imposed on Yugoslavia in 1993, Slobodan Milosevic began cultivating the Chinese leadership in Beijing, and lifted visa requirements for Chinese citizens to travel to Serbia. The snakeheads wasted no time sending their customers to Belgrade by the planeload, knowing full well that from there they could make their way into Western Europe, and onward to Canada or the United States.

Market Saturation

Today, American law enforcement and immigration officials maintain that the snakehead trade has been dramatically curtailed. Whereas the 1990s saw the regular arrival of boatloads of Chinese immigrants on the shores of California and Massachusetts, a series of policy changes ranging from stricter sentences for human smuggling to the detention of undocumented asylum applicants pending resolution of their claims, appears to have brought the problem under control. In addition, it would seem to stand to reason that surging unemployment in the current economic downturn would diminish the appeal of the United States. But interviews in the Fujianese community in New York's Chinatown suggest that new undocumented migrants continue to arrive from Fujian Province every week, and snakeheads continue to operate both in Chinatown and in China. Due in part to the increased risk for the snakeheads themselves, the fee has reached $75,000, which the smugglers often insist must be paid in full before the customer leaves China. The size of the fee and the fact that it is no longer contingent on safe arrival is in part a reflection of the difficulties associated with boat smuggling, which is much more hazardous today, due to increased patrols by the United States Coast Guard. Snakeheads have returned to sending most of their passengers by plane, a route which requires a greater financial investment in the form of airline tickets and counterfeit documents, but also less risk that the customer may not arrive in the destination country. Even so, ships still smuggle migrants out of southern China. Instead of traveling directly to the United States, they go only as far as Central America, where the customers disembark and continue their journey overland.

One interesting question, in light of China's continued economic growth over the past decade, is whether at a certain point the country's new prosperity will trickle down to a degree where it can overcome the effects of relative deprivation. Prosperity that is unevenly distributed may drive people to leave a country. But might sustained, widespread economic growth eventually elevate the standard of living for much of the population and create new incentives for people to stay where they are?

On a research trip to Fujian Province I posed this question to laborers and entrepreneurs in Fuzhou, Changle, Tingjiang, and other traditional sources of undocumented migrants to the United States. All of the individuals I spoke to over a two-week trip had family or friends living in the United States, and many of them reveled in the prosperity that the province, and China in general, have enjoyed in recent years. Most of the people I spoke with maintained that the snakeheads do continue to operate, and that many Fujianese still leave China illegally every year. There was agreement that the trade has slowed in recent years, but the prevailing explanation was not China's economic growth.

Instead, most of the Fujianese I spoke with suggested that the snakehead business has been so effective for so long that the industry has declined only because nearly everyone who might possibly want to emigrate to the United States has already done so — the smugglers have achieved a kind of market saturation. To illustrate the point, several people cited the city of Wenzhou, up the coast in Zhejiang Province, which has supplanted Fuzhou in recent years as the dominant source of irregular out-migration.

Lin Li, the Changle entrepreneur who showed me the monument of the winged sail, observed that the long period of sustained economic growth in China has had an impact not necessarily on the number of people leaving Fujian Province, but on the kinds of people who are leaving. Until recently, she explained, the best and the brightest in the province felt stifled in their villages and towns, and made arrangements, assumed debt, and took great risks to journey to the United States. Those who stayed behind were derided as unambitious, if not downright lazy. But today, the truly enterprising residents of a city like Changle set out to start a textile factory, or build a hotel. They see no point in risking their lives to travel to the United States so that they can live a precarious existence as an undocumented alien on the margins of some American city. Much wiser for them to stay put.

People still pay snakeheads to leave the country, Lin Li continued. But only those who have been unable to find some niche in the new economy, some promising way to make it rich. A decade ago, Lin Li might have paid a snakehead to bring her to America, but today she owns two grocery stores and is investing in a condominium complex that is springing up in town, the new buildings erected by construction workers trucked in from Sichuan, because there are so few low-wage Fujianese manual laborers left — they have all moved on to the United States. Lin Li wrinkled her nose disdainfully at the mention of those who today would avail themselves of a snakehead. "If you can do *anything* here," she concluded, "you stay."

Still, China's migrant labor market is exquisitely sensitive to even the most incremental shifts in the local and global economy. Lin Li is right to observe that the dynamics of out-migration in Fujian Province have changed dramatically over the past longed global recession setting in, it remains an open question what developments the near future holds, and how the potentially mobile segment of China's workforce will react to those developments.

Already, many of the same construction workers who have manned new developments like Lin Li's in recent years are struggling to find jobs as the pace of growth slows. They are now reversing the migration trend, returning west to their hometowns and ancestral farms. If the economy continues to suffer, laborers like these could employ snakeheads to transport them to North America, or Europe, to Africa, or the Middle East — anyplace where they might be more likely to make a decent wage. Fujian could once again become a major source of migrants, either in the form of strivers like Lin Li, who suddenly find that it is not as easy as it once was to start a business or land a contract, or in the form of displaced laborers from the west, who would rather try their luck abroad than return to the villages they left behind. If the price of passage is currently prohibitive to all but a few prospective emigrants, it seems more than likely that the snakeheads, entrepreneurial to the end, will find ways to lower their prices and economize on the costs of the journey. Whatever the outcome of the current financial crisis on China's labor market, chances are good that many migrants will once again turn to the snakeheads. And when they do, the snakeheads are certain to oblige.

The Sex Trade 2

Sean Flynn

Part 1: Pleasure At Any Price

The fat guy smoking Pall Malls, he says he almost married one of those girls. Honest. He met her in a bar one of the last times he was in the Philippines and fell in love, almost bought her a ring and took her home. It didn't work out, though, and he doesn't say why because it doesn't really matter. He shrugs.

The skinny kid with the knobby head understands. Same thing happened to him, sort of. She was 19, beautiful, didn't wear makeup or anything. She was so . . . what's the word? *Simple*. You know? "Just give her the American necessities and those are, like, her luxuries," he tells the fat guy. "Let her live like a queen."

The fat guy grins. His front teeth are missing, and he's got hair like an oil slick, long and black and greasy. Oh yeah, lots of those girls want an American husband, and they're not picky, either. "As long as you're not married and you've got an income," the guy says, "you're good to go."

It's four o'clock in the morning in a Japanese airport, thirteen hours out of Detroit Metro, on a layover in Nagoya before the last 1,700 miles to Manila. The fat guy and the skinny kid found each other in the smoking lounge as if they had picked up a shared scent, a couple of misfit white guys dragging halfway around the planet.

Then another, a fellow traveler in a red running suit, walks over. He's fiftyish and pudgy with gray hair and enough of a beard to cover a weak chin. He's never been to the Philippines before, he tells them, just heard the stories about the bars and the girls, and now that he's divorced, what the hell, treat himself. Still, he's a little nervous about the whole thing.

The skinny kid knows that feeling, too. He was nervous his first time. It's kind of weird, the way you can buy a girl for a couple of bucks, a different one every night, every hour if you want, walk around town with her and not even pretend it's anything more than a cash transaction. "I walk into this place with my arm around this local girl, you know, and there's all these guys sitting around looking at me," he says. "And I'm thinking, I'm gonna get my ass kicked, you know?"

The fat guy's grinning again. He knows where this is going.

"But then they're all like, 'Hey, American, come and drink with us!'"

"Oh yeah," the fat guy says. "And after ten minutes, you're not talking *to* them. You're talking *with* them."

They all nod, even the guy in red.

"Seriously," the skinny kid says. "They *love* Americans."

There's a girl on a small stage in a bar called the G-Spot Lounge in Angeles City, a sprawl of cinder block and tin about an hour northwest of Manila. She's wearing a sky blue bikini that matches the powder Mamasan swabbed on her eyelids, along with enough blush and mascara to make her whole face itch. She hasn't worn makeup since her first Communion, and then not so much.

She has a birth certificate that says she's 19. It's false, and obviously so, because she's only 13, but nobody cares, because in the dark, under all that rouge and shadow, she looks old enough. All the girls — the other ones onstage, the ones waiting tables, the ones cuddling up to customers, sweet-talking foreign men into buying them drinks — look old enough, which isn't very old at all.

An American man is yelling at her. "Hey, you!" he says. "Yeah, you. Dance! You're getting paid to dance."

She doesn't really know how to dance, and the high-heeled boots she's wearing make it even harder to fake it. Her arms are in close, holding her own bare torso in a loose hug, and she shifts her weight from foot to foot, gently twists her shoulders from one side to the other. Is that dancing? Is it close enough? Do they even care, the men watching, the Koreans and the Japanese, the Americans and the Aussies, the fat guys and the skinny kids sucking on stubby bottles of San Miguel?

Mamasan, the bar manager, will pay the girl 120 pesos to wear her bikini from six o'clock in the evening until three o'clock in the morning. She is supposed to dance for half an hour, then go work the room for a while and wait for her next shift onstage. If one of the men in the club buys her a drink, Mamasan will cut her in for fifty pesos, put it toward her debts: 1,300 for the boots, thirty-five more for a week's laundry. Or maybe one of the customers will buy her for the night, give Mamasan 1,000 pesos — "bar fine," they call it here, a term that's both a noun and a verb — to take her out of the G-Spot, maybe to another club or a restaurant first but probably just to his hotel room. The girl would get half of that, about $9 American.

It's her first night at the G-Spot. She'd gone looking for work a few days ago — up Fields Avenue, past Club Fantastic and Camelot and Stinger, past the sidewalk shops selling shirts that say I FUCK ON THE FIRST DATE and I'LL BUY DRINKS FOR SEX, past the shoeshine boys and the peddlers with their bootleg Cialis, past all the other bars looking to hire dancers and waitresses and GROs, which is short for *guest-relations officers*, which is long and awkward for *prostitute*. "Must have happy personality," the signs say, because no horny tourist is going to bar-fine a girl who isn't any fun.

The mamasan at the G-Spot asked the girl how old she was, and she said 19 and showed her the birth certificate that couldn't possibly be legit, and Mamasan hired her, gave her the boots and the bikini and rubbed makeup on her face and put her on a stage. That's how it happened, just like that: A little girl walks into a bar and gets a job.

"Hey." Big Daddy again, out there beyond the strobe of the stage lights. Papasan, the guy who runs the G-Spot. His name is Thomas Glenn Jarrell, an Ohio native who did a tour in the army before settling in a dirty little city that is moderately famous simply because it has bars, dozens of them, and girls, thousands of them, and only eighteen bucks a night. "You're getting paid to dance!"

Seriously, fat guys and skinny kids tell each other in Japanese airports, *they love Americans.*

The girl blinks the itch from her eyes and lets her arms fall to her sides and wiggles her hips. Is that dancing? Is it close enough?

Change her name. It doesn't matter. Make her a little younger or a little older, but never too old. Dress her in a red bikini or a slip or a pleated plaid skirt. Wrap her naked around a pole or put her in a room with a big glass window and a flock of other girls, bored and trying not to look it, waiting to be picked like lobsters from a tank. Move her down to Manila and pay her more, or move her up the coast to a shack on the National Highway and pay her less. Put her thousands of miles away, in Tokyo or Moscow, or put her on the other side of the globe, in Costa Rica or Mexico. It doesn't matter. The story will be the same, the beginning sounding like the setup to an old and dirty joke: *A girl walks into a bar . . .*

So many girls walk into so many bars today that no one even tries to count them all. Cataloging every prostitute on the planet with any accuracy is no more feasible than counting leaves in a forest: The business is by definition largely underground and extremely fluid, the workforce mostly unregistered, untraceable, and ever changing. Instead, there are only guesses, estimates, and extrapolations, worst cases and best cases depending on who's counting and where and why. Statistics for individual countries, individual cities, even specific red-light districts, vary wildly from lowball official figures to almost incredible numbers conjured by aid groups and activists. Thailand, for instance, a notorious and well-studied sexual playground for foreign men, has either 75,000 prostitutes, as the government claims, or depending on which aid group is tossing out numbers, nearly 2 million who generate *up to 14 percent* of the country's gross domestic product — parameters calibrated so widely as to be virtually useless as an accounting tool. The sex-trade data are so imprecise that researchers and government agencies shorthand the global total to a generic tens of millions of women and girls generating tens of billions in cash.

The actual numbers are irrelevant, anyway. A Filipino bar girl doesn't care whether she is one of 50,000 (the low end) or 800,000 (the high end), and a john in a Russian brothel doesn't concern himself with the millions of women he could theoretically be renting, because the ten or twenty at hand are more than enough. The global sex trade, as pure a commodities market as pork bellies or soybean futures, need only be measured in broad sweeps of demand, which is apparently insatiable, and supply, which is seemingly endless.

Within those uncountable numbers are stories of horrific brutality, of women smuggled into foreign lands, beaten into submission, forced to work off infinite, impossible debts. There are stories, too, of breathtaking naïveté, of young Moldovans giddy because they've got contracts to work as cocktail waitresses in Kabul, of peasants in Mindanao who believe a low-rent gangster when he promises to make them cabaret stars in Manila or Tokyo, of foolish girls who actually *want* to be prostitutes because they've seen a bootleg tape of *Pretty Woman*.

The great bulk of the business, though, is far more prosaic, a function of simple economics, the ageless enterprise of women willingly selling their most easily marketed assets. It can be condemned by feminist theory and religious mores, and the key adverb — *willingly* — is terribly relative, especially considering that there is almost always a middleman, a mamasan or a pimp, taking a cut. Yet *oppression* is also a relative term: For people with limited options, the few that remain don't seem so unreasonable. And in any case, business is booming. In an age of easy international travel, when borders are not much sturdier than lines drawn on a map, both sides of the trade — supply and demand — have become industrialized.

If viewed from above, from high in the stratosphere with the whole blue earth rolling and spinning below, the currents of the sex trade would be as obvious as the clouds, swirls of people moving from country to country, continent to continent. There are two dominant streams, intertwining, twirling around each other but moving in opposite directions. The women and the girls are swept out of poor places, from parts of South America and Asia and the former Soviet Union, into wealthier nations and cities, Moscow and Tokyo, Turkey and Dubai, Germany and the United States. The men — "'mongers" or "hobbyists," in the fraternal jargon of the hardcore sex traveler — generally drift in the other direction, from rich to poor, from the United States and Australia and Britain and Japan and the rest of the First World into the Second and Third Worlds. There are small and curious eddies, like the Brits — "whorists," the tabloids call them — who've discovered "tottie tours" through Tallinn, the capital of Estonia, or the drip of Arabs who fly to Chisinau, in desperately impoverished Moldova, to patronize the brothels. But the strongest currents flow to the most entrenched bazaars: To the resort cities of Brazil, Cuba, and a few Caribbean islands; to Central America; and, of course, to Southeast Asia — historically, Thailand and Cambodia and, rising fast over the past twenty years, the Philippines. Many of those countries, particularly in Asia, became destinations in part because they have long cultural histories of prostitution. According to several studies, more than half of Thai men paid to lose their virginity, and more than 400,000 visit brothels each day, estimates that no one seriously disputes. The Philippines, a nation that is at once matriarchal and rotten with machismo, has a similar tradition, an indigenous demand that drives a local market. "It's simply the norm that you have two kinds of women — those you respect and those you can buy and play around with," says Aurora Javate-de Dios, the executive director of the Asia-Pacific chapter of the Coalition Against Trafficking in Women, based in Quezon City.

And that norm has grown into a massive service industry for foreigners. In Balibago, a few dusty blocks of Angeles City on the south side of what used to be Clark Air Force Base, there are 117 bars and a handful of massage parlors, one gaudy facade next to another next to another. "It's all here: alcohol and sexy young women," the neighborhood's semiofficial Web site (www.balibago.com) promises. "Recreational sex is the sport of choice. You can enjoy full privileges with one or more attractive young females regardless of your age, weight, physical appearance, interpersonal skills, wealth, or social class." On Burgos Street in Makati, the high-rent district of Manila, the girls upstairs at Jools wait by the door until men walk in and the lights snap on, and then they all pop up and pose, and the girls at High Heels squeeze onto a melon-wedge stage and sway roughly in sync while others work the high-top tables with red velveteen trim — *you bar-fine me?* — and all the girls at all the other clubs on that strip do the exact same thing. A few congested miles away, in Quezon City, is Air Force One, an enormous neon box the size of a midwest convention center, with inlaid floors and a red-curtained stage and narrow hallways lined with small rooms named for every American president (the George W. Bush cubicle is particularly popular) and girls stocked in two glass-walled displays — first and business classes for the younger and prettier, economy for the older and uglier. And along the northern coast of Subic Bay, in a speck of a town called Calapandayan, underage girls wave from a balcony in striped tube tops while across the street, in a place called Muff Divers, a dozen more girls do a limp waggle for five surly Australians.

The bars are everywhere, and there are girls in every bar. Yet none of the girls are technically prostitutes, because prostitution is illegal in the Philippines. A bar fine, in the national patois, is merely proper compensation for a club to let a girl out the door for a few hours, after which consenting adults can have at it — a ridiculous semantic wink that allows the industry to thrive with official deference if not outright sanction. ("I've had [aid workers] tell me you can't stop it because to do so you'd have to arrest half the senate," says one Western diplomat in Manila.) Indeed, much of the rest of the tourist sector is in on the gag. A guard with a machine gun at Ninoy Aquino International Airport sees a man in a suit with an American passport, grins, nods. "You have a good time, yes? You get some girls, yes?" A driver for the Makati Shangri-La, a five-star hotel, volunteers that he can procure an authentic virgin out in the provinces. Her parents will want 100,000 pesos, but she'll be a real cherry girl, guaranteed, not some university coed faking it for a night because she's short on tuition.

At this point, there is no financial incentive to enforce the laws, anyway. No one knows exactly how much the bars and the girls contribute to the $2 billion tourist trade — immigration does not ask men if they're entering the country to get laid — but it is substantial. An estimated 300,000 Japanese sex tourists visit the Philippines each year; and in 1997, a boom year for tourism, 13,000 Australians traveled to Angeles City alone, a figure reportedly second only to Americans. (And there really is no other appreciable reason to go to Angeles City, other than the bars.) Factor in the businessmen with a few hours to kill, multiply by hotel rooms and restaurant tabs and bar bills . . . It adds up.

Moreover, the bars and the brothels provide jobs in a country that doesn't have nearly enough to go around. Almost a million Filipinos leave the country each year to find employment, and more than 10 percent of the gross domestic product is cash sent home by overseas workers. Most go off to be domestics and laborers, a few are skilled professionals, and some — again, no one knows exactly how many — are imported to be prostitutes in wealthier countries. Until earlier this year, Japan alone granted more than 70,000 visas annually to Filipinos to work as "cultural entertainers," a euphemism so transparent that international pressure finally forced the number to be cut to 8,000. For those who remain on the archipelago, where nearly half the population lives on less than $2 a day, there are menial jobs in the city and field work in the provinces, neither of which is abundant or pays more than a subsistence wage.

Or there are the bars. There are thousands in the big cities and little villages, and dozens that sprouted next to the American naval base at Subic Bay and alongside Clark Air Force Base in Angeles City. Soldiers and sailors and air-men used to come by the thousands, flush with American dollars to spend on cheap beer and pretty girls, and the pretty girls came by the thousands, too, because the money was so much better than anything else they could do, and sometimes — not often, but with the same frequency that sells lottery tickets — a soldier or a sailor fell in love with a girl he met in a bar and married her and took her away. It went on like that for decades, so durable and so vast that it became famous, so famous that even after the bases closed, men kept coming, Americans and Australians and Koreans and Japanese, with their dollars and yen, traveling all the way into the middle of the Pacific just to hump the local women. There are so many tourists bringing so much money that a silly term is invented to make it all legal, and eventually the whole country — the hotel clerks and taxi drivers and airport guards — is winking and nodding, because in a way they're getting a little taste of the action, too.

And then it's simply the norm.

There is another girl, a woman, actually, because she's 23, who works at another club, a different kind of club in Manila, more subdued, classier, the sort that features girls with business cards. The cards are a mottled gold and pink, and they have her cell-phone number in the bottom corner and her name — Wine, that's all, just Wine — above her awkwardly translated and slightly misspelled title, CLIENT'S LIASON ENTERTAINMENT OFFICER.

Wine wears a cocktail dress, size zero because she is tiny, not quite five feet tall. At the start of each shift, she sits with all the other girls in the showroom behind a wide pane of one-way glass in one of the upholstered chairs that are set in long rows, like the littlest theater at the cineplex, and there is a small screen, set low into the front wall, playing videos to keep her from going mad with boredom while she waits. When customers come in, Mamasan draws open the curtains on the other side, and dim light filters in so Wine knows to look up, but she can't see anything on the other side, only shadows. She can count how many men are looking in and sometimes, if one of the silhouettes is especially large, she'll get up and slip out the back.

Most times, though, Wine smiles and tries to look pretty, which she is, and tries to be charming, which is difficult through a sheet of soundproof glass. If a man selects her, Mamasan will push a button on an intercom and call her name, and then Wine will come into the hallway and try even harder to be charming. She will kiss him on the cheek and slip her arm through his, like a new girlfriend on a third date. Mamasan will lead them — Wine and a client, maybe two other girls and their clients, maybe two girls and one client — through a warren of hallways, which are darker and narrower away from the lobster tank, to one of the fifty private rooms. There are banquettes along two or three of the walls, short cocktail tables, a television set, and a karaoke machine.

The club is not a brothel. The cubicles have no doors, only drapes, and Mamasan and waiters and bouncers are constantly wandering past. Some men, especially the Asian men who make up most of Wine's clients, will pay good money to have strange women sing karaoke with them, 800 pesos an hour, of which Wine collects 250. Her client will buy drinks, of course (Wine is a scotch gal), and if he's feeling frisky, he'll drop an additional 400 pesos to have Wine change into a loose and low-cut slip so he can lick salt off her body for a tequila shooter. "Not the naughty parts," Wine says. Only here — she points to her neck — or here — a spot above her left breast — or here — the curve of her hip. She always offers the body-shot option, the same way used-car salesmen offer rustproofing, because she gets paid an extra 150 when she lets a man lick her. A lot of clients paw and grope her anyway, so she may as well collect some pesos for her trouble.

If a man is particularly taken by her, he can pay Mamasan the bar fine, 10,000 pesos — $180, give or take, ten times the price of an Angeles City girl — half of which goes to Wine. But Wine says she does not leave the club with clients. Okay, maybe she does once in a while, but only for dinner in a nice restaurant or a few hours in a casino. She says she is not a prostitute. Her English gets noticeably worse. She changes the subject.

Wine has worked at that club for almost three years, which is unusual only because she admits it. (Dorothy says she has been there for two weeks. Maki says she has been there for two weeks. An astonishing number of girls say they are 19 years old and have worked at their particular bar or club for exactly two weeks, like a default code that says *I'm legal and experienced, but barely*.) She comes in four or five nights a week at seven o'clock and stays until three or four the next morning. On a good night — actually, her best night ever — she will spend five hours with clients. If they all spring for body shots, she will gross 2,000 pesos. Of that, Wine will owe 100 pesos for laundry, 200 for makeup, and an additional 300 or so for food. So if she's very charming and very lucky, Wine will walk out just before dawn, sticky with salt licks, with 1,400 pesos. Thirty bucks, give or take.

It is the best job she has ever had.

She has a 7-year-old son to support. Wine got pregnant when she was 15, gave birth at 16, started working soon after. Odd jobs, menial jobs. She peddled cosmetics, sold bananas from a cart, worked the cashbox at a cockpit. None of them paid well. When she was 19 she told her boyfriend, her baby's father, that she wanted to be an entertainer in Japan. He said no. But she knew someone who had a friend who knew a guy — it's always that complicated — who managed girls who wanted to go get one of those 70,000 cultural-entertainment visas. Wine needed the money more than she needed her boyfriend, so she signed up.

Her manager put her through six months of training, schooling her in rudimentary Japanese culture and etiquette, teaching her the basics of the language, explaining the mysteries of the wider world, like how to behave on an airplane. That all cost money, naturally — "credits," Wine says, when she actually means debts. So did coaching her to pass the Artist Record Book test, which required her to sing three songs — one fast and two slow — ably enough to qualify as a "cultural entertainer," a threshold Wine concedes is not set particularly high because she cannot, in fact, sing very well. Then there was paperwork to arrange, and plane tickets and housing — thousands and thousands of amorphous expenses, all on credit.

She says she spent six months in Kyoto working at a club controlled by local gangsters. That was a good job, too. The mamasan looked out for her, she says, kept her away from the yakuza heavies, never forced her to do anything she didn't want to, like go out on dates with any of the clients. A lot of the other girls did, though. The Russians and the Romanians? Total whores. When Wine talks about that part of the job, she only screws up her pronouns a couple of times, says *I* before she stops and says *she* and changes the subject. Mostly, she says, she hustled drinks from lonely businessmen and rasped Britney Spears songs onstage.

After six months, after paying her living expenses and all of her debts, subtracting everything she owed, she cleared 40,000 pesos, or about $700.

Wine got the job at her current club not long after she came back from Japan. She never meant to stay here so long, but the money's good, better than she'd get anywhere else. She could make even more, work six nights a week, if it weren't for the hangovers. She's trying to cut back on the booze, trying to switch over to fruit shakes like the other girls, which is why she's only having one magnificent tumbler of scotch tonight, not counting the two she had with the guy who was in a couple of hours ago.

Two years pass. The girl from the G-Spot is still only a girl, 15 now, almost 16, which is how old she looks in the twilight on a bluff above Subic Bay, thirty miles southwest of the bars in Angeles City where she used to work. She's wearing a red T-shirt and a thin silver chain that reflects gold in the sunset, and she has dark eyes and dark hair, but her skin is a faint shade lighter than most Filipinos' because her father was a white man, an Australian.

He was a businessman in the north of the country, and he bought fabrics, bolts of silk, from a pretty lady in a market. He kept buying her silks, and soon, maybe even in the first week, he fell in love, *crazy in love*, that's how the girl says it because that's how her father said it. After three years, when they were living as husband and wife, they had a baby daughter — the girl — and later two sons.

When the girl was 4, the family moved to Quezon City, in metro Manila, to be closer to her mother's relatives. The girl had her own room in a two-story house next to a garment shop her father owned, which, along with an ice plant he also owned, paid the bills. She was happy. Her father told her she would grow up to be a doctor.

Then her mother met another man. He was a bad guy, compared with her father anyway, in trouble with the police, in and out of jail, always smoking *shabu*, the Filipino version of crystal meth. Not long after, the girl's parents split up.

They still saw each other, though. According to the girl, her mother would go to her father and ask him for money, say it was to buy food and to raise the girl and her brothers, but she'd use it to post bail for the thief or buy him more *shabu.* The girl's father knew, but he gave her the pesos anyway. "My father," she says, "he is so crazy in love with her."

Until it hurt too much to be crazy in love. On December 15, 2000, the girl's father hanged himself in his apartment.

She ran back north for a while, lived with one of her father's friends, but seven months later she went back to her mother and the man, who by then was her stepfather — a junkie and a criminal sleeping in her father's bed in her father's house. He was strict, wouldn't let her out of the house, and he would hit her, hit her little brothers. "My stepfather, I think he has something wrong with me," she says. "Why does he do these things to me? Why doesn't he let me be a child?"

Her mother took the worst of the beatings. In the summer of 2002, the stepfather threw his wife to the floor, grabbed her by the hair, dragged her into the bathroom, and tried to drown her in the tub. He pulled a knife, held it to her throat, and swore he would kill her. Then the police came, swarming into the house, waving their guns. Days later, when the police said they couldn't hold her stepfather any longer, she packed a bag and headed north again.

She bounced from relative to relative for a few months before going to Angeles City. She had family there, an "uncle" who's actually her mother's cousin. She asked if she could live with his family, and he said no, he couldn't afford another mouth, but she asked again and then a third time, and he finally said yes, okay, she could stay. But she felt guilty because she knew she was a burden. And she worried about her little brothers, left behind in Manila to fend for themselves. "So after so many days," she says, "I decide to work in a bar."

That's how it happens. That's how a girl 13 years old walks into a bar and gets a job.

She worked nine-hour shifts, trying to dance in her bikini, blue one day, maroon the next, eye shadow always matching and always too thick, then coming off the stage, talking to customers, coaxing drinks out of them, fifty pesos a shot for her own pocket. She did not like her job. Some of the men who drank at the G-Spot seemed nice enough, but mainly they were old (everyone seems old to a girl of 13) and fat and horny, the sort of schlubs who read the Web site and believed it because it happens to be true: *You can enjoy full privileges with one or more attractive young females regardless of your age, weight, physical appearance, interpersonal skills, wealth, or social class.*

"Do you know the word *blow job*?" she asks. "And . . . I don't know the word, when you lick the pussy?" The girl blushes, looks away. "I saw some very bad, disgusting . . . *yuck*," she says. "I saw it because I have eyes."

On her third night at the G-Spot, she says, a Japanese businessman and his Filipina assistant bar-fined her, paid a thousand pesos to take her out into Angeles City. Mamasan told the Japanese guy that his date was a cherry girl, which normally would tack a premium onto the price — "cherry popping" is popular among certain connoisseurs of degeneracy — but her tone was firm, a cautionary instruction — *don't fuck her* — instead of a promise. And he did not try. He asked her how old she was, and she said 18, and he didn't believe her, so she said 16, and he did not ask again. Then he took her around the corner to a casino, and the girl just watched while he gambled. She was relieved when he told her to go.

Fifteen years ago, and for decades before that, most of the men in the bars were Americans, the soldiers and sailors on leave or stationed at Clark and Subic Bay. In the '80s, Aurora Javate-de Dios of the Coalition Against Trafficking in Women was in Olongapo on business as the troopships unloaded and thousands of servicemen streamed off the naval base and into the city. She could feel their eyes, all those men looking at her the way they looked at all the other Filipinas. "That was kind of a humiliating moment," she says. " 'Oh, so *this* is how it feels to be commodified.'"

When the US military decamped a few years later, it was assumed by many Filipinos that the sex trade would go with them, that the former bases would be redeveloped with hotels and restaurants, provide decent jobs, and attract less salacious tourists. That has happened to some extent at Subic Bay, but much less so in Angeles City. "We had hoped it would end, but it did not," Javate-de Dios says. "Apparently, the culture and the infrastructure were enough reason for other investors to come in. In fact, now it's more terrible because it's international." The dynamic has been reversed, the supply of bars and girls no longer a reaction to a specific demand — horny American soldiers who were sent there by the shipload — but a self-sustaining industry that creates its own demand. Americans still wander the streets of Angeles City, but so do Koreans and Brits and Australians and Germans.

The moneymen tend to be foreigners as well. The legal papers are fuzzy (which, in turn, makes the legal responsibilities fuzzy, too), but the alleged Pooh-Bah of Fields Avenue is Richard Agnew, a former constable with the Royal Ulster Constabulary. He moved to the Philippines in the mid-'90s and over the following years started running a small empire of clubs — Nero's Forum, Misty's, and at least three others — and the nicest hotel in the neighborhood, the Egyptian-themed Blue Nile Executive Club. An Australian, Terrence George Matthews, and his purported partner, an American named Thomas Glenn Jarrell, apparently owned the G-Spot, Club Fantastic, and other clubs. The girl thought so, anyway. She recognizes Jarrell's picture now. "That's Papasan," she says. That's the guy who yelled at a child for not dancing well enough.

The girl worked four more nights before anyone else paid her bar fine. This time, she says, it was an Australian man with a Filipino wife. Odd, two couples bar-fining an underage girl in a club that serves single men almost exclusively. The Australian had started talking to her in the bar, and she told him how her father had been Australian, too, which was enough for the man to invite her out to dinner. They just talked, the three of them, all through the meal, and when they finished, the Australian thanked her and told her to go home.

She went back to the G-Spot instead, where another man approached her, took her gently by the arm, and asked her to point out Mamasan. The girl did. The man, still holding the girl's arm, took her to Mamasan and said he wanted to pay her bar fine, started dickering over the price, argued, wanted to know exactly how much for the girl.

Cops were everywhere after that, bursting through the door, guns drawn, yelling at everyone not to move. The girl was terrified, but all the adults were likely more dumbfounded than frightened: Police raid the bars in Angeles City about as often as Mount Pinatubo explodes, which is hardly ever. Why would they shake down the G-Spot now?

Because activists from an international nonprofit had been in town for more than a week, crawling through the bars, snooping for underage girls. This wasn't hard to do: UNICEF estimates there are approximately 100,000 minors currently working as prostitutes in the Philippines. The guy who dickered with Mamasan was an undercover cop, one of a squad put together after the activists pestered federal police for help. On November 28, 2002, the National Bureau of Investigation and the Angeles City police raided five bars. The cops took the girl and four others, all 17, out of the G-Spot, and three others — two 17 and one 13 — from Club Fantastic. Jarrell, Matthews, and four Filipina floor managers were arrested. As for the other three clubs, the aid workers could have been wrong — maybe they saw some girls who only *looked* like they were too young to be working as bar girls.

Or maybe the clubs got lucky. Maybe the young ones had the night off.

Change the details. Shuffle the dates, stage the raid in July, when the girl was still in Manila watching a thief beat up her mother. Put the cops in a dozen bars that night, let them grab a hundred underage girls, arrest four foreign papasans and ten mamasans. It doesn't matter. The next day, the story would be the same: *A girl walks into a bar . . .*

For the girl, though, it matters. In a miserable life, she was blessed with small kindnesses and fortunate timing, by a mamasan who protected her cherry-girl status even as she sold her out the door, by missionaries who appeared like wraiths, by a raid orchestrated after she'd spent only a few nights in a bikini. If she'd been off that night, if she'd been out on a bar fine when the police came through the door . . . For her, the details matter.

Yet for Fields Avenue, for Balibago, for Burgos Street, for Makati, for all the other girls in all the other bars and clubs, the details are irrelevant. The girls who were swept away that night could be replaced in the morning. The six girls who were 17 when the cops came? In a few months, all of them would cross that mystical barrier, the age of consent, turn 18, and become, by the flip of a calendar page, legal adults with all the free will in the world to dance in a bar for fat, horny foreigners.

The lure is so strong. Even the youngest among them, the girl with not even two weeks' experience, couldn't stay away. After the raid, she was sent to a group home run by PREDA — the People's Recovery, Empowerment and Development Assistance Foundation, in a villa on a hill above Subic Bay — which a Columban missionary named Father Shay Cullen cofounded thirty years ago after a pimp in Olongapo tried to sell him an 11-year-old. The girl was there for a year. She had a bed in a dormitory, food, school lessons, therapy.

She went back to Angeles City anyway. Took two other girls with her, too.

"My feelings and my mind were mixed-up," is the only way she can explain it. She was too frightened to go back to the G-Spot, so she scouted all the bars and then settled on Bahama Mama's because it had the chubbiest girls loitering outside and, consequently, the fewest men inside. At first she was bored, but after a few days she thought it was fun, like a game, dancing with her big sisters — the senior dancers' names are always preceded by *ate* (*ah*-teh), a familiar form of "big sister" — and any man who paid her bar fine received only the pleasure of buying her margaritas. She's still a cherry girl. Her friends left, but she stayed for a couple weeks, and would have stayed longer if Father Shay hadn't gone looking for her, handing her picture to the police and the tricycle-taxi drivers, loudly announcing that she was a lost child, shaming people with an immunity to shame into looking for her. She finally turned herself in.

No one's looking for Wine. She'd like to get out of the club in Manila where she works, open her own place, something nice down in the Malate district, near the embassies and the waterfront. She's got it all figured out, explains it between sips of scotch, how she'll have three rooms, an Internet café out front, karaoke in the middle, billiards in the back. No go-go girls. No bar fines. Classy. A nice dream. A girl can dream, right?

She takes another drink, rattles the ice in her glass. She knows it'll never happen. "How long will I work here?" she says. "Until my hair is white."

And the arrests? The foreign men hauled off in handcuffs? Change those details, too. Put them in shackles for the cameras, drag them out in chains while the missionaries watch. Shut down their bars. Accuse them of pimping minors, of hiring children to wear bikinis, all of which the Philippines has laws against. It doesn't matter. "We have laws against trafficking, protecting women and children," says Javate-de Dios. "But they're almost always breached in practice." She shakes her head. "You could say our criminal-justice system sucks. Really, *really* sucks." The business is simply too big, the money too good.

On paper, Thomas Glenn Jarrell — who the girl says was the papasan at the G-Spot — faced an apparently serious charge of "willfully, unlawfully, and feloniously" employing a minor as an erotic dancer. His bail was set at 30,000 pesos — $600. To no one's surprise, he posted it. In the almost three years since his arrest, he has not been prosecuted for anything involving the club.

Change the details again. Have a couple of local families complain that their daughters were hired as waitresses in Richard Agnew's clubs and then ordered to have sex with foreign tourists. Make the girls young — 13, 12, 11. Let one of them tell a reporter, "I was a virgin, and I didn't want to go, but I was told I would lose my job if I didn't do it, so I went with him." Let the British papers loose on him, call him sleazy, say he's pimping children. Presume him innocent, but line up all the witnesses; get his employees and get his business partner to say he's the boss, that Agnew owns all the clubs around here. Gather so much evidence that the Philippine police raid his clubs and throw him in jail. Let him sit there for so long facing such an awful charge that he asks to be deported just to make it go away.

All of that happened in September 2003, about the time the girl was drinking margaritas in Bahama Mama's. Agnew denied owning any clubs, still denies it, says he's only a manager, that other people, local people, ran the operations, that he thought all those girls were 18. And it was technically true: His name appeared on none of the clubs' legal papers. And it was true that when he was locked up, he signed papers admitting to owning part of those clubs, but he says he was coerced, that the Filipino cops were all corrupt, that he had to admit something, anything, just to get out of jail.

And yet he's still there in Angeles City, managing bars, bragging about his charity work. Those cops he swears were all corrupt seem to like him very much. The charges were dropped, and in January 2005 a chief from the Philippine National Police presented Agnew with a plaque in gratitude for his contributions to the tourist trade. It was a small moment in a bigger ceremony, one of those details that get buried in the back pages of the newspapers, and one of the only details that actually matter.

Part 2: The Great Sex Migration

Zina and Veronica are on a train traveling east, though the direction doesn't matter, because north or south or west would take them just as surely away from home and toward somewhere else, which is the only place they want to go. They think they are dreaming. They think this, finally, is what it must feel like, dreaming, being cradled in the sway of a railcar, steel track sliding beneath them, something like a future waiting beyond the border, faint and indistinct but shining brighter than anything in their past.

They have never dreamed before. Ask them. Ask Zina and Veronica what they dreamed about when they were girls, after their father left them with their alcoholic mother and an alcoholic brother in three dank rooms along a mud rut of a road in a smudge of a country called Moldova, and they will look at you with wide, blank eyes, as if you'd asked where they stabled their unicorns. "We didn't have a dream, because it was impossible," Zina will tell you. "When you come home from school and there is no food, you can't dream."

When they finished their primary studies, Zina and Veronica wanted only to work, any kind of work, so they could earn money to buy food, but no one would hire them — they were only 15, and it wouldn't have mattered even if they'd been older, because there weren't any jobs anyway. So they planted vegetables in the patch of dirt inside the garden wall and collected apricots from three skinny trees, and they hoped winter would come late and stay mild, because the house would get so cold they would have to close off the largest room and huddle together in the two remaining rooms that, small as they were, the stove could barely heat. They lived like this until Zina was 27 and Veronica was 24, and they expected they always would.

Then, one December day when they were cold and hungry, a woman knocked on their door. Zina and Veronica recognized her from their childhood, only she was dressed better and looked well fed, as if she had some money in her pocket. She told the sisters that she had been to Russia, that there were jobs there, that Zina and Veronica should go at once. They could be vendors in a market in Krasnodar, one of the biggest cities in southern Russia. Or they could wash windows, as Russia has many wealthy people who insist on looking through sparkling-clean glass.

Zina and Veronica thought this was preposterous. True, thousands of people had left their village, Costesti, and some of them must be doing well, making money. See the new houses rising along the crumbling main road, grand and sturdy, two stories of block and timber with arches above the windows? That's how you could tell who had a son on a construction crew in Lisbon or Moscow, a daughter mopping hotel floors in London or Dubai. But they could not go to Russia. They had no passports, no money, no place to stay. The woman said she had friends, Gypsy friends, who would get them passports, lend them money for the train, and give them a place to live.

No, they could not go. Who would take care of Mama?

The woman told them they could send Mama money from Russia. How could they take care of Mama if they had no money?

Zina and Veronica said no again. The woman left, came back, had the same conversation, left again, came back again. She did this for two weeks, kept coming until Zina and Veronica decided she must be right, that they should go to Russia and earn money. It was agreed, then. The Gypsies helped them get their papers in order and booked their passage, and now, finally, they are on a train heading east.

Are they dreaming? Or are they only less desperate?

The train stops in Krasnodar. More Gypsies are waiting for them, as if they know exactly whom to look for — Zina with her huge brown eyes and high cheekbones, Veronica with her short hair and pug nose — as if they know exactly which carriage the pair will climb down from. The Gypsies put the sisters in a sedan and drive them to a two-room apartment. Six other girls are already there. This is where Zina and Veronica will live.

The Gypsies tell them it will take two days, maybe three, to find them an open stall in the market and clear it with the police, with whom the Gypsies suggest they are extremely friendly.

Two days pass. Zina and Veronica do not leave the apartment.

On the third day, the Gypsies tell them there are no openings in the market. No one wants any windows washed. "But you still owe us money," one of the Gypsies says. "So you will do other things. You will be prostitutes."

Zina and Veronica panic. No, they say, we will not be prostitutes; we will not do such an awful thing. They say they are sorry for the trouble they have caused, for the money they have borrowed. They say they will go back to Moldova and find a job, any job, to pay back the Gypsies, pay back every cent.

The Gypsies beat them.

The Gypsies say, "We will cut your fucking hands off."

The Gypsies say, "We will bury you alive."

The Gypsies beat them some more, keep beating them until Zina and Veronica believe that they will, in fact, cut off their hands and bury them alive, beat them until there is no more foolish talk about going back to Moldova, beat them until, as Zina says, "we were destroyed."

The next day, Zina and Veronica are sold to a strip club. Every night, they dance naked on a stage and have sex in the back rooms with strangers who do not care about their bruises. There are old men and young men, rich men and working men, and Zina and Veronica do not know how many, because there are too many to count.

And how many women? How many like Zina and Veronica, forced into prostitution not by circumstance or poverty but by deception, threats, and violence? How many are trafficked from villages to cities, from poor countries to wealthier ones, lured by false promises, bought and sold like chattels?

No one knows. Among the tens of millions of bodies swirling through the global sex trade — the bar girls, the street whores and the escorts — they are surely a minority. Yet the victims, the Zinas and Veronicas, can't be counted because they are nearly always invisible, even in plain sight. Hire a prostitute in Amsterdam or Frankfurt or Los Angeles and you will not know if she has been trafficked. She will look like every other woman in that brothel or on that street corner, her situation no more apparent. A woman such as Zina will not tell the men who pay to have sex with her that a Gypsy has threatened to cut off her hands, because she believes he will. She will not confess her fear because she is afraid. She will not go to the police because she believes they are corrupt, and she will not run away because she has no money and no passport and she's not sure exactly where she is anyway. And because she will not do any of those things, she eventually will confuse her fear with shame, her captivity with complicity, and her shame will make her silent, a slave mistaken for a whore.

The US State Department estimates that between 600,000 and 800,000 people are trafficked — that is, transported by force or fraud — across international borders every year, 80 percent of whom are women and girls and most of whom are destined for the sex trade. UNICEF puts those numbers at between 700,000 and 2 million, also mostly women and also mostly in the sex trade, which it says is the third-most-lucrative black-market business on the planet, behind only weapons and drugs. The International Labour Organization calculates worldwide profits from sex trafficking at $27.8 billion a year, and the Federal Bureau of Investigation says the transnational trade (moving people from one country to another) is worth $9.5 billion.

The problem with those numbers isn't that they're wrong so much as they're impossible to verify. "You have to remember, victims don't stand in line and raise their hands to be counted," says Ambassador John R. Miller of the US State Department's Office of Trafficking in Persons. "So any estimate, I would say — I would *hope* — is an intelligent guesstimate." The body counts are mostly for the benefit of journalists and policymakers and grant dispensers, anyway, none of whom tolerate ambiguity particularly well. (The reports out of Miller's office, even with their fuzzy figures, generate an annual flurry of MODERN SEX SLAVES headlines that would likely never be written if the number were to be reported as a more honest yet less enthralling "a lot.")

There are only hints at the true magnitude, anecdotes and fragments of hard data. For example: In late June, federal agents and state police escorted more than a hundred Korean women out of massage parlors and spas in San Francisco, most if not all of whom were allegedly forced into prostitution to repay enormous debts to smugglers who got them into the country. In Turkey — a country so flush with prostitutes imported from the former Soviet states that they've been given a generic brand name, Natashas, as if they were an exotic subspecies — authorities reportedly identified more than 200 trafficked women last year alone. Two months ago in Phnom Penh, Cambodia, police pulled eighty-eight women out of a hotel massage parlor, including twenty-eight Vietnamese and four Chinese believed to have been trafficked into the country.

All these are just the faintest echoes of a much, much larger trade, tiny blips of radar pinging off a mountain shrouded in fog. But how big is the mountain?

Narrow the focus. Train the lens on one tiny country, Moldova, a ripple of vineyards and croplands barely the size of Maryland, a scant 3.4 million people wedged between Romania and the Ukraine. In the fourteen years since it became an independent nation with the breakup of the Soviet Union, Moldova has been decimated by sex trafficking; it is a place of desperately poor women made easy prey for a black market with a voracious demand for Eastern (read: White) Europeans. Yet even here, in a country so small that it has become a petri dish of sorts for the causes and effects of trafficking, there are still only clues. From the beginning of 2000 through May 2005, for instance, the International Organization for Migration provided counseling, health care, job training, and the like to 1,571 Moldovan women who'd been trafficked out of the country and then escaped or were rescued and returned home (another thirty-five were either trafficked internally — say, from a village to the capital, Chisinau — or were foreigners brought into the country to work as prostitutes). "That's only a fraction" of the actual victims, says Martin Wyss, who is in charge of IOM's Chisinau office.

So narrow the focus even more. Crop out the big cities and all the little towns and villages and leave only Costesti. Shrink the whole globe to the cluster of mud roads and stone houses where Zina and Veronica once briefly dreamed of washing Russian windows. There is a social-service agency here called Compasiune, which means "compassion," and it is run out of an old concrete community center by a sturdy middle-aged woman with short gray hair named Elena Mereacre. She was born in Costesti, and her parents were born in Costesti, and for many years she was the village librarian, so she knows almost everyone who lives there, and she will help anyone who asks: Old people who need food and young people who need to learn how to use computers and kids who just need something to do and, especially, women like Zina and Veronica. She recognizes them as soon as they return, knows what has happened to them even before they tell her. "You didn't even have to ask," she says. "It was written on their faces."

She recognizes those faces because she's seen so many exactly like them in Costesti. Since 2000, Compasiune has taken in fifty-three women and girls who'd been forced into prostitution. That's the hard count from one village of about 10,000 people — the equivalent of every girl on the Hope, Arkansas, high school cheerleading squad, softball team, and soccer team, plus the basketball team's starting five, being snatched away. And it is still only another ping through the fog. How many women never came home? How many came home and were too ashamed to ask for help, too ashamed to be labeled a prostitute in a place where it is not uncommon to raise a bloody sheet the morning after a wedding, the flag of the virgin bride? "Multiply by five," a Western diplomat in Moldova says, "or ten. You won't be wrong, because no one knows."

There are days, and not enough of them, when Ion Bejan drives north out of Chisinau to the village where he was born, where his parents' house still stands, vacant now but immaculate, every table and dish exactly where it should be, where it's always been. A nearby family of Baptists keeps it that way for him, like a museum, like a sanctuary. Bejan goes there to settle into a chair and close his eyes and empty his mind for a little while, maybe walk the edge of the fields he rents out to tenant farmers and allow his past to wrap around him like an old, worn blanket. "It restores my soul," he says. He stays only a few hours, because the drive back to Chisinau is long and his wife and kids are waiting and he has to be in an office early the next morning . . . at which point his soul will begin to be depleted again.

Bejan is the cop in charge of countertrafficking in Moldova. He has twenty-seven officers working for him, but he ultimately is the one responsible for arresting the traffickers and chronicling their crimes. He is a block of a man with enormous, thick-fingered hands and coal black hair swept back on a big, square head, a physical specimen apparently designed to intimidate. Yet he is gregarious by nature and capable of being quite gentle, which his job often requires because the victims he interviews, the women he needs to testify against the bad guys, have been so horribly traumatized.

The woman imprisoned for four years in a cell of a room, nine feet square, with a toilet and a shower and a mattress, forced to have sex with fifteen to twenty men every day, never allowed beyond the door — how does a cop coax her to trust him? "She didn't see the sunlight for four years," Bejan says. "She did not think, did not feel. She did everything automatically." Or the woman sold to a Turkish pimp for $3,000 who got pregnant because men pay more to have sex without a condom, after which the Turk, enraged that she hadn't taken her birth-control pills, beat her unconscious and gouged the fetus from her belly and held up the bloody mess as a warning to the other girls he owned — can she be soothed enough to tell that story in a courtroom, to say it out loud and make it real again? Or the young girl who believes the handsome stranger with the fancy car and some money in his pocket when he says he loves her, who believes she's found a rich boyfriend even after he sells her to a brothel across the border — how can a cop convince her that she's wrong, that a trafficker isn't the same as a boyfriend?

And how many times can he hear such stories before his soul begins to wither and he has to drive north to his sanctuary, before he has to escape, if only briefly, into his past?

In his past, Bejan did not want to be a cop. In his past, he was a dutiful Soviet citizen who did three years in the navy on a sub hunter out of Odessa and then went on to the university in Chisinau to study economics. He worked as an accountant while he continued at the university, earning an engineering degree next, then starting over in law school. The Soviets were good like that, giving away educations to smart young men such as Bejan.

And then there weren't any more Soviets. It happened so fast, or seemed to, the sprawling empire collapsing, all the republics suddenly set free or cut loose, depending how one looked at it. Independence is a beautiful theory, but it can be ugly in practice, especially in the beginning, when the rules aren't clear and the old economy collapses before a new one takes root. It did not go well for Moldova. "Unfortunately," Bejan says, and in such grand understatement that he allows himself a grim smile, "there were some mistakes made during this transition." The nation he watched being born — prior to 1991, Moldova had never really been a sovereign nation — seemed less a democracy than a kleptocracy, "chaotic and barbaric," he says. State-owned factories and businesses were grabbed by the apparatchiks who ran them for the Soviets, stripped down, cashed out. Gangsters backed by a contingent of Russian soldiers would soon claim an industry-rich strip on the eastern border, Transnistria, as a separate, outlaw republic (which still exists, albeit unrecognized by anyone but the Russians). Unemployment soared. The villages — which is to say, most of the country — were devastated. In Costesti, about 6,000 people in what was then a village of 13,000 were promptly unemployed. The croplands were turned over to private owners, but so what? No one had a tractor or fuel or money to pay laborers. The new currency, the leu, was supposedly in such short supply that it was distributed to the outlying areas as photocopies, and no one worried much about counterfeiting because there weren't any copiers. Overnight, Moldova became the poorest country in Europe.

That's when Bejan decided to become a cop, to take his university degrees and get himself assigned to the Ministry of Interior investigating economic crimes. It was both practical — the man needed a job, after all — and patriotic, a small and possibly futile effort to help save his new nation from looters.

Legions of other Moldovans, on the other hand, decided to leave. Thousands of them every month, tens of thousands each year, as many as a million in a decade, so many fleeing so fast that there was no way to keep track of them all. Most found legitimate work abroad, but some were just as surely trafficked, tempted with the promise of a job and then beaten into submission. It's obvious now — of *course* women eager to leave a poor, broken little country would be easy prey for gangster pimps — but no one noticed at the time. No one cared. Each victim was merely another drop in the flood spilling across the border.

Until they started coming back. "Not by the dozens," says Bejan, "but by the hundreds, and some of them in coffins." He remembers seeing a critical mass in 1997 and understanding then what had happened, what was still happening. But there was nothing he could do, nothing any cop could do. Trafficking wasn't a crime in Moldova, and it wouldn't be for another five years.

This is what an international trafficker looks like: Female, petite, hair cut pixie-short and rinsed with cheap sienna dye, wearing a black jacket with a hood that she can zip up around her face, pull her entire head in like a turtle. Her name is Lilea Prajac, and she is 32 years old. Also, she cries easily.

Bejan has produced her like a prop, brought her from a cell in his station in Chisinau so she can confess her crimes — alleged, technically — to a magazine writer. He has already sketched the basics, explained how Lilea recruited girls in the rural north for a woman in Chisinau who then shipped them to brothels in Turkey. Lilea was paid $100 to $300 a head, more for the pretty girls with big breasts, less for the ugly and the chubby, and she says they all knew they would be prostitutes. Bejan is not convinced of that — indentured whoring is an impossibly hard career sell, after all — and in any case, he says a recruit would be beaten if she changed her mind en route. Nor does he know how many women Lilea and her colleagues sent out of the country in the past eight months, though the day she was arrested in April, a 19-year-old and two 25-year-olds were booked on the five o'clock flight to Istanbul.

An officer escorts Lilea into Bejan's office. Bejan comes out from behind his desk and speaks to her softly, as if she were a frightened child. He tells her an officer is going to put handcuffs loosely around her wrists, not because she's dangerous but because he thinks the glint of steel against her black sleeves will make a better picture for the foreign photographer. Apparently, anyway. Everything is being said in Romanian, and by the time each word is translated, the cuffs are out and Lilea's lip is quivering and the photographer is saying, *No, this really isn't necessary*, but by then it's too late: Lilea's face disappears inside her zippered hood, which begins to puff like a nylon lung because she is sobbing.

On paper, in the black and white of official statistics, Bejan and his men have destroyed the trafficking syndicates operating out of Moldova. From 2002, when such crimes were finally made illegal, until April 2005, they arrested 839 people for trafficking in human beings, trafficking in children, or pimping. In that same period, 179 were convicted of one or another of those crimes (which, in a bit of self-congratulatory statistical computation, is exactly equal to the official number of "trafficking networks liquidated").

Off the page, in the gray shades of actual cases, they've grabbed a lot of people like Lilea. In the brief moments after she's been photographed and before she's crying too hard to speak, Lilea explains how she used to support her crippled son by driving to Moscow and buying $1,000 worth of goods to sell in her village, for which she would have to pay $500 to bring past the guards at the border. Talking girls into Turkish brothels simply paid better. A crime, sure, both legally and morally. But can she really be considered an international gangster, in league with arms dealers and drug smugglers? Or take the other woman Bejan arrested at about the same time, Raisa Goreanscaia Axenti, 70 years old and the alleged ringleader of a three-person crew who smuggled people out of the country with bogus documents identifying them as members of the National Federation of Artistic Gymnastics — a headline the next day read SLAVE TRADE NETWORK UNCOVERED IN MOLDOVA. Really? Is she Moldova's Ma Barker? Or is she an old lady making a few bucks by, according to Bejan's dossier, "recruiting people . . . whose wish was to leave the country"?

Bejan and his men are earnest, but they are utterly ineffectual. No one disputes that international trafficking is controlled by seriously bad guys who by definition constitute some level of organized criminal networks — after all, it requires at least two people to get someone out of Moldova and into a foreign brothel. The problem in a place such as Moldova, though, is catching and convicting them, moving beyond the flunkies and the lackeys like Lilea, who are arguably as pitiable as the girls they snare. This is not Bejan's fault. Even if he and his men are squeaky-clean (and aid workers and foreign legal advisers believe they are), the rest of the country isn't. The US State Department, in its most recent summary of trafficking in Moldova, reports that it is "widely suspected" — diplomaticspeak for "We know it's true because it's so damned obvious" — that trafficking investigations have been limited, "due in some instances to pressure from complicit officials at higher levels in the government." In the same paragraph: "Despite continued allegations of trafficking-related corruption among some law-enforcement officials, the government took no action against these officials." There are corrupt cops, corrupt prosecutors, corrupt bureaucrats, even a village mayor who reportedly collected $50 for every pretty girl he put on a bus to Macedonia. Meanwhile, there are actual hard-core gangsters roaming Moldova.

Against all that, Bejan has only twenty-seven officers — the drug unit, by comparison, has a hundred — who are badly paid, barely trained, and ill-equipped; until the Americans gave him six Mitsubishi 4x4s and a couple of sedans, his squad traversed Moldova's decrepit roads in one Soviet-era jalopy and public buses.

"They can only go after the low-hanging fruit," one Western trafficking expert says.

And if they try to go for the big, ripe fruit?

"Best case, you're fired," the expert says. "Worst case, you're dead."

Even the arrests the antitrafficking cops do make — all 839 of them since 2002 — are in the end largely pointless. Moldovan law is officially brutal on traffickers, with sentences starting at seven years in prison and maxing out at life. In practice, no one does life. In fact, hardly anyone does time at all. Of ninety-five convictions last year for "crimes related to trafficking in human beings," a mere sixteen were for trafficking in adults and seven for trafficking in children; only thirteen of those traffickers were sentenced to prison, and none for more than sixteen years. The rest, 75 percent, were for the far less serious charge of pimping, which seems odd considering Bejan's men arrest more than twice as many suspects for trafficking as pimping.

"The judiciary is one of the most corrupt entities in the country," says a diplomat who's worked in Moldova for years. That's an enormous institutional problem, yes. But break it down, reduce the appalling statistics to an individual case, to a single woman beaten and raped and sold overseas, rescued and come home, now finally brave enough to testify. Stand next to her when the judge reduces the charge to pimping. Then listen when she tells him, "I was a victim. And now you've made me a whore."

Now go tell other victims they should testify, too.

There's this kid in Chisinau, a boy maybe 10 years old, begging outside the Hotel Dedeman or in the park across Pushkin Street, in the plaza by the little cathedral. He lurches around, one hand out, and he grunts more than he speaks

— *mister uh uh uh mister uh uh* — because he's stoned out of his skull on glue fumes. He's there every night and most mornings, too, like a tiny zombie, dirty and alone and only half-conscious.

There's another kid just like him on Varlaam Street, down by the bus station, and a small flock of them haunting Stefan cel Mare park, and . . . hell, they're scattered all over Chisinau, all over the country, abandoned by parents who've left Moldova. Bejan guesses there are 25,000 such children in Moldova, a figure that is both low and apparently nothing more than a cop's intuition. Diplomats say a more reasonable estimate is over 125,000 who've been either orphaned or, more commonly, left behind by parents who've gone abroad, either for legitimate work or escorted by traffickers.

"The effects of trafficking," Bejan says, "will be felt for ten, fifteen years."

He means those abandoned kids, but only partly. All this has happened with alarming speed: In only fourteen years, sex trafficking has wreaked — is wreaking — enormous damage not only on individual women but on the entire country. By one estimate, 80 percent of the trafficked women who manage to return are either too old or too reproductively damaged to have children, and the physically healthy ones often suffer such severe mental and emotional traumas that they're incapable of proper parenting anyway. Combine that with the general exodus, officially between 600,000 and 1 million since independence, and Moldova is threatened with a long-term population crisis.

It is as if the country is collapsing in upon itself. The capital city is weakly rebounding, but the outlying areas are a medieval shambles. The unemployment spike that followed independence never receded (officially, rates vary from 6.8 to 11.1 percent, but nobody in Moldova really believes that; aid workers and migration experts put the rate at closer to 50, 60, even 70 percent), and that, in turn, bred all the other textbook social ills — alcoholism and domestic violence and divorce — that thrive among the poor. Then the working-age population fled, which only exacerbated the problems: Moldova's sole natural resource is its land, but it's useless if there are no laborers to tend the fields. And while foreign workers send back almost half a billion dollars every year, hardly any of that money is invested in new businesses to nudge the economy along.

And so the cycle continues, a disaster feeding upon itself and, in turn, feeding the sex trade. Moldova is still the poorest country in Europe. People still want to leave, are still desperate to leave, so desperate they'll leave their children behind to do it. And some of them — again, no one knows exactly how many — will be snatched by the traffickers.

A decade ago, it was easy for the traffickers. No one was paying attention. Sex slavery? Who'd even heard of such a thing? The newspaper ads for waitresses in Italy or dancers in Bosnia requested "pretty girls with no hang-ups," but what did *that* mean? Why would a hungry girl in a village without running water or electricity have any hang-ups, other than wanting to eat? Over the past five years, though, as it became clear the cops and the courts couldn't stop the trade,

Moldova's been awash with prevention programs (paid for almost exclusively by the charity of nonprofits and foreign aid). The International Organization for Migration arranged a screening for nearly every schoolgirl of *Lilya 4-Ever*, a Swedish film about a fictional Russian girl trafficked into prostitution. La Strada, another aid group that shares office space with IOM in Chisinau, set up a hotline for girls to call if they've been offered an overseas job that sounds too good to be true. Counselors tell them to ask basic questions: Will they be given a contract? Will they be allowed to call home?

More than 10,500 girls have dialed that number since September 2001. The staff at La Strada are certain some traffickers have called, too — just look how the ads have changed. "Local contracts!" they promise. "You will be able to call home!" (Context is everything, of course. Olesea, who was sold to a brothel after being lured to Moscow for a construction job, was indeed allowed to call home. Once a month, she told her mother all was well, that she was having a great time, that she would send money home soon. Then the pimp pointing a gun at her head made her hang up the phone.)

The promises are so easy to believe because the girls are so eager to leave. Liuba Revenko, the program manager for Winrock International, another aid group working in Moldova, got a call from an airport security guard in late 2001, shortly after the Americans invaded Afghanistan. He told her there was a charter plane on the tarmac scheduled to fly to Kabul and seventeen girls in the terminal waiting to board.

Revenko drove to the airport. The guy who chartered the plane had gotten spooked and disappeared, leaving the girls behind. They were all young, none more than 20, most of them blond, all quite pretty. And they were pissed. "Their first reaction to me was very negative," Revenko says. The girls told her they had real jobs waiting for them, and they waived their contracts at her to prove it. "Crappy pieces of paper," she says, not worth the ink that printed the words: The girls all believed they were going to work as cocktail waitresses in Kabul.

How do you tell them they're wrong, that they've been played for fools, that they're lucky — *lucky!* — their plane never left the ground? They won't believe it. They won't believe where they were going is worse than where they are.

Zina and Veronica are in the apartment in Krasnodar late on a winter afternoon. The Gypsies are telling them to go to work, go to the strip club and dance naked and have sex with strangers. They have done this every afternoon for more than a year. Sometimes the Gypsies say that if the girls behave, if they do what they're told and don't make trouble, they will be allowed to go home soon. They never say how soon, though, and soon never comes.

Zina feels different today, worse. She doesn't know why, but her heart is pounding. She can't breathe, and she is sweating even though she is cold. She tells the Gypsies she's sick. She tells them she can't go to the club.

The Gypsies beat her. She knew they would, because they have beaten her and Veronica and all the other girls so many times before. Only it's worse now. She is beaten bloody, almost unconscious. One of the pimps drags her to the door, throws her into the street. "I can't do anything with you," he says. "Just go away."

Now she is alone. Zina has no money, no passport, nowhere to go.

So she goes to the police.

This is a terrible risk. The Gypsies told her long ago that the police would never help her. Even if the police aren't corrupt, what will they see when they look at her? A whore? A petty criminal who snuck into the country with no papers? Zina's been in Russia, been in that club, for a year. Now she's a *victim*? How can she explain that?

How can any woman anywhere explain such a thing? One of the reasons it is impossible to quantify the victims of international sex trafficking is the very fact that it is *international*. Laws and mores shift from country to country, and the serious crime of sex slavery is always masked as either a petty local nuisance or a perfectly legal business. In Germany, for instance, authorities last summer were building wooden huts to accommodate the 40,000 prostitutes expected to flow into the country for the 2006 World Cup, if only to keep them from scrogging in the bushes. Common sense — as well as several studies that show a correlation between legalization and trafficking — suggest at least some of those women were forced to show up. But how does anyone sort out the willing from the unwilling? By asking?

Zina tells the police her story, how she and Veronica came to work in a market and were sold to a strip club, how the Gypsies beat them and forced them to be prostitutes. The police see her bloody face and believe her. They take her to the club, tell her to point to her sister; then they take Veronica and Zina away from the Gypsies and send them home to Costesti.

Nothing has changed. The house is still cold, and Mama's still sick, and there still aren't any jobs. They tell the neighbors that, yes, they'd been in Russia but they didn't like it so they came home, and maybe some people believe them. But then the Gypsies drive out from Krasnodar, and they come to the house, rile up the angry little dog chained to a post inside the gate, pound on the door, push inside, drag Zina and Veronica off the stoop and into the garden where they will plant vegetables in the spring. The Gypsies beat them in the yard. "You ruined our business!" they scream. "You cost us money!" It's four o'clock in the morning and bitterly cold, but the neighbors come out to watch. None of them do anything, though. Everyone's afraid of the Gypsies.

The Gypsies leave as abruptly as they came. The next morning, Zina and Veronica tell the villagers who watched that it was simply a business dispute, nothing more. No one believes them. So one thing changes: Their neighbors think they're prostitutes.

It's never easy for a victim to come home. Some of them, usually the ones who've been rescued and repatriated, don't *want* to be home, insist they want to go back to their "boyfriends," their pimps. Change the context just a little and psychologists would call it battered woman syndrome, or maybe Stockholm syndrome. "It's not because she's afraid," says Ana Revenco, the president of La Strada's office in Moldova. "It's because she doesn't know what to do with this freedom."

Yet freedom is relative. Trafficked women go home to husbands who call them whores, to children who no longer recognize them, to babies they can no longer cope with. They return to the same villages where their traffickers — the lackeys and thugs who sent them abroad — still live, where they are intimidated and shamed and stigmatized. They come back diseased and pregnant and racked by anxiety and nightmares. And even if psychologists can treat them, even if job counselors can train them, they're still stuck in Moldova. "So sometimes they are leaving again, hoping it will be better," says Alina Budeci, a social worker at La Strada. "How do you tell a young girl not to do it, not to go? Too many of them see it as their last, best hope."

Zina and Veronica want only to leave Costesti. They move to Chisinau, where they decide they want a profession because that is the first question everyone asks when they look for jobs: What is your profession? Except the man hiring dishwashers in a small restaurant. He doesn't care if they have a profession, and he pays them enough to cover the rent on the tiny room they share. Most weeks, they have enough left over to buy food.

They end the story there. But there's more. Veronica should tell it, but she won't. Elena Mereacre, the woman who runs Compasiune, whispers it later.

Veronica was in love. With a priest, Russian Orthodox, a man she met in Chisinau. They were going to be married. The priest could never understand, though, why Veronica wouldn't take him back to her village, introduce him to her mother. So one day he went by himself, and the villagers saw the stranger and asked who he was, and he told them, and they told him about the Gypsies who beat Veronica in her garden. Then the priest went to Veronica and asked her why she'd been beaten.

Veronica told him.

Was she dreaming? Or was she just desperate for someone to understand?

The priest left her that night.

Global Sex Trafficking

Joni Seager

Women's bodies are commodities in the global sex trade, a multi-billion dollar industry.

The international sex trade thrives on economic disparity — between men and women at all scales, and between regions on a global scale. Globalization has heightened these disparities. New regions and countries enter into the sex trade as their economic fortunes wax or wane. As poverty deepens in Eastern Europe, it becomes a major source region for prostitutes; as wealth expands in China and Malaysia, men in those countries fuel an increased demand for the traffic in women and girls. Large circuits of trafficking operate among the countries of East and Southeast Asia., and from Central and Eastern Europe into Western Europe. The global sex trade is sustained by astounding levels of coercion, torture, rape, and systemic violence. Women are often lured into the sex trade under false pretences — hired as waitresses or maids and then forced into prostitution. Girls are often sold into prostitution by poor families and, increasingly, girls and women are simply kidnapped, often from poverty-stricken regions, to be traded globally as sex slaves and prostitutes.

The AIDS/HIV epidemic is fueling demand for younger and younger girls, as customers try to find "safe" commercial sex partners.

> "We, as [Western] men, are more and more wanting to step back from the types of [Western] women we meet now. With many women taking on the 'me first' feminist agenda and the man continuing to take a back seat to her

desire for power and control many men are turned off by this and look back to having a more traditional woman as our partner."

—*Introduction to goodwife.com*

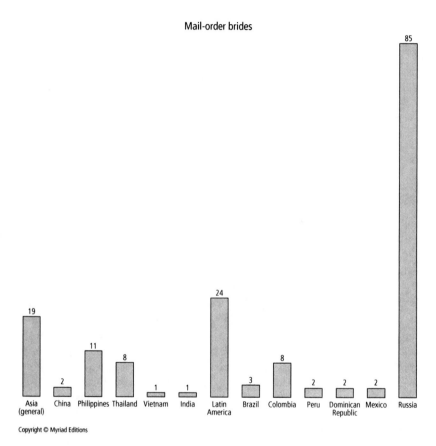

Mail-order brides

Copyright © Myriad Editions

Figure 3.1 Number of introduction sites advertising on goodwife.com *January 2008*; by country of origin of women available

Figure 3.2 Sex Trafficking Flows: Western Hemisphere

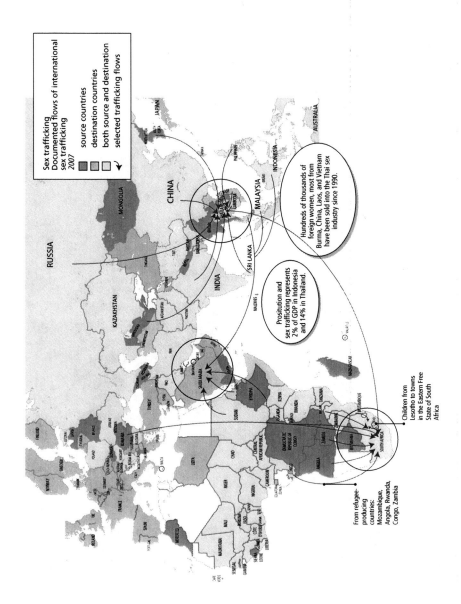

Figure 3.3 Sex Trafficking Flows: Eastern Hemisphere

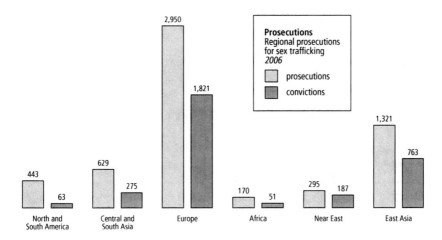

Figure 3.4 Regional prosecutions for sex trafficking 2006

4 The Black Market in Human Organs

Frederike Ambagtsheer

> *"The problem is: organs are just like women, weapons and drugs. There is demand in this world. People are ill; they want an organ. And there is supply. There are poor people in this world who are desperate [. . .] and sell their organ in order to feed their children. Unfortunately demand and supply come together too often in this world."*
>
> *(Nephrologist from the Netherlands)*

There is perhaps no form of crime that is as multifaceted and morally complex as the illegal trade in human organs. Little is known about the organ market. Very few empirical studies have been conducted on the topic and little scientific literature exists. According to Travaini et al., the most consistent source of information about organ trafficking is the media, which sometimes reports rumors as fact. Only occasionally are popular news stories based on official reports or scientific research.[1]

Nevertheless, in recent years an increasing number of publications have been written on the phenomenon, giving some clues into the nature and development of the illegal organ trade. A large amount of information comes from medical professionals publishing in medical journals. In addition, a small number of anthropologists and sociologists conduct fieldwork on organ trafficking in various countries, although they tend to focus only on victims of organ trafficking.[2] International organizations such as the World Health Organization and the European Union have also produced reports giving an overview of the nature and scale of the trade at an international level.[3]

This essay draws upon information from these sources to describe and analyze what happens when demand and supply of human organs come together.

The Demand for Organs

In 1954, doctors performed the first successful human organ transplant, moving a kidney from a donor to his identical twin. For the next 30 years, transplantation remained a risky and experimental procedure, usually used only as a last effort to stave off death.[4] Organ transplantation usually failed in this early period, since the body's immune system attacked and rejected the foreign organ. This changed with the discovery of cyclosporine, an immuno-suppressive drug that moderates the body's response to foreign tissue without suppressing the immune system's reactions to infectious diseases.[5] As a result, organ transplants became widely used medical procedures, leading to higher percentages of successfully performed transplants, particularly in countries with advanced medical facilities.[6] Now, thirty years later, transplantation has become a standard procedure carried out in hospitals and clinics worldwide.[7] Kidneys, livers, hearts, lungs, pancreases and other organs are transplanted regularly both to relieve suffering and to prolong life. Survival rates of trans-plant patients have risen dramatically over the past decades. With increasing transplant capabilities and skilled surgeons able to perform the procedure, patient demand has also risen dramatically. The supply of organs, however, is incapable of keeping pace with demand.[8] With a few exceptions, no country has sufficient organ supply to satisfy its citizens' needs. Thus, a global scarcity of human organs now exists.

Organ shortages have led to both a large and growing backlog of desperate patients, and a complicated waitlist system to determine recipients. In the United States the waitlist for kidneys more than doubled over the past decade. Currently, there are over 80,000 patients waiting for a kidney, 16,000 for a liver and 3,500 for a heart. The average waiting time for a kidney in the United States and in Europe is three to five years. European countries also face a severe shortage of organs. There, 65,000 patients are currently on the waitlist for a kidney, yet only about 25,000 transplants take place each year. The mortality rate on European transplant waitlists is approximately 35%.[9]

The limited availability of legal donor organs drives many patients to turn to the international black market for organs. What is the black market for organs? What are its regional or global trends? And how and why did it develop?

Black Markets

Black markets are "underground," unregulated, and illegal economies that exist parallel to formal, legal markets. Black markets thrive where they fulfill demand for goods that are scarce, such as human organs, and their formal market counterparts cannot or do not supply the good. In the black market for organs, kidneys, livers, hearts and other organs that have been harvested from living or deceased persons are bought, sold or stolen for financial profit.[10] The black market in human organs coexists with other formalized and legal methods of organ procurement, such as the hospital waitlists already mentioned. The organs in these black markets are not inherently illegal; it is the profitable exchange that is prohibited. International and national laws universally forbid commercial transactions of human organs for financial profit. The World Health Organization "Guiding Principles on Human Organ Transplantation" explains the rationale prohibiting organ sales:

Payment for organs is likely to take unfair advantage of the poorest and most vulnerable groups, undermines altruistic donation and leads to profiteering and human trafficking. Such payment conveys the idea that some persons lack dignity, that they are mere objects to be used by others.[11]

Thus, black market organ transactions are forbidden largely for moral and ethical reasons related to the inherent value of each human life.

Both legal and illegal actors are involved in the trade of human organs. Unlike the illegal trade in narcotics, the transplantation of human organs relies upon the participation and cooperation of *legal* professionals and institutions, like surgeons and hospitals. Organs have an extremely short shelf life. A successful harvest and transplantation requires the expertise of medical specialists such as nephrologists and transplant surgeons. In addition, proper medical technology, access to sterile facilities and reliable, rapid transportation is needed. Because organs can only be preserved for a short time, transplant operations must be performed in close proximity to both the donor and the recipient. These requirements are necessary *regardless of* whether the transplantation occurs under legal or illegal circumstances. This means that illegal organ transaction cannot be successfully established without the participation of surgeons, nephrologists and other specialized physicians, ambulance drivers, morticians and undertakers.

In addition to these legal actors, so-called 'illicit' actors are also involved in illegal organ trade. Brokers, intermediaries and middlemen of various sorts recruit donors, identify patients desperate enough to buy black market organs, and match donors with recipients, while traffickers facilitate transportation. The lack of established case law and reliable data on illegal organ trade and trafficking makes it difficult to know how these people operate. Most descriptions of the degree of organization of this illegal trade in organs is therefore fairly speculative.

Whether the organ trade is formally legal or illegal, and whether it is connected to larger criminal enterprises, varies widely from one geography to another. Some authors claim that the illegal organ trade is run by international criminal organizations, and that the illicit actors involved in organ traffic began in drug trafficking networks that then diversified into the organ trade.[12] Many reports speculate on the inner workings of these criminal organizations, leading to some differences in the accounts. For instance, in her book on the illegal body part trade in the United States, Goodwin explains that illegal organ trade often occurs clandestinely.[13] Whereas this might be the case in the United States, publications written on organ trade in countries such as China, India and Pakistan highlight the "open" nature of organ trafficking there.[14] Whether organ trade occurs underground or overtly largely depends on the social and political structures in a country. For instance, organ trafficking is widespread and "open" in areas that have access to large populations of organ sellers, where systems of medical regulation are lax or nonexistent, and where law enforcement is compromised either by widespread corruption or lack of enforcement capabilities. By contrast, in countries with strong medical regulations and law enforcement (such as the United States) organ trade is more likely to occur underground.

According to most accounts, coercion of kidney vendors sometimes occurs. The more covert the illegal organ trade is, and the more lax the law enforcement in a country, the larger the likelihood that coercion will result in violence.[15] In the illicit organ trade, the victims are usually the organ "donors" or organ sellers, some of whom have been forced to give away their organs. This is particularly true in the kidney trade, since most people can function normally with only one kidney — removing the other does not therefore inherently threaten their lives.[16] Pearson states that:

There is certainly a much more significant pattern of organ trafficking in terms of people being deceived and coerced into selling organs. Most [people] consent to sell a kidney, but there is deception as to the amount of payment for the kidney, and in some cases no payment at all.[17]

In addition to donors, patients (organ recipients) can also be harmed.

An increasing number of medical publications present transplant outcomes in patients who are thought to have obtained organs on the black market. These patients often travel overseas to receive a transplant, a phenomenon commonly referred to as transplant tourism The majority of these publications report inferior patient and graft (organ) survival, including a higher incidence of unconventional and life-threatening infections such as malaria, invasive fungal infections, pneumonia, HIV and hepatitis and a markedly increased incidence of postoperative surgical complications.[18] Other publications present better outcomes of patients transplanted overseas. The reasons for these varied outcomes remain unclear. Possibly, negative post-transplant outcomes are a consequence of compromised health conditions that already existed *prior to* the transplant. Some patients travel abroad for a transplant because they are considered too ill to qualify for a transplant in their home country. While a black market transaction is not a prerequisite for negative transplant outcomes to occur, it can be presumed that underground transplant procedures are less likely to take account of safety measures, thus increasing the likelihood of inferior patient and graft survival. In conclusion, much will depend on the patient's medical condition and the circumstances of the hospital or clinic where the transplant takes place.

Organ Trade and Its Asymmetries

What contributes to the development of the black market in human organs? As explained before, the legal supply of organs for transplantation is unable to keep up with the demand for them. As such, patients turn to the black market. Clearly, processes of globalization have resulted in lower international transportation costs and time, and technological innovations have made surgery safer. While these are frequently sited as facilitating transnational legal economies and enterprises, they also contribute to the expansion of illegal businesses.

More importantly, however, Passas' analysis of so-called "criminogenic asymmetries" helps to explain the causes of the black market in human organs. Passas defines criminogenic asymmetries as *"structural disjunctions, mismatches and inequalities in the spheres of politics, culture, the economy and the law."*[19] First, these asymmetries cause or strengthen the demand for illegal goods or services. With regard to organ trade, this relates to, for instance, the inability of governments to provide sufficient organ supply to fulfill patients' needs.

The second asymmetry relates to motives generated for particular actors to participate in illegal businesses. The lack of organs coupled with high demand, increases their value and thus their potential profit. This profit potential increases the likelihood of people getting involved to benefit from the trade. Global income disparities between countries, as well as high rates of abject poverty in many poor countries, facilitate organ trade. In conditions of extreme poverty, there exist people desperate enough for money that they are willing to risk their lives by undergoing complex surgery and living with reduced organ functionality. Most of the organs in the illicit organ trade are thought to stem from this sort of individual — people who, many might argue, lack alternative sources of income at the level selling organs brings. These people tend to live in countries with lax law enforcement. On the other side of the equation, wealthy individuals able to pay for illicit organs may not know (or care) about the origin of their organ. The global uneven distribution of wealth brings about an uneven distribution in organ supply, rendering the trade into an international one. A case example will help to illuminate how the trade functions. In 2003, an international organ trafficking syndicate was discovered, seemingly involving the sale and purchase of kidneys in three countries. At the donor end of the trade were poor Brazilians, who were willing to sell one kidney for approximately $10,000. At the other end, the kidney recipients were Israelis, who paid up to $100,000 for the same organs. Both donors and patients traveled to South Africa, where all the surgeries took place in one hospital. Prior to surgery, both donors and patients willingly signed fraudulent documents stating that they were related.[20] These operations were organized and facilitated by middlemen, and were conducted by surgeons, nephrologists, and other medical staff. The intermediaries — who profit from the up to ten-fold markup in organ price from donor to recipient — matched donors to recipients and arranged logistics in South Africa.[21]

This is where Passas' second asymmetry, regarding the motives of different participants, comes into play. The primary motive of all actors in the organ trade is financial profit. Similar to legal markets, when the demand for certain goods increases and supply is lower than demand, prices go up. The high price that patients are willing to pay for organs relative to the low price that they can be purchased for in poor countries creates a strong incentive for actors to become involved in the trade as middlemen. Physicians can make high profits from commercial, illegal transactions. Donors' motives are most often also financial. Many studies have been conducted on the reasons donors sell kidneys. These reports indicate that donors sell their kidney as a way out of a desperate financial situation. Often, kidney sellers are in deep financial debt and see no alternative than to sell their kidney.

According to the Coalition for Organ Failure Solutions, the level of compensation donors receive for their kidneys varies by region. In South Africa, living donors are said to receive only $700. Prices increase from there, as indicated in the table below.[22] Patients often pay ten times the amount that donors receive.

Country	Donor Compensation
South Africa	$700
India	$1000–$1200
Philippines	$1200–$2000
Moldova	$2700
Egypt	$1700–$2700
Turkey	$5000–$10,000
Peru	$8000
United States	$30,000

Finally, the motive of the patient cannot be overlooked. Waiting three to five years for an organ while one's health deteriorates drives patients to seek non-legal opportunities and solutions. Out of desperation, they take the risk of buying an organ on the black market. In the abovementioned case, the Israeli patients faced larger than usual obstacles at home, since organ donation is extremely low in the country for religious reasons. Many Israeli recipients therefore have little choice but to travel abroad and pay for an organ if they wish to have a transplant.

The third and last asymmetry refers to the inability of authorities to control transnational illegal activities.[23] Although some countries have the legislative interest and willingness to prohibit illegal organ trade, a lack of enforcement capacity may hamper a government's capability to effectively control, prevent and punish the illegal trade. Other countries, like the Philippines and Iran, prefer to allow and regulate organ trade, rather than prohibit it. Until one year ago, Israel was unwilling to control the illegal organ trade, due to low national donation rates. Indeed, it allowed national insurance companies to offer 'transplant packages' for its citizens to purchase kidneys from living donors in countries such as South Africa, the United States, Turkey, Russia, and Moldova. For an estimated $120,000 to $200,000, Israeli insurance companies covered the costs of transportation, accommodation, surgery (of both donor and recipient), "fees" to bribe airport and customs officials, and the rental of operating and recovery rooms. The Israeli government, however, recently passed a law that prohibits these practices.

Global Patterns of Organ Trade

Organ trade occurs with human organs that have been harvested from both deceased and living donors. While many people in the US may be familiar with voluntary organ donation, sometimes organs are harvested from deceased people without their prior consent. These organs are usually then sold to biomedical companies for research or are used in transplantation. Instances of these forms of trade are known to have occurred in the United States in 2004 and 2009,[24] and are considered to be more common in China. Some researchers assert that the removal of kidneys, cornea, liver tissue and heart valves from executed prisoners without their prior consent is a routine procedure undertaken by the government in China.[25] Others report that the Chinese state harvests the organs of Falun Gong practitioners, sometimes while they are still alive, as a form of torture.[26] Organs from Falun Gong practitioners are said to be sold to wealthy foreigners or politicians.[27] In April 2007 China published new laws governing human organ transplants, which include a ban on both the sale of human organs for profit and donations by people younger than 18 years of age. Critics argue that while the new law represents China's response to international pressure, its language is vague enough to leave some leeway for organ harvesting, as with the issue of informed, consensual harvesting from executed prisoners.[28] Time will tell if these rules will remain on paper only, or if the government will put the law into effect.

Organ harvesting from living donors occurs as well in India, Pakistan and Iran. Iran, one of the few countries where the organ trade is legal and regulated, coordinates organ sales through a state organization called the Charity Association for Support of Kidney Patients (CASKP). In Iran, there are two contracts negotiating payment between the donor and the recipient. One is the official contract, which confirms that the donor receives approximately $1220 from the government as payment. The other contract is between the donor and recipient, detailing any additional payment the donor received, and is usually arranged via a broker. This payment level has fluctuated over the years, according to the supply and demand of the market.[29]

Unlike Iran, India has not been successful in controlling the illegal trade in kidneys in the country. Although the government enacted the Transplantation of Human Organs Act in 1994, which prohibits profiting from the sale of living donor organs, the government has not been able to successfully enforce the Act. Instead, the organ trade has merely become more clandestine.[30] The Act's ambiguous language contributes to this problem, as it contains a clause stating that a person unrelated to a recipient may donate his or her kidney for reasons of affection towards the recipient, provided that the government's Authorization Committee approves the donation. This clause produces an effective loophole for the continued sale of illegal kidneys since the Act came into force.[31] In addition, both negligence and the lack of enforcement capability by public officials in India have facilitated a flourishing organ trade in a number of places throughout the country.[32] Organ trafficking is so prevalent in some locations that they have garnered nicknames like, "Organ Bazaar," "The Kidney District" and "the warehouse for kidneys."[33] Media investigations into these areas have uncovered widespread corruption involving donors, recipients and brokers, as well as doctors and high-ranking police officers.[34]

Organ trade does not only occur in the poorer countries of Asia. According to the Social and Economic Council of the UN, various European countries have encountered organ trafficking cases.[35] For example, the Czech Republic reported one case of illegal post-mortem removal and abuse of human organs and tissues. Finland also reported a case where a Russian citizen was suspected of trafficking children from Russia to Spain for organ harvesting. Germany, Latvia, Romania, Slovakia and Ukraine have also reported incidents of organ trade in which physicians harvested human tissue without the donors' prior consent.

As previously stated, the illicit market for human organs has an important cross-border component. Transplant tourism involves recipients traveling internationally, to countries where organs are abundant, organ commerce is legal, or where illegal organ commerce is inefficiently controlled.[36] Although there is some variation in the structure of organ trade and transplant tourism, kidneys generally travel from South to North, from East to West, from poorer to richer persons, from female to male, and from poor, low status men to more affluent men.[37] Seldom are women the recipients of purchased organs, yet in places like India, females usually act as donors for male recipients.[38] It is important to note, however, that demand is not confined to individuals from developed nations. Patients with sufficient economic means from around the world are known to have traveled to clinics in India, China, Turkey, South Africa, and Russia in order to purchase illegally harvested organs. And kidneys can be purchased in countries such as India, Thailand, Moldova, Bosnia-Herzegovina, and most recently, Iraq.

As was demonstrated in the example early in this chapter, transplant tourism may involve three countries: The country where the donor is recruited, the country of the recipient's origin and the country where the surgery takes place. There are strong regional trends and dimensions of transplantation routes. In the Pacific, Koreans, Japanese and Taiwanese, along with residents from Hong Kong, Malaysia and Singapore travel to China.[39] Wealthy foreigners from Botswana and Namibia travel to South Africa to receive kidneys. Residents of Israel, Saudi Arabia, Oman, Kuwait, Egypt, Malaysia, and Bangladesh go to India, Iran, Iraq, Russia, Romania, Moldova, Georgia, and Turkey.[40] Brazil dominates the trade in human organs in South America, and affluent South Americans go to Cuba. Well-off patients from Japan go to North America.[41] Italians and Israeli's go to Belgium. American and Canadian patients travel to China to receive kidney transplants. From the Netherlands, patients also travel overseas for commercial transplants.

The cross-border element of organ trade makes it very difficult to tackle. International cooperation, prioritization and control are necessary elements to effectively prevent and fight the international trade.

Notes

1. G.V. Travaini, V. Garibaldo, V. Arcari, & R. Molteni, "International Trafficking in Human Organs" in: *Organised Crime, Trafficking, Drugs*, selected papers presented at the Annual Conference of the European Society of Criminology, Helsinki, Sami Nevala & Kauko Aromaa, (2003).
2. F. Moazam, *Conversations with Kidney Vendors in Pakistan. An Ethnographic Study*, Hasting Center Report, (2009), www.thehastingcenter.org; Coalition for Organ Failure Solutions (2009), www.cofs.org.
3. World Health Organization, *Human Organ and Tissue Transplantation. Report by the Secretariat*, Executive Board, 113th Session, (2003), http://www.who.int/ethics/en/EB113_14.pdf; European Commission, *Organ Donation and Transplantation: Policy options at EU level*, (2006).

4. D. Rothman, *The International Organ Traffic*, 10th Annual Conference on "The Individual vs. the State," Budapest, Central European University, (2002).

5. Ibid; D. Barney & R.L. Reynolds, "An Economic Analysis of Transplant Organs," *AEJ* 17 (1989): 3.

6. N. Scheper-Hughes, "Parts Unknown: Undercover ethnography of the organs-trafficking underworld," *Ethnography*, 5, 1 (2004): 29–73.

7. D. Rothman, *The International Organ Traffic*; M. Defever, "The policies of organ transplantation in Europe: Issues and problems," *Health Policy*, 16 (1990): 95–103.

8. D. Rothman, E. Rose, T. Awaya, B. Cohen, A. Daar, S.L. Dzemeshkevich, Lee, et al., "The Bellagio Taskforce Report on Transplantation, Bodily Integrity and the International Traffic in Organs," *Transplantation Proceedings*, 29 (1997): 2739–45; H. Rigter, & M.A. Bos, "The diffusion of organ transplantation in Western Europe," *Health Policy*, 16 (1990): 133–145; and H.D.C. Roscam-Abbing, "Organ Donation, the legal framework," *Health Policy*, 16 (1990): 105–115.

9. European Commission, *Organ Donation and Transplantation.*

10. N. Scheper-Hughes, "The Global Traffic in Human Organs," *Current Anthropology*, 41 (2000): 2; Economic and Social Council, *Preventing, combating and punishing trafficking in human organs*, Report of the Secretary-General, United Nations, Commission on Crime Prevention and Criminal Justice, (Vienna: UN, 2006).

11. World Health Organization. *Guiding Principles on Human Organ Transplantation*, (2008), *www.who.int.*

12. Economic and Social Council, *Preventing, combating and punishing trafficking*; R.G. Vermot-Mangold, Parliamentary Assembly. Council of Europe, *Trafficking in Organs in Europe*. Doc. 9822, (2003); and N. Scheper-Hughes, "The Ends of the Body: Commodity Fetishism and the Global Traffic in Organs," *SAIS Review*, 22 (2002): 1.

13. M. Goodwin, *Black Markets: The Supply and Demand of Body Parts*, (Depaul University College of Law, New York: Cambridge University Press, 2006).

14. D Matas, & D. Kilgour, *Bloody Harvest: Revised Report into Allegations of Organ Harvesting of Falun Gong Practitioners in China*. Organ Harvesting Investigation (2009), http://organ-harvestinvestigation.net; F. Moazam, *Conversations with Kidney Vendors.*

15. N. Passas, "Cross-border crime and the interface between legal and illegal actors," in: P. van Duyne, K. von Lampe and N. Passas (eds.), *Upperworld and Underworld in Cross-border Crime* (Nijmegen: Wolf Legal Publishers, 2002).

16. Of all forms of organ trade, illegal kidney trade occurs most frequently, since unlike other organs, human beings are capable of living with one kidney. This means that it is possible for living people to donate one whole kidney to another person who is in need of a kidney transplant. Kidneys can also be harvested from cadavers, but at present, this supply does not meet demand.

17. E. Pearson, *Coercion in the Kidney Trade*, A background study on trafficking in human organs worldwide, Sector project against trafficking in women, (2004), 5.

18. A.K. Salahudeen, H.F. Woods, A. Pingle, M. Nur-El-Huda Suleyman, K. Shakuntala, Nandakumar, et al., "High mortality among recipients of bought living-unrelated donor kidneys," *The Lancet*, 336 (1990): 725–728.

    I. Sajjad, L.S. Baines, P. Patel, M.O. Salifu, R.M. Jindal, "Commercialization of Kidney Transplants: A Systematic Review of Outcomes in Recipients and Donors," *Americam Journal of Nephrology*, 28 (2008): 744–754.

19. N. Passas, "Cross-border crime."

20. South Africa prohibits commercial organ transactions between donors and recipients who are unrelated.

21. Sidley, "South African doctors charged with involvement in organ trade," *British Medical Journal*, 329 (2004): 190.
22. Coalition for Organ Failure Solutions (COFS), (2009), www.cofs.org.
23. N. Passas, "Cross-border crime."
24. New Jersey Real-Time News, *N.J. Corruption Probe includes first organ trafficking case.* (July 24, 2009).
    http://www.nj.com/news/index.ssf/2009/07/nj_corruption_probe_includes_f.html
25. D. Rothman, *The International Organ Traffic*; and N. Scheper-Hughes, "The Global Traffic in Human Organs."
26. Falun Gong is a religious practice that is condemned by the Chinese government.
27. D. Matas, & D. Kilgour, *Bloody Harvest: Revised Report.*
28. International Herald Tribune, 2007.
29. G.V. Travaini, et al., "International Trafficking in Human Organs."
30. N. Scheper-Hughes, "The Global Traffic in Human Organs," 8; E. Young, "Laws fail to stop India's organ trade," *New Scientist*, (10/21/05), retrieved June 15, 2007 from http://www.newscientist.com/article.ns?id=mg18825224.500.
31. Travaini, G. V., Garibaldo, V., Arcari, V. & Molteni, R. 2003 op cit.
32. Ibid.; G. Mudur, "Kidney trade arrest exposes loopholes in India's transplant laws," *British Medical Journal*, 328 (2003): 246; E. Pearson, *Coercion in the Kidney Trade.*
33. G.V. Travaini, et al., "International Trafficking in Human Organs;" N. Scheper-Hughes, "The Global Traffic in Human Organs."
34. E. Pearson, *Coercion in the Kidney Trade.*
35. Economic and Social Council, *Preventing, combating and punishing trafficking.*
36. G.V. Travaini, et al., "International Trafficking in Human Organs."
37. M. Goodwin, *Black Markets.*
38. N. Scheper-Hughes, "Keeping an eye on the global traffic in human organs," *The Lancet*, 361 (2003): 1645–1648.
39. E. Pearson, *Coercion in the Kidney Trade*; D. Rothman, *The International Organ Traffic.*
40. N. Scheper-Hughes, "The Global Traffic in Human Organs."
41. D. Rothman, *The International Organ Traffic*; N. Scheper-Hughes, "The Global Traffic in Human Organs."

The Dark Side of Dubai 5

Johann Hari

The wide, smiling face of Sheikh Mohammed — the absolute ruler of Dubai — beams down on his creation. His image is displayed on every other building, sandwiched between the more familiar corporate rictuses of Ronald McDonald and Colonel Sanders. This man has sold Dubai to the world as the city of One Thousand and One Arabian Lights, a Shangri-La in the Middle East insulated from the dust storms blasting across the region. He dominates the Manhattan-manqué skyline, beaming out from row after row of glass pyramids and hotels smelted into the shape of piles of golden coins. And there he stands on the tallest building in the world — a skinny spike, jabbing farther into the sky than any other human construction in history.

But something has flickered in Sheikh Mohammed's smile. The ubiquitous cranes have paused on the skyline, as if stuck in time. There are countless buildings half-finished, seemingly abandoned. In the swankiest new constructions — like the vast Atlantis hotel, a giant pink castle built in 1,000 days for $1.5bn on its own artificial island — where rainwater is leaking from the ceilings and the tiles are falling off the roof. This Neverland was built on the Never-Never — and now the cracks are beginning to show. Suddenly it looks less like Manhattan in the sun than Iceland in the desert.

Once the manic burst of building has stopped and the whirlwind has slowed, the secrets of Dubai are slowly seeping out. This is a city built from nothing in just a few wild decades on credit and ecocide, suppression and slavery. Dubai is a living metal metaphor for the neo-liberal globalised world that may be crashing — at last — into history.

An Adult Disneyland

Karen Andrews[1] can't speak. Every time she starts to tell her story, she puts her head down and crumples. She is slim and angular and has the faded radiance of the once rich, even though her clothes are as creased as her forehead. I find her in the car park of one of Dubai's finest international hotels, where she is living, in her Range Rover. She has been sleeping here for months, thanks to the kindness of the Bangladeshi car park attendants who don't have the heart to move her on. This is not where she thought her Dubai dream would end.

Her story comes out in stutters, over four hours. At times, her old voice — witty and warm — breaks through. Karen came here from Canada when her husband was offered a job in the senior division of a famous multinational. "When he said Dubai, I said — if you want me to wear black and quit booze, baby, you've got the wrong girl. But he asked me to give it a chance. And I loved him."

All her worries melted when she touched down in Dubai in 2005. "It was an adult Disneyland, where Sheikh Mohammed is the mouse," she says. "Life was fantastic. You had these amazing big apartments, you had a whole army of your own staff, you pay no taxes at all. It seemed like everyone was a CEO. We were partying the whole time."

Her husband, Daniel, bought two properties. "We were drunk on Dubai," she says. But for the first time in his life, he was beginning to mismanage their finances. "We're not talking huge sums, but he was getting confused. It was so unlike Daniel, I was surprised. We got into a little bit of debt." After a year, she found out why: Daniel was diagnosed with a brain tumor.

One doctor told him he had a year to live; another said it was benign and he'd be okay. But the debts were growing. "Before I came here, I didn't know anything about Dubai law. I assumed if all these big companies come here, it must be pretty like Canada's or any other liberal democracy's," she says. Nobody told her there is no concept of bankruptcy. If you get into debt and you can't pay, you go to prison.

"When we realized that, I sat Daniel down and told him: listen, we need to get out of here. He knew he was guaranteed a pay-off when he resigned, so we said — right, let's take the pay-off, clear the debt, and go." So Daniel resigned — but he was given a lower pay-off than his contract suggested. The debt remained. As soon as you quit your job in Dubai, your employer has to inform your bank. If you have any outstanding debts that aren't covered by your savings, then all your accounts are frozen, and you are forbidden to leave the country.

"Suddenly our cards stopped working. We had nothing. We were thrown out of our apartment." Karen can't speak about what happened next for a long time; she is shaking.

Daniel was arrested and taken away on the day of their eviction. It was six days before she could talk to him. "He told me he was put in a cell with another debtor, a Sri Lankan guy who was only 27, who said he couldn't face the shame to his family. Daniel woke up and the boy had swallowed razor blades. He banged for help, but nobody came, and the boy died in front of him."

Karen managed to beg from her friends for a few weeks, "but it was so humiliating. I've never lived like this. I worked in the fashion industry. I had my own shops. I've never . . ." She peters out.

Daniel was sentenced to six months' imprisonment at a trial he couldn't understand. It was in Arabic, and there was no translation. "Now I'm here illegally, too," Karen says. "I've got no money, nothing. I have to last nine months until he's out, somehow." Looking away, almost paralyzed with embarrassment, she asks if I could buy her a meal.

She is not alone. All over the city, there are maxed-out expats sleeping secretly in the sand dunes or the airport or in their cars.

"The thing you have to understand about Dubai is — nothing is what it seems," Karen says at last. "Nothing. This isn't a city, it's a con-job. They lure you in telling you it's one thing — a modern kind of place — but beneath the surface it's a medieval dictatorship."

Tumbleweed

Thirty years ago, almost all of contemporary Dubai was desert, inhabited only by cactuses and tumbleweed and scorpions. But downtown there are traces of the town that once was, buried amidst the metal and glass. In the dusty fort of the Dubai Museum, a sanitized version of this story is told.

In the mid-18th century, a small village was built here, in the lower Persian Gulf, where people would dive for pearls off the coast. It soon began to accumulate a cosmopolitan population washing up from Persia, the Indian subcontinent, and other Arab countries, all hoping to make their fortune. They named it after a local locust, the *daba*, who consumed everything before it. The town was soon seized by the gunships of the British Empire, who held it by the throat as late as 1971. As they scuttled away, Dubai decided to ally with the six surrounding states and make up the United Arab Emirates (UAE).

The British quit, exhausted, just as oil was being discovered, and the sheikhs who suddenly found themselves in charge faced a remarkable dilemma. They were largely illiterate nomads who spent their lives driving camels through the desert — yet now they had a vast pot of gold. What should they do with it?

Dubai only had a dribble of oil compared to neighboring Abu Dhabi — so Sheikh Maktoum decided to use the revenues to build something that would last. Israel used to boast it made the desert bloom; Sheikh Maktoum resolved to make the desert boom. He would build a city to be a centre of tourism and financial services, sucking up cash and talent from across the globe. He invited the world to come tax-free — and they came in their millions, swamping the local population, who now make up just 5 per cent of Dubai. A city seemed to fall from the sky in just three decades, whole and complete and swelling. They fast-forwarded from the 18th century to the 21st in a single generation.

If you take the Big Bus Tour of Dubai — the passport to a pre-processed experience of every major city on earth — you are fed the propaganda-vision of how this happened. "Dubai's motto is 'Open doors, open minds,'" the tour guide tells you in clipped tones, before depositing you at the souks to buy camel tea-cozies. "Here you are free. To purchase fabrics," he adds. As you pass each new monumental building, he tells you: "The World Trade Centre was built by His Highness . . ."

But this is a lie. The sheikh did not build this city. It was built by slaves. They are building it now.

Hidden in Plain View

There are three different Dubais, all swirling around each other. There are the expats, like Karen; there are the Emiratis, headed by Sheikh Mohammed; and then there is the foreign underclass who built the city, and are trapped here. They are hidden in plain view. You see them everywhere, in dirt-caked blue uniforms, being shouted at by their superiors, like a chain gang — but you are trained not to look. It is like a mantra: The Sheikh built the city. The Sheikh built the city. Workers? What workers?

Every evening, the hundreds of thousands of young men who build Dubai are bussed from their sites to a vast concrete wasteland an hour out of town, where they are quarantined away. Until a few years ago they were shuttled back and forth on cattle trucks, but the expats complained this was unsightly, so now they are shunted on small metal buses that function like greenhouses in the desert heat. They sweat like sponges being slowly wrung out.

Sonapur is a rubble-strewn patchwork of miles and miles of identical concrete buildings. Some 300,000 men live piled up here, in a place whose name in Hindi means "City of Gold." In the first camp I stop at — riven with the smell of sewage and sweat — the men huddle around, eager to tell someone, anyone, what is happening to them.

Sahinal Monir, a slim 24-year-old from the deltas of Bangladesh. "To get you here, they tell you Dubai is heaven. Then you get here and realize it is hell," he says. Four years ago, an employment agent arrived in Sahinal's village in Southern Bangladesh. He told the men of the village that there was a place where they could earn 40,000 takka a month (£400) just for working nine-to-five on construction projects. It was a place where they would be given great accommodation, great food, and treated well. All they had to do was pay an up-front fee of 220,000 takka (£2,300) for the work visa — a fee they'd pay off in the first six months, easy. So Sahinal sold his family land, and took out a loan from the local lender, to head to this paradise.

As soon as he arrived at Dubai airport, his passport was taken from him by his construction company. He has not seen it since. He was told brusquely that from now on he would be working 14-hour days in the desert heat — where western tourists are advised not to stay outside for even five minutes in summer, when it hits 55 degrees — for 500 dirhams a month (£90), less than a quarter of the wage he was promised. If you don't like it, the company told him, go home. "But how can I go home? You have my passport, and I have no money for the ticket," he said. "Well, then you'd better get to work," they replied.

Sahinal was in a panic. His family back home — his son, daughter, wife and parents — were waiting for money, excited that their boy had finally made it. But he was going to have to work for more than two years just to pay for the cost of getting here — and all to earn less than he did in Bangladesh.

He shows me his room. It is a tiny, poky, concrete cell with triple-decker bunk beds, where he lives with 11 other men. All his belongings are piled onto his bunk: Three shirts, a spare pair of trousers, and a cell phone. The room stinks, because the lavatories in the corner of the camp — holes in the ground — are backed up with excrement and clouds of black flies. There is no air conditioning or fans, so the heat is "unbearable. You cannot sleep. All you do is sweat and scratch all night." At the height of summer, people sleep on the floor, on the roof, anywhere where they can pray for a moment of breeze.

The water delivered to the camp in huge white containers isn't properly desalinated: It tastes of salt. "It makes us sick, but we have nothing else to drink," he says.

The work is "the worst in the world," he says. "You have to carry 50 kg bricks and blocks of cement in the worst heat imaginable . . . This heat — it is like nothing else. You sweat so much you can't pee, not for days or weeks. It's like all the liquid comes out through your skin and you stink. You become dizzy and sick but you aren't allowed to stop, except for an hour in the afternoon. You know if you drop anything or slip, you could die. If you take time off sick, your wages are docked, and you are trapped here even longer."

He is currently working on the 67th floor of a shiny new tower, where he builds upwards, into the sky, into the heat. He doesn't know its name. In his four years here, he has never seen the Dubai of tourist-fame, except as he constructs it floor-by-floor.

Is he angry? He is quiet for a long time. "Here, nobody shows their anger. You can't. You get put in jail for a long time, then deported." Last year, some workers went on strike after they were not given their wages for four months. The Dubai police surrounded their camps with razor wire and water cannons and blasted them out and back to work.

The "ringleaders" were imprisoned. I try a different question: Does Sohinal regret coming? All the men look down, awkwardly. "How can we think about that? We are trapped. If we start to think about regrets . . ." He lets the sentence trail off. Eventually, another worker breaks the silence by adding: "I miss my country, my family and my land. We can grow food in Bangladesh. Here, nothing grows. Just oil and buildings."

Since the recession hit, they say, the electricity has been cut off in dozens of the camps, and the men have not been paid for months. Their companies have disappeared with their passports and their pay. "We have been robbed of everything. Even if somehow we get back to Bangladesh, the loan sharks will demand we repay our loans immediately, and when we can't, we'll be sent to prison."

This is all supposed to be illegal. Employers are meant to pay on time, never take your passport, give you breaks in the heat — but I met nobody who said it happens. Not one. These men are conned into coming and trapped into staying, with the complicity of the Dubai authorities.

Sahinal could well die out here. A British man who used to work on construction projects told me: "There's a huge number of suicides in the camps and on the construction sites, but they're not reported. They're described as 'accidents.'" Even then, their families aren't free: They simply inherit the debts. A Human Rights Watch study found there is a "cover-up of the true extent" of deaths from heat exhaustion, overwork and suicide, but the Indian consulate registered 971 deaths of their nationals in 2005 alone. After this figure was leaked, the consulates were told to stop counting.

At night, in the dusk, I sit in the camp with Sohinal and his friends as they scrape together what they have left to buy a cheap bottle of spirits. They down it in one ferocious gulp. "It helps you to feel numb," Sohinal says through a stinging throat. In the distance, the glistening Dubai skyline he built stands, oblivious.

Mauled by the Mall

I find myself stumbling in a daze from the camps into the sprawling marble malls that seem to stand on every street in Dubai. It is so hot there is no point building pavements; people gather in these cathedrals of consumerism to bask in the air conditioning. So within a ten-minute taxi-ride, I have left Sohinal and I am standing in the middle of Harvey Nichols, being shown a £20,000 taffeta dress by a bored salesgirl. "As you can see, it is cut on the bias . . ." she says, and I stop writing.

Time doesn't seem to pass in the malls. Days blur with the same electric light, the same shined floors, the same brands I know from home. Here, Dubai is reduced to its component sounds: Do-buy. In the most expensive malls I am almost alone, the shops empty and echoing. On the record, everybody tells me business is going fine. Off the record, they look panicky. There is a hat exhibition ahead of the Dubai races, selling elaborate headgear for £1,000 a pop. "Last year, we were packed. Now look," a hat designer tells me. She swoops her arm over a vacant space.

I approach a blonde 17-year-old Dutch girl wandering around in hotpants, oblivious to the swarms of men gaping at her. "I love it here!" she says. "The heat, the malls, the beach!" Does it ever bother you that it's a slave society? She puts her head down, just as Sohinal did. "I try not to see," she says. Even at 17, she has learned not to look, and not to ask; that, she senses, is a transgression too far.

Between the malls, there is nothing but the connecting tissue of asphalt. Every road has at least four lanes; Dubai feels like a motorway punctuated by shopping centers. You only walk anywhere if you are suicidal. The residents of Dubai flit from mall to mall by car or taxis.

How does it feel if this is your country, filled with foreigners? Unlike the expats and the slave class, I can't just approach the native Emiratis to ask questions when I see them wandering around — the men in cool white robes, the women in sweltering black. If you try, the women blank you, and the men look affronted, and tell you brusquely that Dubai is "fine". So I browse through the Emirati blog-scene and found some typical-sounding young Emiratis. We meet — where else? — in the mall.

Ahmed al-Atar is a handsome 23-year-old with a neat, trimmed beard, tailored white robes, and rectangular wire glasses. He speaks perfect American English, and quickly shows that he knows London, Los Angeles and Paris better than most westerners. Sitting back in his chair in an identikit Starbucks, he announces: "This is the best place in the world to be young! The government pays for your education up to PhD level. You get given a free house when you get married. You get free healthcare, and if it's not good enough here, they pay for you to go abroad. You don't even have to pay for your phone calls. Almost everyone has a maid, a nanny, and a driver. And we never pay any taxes. Don't you wish you were Emirati?"

I try to raise potential objections to this Panglossian summary, but he leans forward and says: "Look — my grandfather woke up every day and he would have to fight to get to the well first to get water. When the wells ran dry, they had to have water delivered by camel. They were always hungry and thirsty and desperate for jobs. He limped all his life, because he there was no medical treatment available when he broke his leg. Now look at us!"

For Emiratis, this is a Santa Claus state, handing out goodies while it makes its money elsewhere: Through renting out land to foreigners, soft taxes on them like business and airport charges, and the remaining dribble of oil. Most Emiratis, like Ahmed, work for the government, so they're cushioned from the credit crunch. "I haven't felt any effect at all, and nor have my friends," he says. "Your employment is secure. You will only be fired if you do something incredibly bad." The laws are currently being tightened, to make it even more impossible to sack an Emirati.

Sure, the flooding-in of expats can sometimes be "an eyesore," Ahmed says. "But we see the expats as the price we had to pay for this development. How else could we do it? Nobody wants to go back to the days of the desert, the days before everyone came. We went from being like an African country to having an average income per head of $120,000 a year. And we're supposed to complain?"

He says the lack of political freedom is fine by him. "You'll find it very hard to find an Emirati who doesn't support Sheikh Mohammed." Because they're scared? "No, because we really all support him. He's a great leader. Just look!" He smiles and says: "I'm sure my life is very much like yours. We hang out, have a coffee, go to the movies. You'll be in a Pizza Hut or Nando's in London, and at the same time I'll be in one in Dubai," he says, ordering another latte.

But do all young Emiratis see it this way? Can it really be so sunny in the political sands? In the sleek Emirates Tower Hotel, I meet Sultan al-Qassemi. He's a 31-year-old Emirati columnist for the Dubai press and private art collector, with a reputation for being a contrarian liberal, advocating gradual reform. He is wearing Western clothes — blue jeans and a Ralph Lauren shirt — and speaks incredibly fast, turning himself into a manic whirr of arguments.

"People here are turning into lazy, overweight babies!" he exclaims. "The nanny state has gone too far. We don't do anything for ourselves! Why don't any of us work for the private sector? Why can't a mother and father look after their own child?" And yet, when I try to bring up the system of slavery that built Dubai, he looks angry. "People should give us credit," he insists. "We are the most tolerant people in the world. Dubai is the only truly international city in the world. Everyone who comes here is treated with respect."

I pause, and think of the vast camps in Sonapur, just a few miles away. Does he even know they exist? He looks irritated. "You know, if there are 30 or 40 cases [of worker abuse] a year, that sounds like a lot but when you think about how many people are here . . ." Thirty or 40? This abuse is endemic to the system, I say. We're talking about hundreds of thousands.

Sultan is furious. He splutters: "You don't think Mexicans are treated badly in New York City? And how long did it take Britain to treat people well? I could come to London and write about the homeless people on Oxford Street and make your city sound like a terrible place, too! The workers here can leave any time they want! Any Indian can leave, any Asian can leave!"

But they can't, I point out. Their passports are taken away, and their wages are withheld. "Well, I feel bad if that happens, and anybody who does that should be punished. But their embassies should help them." They try. But why do you forbid the workers — with force — from going on strike against lousy employers? "Thank God we don't allow that!" he exclaims. "Strikes are in-convenient! They go on the street — we're not having that. We won't be like France. Imagine a country where they the workers can just stop whenever they want!" So what should the workers do when they are cheated and lied to? "Quit. Leave the country."

I sigh. Sultan is seething now. "People in the West are always complaining about us," he says. Suddenly, he adopts a mock-whiny voice and says, in imitation of these disgusting critics: "Why don't you treat animals better? Why don't you have better shampoo advertising? Why don't you treat laborers better?" It's a revealing order: Animals, shampoo, then workers. He becomes more heated, shifting in his seat, jabbing his finger at me. "I gave workers who worked for me safety goggles and special boots, and they didn't want to wear them! It slows them down!"

And then he smiles, coming up with what he sees as his killer argument. "When I see Western journalists criticize us — don't you realize you're shooting yourself in the foot? The Middle East will be far more dangerous if Dubai fails. Our export isn't oil, it's hope. Poor Egyptians or Libyans or Iranians grow up saying — I want to go to Dubai. We're very important to the region. We are showing how to be a modern Muslim country. We don't have any fundamentalists here. Europeans shouldn't gloat at our demise. You should be very worried . . .. Do you know what will happen if this model fails? Dubai will go down the Iranian path, the Islamist path."

Sultan sits back. My arguments have clearly disturbed him; he says in a softer, conciliatory tone, almost pleading: "Listen. My mother used to go to the well and get a bucket of water every morning. On her wedding day, she was given an orange as a gift because she had never eaten one. Two of my brothers died when they were babies because the healthcare system hadn't developed yet. Don't judge us." He says it again, his eyes filled with intensity: "Don't judge us."

The Dunkin' Donuts Dissidents

But there is another face to the Emirati minority — a small huddle of dissidents, trying to shake the Sheikhs out of abusive laws. Next to a Virgin Megastore and a Dunkin' Donuts, with James Blunt's "You're Beautiful" blaring behind me, I meet the Dubai dictatorship's Public Enemy Number One. By way of introduction, Mohammed al-Mansoori says from within his white robes and sinewy face: "Westerners come here and see the malls and the tall buildings and they think that means we are free. But these businesses, these buildings — who are they for? This is a dictatorship. The royal family think they own the country, and the people are their servants. There is no freedom here."

We snuffle out the only Arabic restaurant in this mall, and he says everything you are banned — under threat of prison — from saying in Dubai. Mohammed tells me he was born in Dubai to a fisherman father who taught him one enduring lesson: Never follow the herd. Think for yourself. In the sudden surge of development, Mohammed trained as a lawyer. By the Noughties, he had climbed to the head of the Jurists' Association, an organization set up to press for Dubai's laws to be consistent with international human rights legislation.

And then — suddenly — Mohammed thwacked into the limits of Sheikh Mohammed's tolerance. Horrified by the "system of slavery" his country was being built on, he spoke out to Human Rights Watch and the BBC. "So I was hauled in by the secret police and told: Shut up, or you will lose you job, and your children will be unemployable," he says. "But how could I be silent?"

He was stripped of his lawyer's license and his passport — becoming yet another person imprisoned in this country. "I have been blacklisted and so have my children. The newspapers are not allowed to write about me."

Why is the state so keen to defend this system of slavery? He offers a prosaic explanation. "Most companies are owned by the government, so they oppose human rights laws because it will reduce their profit margins. It's in their interests that the workers are slaves."

Last time there was a depression, there was a starburst of democracy in Dubai, seized by force from the sheikhs. In the 1930s, the city's merchants banded together against Sheikh Said bin Maktum al-Maktum — the absolute ruler of his day — and insisted they be given control over the state finances. It lasted only a few years, before the Sheikh — with the enthusiastic support of the British — snuffed them out.

And today? Sheikh Mohammed turned Dubai into Creditopolis, a city built entirely on debt. Dubai owes 107 percent of its entire GDP. It would be bust already, if the neighboring oil-soaked state of Abu Dhabi hadn't pulled out its checkbook. Mohammed says this will constrict freedom even further. "Now Abu Dhabi calls the tunes — and they are much more conservative and restrictive than even Dubai. Freedom here will diminish every day." Already, new media laws have been drafted forbidding the press to report on anything that could "damage" Dubai or "its economy". Is this why the newspapers are giving away glossy supplements talking about "encouraging economic indicators"?

Everybody here waves Islamism as the threat somewhere over the horizon, sure to swell if their advice is not followed. Today, every imam is appointed by the government, and every sermon is tightly controlled to keep it moderate. But Mohammed says anxiously: "We don't have Islamism here now, but I think that if you control people and give them no way to express anger, it could rise. People who are told to shut up all the time can just explode."

Later that day, against another identikit-corporate backdrop, I meet another dissident — Abdulkhaleq Abdullah, Professor of Political Science at Emirates University. His anger focuses not on political reform, but the erosion of Emirati identity. He is famous among the locals, a rare outspoken conductor for their anger. He says somberly: "There has been a rupture here. This is a totally different city to the one I was born in 50 years ago."

He looks around at the shiny floors and Western tourists and says: "What we see now didn't occur in our wildest dreams. We never thought we could be such a success, a trendsetter, a model for other Arab countries. The people of Dubai are mighty proud of their city, and rightly so. And yet . . ." He shakes his head. "In our hearts, we fear we have built a modern city but we are losing it to all these expats."

Adbulkhaleq says every Emirati of his generation lives with a "psychological trauma." Their hearts are divided — "between pride on one side, and fear on the other." Just after he says this, a smiling waitress approaches, and asks us what we would like to drink. He orders a Coke.

Dubai Pride

There is one group in Dubai for whom the rhetoric of sudden freedom and liberation rings true — but it is the very group the government wanted to liberate least: Gays.

Beneath a famous international hotel, I clamber down into possibly the only gay club on the Saudi Arabian peninsula. I find a United Nations of tank tops and bulging biceps, dancing to Kylie, dropping ecstasy, and partying like it's Soho. "Dubai is the best place in the Muslim world for gays!" a 25-year old Emirati with spiked hair says, his arms wrapped around his 31-year old "husband". "We are alive. We can meet. That is more than most Arab gays."

It is illegal to be gay in Dubai, and punishable by 10 years in prison. But the locations of the latest unofficial gay clubs circulate online, and men flock there, seemingly unafraid of the police. "They might bust the club, but they will just disperse us," one of them says. "The police have other things to do."

In every large city, gay people find a way to find each other — but Dubai has become the clearing-house for the region's homosexuals, a place where they can live in relative safety. Saleh, a lean private in the Saudi Arabian army, has come here for the Coldplay concert, and tells me Dubai is "great" for gays: "In Saudi, it's hard to be straight when you're young. The women are shut away so everyone has gay sex. But they only want to have sex with boys — 15- to 21-year-olds. I'm 27, so I'm too old now. I need to find real gays, so this is the best place. All Arab gays want to live in Dubai."

With that, Saleh dances off across the dance floor, towards a Dutch guy with big biceps and a big smile.

The Lifestyle

All the guidebooks call Dubai a "melting pot," but as I trawl across the city, I find that every group here huddles together in its own little ethnic enclave — and becomes a caricature of itself. One night — in the heart of this homesick city, tired of the malls and the camps — I go to Double Decker, a hangout for

British expats. At the entrance there is a red telephone box, and London bus-stop signs. Its wooden interior looks like a cross between a colonial clubhouse in the Raj and an Eighties school disco, with blinking colored lights and cheese blaring out. As I enter, a girl in a short skirt collapses out of the door onto her back. A guy wearing a pirate hat helps her to her feet, dropping his beer bottle with a paralytic laugh.

I start to talk to two sun-dried women in their sixties who have been getting gently sozzled since midday. "You stay here for The Lifestyle," they say, telling me to take a seat and order some more drinks. All the expats talk about The Lifestyle, but when you ask what it is, they become vague. Ann Wark tries to summaries it: "Here, you go out every night. You'd never do that back home. You see people all the time. It's great. You have lots of free time. You have maids and staff so you don't have to do all that stuff. You party!"

They have been in Dubai for 20 years, and they are happy to explain how the city works. "You've got a hierarchy, haven't you?" Ann says. "It's the Emiratis at the top, then I'd say the British and other Westerners. Then I suppose it's the Filipinos, because they've got a bit more brains than the Indians. Then at the bottom you've got the Indians and all them lot."

They admit, however, they have "never" spoken to an Emirati. Never? "No. They keep themselves to themselves." Yet Dubai has disappointed them. Jules Taylor tells me: "If you have an accident here it's a nightmare. There was a British woman we knew who ran over an Indian guy, and she was locked up for four days! If you have a tiny bit of alcohol on your breath they're all over you. These Indians throw themselves in front of cars, because then their family has to be given blood money — you know, compensation. But the police just blame us. That poor woman."

A 24-year-old British woman called Hannah Gamble takes a break from the dance floor to talk to me. "I love the sun and the beach! It's great out here!" she says. Is there anything bad? "Oh yes!" she says. Ah: One of them has noticed, I think with relief. "The banks! When you want to make a transfer you have to fax them. You can't do it online." Anything else? She thinks hard. "The traffic's not very good."

When I ask the British expats how they feel to not be in a democracy, their reaction is always the same. First, they look bemused. Then they look affronted. "It's the Arab way!" an Essex boy shouts at me in response, as he tries to put a pair of comedy antlers on his head while pouring some beer into the mouth of his friend, who is lying on his back on the floor, gurning.

Later, in a hotel bar, I start chatting to a dyspeptic expat American who works in the cosmetics industry and is desperate to get away from these people. She says: "All the people who couldn't succeed in their own countries end up here, and suddenly they're rich and promoted way above their abilities and bragging about how great they are. I've never met so many incompetent people in such senior positions anywhere in the world." She adds: "It's absolutely racist. I had Filipino girls working for me doing the same job as a European girl, and she's paid a quarter of the wages. The people who do the real work are paid next to nothing, while these incompetent managers pay themselves £40,000 a month."

With the exception of her, one theme unites every expat I speak to: Their joy at having staff to do the work that would clog their lives up Back Home. Everyone, it seems, has a maid. The maids used to be predominantly Filipino, but with the recession, Filipinos have been judged to be too expensive, so a nice Ethiopian servant girl is the latest fashionable accessory.

It is an open secret that once you hire a maid, you have absolute power over her. You take her passport — everyone does; you decide when to pay her, and when — if ever — she can take a break; and you decide who she talks to. She speaks no Arabic. She cannot escape.

In a Burger King, a Filipino girl tells me it is "terrifying" for her to wander the malls in Dubai because Filipino maids or nannies always sneak away from the family they are with and beg her for help. "They say — 'Please, I am being held prisoner, they don't let me call home, they make me work every waking hour seven days a week.' At first I would say — my God, I will tell the consulate, where are you staying? But they never know their address, and the consulate isn't interested. I avoid them now. I keep thinking about a woman who told me she hadn't eaten any fruit in four years. They think I have power because I can walk around on my own, but I'm powerless."

The only hostel for women in Dubai — a filthy private villa on the brink of being repossessed — is filled with escaped maids. Mela Matari, a 25-year-old Ethiopian woman with a drooping smile, tells me what happened to her — and thousands like her. She was promised a paradise in the sands by an agency, so she left her four year-old daughter at home and headed here to earn money for a better future. "But they paid me half what they promised. I was put with an Australian family — four children — and Madam made me work from 6am to 1am every day, with no day off. I was exhausted and pleaded for a break, but they just shouted: 'You came here to work, not sleep!' Then one day I just couldn't go on, and Madam beat me. She beat me with her fists and kicked me. My ear still hurts. They wouldn't give me my wages: they said they'd pay me at the end of the two years. What could I do? I didn't know anybody here. I was terrified."

One day, after yet another beating, Mela ran out onto the streets, and asked — in broken English — how to find the Ethiopian consulate. After walking for two days, she found it, but they told her she had to get her passport back from Madam. "Well, how could I?" she asks. She has been in this hostel for six months. She has spoken to her daughter twice. "I lost my country, I lost my daughter, I lost everything," she says.

As she says this, I remember a stray sentence I heard back at Double Decker. I asked a British woman called Hermione Frayling what the best thing about

Dubai was. "Oh, the servant class!" she trilled. "You do nothing. They'll do anything!"

The End of The World

The World is empty. It has been abandoned, its continents unfinished. Through binoculars, I think I can glimpse Britain; this sceptred isle barren in the salt-breeze.

Here, off the coast of Dubai, developers have been rebuilding the world. They have constructed artificial islands in the shape of all planet Earth's landmasses, and they plan to sell each continent off to be built on. There were rumors that the Beckhams would bid for Britain. But the people who work at the nearby coast say they haven't seen anybody there for months now. "The World is over," a South African suggests.

All over Dubai, crazy projects that were Under Construction are now Under Collapse. They were building an air-conditioned beach here, with cooling pipes running below the sand, so the super-rich didn't singe their toes on their way from towel to sea.

The projects completed just before the global economy crashed look empty and tattered. The Atlantis Hotel was launched last winter in a $20m fin-de-siècle party attended by Robert De Niro, Lindsay Lohan and Lily Allen. Sitting on its own fake island — shaped, of course, like a palm tree — it looks like an immense upturned tooth in a faintly decaying mouth. It is pink and turreted — the architecture of the pharaohs, as reimagined by Zsa-Zsa Gabor. Its Grand Lobby is a monumental dome covered in glitter balls, held up by eight monumental concrete palm trees. Standing in the middle, there is a giant shining glass structure that looks like the intestines of every guest who has ever stayed at the Atlantis. It is unexpectedly raining; water is leaking from the roof, and tiles are falling off.

A South African PR girl shows me around its most coveted rooms, explaining that this is "the greatest luxury offered in the world." We stroll past shops selling £24m diamond rings around a hotel themed on the lost and sunken continent of, yes, Atlantis. There are huge water tanks filled with sharks, which poke around mock-abandoned castles and dumped submarines. There are more than 1,500 rooms here, each with a sea view. The Neptune suite has three floors, and — I gasp as I see it — it looks out directly on to the vast shark tank. You lie on the bed, and the sharks stare in at you. In Dubai, you can sleep with the fishes, and survive.

But even the luxury — reminiscent of a Bond villain's lair — is also being abandoned. I check myself in for a few nights to the classiest hotel in town, the Park Hyatt. It is the fashionistas' favorite hotel, where Elle Macpherson and Tommy Hilfiger stay, a gorgeous, understated palace. It feels empty. Whenever

I eat, I am one of the only people in the restaurant. A staff member tells me in a whisper: "It used to be full here. Now there's hardly anyone." Rattling around, I feel like Jack Nicholson in The Shining, the last man in an abandoned, haunted home.

The most famous hotel in Dubai — the proud icon of the city — is the Burj al Arab hotel, sitting on the shore, shaped like a giant glass sailing boat. In the lobby, I start chatting to a couple from London who work in the City. They have been coming to Dubai for 10 years now, and they say they love it. "You never know what you'll find here," he says. "On our last trip, at the beginning of the holiday, our window looked out on the sea. By the end, they'd built an entire island there."

My patience frayed by all this excess, I find myself snapping: Doesn't the omnipresent slave class bother you? I hope they misunderstood me, because the woman replied: "That's what we come for! It's great, you can't do anything for yourself!" Her husband chimes in: "When you go to the toilet, they open the door, they turn on the tap — the only thing they don't do is take it out for you when you have a piss!" And they both fall about laughing.

Taking on the Desert

Dubai is not just a city living beyond its financial means; it is living beyond its ecological means. You stand on a manicured Dubai lawn and watch the sprinklers spray water all around you. You see tourists flocking to swim with dolphins. You wander into a mountain-sized freezer where they have built a ski slope with real snow. And a voice at the back of your head squeaks: This is the desert. This is the most water-stressed place on the planet. How can this be happening? How is it possible?

The very earth is trying to repel Dubai, to dry it up and blow it away. The new Tiger Woods Golf Course needs four million gallons of water to be pumped on to its grounds every day, or it would simply shrivel and disappear on the winds. The city is regularly washed over with dust storms that fog up the skies and turn the skyline into a blur. When the dust parts, heat burns through. It cooks anything that is not kept constantly, artificially wet.

Dr Mohammed Raouf, the environmental director of the Gulf Research Centre, sounds somber as he sits in his Dubai office and warns: "This is a desert area, and we are trying to defy its environment. It is very unwise. If you take on the desert, you will lose."

Sheikh Maktoum built his showcase city in a place with no useable water. None. There is no surface water, very little aquifer, and among the lowest rainfall in the world. So Dubai drinks the sea. The Emirates' water is stripped of salt in vast desalination plants around the Gulf — making it the most expensive water on earth. It costs more than petrol to produce, and belches vast amounts of carbon dioxide into the atmosphere as it goes. It's the main reason why a resident of Dubai has the biggest average carbon footprint of any human being — more than double that of an American.

If a recession turns into depression, Dr Raouf believes Dubai could run out of water. "At the moment, we have financial reserves that cover bringing so much water to the middle of the desert. But if we had lower revenues — if, say, the world shifts to a source of energy other than oil . . ." he shakes his head. "We will have a very big problem. Water is the main source of life. It would be a catastrophe. Dubai only has enough water to last us a week. There's almost no storage. We don't know what will happen if our supplies falter. It would be hard to survive."

Global warming, he adds, makes the problem even worse. "We are building all these artificial islands, but if the sea level rises, they will be gone, and we will lose a lot. Developers keep saying it's all fine, they've taken it into consideration, but I'm not so sure."

Is the Dubai government concerned about any of this? "There isn't much interest in these problems," he says sadly. But just to stand still, the average resident of Dubai needs three times more water than the average human. In the looming century of water stresses and a transition away from fossil fuels, Dubai is uniquely vulnerable.

I wanted to understand how the government of Dubai will react, so I decided to look at how it has dealt with an environmental problem that already exists — the pollution of its beaches. One woman — an American, working at one of the big hotels — had written in a lot of online forums arguing that it was bad and getting worse, so I called her to arrange a meeting. "I can't talk to you," she said sternly. Not even if it's off the record? "I can't talk to you." But I don't have to disclose your name . . . "You're not listening. This phone is bugged. I can't talk to you," she snapped, and hung up.

The next day I turned up at her office. "If you reveal my identity, I'll be sent on the first plane out of this city," she said, before beginning to nervously pace the shore with me. "It started like this. We began to get complaints from people using the beach. The water looked and smelled odd, and they were starting to get sick after going into it. So I wrote to the ministers of health and tourism and expected to hear back immediately — but there was nothing. Silence. I hand-delivered the letters. Still nothing."

The water quality got worse and worse. The guests started to spot raw sewage, condoms, and used sanitary towels floating in the sea. So the hotel ordered its own water analyses from a professional company. "They told us it was full of fecal matter and bacteria 'too numerous to count'. I had to start telling guests not to go in the water, and since they'd come on a beach holiday, as you can imagine, they were pretty pissed off." She began to make angry posts on the expat discussion forums — and people began to figure out what was happening. Dubai had expanded so fast its sewage treatment facilities couldn't keep up.

The sewage disposal trucks had to queue for three or four days at the treatment plants — so instead, they were simply drilling open the manholes and dumping the untreated sewage down them, so it flowed straight to the sea.

Suddenly, it was an open secret — and the municipal authorities finally acknowledged the problem. They said they would fine the truckers. But the water quality didn't improve: It became black and stank. "It's got chemicals in it. I don't know what they are. But this stuff is toxic."

She continued to complain — and started to receive anonymous phone calls. "Stop embarrassing Dubai, or your visa will be cancelled and you're out," they said. She says: "The expats are terrified to talk about anything. One critical comment in the newspapers and they deport you. So what am I supposed to do? Now the water is worse than ever. People are getting really sick. Eye infections, ear infections, stomach infections, rashes. Look at it!" There are feces floating on the beach, in the shadow of one of Dubai's most famous hotels.

"What I learnt about Dubai is that the authorities don't give a toss about the environment," she says, standing in the stench. "They're pumping toxins into the sea, their main tourist attraction, for God's sake. If there are environmental problems in the future, I can tell you now how they will deal with them — deny it's happening, cover it up, and carry on until it's a total disaster." As she speaks, a dust storm blows around us, as the desert tries, slowly, insistently, to take back its land.

Fake Plastic Trees

On my final night in the Dubai Disneyland, I stop off on my way to the airport, at a Pizza Hut that sits at the side of one of the city's endless, wide, gaping roads. It is identical to the one near my apartment in London in every respect, even the vomit-colored decor. My mind is whirring and distracted. Perhaps Dubai disturbed me so much, I am thinking, because here, the entire global supply chain is condensed. Many of my goods are made by semi-enslaved populations desperate for a chance 2,000 miles away; is the only difference that here, they are merely two miles away, and you sometimes get to glimpse their faces? Dubai is Market Fundamentalist Globalization in One City.

I ask the Filipino girl behind the counter if she likes it here. "It's OK," she says cautiously. Really? I say. I can't stand it. She sighs with relief and says: "This is the most terrible place! I hate it! I was here for months before I realized — everything in Dubai is fake. Everything you see. The trees are fake, the workers' contracts are fake, the islands are fake, the smiles are fake — even the water is fake!" But she is trapped, she says. She got into debt to come here, and she is stuck for three years: An old story now. "I think Dubai is like an oasis. It is an illusion, not real. You think you have seen water in the distance, but you get close and you only get a mouthful of sand."

As she says this, another customer enters. She forces her face into the broad, empty Dubai smile and says: "And how may I help you tonight, sir?"

Note

1. Some names in this article have been changed.

DRUGS

Smuggling Made Easy: Landlocked Paraguay Emerges as a Top Producer of Contraband Tobacco

6

Marina Walker Guevara,
Mabel Rehnfeldt, Marcelo Soares

Guaíra sits on the edge of the sluggish, muddy, mile-wide Paraná River that cuts a natural border between Brazil and Paraguay. Here the soil is red, the terrain is flat with ample soybean and mate leaf plantations. On its face, Guaíra is a well-kept Western Brazilian city of 30,000. Men chatter among themselves sitting in small plazas and barbershops. The streets downtown are clean, the houses are freshly painted and pay phones are decorated with natural motifs — you can call from the gut of a fish or the chest of a parrot.

Beneath this surface, however, the city shows a more disturbing element.

Last September, Guaíra made headlines across Brazil when 15 people were murdered at a makeshift riverside warehouse. The killings were the result of a vendetta among drug smugglers and, officials here say, they weren't all that unusual. Just 150 miles north from the notorious Tri-Border Area, where Brazil, Paraguay and Argentina meet, Guaíra is today a major weapons and drugs corridor in the region. But no product, police say, is more widely smuggled through this city, and more profitable to smugglers, than Paraguayan cigarettes.

Dozens of motorboats crammed with tobacco cross the Paraná River daily from the neighboring Paraguayan city of Salto del Guairá. The smugglers feed an illicit trade that injects billions of cigarettes into Sao Paulo, Rio de Janeiro, and other large Brazilian cities, where the cheap, untaxed Paraguayan sticks account for 20 percent of the entire cigarette market. Guaíra sits at the heart of this trade, a strategic gateway and a place where many residents — up to half its population, locals say — rely directly or indirectly on smuggling for their livelihood. A few reap millions from the illicit trade. Guaíra's most famous criminal son, Roque Fabiano Silveira, made a fortune and a name, trafficking Paraguayan cigarettes thousands of miles away.

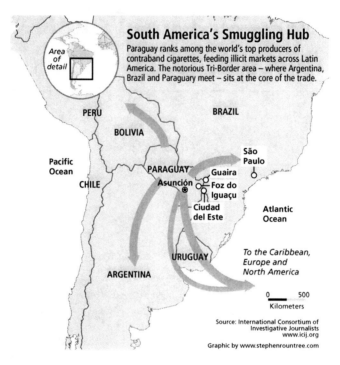

Figure 6.1 South America's Smuggling Hub. Paraguay ranks among the world's top producers of contraband cigarettes, feeding illicit markets across Latin America. The notorious Tri-Border area — where Argentina, Brazil and Paraguay meet — sits at the core of the trade.

Silveira, 44, nicknamed Zero Um ("The Kingpin"), is a larger-than-life border boss who fled to Paraguay after being charged in Guaíra with orchestrating the 1996 murder of a businessman. In Paraguay his cigarette business took off, and in 1999 he opened a sizable cigarette factory on the outskirts of the country's capital, Asunción, which soon became the operational base for a smuggling network that spanned two continents and reached deep into the United States. Starting in 2003, Silveira cut deals with tobacco traders in Arizona and smoke shop owners in Indian reservations in Washington state to smuggle millions of Paraguayan-made contraband cigarettes through the ports of Miami, Norfolk, and Baltimore. The sticks were then distributed across the country and the profits were laundered to bank accounts in Paraguay and the United States. Silveira not only manufactured the cigarettes, US prosecutors said, but also greased political and law enforcement hands in South America that guaranteed swift passage north for the cargoes. His former associates describe him as smart and cold, with an eye for fine suits.

The tale of Roque Silveira is emblematic of the criminal nature and global reach of the teeming Paraguayan cigarette industry, one that experts and law enforcement officials say is, largely, set up for and devoted to transnational smuggling. Fifteen years ago cigarette manufacturing was minimal in Paraguay, one of South America's poorest countries and a place notorious for corruption and trading in counterfeit goods. Today Paraguay, a landlocked, California-sized country, ranks among the world's top producers of contraband cigarettes, responsible for 10 percent of the world's contraband tobacco, experts estimate.

Paraguay's factories churned out 68 billion cigarettes in 2006, more than 20 times what the country consumes, according to a study by the Centro de Investigación de la Epidemia de Tabaquismo (CIET), a Uruguay-based NGO that tracks the economics of the region's tobacco market. The vast majority of the cigarettes — up to 90 percent of production, worth an estimated $1 billion — disappear in the black market, law enforcement officials say. The cigarettes are flooding Brazil and Argentina, where taxes are much higher than in Paraguay, and have turned up as far away as Ireland.

Fidel, Hamlet, and Opus Dei

Once dominated by multinational tobacco companies, the global illicit cigarette trade today involves an array of crime syndicates which, much like the Silveira network, rob governments of billions of dollars in much-needed tax money, fuel organized crime, and help spread addiction by placing cheap cigarettes in the world's black markets. The steep growth of Paraguay's cigarette industry alarms law enforcement agencies and health officials alike, who fear that the South American nation could become the next nightmare in global cigarette trafficking. Industry sources say manufacturing cigarettes in Paraguay today is cheaper than in China — the top producer of contraband smokes — while the quality of the product is far superior.

"There is a real danger that this situation could escalate very rapidly," says Austin Rowan, head of the anti-tobacco smuggling operations at the European Union's Anti-Fraud Office (OLAF). What's distinctive about Paraguay, investigators say, is the massive number of obscure, cheap brands its factories produce — more than 2,600 brands have been registered with the Ministry of Industry and Commerce, including the likes of "Dirty," "Fidel," "Hamlet," and "Opus Dei" — which makes it harder for investigators to track the trade. In contrast, only a handful of local brands are sold in the domestic market, where smokers pay some of the lowest cigarette taxes in the world.

Multinational tobacco firms are alarmed at the size and speed at which the Paraguayans have built up an off-the-books industry. Investigators for Big Tobacco say Paraguayan cigarettes are shipped to known Caribbean smuggling hubs like Aruba and Panama, where they believe the shipments enter the black market. In 2006 Irish customs seized a container loaded with five million Paraguayan cigarettes concealed in bales of plywood. While making inquiries about the case among his EU peers, David Godwin of Irish Customs says he was told: "'If you think you have problems with China, the Middle East, and the rest, brace yourself because you haven't seen anything. . . . The capacity is just endless in South America.'"

Tobacco factories in Paraguay range from sprawling, state-of-the-art manufacturing plants that boast cutting-edge technology to miniature "mobile" factories — also called submarines — which are assembled inside of trucks. Paraguayan government officials say that if all cigarette-making machines in Paraguay were to work at maximum output, the country could produce up to 100 billion sticks annually — enough to supply about two-thirds of the Brazilian market.

Smuggling is made easy in Paraguay, officials confide. There is virtually no industry regulation, and illegal manufacturers and traffickers are often insulated from prosecution by those in power. Bankers, politicians, and soccer club barons are themselves involved in the business and make hefty campaign contributions. Although the administration of President Fernando Lugo — a former Catholic bishop who in 2008 unseated the powerful Colorado Party after more than 60 years in power — has pledged to change the country's reputation as a smuggling haven, there already have been some mishaps. In February, the president named a convicted cigarette smuggler as his Air Force intelligence chief. Lugo later backed off amidst intense criticism.

A Smuggler's Paradise

Cigarettes are just another commodity peddled through Paraguay's decades-old underground economy, which flourished during the 35-year dictatorship of Alfredo Stroessner. Before he was forced from power in 1989 in a military coup, Stroessner made the country a sanctuary for Nazi war criminals, deposed dictators, and smugglers.

The Tri-Border Area of Paraguay, Brazil, and Argentina is the epicenter of this contraband culture. A corridor for drugs, weapons, stolen cars, and any imaginable knock-off — from CDs to Viagra — this region of thick, green rainforests and spectacular waterfalls has also become the backdrop for the booming trade in smuggled and counterfeit cigarettes made in Paraguay.

"The only thing that flourishes here is illegality," says Humberto Rosetti, a prosecutor in Ciudad del Este, the commercial center of the Tri-Border Area, often regarded as one of the most lawless places on earth. The city's downtown is a bustling labyrinth of narrow streets cluttered with thousands of street stands, money exchange houses and shops, where anything from exotic pets to AK-47s can be obtained with almost equal ease. Late-model Mercedes and BMWs sporting polarized windows rush by and scores of motor scooters, some of them transporting entire families, weave through the ubiquitous traffic jams. In the Calle de los Cigarrilleros, as locals have christened one of the city streets, boxes of Eight, Te, Rodeo, Calvert — the smugglers' favorite brands — are stacked high along the sidewalk. "Our hands are pretty much tied," says Rosetti, who has directed several cigarette seizures in recent months, only to see judges and customs officials promptly return the loads to smugglers.

US officials regard Paraguay as a principal money-laundering center for the proceeds of drugs, arms, and cigarette trafficking in South America — and Ciudad del Este sits at the core of that trade. Cigarette factories are often linked to money exchange houses where profits of the contraband are laundered, according to former factory managers and court records. So impenetrable is Ciudad del Este's financial system that American undercover agents who infiltrated Roque Silveira's US smuggling ring were unable to find the money they helped the group launder. "We tried to track the proceeds," says Assistant US Attorney James Warwick. "Did we succeed? No."

Several Paraguayan cigarette firms have conveniently built factories in Ciudad del Este and nearby Hernandarias. From there, cigarettes for years were smuggled to Brazil in vans, trucks, and buses through the shabby Friendship Bridge that connects Ciudad del Este with its Brazilian counterpart, the city of Foz do Iguaçu. Brazilians stepped up controls at the border in 2005, so smugglers switched from the road to the water. Starting at dusk, motor boats leave through any of the more than 300 makeshift piers fashioned along the nearby Lake Itaipú, formed by the dam of one of the world's largest hydrological power plants, built on the Paraná River. To reach some of these illicit piers, one must navigate a maze of tortuous and narrow red-dirt paths through dense underbrush. One afternoon in March, ICIJ reporters visiting the seemingly deserted Codorso Pier came across a government worker smoothing out the smugglers' trail with the help of his tractor. Reporters were told the smugglers were taking the day off to mourn one of their own, a former policeman, who had died in a car accident the day before.

"We close one pier, and two more pop up overnight," says Gilberto Tragancin, chief of Brazil customs service in Foz do Iguaçu. With a shoreline of nearly 1,000 miles, Lake Itaipú is almost impossible to patrol in its entirety, Tragancin explains. A few yards outside of Tragancin's office, a 'cigarette trashing' machine was in motion. The loud contraption pulverizes about 500,000 seized cigarette packs every day — the remains of which are used in fertilizers and to build roads. The flow of Paraguayan contraband cigarettes to Brazil is 20–30 billion sticks annually, experts estimate. In contrast, says Tragancin, legal exports of cigarettes to Brazil are zero.

Besides the public health threat it poses, cigarette smuggling is also bolstering violent organized crime groups that operate complex networks along the border with Brazil. Tragancin says these groups are now using the cigarette smuggling channels to supply weapons and munitions to some of Brazil's most dangerous syndicates, including the First Command of the Capital (PCC), the leading criminal gang in Sao Paulo prisons.

The Trade Goes Global

International smugglers quickly spotted an opportunity in the booming Paraguayan illicit tobacco trade. Washington state-based cigarette wholesaler Stormmy Paul, a Tulalip Indian, flew to Paraguay in 2003 to cut a deal. He had been buying Chinese cigarettes, including counterfeit Marlboros, and re-selling them tax-free to smoke shops in his state, but he wanted a better combination of price and quality. A business partner from Brazil offered to make some introductions south of the border.

In Paraguay, Paul visited a handful of cigarette factories. One facility stood out: The heavily guarded Tabacalera Central in the outskirts of Asunción. The visitors were greeted by owner Roque Silveira and feted with a lavish barbecue. By the time dinner was completed an agreement had been sealed. Paul would pay $2 for each carton of cigarettes manufactured at Silveira's facility and an additional $2 per carton to a middleman in Maryland who altered customs forms to avoid controls, and taxes, at US ports. The deal still left Paul a $2 per-carton profit.

"I loved it down there," said Paul, an enterprising, voluble fellow who leads a weekly ritual at a sweat lodge on the Tulalip reservation, north of Seattle. He found Silveira impressive. "He is a really sharp business guy," said Paul of Silveira. "There is a certain class about him — Roque looks successful."

Starting in late 2003, the ring of 11 people, most of them American tobacco traders, smuggled into the United States more than 120 million Paraguayan cigarettes, for distribution from California to North Carolina, according to court records. The ring was brought down in spring 2005 as the smugglers convened in Las Vegas. Silveira, Paul, and the others were indicted on a total of 50 counts of conspiracy, smuggling, trafficking, and money laundering. US officials jailed Silveira for two months after his arrest at the Miami airport, but the Brazilian pledged to cooperate with authorities and was handed a probationary sentence. Silveira paid a fine and, to the amazement of Paraguayans, was let go.

River of the Dead

Around the same time the Americans gave Silveira a slap on the wrist, Brazilian prosecutors indicted him in one of the largest-ever cigarette smuggling investigations in that country. Codenamed Operation Fireball, the sting rounded up more than 90 people in 11 Brazilian states. In the indictment for the case, Silveira was fingered as a major supplier of contraband cigarettes who allegedly controlled three different networks that delivered the sticks to the populous Rio Grande do Sul state. Silveira managed to evade the law simply by staying in Paraguay, where, Brazilian prosecutors alleged, he has "a vast network of contacts and the financial capability to live underground."

Silveira had become the top dog in the traffic of cigarettes from Paraguay to Brazil following the 2003 arrest and subsequent conviction of legendary cigarette smuggler Roberto Eleuterio "Lobão" Da Silva, a Brazilian who wore plenty of bling and looked like Mr. T, Brazilian police say. From that point on, in smuggling parlance, Silveira "owned" the routes that led to millions of smokers in Brazil's largest cities.

Two weeks after Operation Fireball, a Brazilian customs agent was murdered in a bleak, sparsely populated region of the border called Rio do Morte — River of the Dead. An anonymous caller tipped local police to a burned-out SUV on the road. So charred was the corpse in the passenger's seat that police couldn't readily identify the victim, who had been burned alive. Forensic experts eventually said the dead man was Carlos Renato Zamo, a resident of Mundo Novo, a city just north of Guaíra. He was one of thousands of customs agents working Brazil's porous borders. Throughout the years, however, Zamo reportedly had grown far richer than most on a typical border agent's salary. He accumulated real state investments in Sao Paulo and Mato Grosso do Sul. He even owned a plane.

Brazilian police discovered that Zamo had worked for Silveira and other cigarette smugglers, who allegedly paid the agent $8,000 a month to assure their cigarette cargoes passed uninspected through border checkpoints. But Zamo had begun to fear discovery and finally backed out of the ring, police said. In a meeting, the smugglers allegedly offered to raise his payment, but he refused and tipped off customs about the group's shipments, according to Brazilian police.

Four men were eventually arrested in connection to Zamo's murder, but not Silveira, who was wanted by Brazilian authorities but remained at large in Paraguay. The day police officials announced the arrests, they addressed Silveira directly, calling him "the big head" of cigarette smuggling in the region. "Everything happens under his orders," they said.

Through his attorney in Asunción, Silveira declined to comment for this article.

Filling Big Tobacco's Shoes

Paraguayan cigarette manufacturers like to point out that they are just filling a void created by large multinational tobacco companies. In the 1990s, British American Tobacco and Philip Morris ran independent schemes in which their subsidiaries in Brazil and Argentina legally exported billions of cigarettes to Paraguay. The sticks were then smuggled back to these two higher-tax countries and sold on the black market. The practice ended in 1999 when the Brazilian government raised the cigarette export taxes dramatically to discourage the illegal trade. Following the tax increase, dozens of cigarette factories opened in Paraguay, many of them owned fully or in part by Brazilians. Within three years, Paraguay was home to more than 30 cigarette manufacturing plants, some of which counterfeited well-known international brands.

The local counterfeiting business has dropped markedly in recent years as cigarette makers realized that there was a market — in Brazil and around the world — for the cheap Paraguayan brands. The practice also carries less risk of being pursued by Big Tobacco companies for trademark violation. Today the number of manufacturing facilities has more than halved, but not so production.

Tabacalera del Este (Tabesa) is Paraguay's top cigarette factory, a modern, sprawling 183,000 square-foot facility that can pump out up to 1.5 billion cigarettes a month — or 579 cigarettes per second. The factory, located a short drive north from Ciudad del Este in the city of Hernandarias, supplies almost half of the Paraguayan market with its two flagship brands, Kentucky and Palermo. But at the same time as it serves a legitimate market, the company allegedly supplies large quantities of cigarettes that end up smuggled to Brazil and Argentina. Customs officials in those two countries told ICIJ they seize more contraband cigarettes from Tabesa than any other Paraguayan company. In 2006, Tabesa was mentioned in Operation Fireball as one of the factories whose cigarettes were allegedly smuggled to Brazil.

Paraguayan businessman Horacio Manuel Cartes is widely reported to be the owner of Tabesa, and is listed as a top shareholder and director by Informconf, a Paraguay business database. Cartes started as a cigarette distributor two decades ago. Since then he has built an empire that includes a bank, a soccer club, and several agricultural ventures — some of these formally owned by family members and business associates.

Tabesa's CEO José Ortiz talked to ICIJ reporters about the company's business.

"We don't know where our cigarettes are consumed, and it's not our problem," said Ortiz when asked about the presence of Tabesa's cigarettes in Brazil and Argentina, two markets to which the company does not legally export. "We sell our products in Paraguay and pay all local taxes," he added, sitting in his office at Tabesa's manufacturing plant, which features high-end German cigarette machinery. What happens once the cigarettes leave the factory is not Tabesa's responsibility, said Ortiz, a view shared by other cigarette makers in Paraguay. "My job is to supply the market."

Ortiz said the Tabesa does not sell directly to vendors but rather to four or five wholesale distributors. He named two wholesale firms, one of which, Tabacos del Paraguay, is affiliated with Tabesa. "The rest, I don't remember," he said, reclining on his large black leather office chair and switching the focus to multinational tobacco companies: "They are the parents and the grandparents of the creature," said Ortiz of BAT and Philip Morris' smuggling in the 1990s. "We are replacing that market they abandoned."

Last year, the company broke into the US market with its Palermo brand and is now certified to sell in at least eight states, including Maryland and California. Palermo is also available online through websites selling cigarettes from Indian reservations in New York, but Ortiz denied that Tabesa is selling to Native Americans directly. US officials have identified New York reservations as major hubs for cigarette smuggling.

Guaíra: No Man's Land

Brazilian prosecutors and police place the Paraguayan factories at the top of the "criminal enterprise," which they say runs high-volume cigarette smuggling in the region. Érico Saconato, head of the Brazilian federal police in Guaíra, said that the factories work hand in hand with "managers" on both sides of the border who acquire trucks and boats, bribe public servants, and hire scores of youths, fishermen, and farmers to transport the cigarette loads. In one of the cases involving Silveira, prosecutors said in court documents that the ring acquired large quantities of contraband cigarettes "directly from the Paraguayan factories" for distribution in Rio Grande do Sul and border cities of Argentina.

"All the smugglers, big-time traffickers, in this region are businessmen and politicians, who have good lawyers, fancy cars, family," says Saconato. "Some even are leaders of evangelical churches."

Roque Silveira's hometown of Guaíra gained prominence in the cigarette trade when controls tightened in the Tri-Border Area, starting in 2005. Today large portions of the population there, Guaíra officials say, rely on smuggling for their livelihood, whether it's renting space in their homes for the smugglers to store their loads, working as lookouts, or passing cigarettes across the Paraná River. The "paseros," or crossers, make about $300 a week, one and a half times the minimum monthly wage in Brazil.

Police in Guaíra say they feel overwhelmed. Saconato says 700 people were arrested in 2007 in connection with smuggling, yet only two men were convicted. When the district attorney shut down a riverside bar, Tininha's, which allegedly was widely used by smugglers to plan their business, a federal prosecutor reversed the order and sued the city. That night smugglers celebrated by launching fireworks on the riverside, officials say.

"Guaíra is practically abandoned," says Saconato, who anticipates record cigarette seizures this year due to the global financial crisis and a recent rise in cigarette taxes in Brazil. In the kiosks of Sao Paulo or Rio de Janeiro, the cheapest Brazilian cigarette pack (valued at roughly $1.50) costs three times as much as the contraband Paraguayan brands.

"A Big Duty Free Store"

No policeman in Guaíra has seen Silveira in recent years, Saconato says. He has become a mythical character of sorts, with town residents claiming from time to time to have spotted him. His 1996 murder case is still meandering through Guaíra's courts. After Operation Fireball, Silveira became a ghost, Brazilian police say, but no one believes he has retired from the cigarette trade. Some of Silveira's former associates now manage large portions of the smuggling on both sides of the border, according to Brazilian police.

The latest traces of Silveira in Paraguay's courts are from July 2007, when he beat the legal system again. On that occasion, Paraguay's Supreme Court denied an extradition request by Brazilian prosecutors who accused him of conspiracy, cigarette smuggling and money laundering.

Just the mention of Silveira's name in Paraguay's tobacco circles raises eyebrows and causes interviewees to clear their throats repeatedly before offering a noncommittal "His name sounds familiar," or "Didn't he own a cigarette factory around here?"

One man in Salto de Guairá, a Paraguayan city located just across the river from Guaíra, is not hesitant to talk about Silveira. Sidronio Talavera, a professional harpist who once played with one of Paraguay's most famous bolero bands, sits in a small office from where he manages his cigarette factory, Cosmopolita S.A. The facility is rather old and the cigarette-making machines are housed in a warehouse across a dirt yard from Talavera's office. A truck was picking up cigarettes at the factory the afternoon ICIJ reporters visited in March. Talavera says he not only knows Silveira, he is also his business associate. "He is one of the nicest people I have ever met," beams Talavera, who was convicted last year of tax evasion. Paraguayan prosecutors accused Talavera of reporting fake cigarette exports to Brazil in order to avoid paying taxes on imported cigarette manufacturing supplies. He has also been fingered by Paraguayan officials as a counterfeiter, a charge he denies.

Talavera says he sells to anybody who knocks on his factory's door, and he's well aware that some of the buyers are smugglers or work with smugglers. "Good for them if they send the cigarettes to Brazil," he says slapping his hands down on his desk. "If I have too many requirements, I will starve." Talavera boasts that his Latino cigarettes have found a market as far away as Dubai. He says that wholesalers based in Panama buy from him and then ship the cigarettes overseas. "I don't know if from Panama they are smuggled elsewhere or re-sold legally, and I don't care. I care that I sell."

As for Silveira, Talavera says he is still the trade's big intermediary, the middleman who acquires large quantities of cigarettes from the Paraguayan factories and arranges the deliveries in Brazil. "He works with everybody!" he says when told that other cigarette makers seem oblivious these days to Silveira's whereabouts. "He is smart, the Mafioso. He fooled the Americans," says Talavera.

As things stand, the Paraguayan government, which says it's determined to bring the cigarette industry under compliance, has its work cut out for it. Ortiz, Tabesa's CEO, put it simply. "Paraguay is like a big duty free store," he said. "And it's a great deal."

West Africa's International Drug Trade

7

Stephen Ellis

A report published by the United Nations office on drugs and crime (UNODC) in December 2007 has drawn unprecedented international attention to West Africa's role as an intermediary in the cocaine trade between Latin America and Europe.[1] Major newspapers have carried full-page articles on the subject.[2] But law-enforcement officers have long been aware of the reach of West African drug-trading networks, and the UNODC and other official bodies have for some years been observing a sharp rise in cocaine exports from Latin America to West Africa. The roots of the current collaboration between drug traders in these two sub-continents in fact go back for more than a decade, as this article will demonstrate.

According to the UNODC's estimate, about a quarter of Europe's annual consumption of 135 to 145 tons of cocaine,[3] with a wholesale value of some $1.8 billion,[4] currently transits via West Africa. In addition to the cocaine trade, West Africa is also a transit point for much smaller quantities of heroin exported from Asia to North America, as well as being a producer and exporter of cannabis products and perhaps amphetamines.

Needless to say, this trade is entirely illegal, and yet the proceeds are so great as to have a considerable impact on West African economies.

A major change in the global cocaine trade is taking place. South American cocaine traders are reacting against the saturation of the North American market, the growing importance of Mexican drug gangs, and effective interdiction along the Caribbean smuggling routes. These factors have induced them to make a strategic shift towards the European market, making use of

West Africa's conducive political environment and the existence of well-developed West African smuggling networks. Some leading Latin American cocaine traders are even physically relocating to West Africa[5] and moving a considerable part of their business operations to a more congenial location, just as any multinational company might do in the world of legal business. Most recently, since a coup in Guinea in December 2008, there have been reports[6] of Latin American cocaine traders moving in significant numbers to Conakry, where some relatives of the late President Lansana Conte have an established interest in the cocaine trade. Some observers believe that the next step for Latin American cocaine traders might be to commence large-scale production in West Africa. Some African law-enforcement officers are deeply concerned by the likely effects of the drug trade and drug money on their own societies,[7] and indeed there is evidence that drug money is funding political campaigns and affecting political relations in several West African countries. Diplomats and other international officials worry that some West African countries could develop along similar lines to Mexico,[8] where drug gangs have a symbiotic relationship with political parties and with the state and drug-related violence results in thousands of deaths every year.

Research by the present author shows that Lebanese smugglers were using West Africa as a transit point to transport heroin to the USA as early as 1952.[9] A decade later, Nigerian and Ghanaian smugglers in particular began exporting African-grown marijuana to Europe on a scale large enough to attract sustained official attention. By the early 1980s, some had graduated to the global cocaine and heroin business. Since then, successful Nigerian and Ghanaian drug traders have established themselves in most parts of the world, including other West African countries, where they work with local partners in Benin, Côte d'Ivoire and elsewhere. Very large shipments of cocaine from South America to West Africa have been recorded for the last ten years. In short, West Africa's role in the international drug trade has historical roots going back for over half a century and has been a matter of significant concern to law-enforcement officers worldwide for decades rather than years. Latin American traders who see some benefit in moving part of their operations to West Africa can find local partners with well-established networks who provide them with safe houses, banking, storage space, and a host of other facilities in return for a suitable financial arrangement or for payment in kind.[10]

Not only is West Africa conveniently situated for trade between South America and Europe, but above all it has a political and social environment that is generally suitable for the drug trade.[11] Smuggling is widely tolerated, law enforcement is fitful and inefficient, and politicians are easily bribed or are even involved in the drug trade themselves. Many officials throughout the region are deeply concerned by the effects of the drug trade, but are often confronted by people and networks more powerful than they, with other priorities. The recent emergence of a sophisticated financial infrastructure in Ghana and Nigeria is a further reason for the enhanced importance of West Africa in global drug trafficking. All of the above draws attention to a point made by Jean-François Bayart and others more than ten years ago,[12] namely that expertise in smuggling, the weakness of law-enforcement agencies, and the official tolerance of, or even participation in, certain types of crime, constitute a form of social and political capital that accumulates over time.

The Origins of the West African Drug Trade

It is sometimes said that West Africa was introduced to the cultivation of cannabis and consumption of the plant's leaves by veterans returning from military service in Asia at the end of the Second World War. Yet a pioneering article published in *African Affairs* in 2005 by the historian Emmanuel Akyeampong[13] pointed out that a small trade in cannabis products from West Africa existed in the first half of the twentieth century. In Nigeria, later to emerge as the hub of West Africa's illicit drugs trade, the colonial authorities in 1934 were experimenting with the cultivation of the coca plant in the botanical gardens in Calabar and at various other stations in the south of the country.[14] By the mid-1950s, there were occasional arrests of farmers in southwest Nigeria for growing cannabis,[15] and small quantities of locally grown marijuana were being shipped from the region to Europe and the USA. At the same time, Nigerian marijuana smokers were also buying small amounts imported from South Africa and the Belgian Congo.[16]

The first documented use of West Africa as a staging post for heroin smuggling dates from 1952, when US officials noted that parcels of the drug were being transported by a Lebanese syndicate from Beirut to New York via Kano and Accra, using couriers on commercial airlines.[17] One of those implicated at the Beirut end of the pipeline was reported to be an Italian intelligence officer; it was not clear whether he was operating with the approval of his superiors. The US consul-general in Lagos was told by a Lebanese source, described as "a competent narcotics and diamond smuggler,"[18] that the existing "heavy dope traffic" from the Near East to the US via Europe was being diverted to Nigeria "to an increasing extent" to avoid the attention of law-enforcement officers on the European route.[19] Given the use of West Africa by Lebanese smugglers in more recent times, it is an intriguing question whether there has been a highly discreet narcotics pipeline linking Lebanon and West Africa to the consumer markets of North America and Western Europe in continuous operation for more than fifty years. The presence of a murky official element in the person of an Italian intelligence officer is also of interest, as narcotics smuggling the world over seems to have become intertwined with the work of secret intelligence agencies from an early period.[20]

Generally speaking, however, the roots of West Africa's emergence as a major transit point for a more broadly based trade in illegal drugs may be traced to the 1960s. This was the era of the Beatles, youth rebellion and Swinging London, when a mass market for illicit drugs was developing in the United Kingdom and some other parts of Europe. Marijuana was particularly fashionable. It was in this context that the first reports emerged of locally grown cannabis being exported from Nigeria to Europe in significant quantities. In 1966, Nigeria's first military government took this problem seriously enough to decree ten-year jail terms for persons found guilty of exporting cannabis, although it is not clear that anyone was actually convicted under the terms of this legislation. In 1971, Nigeria's Federal Commissioner for Health, Dr J. O. J. Okezie, described marijuana smuggling from Nigeria and other African countries as "rampant."[21] By the end of the decade, a Nigerian Federal Ministry of Information official claimed that drug smuggling had become so common that "Nigerian travelers are often subjected to rigorous search each time they travel abroad."[22]

Early West African marijuana traffickers seem to have been mostly individuals travelling by air to the United Kingdom in particular, carrying relatively small quantities of the drug hidden in their personal baggage or in cargo. A Nigerian government information leaflet concerning trade in cannabis "across the border and overseas" claimed that some smugglers made use of unwitting couriers by persuading innocent passengers to carry parcels on their behalf, not revealing the true contents of the packages.[23] Significantly, among Nigerians arrested for smuggling cannabis in 1972 were pilgrims travelling to Saudi Arabia for the *hajj*.[24] This is important for the light it throws on an aspect of Nigerian drug trafficking that appears to be almost completely unresearched, as most reports on West African drug traders over the last forty years, whether by law-enforcement agencies or emanating from other sources, have concerned the supply of consumer markets in North America and Western Europe. The West African trade route to these destinations appears to have been largely in the hands of people from southern Nigeria from its inception. It is therefore interesting to note that, in the 1980s, Saudi Arabia already figured prominently on the list of countries where Nigerians had been arrested for drug offences, in third place behind the US and the United Kingdom.[25] The transport of illegal drugs by Nigerians to the Middle East, including under cover of the *hajj*, is far more likely to involve people of Northern Nigerian origin than the North Atlantic trade, given the historic links between northern Nigeria and the Muslim world.

A significant case from the early period of West African marijuana trafficking concerns the conviction by a court in the United Kingdom of a 33-year-old Nigerian woman, Iyabo Olorunkoya, found guilty in 1974 of importing 78 kilograms of marijuana. The woman, said to be well-connected in Lagos high society, named as her accomplices two Nigerian army officers.[26] One of the two was Brigadier Benjamin Adekunle, known to the Nigerian press as "the Black Scorpion," a hero of the federal army during the Biafra war. He was suspended from duty on account of the case, although his alleged role was not proved.[27] He never resumed his military career.

The smuggling of relatively small quantities of marijuana by individual traders, some of whom may have had connections to senior officials, was the precursor of the narcotics trade that emerged on a much larger scale in the early 1980s. This too appears to have been largely the work of individual Nigerian and Ghanaian traders, who penetrated the international narcotics market with extraordinary speed. They travelled to South America or Asia to buy small quantities of cocaine or heroin that they could carry to West Africa in their personal luggage for onward transmission to the consumer markets of the North Atlantic, or they took up residence in producer countries and recruited couriers to carry the packages for them. They developed the technique of swallowing cocaine and heroin sealed in condoms, soon to become a hallmark of the West African carrying trade. The large-scale involvement of West Africans in the cocaine and heroin trade is often said to have begun when West African students living in Europe and North America failed to receive payments of their study grants.[28] The US Drug Enforcement Administration has claimed that the trade was pioneered by Nigerian naval officers undergoing training in India, who bought heroin at source and sent it back to West Africa with couriers whom they had recruited from among Nigerian students there.[29] Whatever the exact origin, it is certainly the case that, in the early 1980s, there were already individual West Africans — overwhelmingly Nigerians, plus a few Ghanaians — who were settling in the main areas of narcotics supply. Nigerian smugglers were sending heroin by air courier from Pakistan to Nigeria, where it was repackaged and re-exported to the US.[30] One Pakistani heroin dealer was reported in 1985 as saying that he had made regular sales of heroin to a locally based Nigerian for eight months.[31] There was also a small Nigerian community resident in Bangkok. This early cohort of heroin and cocaine traders was presumably ignorant of the fact that a Lebanese syndicate had been doing something similar a generation previously.

"Prior to 1982," the US embassy in Lagos stated, "Nigerians played an insignificant role in the marketing of narcotics and dangerous drugs in the United States."[32] That year, US authorities arrested 21 Nigerians for narcotics offences, with figures rising rapidly thereafter.[33] A similar pattern emerged in Europe, where an official of the West German Interior Ministry reportedly stated in 1983 that Hamburg was importing significant quantities of drugs from West Africa, including one and a half tons from Ghana (presumably of marijuana), and that a ship from Nigeria carrying cocaine, heroin, and marijuana had also docked there.[34] A year later, the director of West Germany's customs service, Georg Wolt, stated that Nigeria was one of the top six importers of cocaine to his country.[35] Also in 1983, Thailand witnessed its first known case of a Nigerian convicted of possessing heroin.[36] The great advantage of West African smugglers in the early days of this trade was that European and North American law-enforcement officers were not expecting heroin and cocaine to be imported from West Africa, since it was not a producing area. However, the reputation of Nigeria in particular soon changed, to the extent that, by 1985, British customs agents were said to be systematically searching, and sometimes strip-searching, Nigerians entering the country.[37]

A small market for cocaine soon emerged in Nigeria itself, to the extent that a Nigerian newspaper in 1983 reported the existence of what it called "a tiny cocaine world" in fashionable Lagos society.[38] In view of this, it is interesting to note persistent reports as early as 1983 that one very senior military officer, married to a high society lady, had developed an active interest in narcotics trafficking.[39] The drug connection was already becoming a factor in Nigerian politics. A coup on 31 December 1983 brought to power the austere General Muhammadu Buhari, who justified his assumption of power, in the customary manner, with the claim that he was going to clean up corruption in Nigeria with military rigor. Within months, the new military junta introduced a decree making drug trafficking punishable by death, and by the end of 1984 a number of minor drug smugglers had been publicly executed by firing squad in Lagos. In general, the reaction of the Nigerian public was not favorable to the severe penalties decreed by General Buhari's military government. Those West Africans who had heard of cocaine and heroin at all appear to have regarded them as luxury products that were consumed in the rich world. In Nigeria at least, little social stigma was attached to people who simply transported them from one part of the world to another in an effort to earn a living. To this day, Nigerians often say that, since the drug trade involves willing sellers and willing buyers at every stage of the chain, it is essentially a legitimate form of commerce. As for the fact that it is illegal, Nigerian drug dealers often "view the black market as the only way to redistribute wealth from the north to the south, arguing that mainstream commercial channels are effectively occupied."[40]

The 1980s were years of rapid economic decline in West Africa, including in Nigeria, the region's only major oil producer at that time, where problems were compounded by the corruption and incompetence of the civilian government in office from 1979 to 1983. Most West African countries, in financial difficulties as a result of the global convulsions of the period and their own profligacy in earlier, more favorable times, were obliged to borrow money from the International Monetary Fund and the World Bank and to undergo the process of economic liberalization known as structural adjustment. This required deep cuts in public expenditure and the sacking of public employees. Whether imposed by the international financial institutions or from domestic necessity, drastic reductions in public budgets plunged many people into acute financial difficulty, and this was undoubtedly an incentive to some to make money by any means possible. Those who went abroad in search of new sources of income tended not to be the poorest members of society — generally people from rural areas or without education — but rather those who had lived in towns and, being relatively well educated, spoke good English and were familiar with the workings of state bureaucracies. "Let us call a spade a spade," said Nuhu Ribadu, Nigeria's later top anti-corruption official, referring to his country's Second Republic of 1979–83. "This is the period when we started hearing about 419,[41] it is the period we started having drug problems."[42] It was indeed a critical moment in West Africa's insertion into global patterns of crime, even if Nigeria in particular had developed a role in the international marijuana trade well before the financial crisis of the early 1980s.

While General Buhari's decree of the death penalty for drug trafficking was regarded by many Nigerians as too severe, his campaign against crime and corruption seriously threatened the interests of some in the military, including the small group with interests in the drug trade. Another coup in August 1985 introduced a less stringent regime. The new head of state, General Ibrahim Babangida, revoked the death penalty as a punishment for drug trafficking and replaced it with life imprisonment. His period in government is recognized as having marked a transformation in Nigeria's already notorious corruption, turning it into a generalized instrument of government. "[D]irect disbursals and administrative favors were increasingly supplanted by politically-influenced arbitrage in a variety of domestic markets," according to one analysis, in a process more simply described as "Zaïrianization."[43] Nigeria became more than ever a literal kleptocracy, a system of government by theft and bribery. The word "kleptocracy" had been invented some years earlier by the brilliant Anglo-Polish sociologist Stanislav Andreski, who taught for some years at a Nigerian university.[44]

Among the many scandals of the Babangida years was the murder by parcel-bomb of the newspaper editor Dele Giwa. It is widely believed in Nigeria that Giwa's death was connected to his investigations into elite drug trading. Specifically, he is said to have been targeted as a result of an interview he had conducted with a former drug courier, one Gloria Okon, who had worked for principals in very senior positions of the state bureaucracy or for their families. Years later, when Nigeria staged its own truth commission, one of the country's leading human rights lawyers and one of its most senior journalists jointly petitioned the members of the Human Rights Violations Investigation Commission, popularly called the "Oputa Panel," requesting this body to charge General Babangida and others with murder.[45] It was also during the Babangida period that the Bank of Credit and Commerce International, which had arrived in Nigeria in 1979, became integrated into a practice of financial corruption and money laundering that was "systemic and endemic."[46] The chairman of BCCI (Nigeria) Ltd was Ibrahim Dasuki, one of General Babangida's closest associates, whom the head of state later appointed as Sultan of Sokoto. By the end of 1987, BCCI had no less than 33 branches in Nigeria.[47] When BCCI subsequently collapsed, in what was then the world's biggest-ever bank failure, the full extent of its criminal dealings became known.

In the general atmosphere of corruption and manipulation that character-ized General Babangida's years as head of state, from 1985 to 1993, the country's role in the global narcotics trade grew. Nigeria was home to what a US govern-ment official called "a vast commercial sector, immune to most regulations and well suited to illegal activities."[48] When the head of the Ghanaian drug police visited Bangkok in 1986, he found "a lot of Ghanaians and Nigerians' in prison for drug offences.[49] By 1988, some 2,000 Nigerians were reported to be serving sentences for drug offences abroad.[50] US authorities reportedly arrested 851 Nigerians for drug offences between 1984 and 1989, and reckoned that 55 percent of the heroin arriving at New York's John F. Kennedy airport was being carried by Nigerians.[51] In 1991, Nigeria's own Ministry of Justice reported that 15,433 Nigerians had been arrested worldwide for drug offences since 1984.[52] Of these, 4,802 had been convicted.[53] According to a statement attributed to the deputy director-general of the Ministry of External Affairs, Nigerians were the leading nationality arrested for drug offences in India, Pakistan, Saudi Arabia, and Thailand.[54]

Nigerian traders showed great ingenuity in switching their smuggling techniques and routes, for example exporting from Thailand overland to Malaysia or by sea to Taiwan or Hong Kong for onward transmission to Europe and North America.[55] Professional drug traders were constantly adapting and improving their methods. The Nigerians' commercial skills were also attracting the attention of fellow-traffickers from other continents. Scrutiny of arrest figures suggests that the Colombian drug cartels, reacting to the saturation of the US market, had begun seeking relationships with West African traders even by the late 1980s,[56] interested in using the West Africans' highly developed mar-keting channels as a way of penetrating new areas, notably in Europe. Among Nigerians involved in the drug trade were figures of privilege and influence, as became clear in 1989 when a former member of Nigeria's Senate was arrested in New York for heroin trafficking and subsequently convicted. He had previously offered $20 million of his own money, purportedly as a patriotic gesture, to pay a debt owed by Nigerian Airways that had caused French authorities to impound a Nigerian Airways Airbus. Although this scheme did not succeed, his intention had apparently been to use the plane to transport drug cargoes. For some time thereafter Lagos heroin dealers referred to their product as "senator."[57] A later member of the upper house of Nigeria's legislature, who had previously held a senior position in the police, once alleged that the Senate was infested with ex-419ers and drug traders.[58] Even the law-enforcement agencies were not immune to the lure of drug money. A head of the Nigerian Drug Law Enforcement Agency (NDLEA), a unit established in 1990 largely as a concession to US pressure, reportedly stated in 1994 that "those charged with the responsibility of eliminating drug trafficking are by far more interested in drug trafficking than the professional traffickers."[59] One of his predecessors had acquired a particular notoriety in this regard.[60]

The Regional Pattern

Nigeria was not alone. From the late 1970s there were reports of individuals in various West African countries importing narcotics for eventual re-export. Many traffickers appear to have been acting on their own initiative or at any rate without the support of extensive networks. Some powerful external interests also discovered the commercial potential of small West African states that attracted little international attention, and whose authorities could be bought or manipulated. In Sierra Leone, the most prominent members of the commercially powerful Lebanese community in the mid-1980s found themselves under surveillance from Israeli security officers responding to their role in funding various factions in Lebanon's civil war. They were confronted with a sudden influx of mobsters from the Soviet Union, some of them with connections to Israeli intelligence.[61] The most formidable of the newcomers was Marat Balagula, who later migrated to the US, where he became a pioneer of Russian mafia influence, serving a prison sentence before being murdered in March 2008. Balagula and his colleagues used Sierra Leone as a freeport facility, smuggling in diamonds from the USSR and swapping them for heroin from Thailand for onward transmission to the US. They also managed President Joseph Momoh's election campaign.[62]

Trafficking networks with high-level government connections emerged in other countries too. One example involved a group of Ghanaians and a diplomat from Burkina Faso, the latter providing members of the syndicate with diplomatic passports. This team imported heroin from Mumbai to Abidjan for onward transmission to Europe. One of the Ghanaians involved, a certain Emmanuel Boateng Addo, revealed some details of this operation in 1993 after his release from a French prison.[63] The Burkinabe diplomat at the heart of this syndicate was also a close associate of Charles Taylor, subsequently to become president of Liberia. In 1986–7 Taylor was one of several Liberian exiles living in Ghana and plotting against the Liberian government. He was twice detained by the Ghanaian government on political grounds. On the second of these occasions, it was his friend the Burkinabe diplomat who secured Taylor's release from prison.[64] A Ghanaian who shared Taylor's prison-cell in Accra recalled Taylor's opinions on the drug trade:

> In one of our numerous, prolonged arguments whilst in cells he was critical about what he called unwarranted vigilance and the arrest of drug traffickers in Ghana. I begged to differ from him but he insisted that the major concern of African governments should be the prevention of domestic consumption

of hard drugs. Once people are exporting such drugs from Africa, they should be allowed. He further stressed that we should think of cultivating coca and marijuana in Ghana as major exports. He was particularly peeved about the fact that African governments complain of lack of capital when they have the easy option of granting banking facilities to drug barons who have billions of dollars for laundering.[65]

Charles Taylor achieved his ambition of becoming head of state when he became President of Liberia in 1997. True to his earlier ideas, he proceeded to associate with professional criminals from a wide variety of countries.[66] His predecessor, Samuel Doe, had allowed Liberia to be used for drug trafficking, as an earlier government may also have done.[67] Other West African heads of state said by police sources to have been implicated in drug smuggling include the late president of Togo, Gnassingbé Eyadema.[68]

Over the years, West Africa's most prominent traffickers, the Nigerians, developed footholds in many other countries where imported narcotics could be stored and repacked for onward travel. From the early 1990s South Africa became one such base, as it offered the advantages of an excellent transport infrastructure and a good banking system. Before 1990, the drug trade in South Africa was largely confined to mandrax and locally produced marijuana. The South African police, preoccupied by political matters, were extraordinarily inattentive to the risk posed by international traffickers, who flocked to the country from Eastern Europe and from the rest of Africa especially. By 2005, there were between 40,000 and 100,000 Nigerians living in South Africa, as many as 90 percent of them illegally. The drug dealers among them were described as "the most prolific of the organized crime groups operating in the country."[69]

Nigerian traders also established operational centers in Cotonou and Abidjan, which were home to Beninese, Ivorian, and other nationals who had entered the narcotics business. In March 1998, the US government described Nigeria as "the hub of African narcotics trafficking," noting also "traffickers" expansion into bulk shipments into Nigeria's neighbours.[70] After Nigeria had dispatched a peacekeeping force to Liberia in 1990, under the auspices of the Economic Community of West African States (ECOWAS), some members of the Nigerian expeditionary force developed interests in the narcotics trade. Their control of Liberia's seaports and of its international airport provided ideal transport facilities. A further attraction was Liberia's use of the US dollar as an official currency.[71] The Nigerian military, in power almost continuously for three decades, had by this time developed a high degree of impunity. In 1998, NDLEA director Musa Bamaiyi complained that his agents were not allowed to search military barracks, despite the fact that, according to him, "a lot" of military officers were involved in the drug business. He had sent a list of names of military suspects to the presidency.[72] Bamaiyi, generally well regarded by international law-enforcement agents with whom he collaborated, had himself served in the Nigerian peacekeeping contingent in Liberia.[73] Being also a brother of his country's chief of army staff, he was particularly well placed to make such a judgment about the Nigerian military's involvement in drug trafficking.

Nigerian traders especially were truly global. They took over heroin retailing in Moscow. According to one veteran journalist, "the Central Asians . . . were being displaced from 1997 onwards by Africans, especially Nigerians, who have established efficient and well-concealed networks for selling heroin and cocaine in Moscow's student living areas and university residences."[74] Nigerians were particularly prominent in the North American heroin trade until being displaced in recent years. In 1999, the US Department of Justice said it was looking for two Nigerians who were said to be running a network importing "up to 80 percent of the white heroin entering the US from Southeast Asia."[75] This high figure is less noteworthy than might appear at first sight, as the US market for Asian heroin has lost ground to imports from Latin America. In 2002, Dutch customs officers, in a controlled experiment, for a period of ten days searched every Nigerian arriving in Amsterdam from Aruba and the Dutch Antilles, a route used by many of the 1,200 drug couriers arrested annually at Schiphol airport. They found that of the 83 Nigerian passengers using this route during that period, no fewer than 63 were carrying drugs.[76] In the same year, Nigeria's NDLEA arrested two Nigerians and one foreigner with 60 kilograms of cocaine, the agency's largest-ever cocaine find, on board a Brazilian vessel at Tin Can Island wharf in Lagos.[77] Substantial though this haul was, perhaps its chief significance lies in the evidence it presents of direct seaborne transport from Latin America.

There was evidence that knowledge of the drug trade was being passed from one generation to the next. Also in 2002, a twelve-year-old Nigerian boy with US citizenship was reportedly arrested at New York's John F. Kennedy airport with 87 condoms of heroin. He was the son of one Chukwunwieke Umegbolu, who had been convicted in 1995 for his part in importing more than $33 million of heroin in a period of more than a decade.[78]

By the mid-1990s, thus, some Nigerian drug traffickers in particular had not only developed the means to invest in bulk shipments of narcotics, but had also become fully global, having business associates in both producing and consuming countries as well as other facilities in countries outside Nigeria. The same was true on a smaller scale of traffickers from other West African countries, notably Ghana. By the same token, non-African traffickers had become interested in the commercial advantages offered by West Africa. Lebanese smugglers, Soviet gangsters, and South American drug syndicates were among a variety of external interests attracted to the region on account of its usefulness as an entrepôt.[79] In 2003, Senegal expelled a senior member of the Sicilian mafia, Giovanni Bonomo, who was subsequently arrested in Italy. A known money launderer and drug trafficker, he was said to have visited South Africa and Namibia regularly.[80]

The Structure of the Nigerian Drug Trade

A senior US anti-drugs official, Robert S. Gelbard, described Nigerian drug networks as "some of the most sophisticated and finely-tuned transshipment, money-moving and document-forging organizations in the world." He pointed out that "they are sought out by both Asian and Latin American drug producers" on account of their commercial skills.[81] The Nigerian drug trade is characterized by a distinctive business structure that has developed over decades, and which gives depth to the emerging cooperation with traders from other countries and continents.

Crucial to the success of Nigerian drug traders is their highly flexible mode of operation, as those involved constantly form and re-form their business relationships from among a wide pool of acquaintances. This modus operandi closely resembles a so-called "adhocracy," able "to fuse experts drawn from different disciplines into smoothly functioning ad hoc project teams"[82] in a way that, according to some management gurus, is particularly suited to the modern business environment. It stands in contrast to the more corporate-style relations of classic American "mafias" that have exerted such a powerful influence on popular ideas about how organized crime works via films like *The Godfather* or the TV series *The Sopranos*.

The following paragraphs will briefly describe the classic structure of the Nigerian drug trade, starting at the top of the ladder, so to speak, by considering the category often labeled drug "barons." In the words of a senior Nigerian drug law-enforcement officer,[83] a Nigerian drug baron requires at least three assets. First, he, or she, needs to be able to buy drugs cheaply at source. As we have seen, from an early date, there were Nigerians who travelled to producer countries in South America and Southeast Asia to buy drugs. In 2003, some 330 Nigerians were said to be serving prison sentences in Thailand for drug-related offences.[84] Hundreds of Nigerians were living in Bangkok, notably in the city's Pratunum district that is home to an African community some 500–800 strong. Many of these are occupied in the textile or jewelry trades, but a significant number are alleged to have interests in crime.[85] There are also substantial Nigerian communities in the south Asian subcontinent, with over 2,000 Nigerians in Mumbai alone.[86] There is even a small Nigerian community in Afghanistan. A drug baron who lives in one of these locations or has stayed there long enough to build excellent local contacts is well placed to buy heroin. Sometimes, a baron who has the wherewithal to buy a large quantity of cocaine or heroin at source may sell this to a syndicate of smaller operators pooling their resources for such a major purchase. In December 1997, John Ikechukwe, a Nigerian who had immigrated to South Africa and become rich working the South American route, was murdered after cheating some fellow-traders in such a scheme. According to the South African police, 28 Nigerians were killed in Johannesburg alone in the first quarter of 1998.[87]

A second requirement for a drug baron is a good contact in the receiving country, generally North America in the case of heroin, or Europe in the case of cocaine. North America and Europe have substantial Nigerian communities, some of the millions of Nigerians who live outside their own country. Even if most of these people live blameless lives, earning their keep in respectable occupations, the existence of this diaspora nevertheless constitutes a medium in which traffickers can move. Many Nigerian drug barons keep a very low profile in order not to attract attention. The third necessity for a drug baron is a substantial supply of capital to finance operations. This poses little problem to anyone who has already made a couple of successful transactions. An example is Ekenna O, first arrested in 1995 and sentenced to one year's imprisonment, and rearrested in October 2005. At that point, his assets were over 500 million naira, or $4.16 million. He owned three properties in Nigeria and several companies.[88]

For purposes of transportation, a drug baron works with a second layer of operators, known as "strikers." This word is used in Nigeria in regard not only to the drug trade, but also to a range of other criminal enterprises in which a high degree of logistical expertise is necessary. A striker is someone who can strike deals, quite likely a former courier who has entered the business at the lowest level and worked his way up, acquiring an excellent network of contacts. Many strikers are middle-aged, from their late thirties upwards. A striker knows exactly who is the best person to approach for forged documents or who is an expert packer of drugs. He receives a fee for performing this type of service on behalf of a baron, and will typically work with several such barons while remaining essentially self-employed. One of the striker's most important tasks is the recruitment of couriers, and one of the features of the Nigerian system that makes effective police detection so difficult is that the use of independent specialists provides a vital cut-out between the top level of operation and the humble courier. A courier is normally ignorant of the name, or even the very existence, of the baron who is the real initiator of a drug transaction. If a courier is arrested, he or she therefore cannot be prevailed upon to give vital information to police officers. For this reason, strikers often try to recruit a stranger as a courier, although friends and family may also be approached. A Nigerian striker based in South Africa, for example, may recruit South African nationals, or even better, South Africans with British passports. Gambia is a useful transit point because of the existence of a substantial tourist trade, which makes it easy for a courier to travel with a planeload of tourists, or to recruit a holidaymaker and persuade or trick them into acting as a courier. The favorite recruits for strikers based in Nigeria itself are fellow-countrymen who have residence permits for European or North American countries, or Nigerians who possess foreign passports, the more prestigious the better. Having recruited a courier, a striker will stay with the person until the point of departure, a period often between a couple of days and a week, to make sure they do not lose their nerve. In some cases, couriers are escorted to religious oracles during this period to swear an oath. Relatives or home-boys who have been recruited, and made to swear a solemn oath of loyalty, do not easily betray their associates. They can also speak on the phone in "deep" dialects of African languages, difficult for foreign police services to interpret if the conversations are intercepted.

The lowest level of transportation is the couriers or mules, mostly people in desperate need of money. Couriers recruited by Nigerian barons, via a striker, usually carry a small parcel of drugs on their person, in return for cash payment. There are also freelancers, individuals who try their luck at buying and smuggling drugs on their own. The 21-year old Iwuchukwu Amara Tochi, who was hanged in Singapore on Friday 26 January 2006 after being caught in possession of 727 grams of diamorphine, was one such unfortunate. He was just eighteen at the time of his arrest. He had gone to Asia in the hope of pursuing a career as a professional footballer, but had been recruited as a courier by a fellow Nigerian for a fee of $2,000.[89] Of 316 people arrested at Lagos international airport in possession of cocaine or heroin between January 2006 and 5 September 2007, according to a Nigerian police report,[90] no less than 69 percent were so-called 'swallowers', people who had ingested condoms filled with hard drugs. Only 31 percent had packed them in baggage. Of the fifty-five people arrested at the same airport for similar reasons in the third quarter of 2007, most were in their thirties. According to police analysts, this is a vulnerable age because it corresponds to people losing the support of their parents and having to make major life choices. The preferred destination for couriers in recent times is Spain, on account of its relatively lax residence rules. An applicant can get a temporary residence permit after just six months, which makes him or her far less likely to be searched on entry as it is assumed that adequate checks have been made. Thus, between January 2006 and 5 September 2007, out of 273 people arrested in Nigeria on suspicion of exporting drugs, 29 percent were heading for Spain.[91]

Various attempts have been made to profile Nigerian drug traffickers. There is a general consensus among those who have attempted this that the Nigerian narcotics trade is dominated by Igbo people. The Swiss police are reported to have produced a more exact profile, even down to villages of origin, via an analysis of patterns of arrest. Among Igbos themselves, it is sometimes said that most narcotics traffickers come from one particular Local Government Area. Ninety percent of those arrested are male.[92] However, the profiles that are widely used by European, North American and south-east Asian authorities do not appear to include data from the considerable number of Nigerians arrested for drug offences in Saudi Arabia, which may well reveal a different social background.

The ethnic concentration of Nigerian drug traders is not unusual, as some other illegal trades, as well as many legal ones, are also notable for being dominated by people of just one geographical origin, such as the trade in prostitutes from Nigeria to Europe, which is overwhelmingly in the hands of people from Edo State, just one of Nigeria's 36 states.[93] In many legal businesses too, an individual entrepreneur, when he or she needs assistance, often turns to someone from their home area. This may be someone to whom they are related either closely or more distantly, or it may be someone who has property in the same village of origin, or a former school classmate. Entrepreneurs compete with one another but are also able to cooperate when circumstances require this.[94] Social networks that refer to a village of origin are sustained even when people live in Lagos or further afield, with the village remaining a moral point of reference. It is for this reason, too, that when an important bargain is made, including in regard to commerce or politics, the parties to the deal may swear a solemn oath on a traditional oracle, such as the Okija shrine that gained national attention in Nigeria in 2004.[95]

Igbos themselves often explain their general prominence in trade by reference to the civil war of 1967–70, alleging that they have subsequently had a semi-detached status within Nigeria that obliges them to seek their livelihood outside the ambit of the state. However, the Igbo ethos of enterprise also has older roots, in an area once known both for the productivity of its agriculture and for its role in the Atlantic slave trade. The establishment of colonial government and missionary education in the early twentieth century opened an avenue of economic advancement and social promotion for Igbos, whose political organization was traditionally republican, without powerful chiefs or any aristocratic class. During the past hundred years, the population of Igboland has increased dramatically, and the exhausted soil can no longer support even those who stay behind and farm. Still, it remains the ambition of many Igbo men to make money and buy land and build an impressive house in their home village as a mark of their success. "Rich cocaine pushers" who hold extravagant parties to celebrate the acquisition of a chieftaincy title are a recognizable social type.[96] According to Nigerian police officers, those Igbos who dominate the drug trade do not normally choose this career in order to become professional criminals in the Western sense, but primarily as an avenue to wealth and social esteem. Their use of both traditional oracles and Christian rituals is thought to favor the drive to personal achievement and social success.

The employment by Nigerian drug traders of large numbers of couriers carrying small parcels of cocaine or heroin endows them both with a high degree of "vertical" integration of their marketing channel from purchase to sale, and with the means to penetrate any customs service in the world. However, this method involves a high human cost, and not only in the sense that it supplies drug users who may have their lives ruined or cut short, as the growing numbers of addicts in West Africa testifies. The courier system also carries a high risk of arrest for those who actually transport drugs through customs controls. The number of West Africans sitting in jails all over the world after being arrested in possession of illegal drugs is probably disproportionate to the volume of narcotics seized, in consequence of the human-wave tactics often used by drug barons.

The New Bulk Trade

The first recorded case of a Nigerian smuggler transporting heroin in bulk is that of Joe Brown Akubueze, who imported some 250 kilograms of heroin from Thailand by sea, packed in water coolers, in December 1993. He was arrested in Nigeria after a tip-off, and sentenced by a court to 115 years in prison, of which he served ten years before being released.[97] In retrospect, this was an early indicator of a move towards very large shipments by air and sea, although the classic Nigerian courier trade still remains as strong as ever. From the late 1990s, there were growing reports of "very large consignments" of drugs heading to West Africa "by ship or commercial containers," according to a police officer working for the UN.[98] In 2000, Cape Verdean authorities reported the interception of a ship in the Caribbean heading to their country with 2.3 tons of cocaine.[99] In 2003, a massive cargo of 7.5 tons of cocaine was intercepted on a ship en route to Spain via Cape Verde and Senegal.[100] In 2004, six people were arrested in the Ghanaian port-city of Tema in possession of 588 kilograms of cocaine from Colombia via Venezuela.[101] This was a particularly notorious case because of the action of a judge who, amazingly, granted bail to the accused, raising suspicions of corruption. In 2006, a boat was intercepted heading for the Canary Islands, 80 miles from the coast of Senegal, with 3.7 tons of cocaine from Colombia, apparently belonging to a Dutch syndicate and destined for the British market.[102] Major Dutch criminals had long had an interest in Liberia and Sierra Leone, in particular for the trans-shipment of hashish cargoes from Asia.[103] This particular shipment had travelled from Venezuela via the Dutch Antilles. On 31 January 2008, 2.4 tons of cocaine were on board the *Blue Atlantic* when it was intercepted by the French navy off the Liberian coast, en route to Nigeria.[104] Cargoes of comparable size have been detected in or close to the offshore waters of Cape Verde, Senegal, Mauritania, Guinea-Bissau, Guinea, Liberia, Sierra Leone, Ghana, and Benin.

An authoritative view is that of Antonio Mazzitelli, a senior UN drug law-enforcement officer in West Africa, who sees 2005 as the year in which a major change of scale became visible. He lists the total seizures in West Africa of cocaine as going from 1.2 tons in 2005 to 4.3 tons in the first seven months of 2007.[105] The UNODC has given higher figures, reporting that the Spanish and British navies seized 9.9 tons of cocaine on five ships in international waters off West Africa in 2006, and that 5.7 tons were seized in West Africa in the first three quarters of 2007.[106] In June 2007, Venezuelan authorities seized 2.5 tons of cocaine on a private plane about to take off for Sierra Leone.[107] None of these sources appears to include a case from 2006, when Nigeria's drug police, the NDLEA, was reported to have seized no less than 14.2 tons of cocaine located in a container on a ship, the *MSV Floriana*, berthed at Lagos's Tin Can Island port. According to press reports, the ship had originally come from Peru via the US and Cameroon. However, several features of this case as reported by the press are puzzling.[108]

By most accounts, the West African country that has become most completely immersed in the drug trade is Guinea-Bissau. A Nigerian drug law-enforcement official has stated that the Bissau-Guinean army cooperates with drug traffickers to the extent of using military premises to stockpile cocaine awaiting shipment to Europe.[109] The UNODC has recorded private planes flying into a military airstrip.[110] In April 2007, two Colombians, Juan Pablo Rubio Camacho and Luis Fernando Arango Mejia, were arrested in connection with the discovery of a large consignment of cocaine. According to US law-enforcement officers, both men are officials of the FARC, the Revolutionary Armed Forces of Colombia.[111] (Other sources confirm only one of the two as a member of the Colombian guerrilla force.) Both suspects were released on bail; both subsequently disappeared, and are presumed to be at liberty once more. The former head of Guinea-Bissau's judicial police, Orlando Antonio da Silva, says that he was reprimanded by his boss, the country's Interior Minister, and fired on account of his investigations into this case. The country's Attorney-General has received death threats, and also confirms the army's interest in the drug trade.[112] Political upheavals, infighting between rival security forces, and attempted coups in Guinea-Bissau throughout 2008 testify to the effect of the drug trade on the country's politics.[113]

Guinea-Bissau is not the only country in West Africa where Venezuelan and Colombian traffickers, including even FARC operatives, have taken up residence. Similar reports come from Accra, Conakry, Monrovia, and other capital cities. Throughout the region, the Latin Americans' key local partners are often Nigerian drug traffickers who have longstanding connections in South America, and who are paid for their logistical services with cocaine in lots of up to 200 kilograms. The Nigerians can then use this to operate their traditional courier service to European markets. Thus, in December 2006, 32 cocaine mules travelling from Guinea-Conakry via Morocco were arrested at Amsterdam airport. No fewer than 28 of the 32 were Nigerians.[114] Ghana, often seen by donors as a "virtuous" state (high growth rate, freedom of speech, and democratic politics), has been extensively penetrated by drug money. According to Ghanaian law-enforcement officers, many of the country's politicians have interests in the drug trade, and some of Accra's impressive building boom is being financed with the proceeds of drug deals.[115] On 12 November 2005, US officials arrested a Ghanaian Member of Parliament, Eric Amoateng, in possession of 136 pounds of heroin. He was convicted in 2007.[116] There are reports of drug refining taking place in Ghana on a small scale, with precursor chemicals being imported from South Africa.[117]

In the Niger Delta, the home of Nigerian oil, local militias smuggling crude oil to tankers moored offshore are paid not only with cash and weapons, but also with cocaine.[118] Some of the cocaine imported into Nigeria in this process is consumed by foot soldiers in the militias that have sprung up in the Niger Delta, and towns like Warri and Port Harcourt have now become drug centers. However, it is improbable that all the cocaine imported into Nigeria by this relatively new route is consumed locally. It is likely that some at least is sold on or bartered in the complex international trade in oil, arms and drugs that is now connecting centers all along the Gulf of Guinea, from Luanda to Dakar.

Nigerian middlemen are also playing a leading role in the development of a trans-Saharan route for smuggling cocaine into Europe, using Tuareg guides. In early 2008, Malian authorities seized 750 kilos of cocaine at Tin Zawatine in the middle of the Sahara.[119] Intelligence officers of various nationalities claim that the Algerian armed opposition groups today known as Al-Qaeda in the Islamic Maghreb "earn their living" from taxes on this route.[120] Once cocaine has reached North Africa, established Moroccan hashish smugglers can take it to Europe. A US investigation codenamed Operation Titan unraveled a Lebanese-dominated syndicate that linked members of the Lebanese diasporas in North and South America and Nigeria with partners in their Mediterranean homeland, together involved in the transport of hundreds of millions of dollars' worth of merchandise to the US.[121] In this case, an element of continuity in the drug trade becomes apparent, since it was a Lebanese syndicate that was first recorded using West Africa as a transit zone for heroin over fifty years ago.

The Drug Trade and the Long Term

The UNODC has pointed out[122] that the relocation of a substantial part of the Latin American cocaine business to West Africa, including even some senior management functions, is not best understood as a consequence simply of comparative advantage in pricing. A more important reason for this development, which has been taking place for over a decade, is the exceptionally favorable political context offered by ineffective policing, governments that have a reputation for venality, and the relative lack of international attention given to West Africa. A pliable sovereign state is the ideal cover for a drug trafficker. The Colombian economist Francisco Thoumi states that "[p]rofitable illegal economic activity requires not only profitability, but also weak social and state controls on individual behavior, that is, a society where government laws are easily evaded and social norms tolerate such evasion."[123] In short, "[i]llegality generates competitive advantages in the countries or regions that have the weakest rule of law."[124] Drug production is not primarily to be explained by prices, but by reference to "institutions, governability and social values."[125] This is consistent with the "new" international trade theory, which emphasizes the role of technical knowledge, public infrastructure, and the qualities of institutions in encouraging trade, supporting the view that "institutional and structural weaknesses and cultural aspects determine the competitive advantage in illegal goods and services."[126]

As the present article has shown, the development of the drug trade in West Africa has quite deep historical roots and has been enmeshed with politics in some countries for many decades. When the executive director of the UNODC, Antonio Maria Costa, sounds an alarm about the risk of drug money "perverting economies and rotting society"[127] and of drug profits possibly financing insurgency,[128] he is really describing an existing state of affairs rather than some future nightmare. Liberia, to name just one example, was already a fully criminalized state under Charles Taylor, the country's head of state from 1997 to 2003. The financing of insurgency appears to be an established fact, in the case of both the Sahara and the Niger Delta. It is not hard to see why powerful people may nonetheless tolerate the drug trade in West Africa. For countries as poor as Guinea-Bissau or Guinea-Conakry, it makes a huge, though unofficial, contribution to national income. The UNODC, however, warns that crime hinders development, which it defines as "the process of building societies that work."[129] Crime is said to destroy social capital, and therefore to be anti-development.[130]

In purely technical terms, the emergence of the drug trade in West Africa over a period of fifty years or more is an astonishing feat. West African traders, with Nigerians in the forefront, have created for themselves an important role in a business characterized by competition that is cutthroat — literally — and by high profits. They have penetrated drug markets in every continent. Their success, and their growing ability to cooperate with organized crime groups elsewhere in the world, is inextricably linked not only to globalization and new patterns of international migration,[131] but also to specific experiences of rapid economic liberalization in the late twentieth century. Nigerians especially were playing a significant role in the illegal drug trade in the 1970s, before the era of structural adjustment. Subsequently, the manner in which new financial and economic policies were implemented in West Africa in the 1980s contributed greatly to the formation of what has been called "a shadow state," in which rulers draw authority "from their abilities to control markets and their material rewards."[132] Dismantling large parts of the bureaucratic apparatus inherited from colonial times, and the formal economic activity that went with it, rulers became intent on identifying new shadow state networks, sometimes drawing in foreign investors.[133] West Africa's "shadow states" are thus relatively new, but they draw heavily on older traditions. These include not only the existence since pre-colonial times of initiation societies that are sites of power, but also the colonial practice of indirect rule, which sometimes resulted in local authorities operating unofficial networks of governance rooted in local social realities, hidden from the view of European officials whose attention was focused on the official apparatus of government.[134]

The emergence of shadow states with networks that have become globalized through commerce and migration opens up an important debate in historical sociology concerning the degree to which a turn to predation in the last quarter of the twentieth century was the consequence of a specific context in the 1980s, and the extent to which its historical roots go much deeper.[135] The recent emergence of China as a major diplomatic and business operator in Africa, and the arrival in the continent of substantial numbers of Chinese expatriates and even settlers, adds a further element to this chemistry. Chinese crime gangs have a long history in Africa. Their enhanced presence in the continent can be expected to result in collaboration with African interests, and the development of new illicit markets in China itself.[136]

Notes

1. UNODC, *Cocaine Trafficking in West Africa: The threat to stability and development*, (UNODC: Vienna, 2007), <http://www.UNODC.org/documents/data-and-analysis/west_africa_cocaine_report_2007-12_en.pdf> (Accessed 31 January 2008).

2. For example: *NRC Handelsblad* (Rotterdam), 4 August 2008; *Financial Times*, 4 November 2008.

3. UNODC, *Cocaine Trafficking in West Africa*, 8.

4. Ibid., 3.

5. David Blair, "Special report: West Africa welcomes Latin America's drug barons," *Daily Telegraph*, <www.telegraph.co.uk/new/worldnews/africaandindianocean/senegal/3456011/S> (Accessed 9 December 2008).

6. Gleaned during a visit to Monrovia, 11–14 January 2009.

7. Interview, law-enforcement officer, Accra, 31 August 2008.

8. Interviews, US government officials, Washington DC, 6 June 2008.

9. US National Archives and Records Administration [NARA II], Maryland, RG 84, general records of foreign ser vice posts: Records of the consulate-general, Lagos, 1940–63, box 2, "Smuggling of narcotics."

10. Antonio L. Mazzitelli, "Transnational organized crime in West Africa: The additional challenge," *International Affairs* 83, 6 (2007): 1075–6.

11. UNODC, *Cocaine Trafficking in West Africa*, 11–16.

12. Jean-François Bayart, Stephen Ellis, and Béatrice Hibou. *The Criminalization of the State in Africa*, (James Currey: Oxford, 1999), especially Bayart's Chapter 2.

13. Emmanuel Kwaku Akyeampong, "Diaspora and drug trafficking in West Africa: A case study of Ghana," *African Affairs* 104, 416 (2005): 429–47.

14. National Archives, Ibadan, Oyo Prof 1/1321: Correspondence concerning coca cultivation.

15. National Archives, Ibadan, Ekiti Div 1/1, 1085, Indian hemp: Circular from Acting Permanent Secretary, Ministry of Local Government, Western Region, 7 December 1954.

16. NARA II, RG 84, records of the consulate-general, Lagos, 1940–63, box 2, "Smuggling of narcotics": Erwin P. Keeler to Department of State, 3 February 1954.
17. Ibid.: Erwin P. Keeler to Department of State, 4 December 1952.
18. Ibid.: Memorandum for Mr. Ross, 21 August 1952, attached to Robert W. Ross to Department of State, 28 August 1952.
19. Ibid.: Erwin P. Keeler to Department of State, 4 December 1952.
20. Cf. Alfred W. McCoy, *The Politics of Heroin: CIA complicity in the global drug trade*, (Lawrence Hill Books: New York, 1991).
21. Press release number 295, Federal Ministry of Information, Lagos, 22 March 1971, contained in press cuttings file in Nigerian Institute of International Affairs, Lagos.
22. "The cost of war against smuggling," *New Nigerian*, 31 August 1979.
23. "Avoid Indian Hemp," leaflet c. 1974, in "Nigeria: Drugs, 1979–," press cuttings file in Nigerian Institute of International Affairs, Lagos.
24. Umoh James Umoh and Alhaji Nurudeen Adio-Saka, "The problem of smuggling among pilgrims," *Daily Times*, 13 July 1972. In 1972, 44,061 Nigerians officially went on the *hajj*, the second-largest national contingent after Yemenis.
25. Penny Green, *Drugs, Trafficking and Criminal Policy: The scapegoat strategy*, (Waterside Press: Winchester, 1998), 46.
26. *Sunday Times* (Lagos), 10 March 1974; "The redeemer is not near," *Daily Sketch* (Lagos), 28 July 1974.
27. National Archives of the United Kingdom, Kew: FCO 65/1530: Reuters report, 23 August 1974.
28. "Organized crime: Nigeria." Paper presented at UNODC workshop on West African organized crime, Dakar, 2–3 April 2004.
29. Mark Shaw, *Crime as Business, Business as Crime: West African criminal networks in southern Africa*, (South African Institute of International Affairs: Johannesburg, 2003), 11.
30. Statement by US Embassy, Lagos, published in *Daily Times* (Lagos), 10 December 1984, 3.
31. Rasheed Williams, "Nigeria, a leading heroin market," *National Concord* (Lagos), 8 April 1985.
32. Statement by US Embassy, Lagos, published in *Daily Times*, 10 December 1984, 3.
33. Ibid.
34. Quoted in the *Daily Times*, 26 November 1984.
35. Quoted in ". . . and its Nigerian connection," *Guardian* (Lagos), 30 December 1984.
36. According to the newsletter *Drug Force*, the official publication of the Nigerian Drug Law Enforcement Agency, quoted in *Daily Champion* (Lagos), 9 May 1993.
37. "2,000 Nigerians in foreign jails for drug offences," *New Nigerian*, 13 May 1988.
38. *The Guardian* (Lagos) carried a series of reports on this matter in May and June 1983. See also Axel Klein, "Trapped in the traffic: Growing problems of drug consumption in Lagos," *Journal of Modern African Studies* 32, 4 (1994): 657–77.
39. Address by Alain Labrousse, director of Observatoire Géopolitique des Drogues, Bordeaux, 28 April 1994; interviews, US law-enforcement officer, Bangkok, 16 May 2005, and former Liberian presidential aide, Amsterdam, 4 November 2004.
40. Mark Shaw, "The political economy of crime and conflict in sub-Saharan Africa," *South African Journal of International Affairs* 8, 2 (2001): 66.
41. A reference to the notorious Four One Nine advance fee fraud. See Daniel Jordan Smith, *A Culture of Corruption: Everyday deception and popular discontent in Nigeria*, (Princeton University Press: Princeton, NJ, 2007), especially Chapter 1.

42. Speech on 19 January 2006, reported in *Punch* (Lagos), 20 January 2006.
43. Peter Lewis, "From prebendalism to predation: The political economy of decline in Nigeria," *Journal of Modern African Studies* 34, 1 (1996): 97. The reference to "Zaïrianisation" is on p. 80.
44. Stanislav Andreski, *The African Predicament: A study in the pathology of modernization*, (Michael Joseph: London, 1968). A definition of "kleptocracy" is on p. 109.
45. See the unofficial version of the Oputa Panel report released on 1 January 2005 by the National Democratic Movement (Washington, DC), Vol. 4, 104, <http://www.dawodu.com/oputa1. htm> (Accessed 24 November 2008). Further information is in Richard Akinnola (ed.), *The Murder of Dele Giwa: Cover-up — revelations*, (Human Rights Publications: Lagos, 2001).
46. John Kerry and Hank Brown, Senators, *The BCCI Affair: A report to the Committee on Foreign Relations, United States Senate*, (US Government Printing Office: Washington DC, 1993), 99-104. The quotation is on p. 49.
47. Peter Truell and Larry Gurwin, *False Profits: The inside story of BCCI, the world's most corrupt financial empire*, (Houghton Mifflin: Boston and New York, 1992), 162.
48. United States Information Service (USIS) press release, 2 March 1998, quoted in *Punch*, 5 March 1998.
49. Kofi Bentsum Quantson, *Travelling and Seeing: Johnny just come*, (NAPASVIL Ventures: Accra, 2002), 67.
50. "2,000 Nigerians in foreign jails for drug offences," *New Nigerian*, 13 May 1988.
51. Jonas Okwara, "Three Nigerians held weekly in US on drug charges," *Guardian*, 15 July 1990.
52. Jackson Akpasubi, "US says 'no' to Nigeria," *Sunday Concord*, 30 June 1991; Eric Fottorino, *La Piste blanche: L'Afrique sous l'emprise de la drogue*, (Balland: Paris, 1991), 19, gives the same figure of 15,433 for Nigerians arrested for drug offences between 1979 and 1989.
53. Eric Fottorino, *La Piste blanche*, 19.
54. Segun Babatope, "Drug trafficking: A nation under siege," *National Concord*, 3 February 1992.
55. Nnamdi Obasi, "Drug trafficking," *Weekend Concord*, 1 June 1991.
56. Penny Green, *Drugs, Trafficking and Criminal Policy*, 48.
57. "Adegoke's ill-fated deal with skypower," *National Concord*, 30 April 1989.
58. Editorial, *Nigerian Tribune*, 24 March 2006.
59. "NDLEA stinks — Bamaiyi," *Daily Times*, 18 February 1994.
60. Eric Fottorino, *La Piste blanche*, 57, 60.
61. Stephen Ellis, "Les prolongements du conflit israélo-arabe: le cas du Sierra Leone," *Politique Africaine* 30 (1988), 69-75.
62. Robert I. Friedman, *Red Mafiya: How the Russian mob has invaded America*, (Little, Brown: Boston, MA, 2000), 57-8.
63. Emmanuel Kwaku Akyeampong, "Diaspora and drug trafficking," 441.
64. Author's interviews with former aide to President Charles Taylor, 2002-4.
65. Kwesi Yankah and Lazarus D. Maayang, "Charles Taylor: Dark days in Ghana," *Uhuru* (Accra). 3 (1990), 40.
66. The International Consortium of Investigative Journalists, *Making a Killing: The business of war*, (Public Integrity Books: Washington, DC, 2003), especially chapters 7 and 10.
67. Nya Kwiawon Taryor (ed.), *Justice, Justice: A cry of my people*, (Strugglers' Community Press: Chicago, IL, 1985), 54; phone interview, former aide to Charles Taylor, 4 November 2004.
68. Interview, Ghanaian police officer, Accra, 31 August 2008.

69. *Jane's Intelligence Review*, 1 July 2005; Antony Altbeker, *A Country at War with Itself: South Africa's crisis of crime*, (Jonathan Ball: Johannesburg and Cape Town, 2007), 124–5, argues that South Africans often exaggerate the impact of foreign organized crime in their own country. However, his concern in this passage is to refute any suggestion that South African crime is foreign rather than homegrown.

70. USIS press release, 2 March 1998, quoted in *Punch*, 5 March 1998.

71. Eric Fottorino, *La Piste blanche*, 60–1; see also allegations in *Liberian Diaspora* 3:12 (1993), 4 (to be viewed with caution, as this was a propaganda sheet for Charles Taylor).

72. "Drug: NDLEA sends officers' names to presidency," *Guardian*, 9 November 1998.

73. See interview with General Bamaiyi in *Sunday Champion*, 20 June 1999.

74. John K. Cooley, *Unholy Wars: Afghanistan, America and international terrorism*, third edition, (Pluto Press: London and Sterling, VA, 2002), 143.

75. Laolu Akande, "Nigeria high on US fraud, drugs list," *Guardian*, 18 August 1999.

76. UNODC. *Transnational Organized Crime in the West African Region*. New York, NY, (2005), 21.

77. Sisca Agboh, "NDLEA impounds N1b worth of cocaine," *Post Express* (Lagos), 31 August 2002.

78. Laolu Akande, "Nigerian boy, 12, swallows 87 condom wraps of heroin," *Guardian*, 13 April 2002.

79. UNODC, *Transnational Organized Crime in the West African Region*, 48.

80. "Italy police arrest mafia suspect," *BBC News*, 14 November 2003, <http://news.bbc. co.uk/2/hi/europe/3270935.stm> (Accessed 24 November 2008).

81. Statement to the Senate Foreign Relations Committee Subcommittee on African Affairs, 20 July 1995, obtained from the US Information Resource Center, US Embassy, The Hague.

82. Henry Mintzberg, *Structure in Fives: Designing effective organizations*, second edition, (Prentice Hall: Englewood Cliffs, NJ, 1983), 254. The term 'adhocracy' was coined by Alvin Toffler in his bestseller *Future Shock*, (Bantam Books: New York, NY, 1972).

83. Interview, Lagos, 24 October 2007.

84. "237 Nigerian drug convicts in arrive [sic] today," *Guardian*, 29 March 2003.

85. "African community at Pratunum, Bangkok." Paper presented by Royal Thai Police, African Criminal Networks conference, Bangkok, 16–19 May 2005.

86. "Dongri nightlife," *Time Out Mumbai* 2, 24 (July–August 2006), <http://www.timeoutmumbai.net/mumbailocal/mumbailocal_details.asp?code=11&source=1> (Accessed 24 November 2008).

87. "Nigerian drug barons invade South Africa," *Guardian*, 11 April 1998.

88. The name has been suppressed for legal reasons. Information obtained from official source, Lagos, 24 October 2007.

89. Reuben Abati, "The hanging of Amara Tochi in Singapore," *Guardian*, 28 January 2006.

90. Nigerian Drug Law Enforcement Agency (NDLEA), "An analysis of the drug trafficking issues and trends at the Murtala Muhammed International airport, Ikeja, Lagos (MMIA)" (unpublished paper, 7 pp., September 2007).

91. Ibid.

92. Ibid.

93. Franco Prina, Chapter 1 of "Trade and exploitation of minors and young Nigerian women for prostitution in Italy," 2003, <http://www.unicri.it/wwd/trafficking/nigeria/docs/rr_prina_eng.pdf> (Accessed 24 November 2008).

94. Cf. Kate Meagher, "Social capital, social liabilities, and political capital: Social networks and informal manufacturing in Nigeria," *African Affairs* 105, 421 (2006): 553–82.

95. Stephen Ellis, "The Okija shrine: Death and life in Nigerian politics," *Journal of African History* 49, 3 (2008): 445–66.

96. Joe Igbokwe, *Igbos: 25 years after Biafra*, (Advent Communications: No place given, 1995), 40.

97. Joe Brown Akubueze v The Federal Republic of Nigeria, 4 March 2003. Available via Toma Micro Publishers Ltd., <http://www.tomalegalretrieve.org/phplaw/site/index.php> (Accessed 23 July 2008).

98. Flemming Quist, "Drug trafficking in West Africa 2000–2004 in an international perspective" (UNODC workshop on West African organized crime, Dakar, 2–3 April 2004).

99. Ibid.

100. Ibid.

101. Ibid.

102. Johan van den Dongen and Bart Olmer, "Vloedgolf van drugs," *De Telegraaf* (Amsterdam), 26 October 2006.

103. Interview, Dutch judicial officer, Amsterdam, 13 December 2006; cf. Bart Middel-burg and Paul Vugts (eds.), *De Endstra-Tapes: De integrale gesprekken van Willem Endstra met de Recherche*, (Nieuw Amsterdam publishers: Amsterdam, 2006), 324, a record of police interviews with a leading figure of the Dutch underworld, the late Willem Endstra.

104. ISN Security Watch, 27 February 2008, <www.isn.etnz.ch> (28 February 2008).

105. Antonio L. Mazzitelli, "Transnational organized crime," 1075.

106. UNODC, "Cocaine trafficking in western Africa, situation report," (October 2007), 3–5, <http://www.google.com/search?hl=en&q=UNODC±Situation±Report%E2%80%99%2C± October±2007&btnG=Search> (Accessed 24 November 2008).

107. Ibid., 5.

108. *This Day*, 10, 13, 15 June 2006.

109. Interview, Lagos, 24 October 2007.

110. UNODC, "Cocaine trafficking in Western Africa," 6.

111. Presentation by DEA agent, Washington DC, 6 June 2008.

112. "Bissau drugs probe death threats," *BBC News*, 30 July 2008, <http://news.bbc.co.uk/go/pr/ fr/-/2/hi/africa/7532466.stm> (Accessed 31 July 2008).

113. International Crisis Group, *Guinee-Bissau: Besoin d'Etat* (Africa report No.142, Dakar/Brussels, July 2008).

114. Antonio L. Mazzitelli, "Transnational organized crime," 1076, note 23; UNODC, "Drug Trafficking as a Security Threat in West Africa" (November 2008), 13, gives the origin as Guinea-Bissau, <http://www.unodc.org/unodc/en/frontpage/drug-trafficking-as-a-security-threat-in-west-africa.html> (Accessed 4 February 2009).

115. Interviews, Accra, 31 August 2008; "West Africa/drugs," *Africa Confidential* 49:6 (14 March 2008).

116. Alistair Thomson, "Drug trade threatens to corrode Ghana's image," *International Herald Tribune*, 23 December 2008.

117. "West Africa/drugs," *Africa Confidential* 49:6 (14 March 2008).

118. Interviews, Lagos and Abuja, October 2007; "'Blood oil' dripping from Nigeria," *BBC News*, 27 July 2008, <http://news.bbc.co.uk/2/hi/africa/7519302.stm> (Accessed 25 November 2008).

119. "Mali cocaine haul after firefight," *BBC News*, 4 January 2008, <http://news.bbc.co.uk/2/hi/

africa/7171219.stm> (Accessed 17 January 2008); UNODC, "Drug Trafficking as a Security Threat," 32, reports the discovery of a similar amount of hashish. It is not clear if this is a coincidence or a reporting error.

120. Heba Saleh, "Islamist militants rise again in Algeria," *Financial Times*, 1 September 2008; cf. International Crisis Group, *Islamist Terrorism in the Sahel: Fact or fiction?* (Africa report No. 92, Dakar/Brussels, 2005), 18–19.

121. Presentation by DEA officers, Washington DC, 6 June 2008.

122. UNODC, *Cocaine Trafficking in West Africa*, 20.

123. Francisco E. Thoumi, "The rise of two drug tigers: The development of the illegal drugs industry and drug policy failure in Afghanistan and Colombia," in F. Bovenkerk and M. Levi (eds.), *The Organized Crime Community: Essays in honor of Alan A. Block*, Studies of Organized Crime No. 6, Springer Science and Business Media: New York, NY, (2007), 126.

124. Ibid.

125. Ibid.

126. Ibid., 127.

127. UNODC, *Cocaine Trafficking in West Africa*, 1.

128. "UN fears over West Africa drugs," *BBC News*, 27 November 2007, <http://news.bbc.co.uk/2/hi/africa/7114593.stm> (Accessed 25 November 2008).

129. UNODC, *Crime and Development in Africa*, (UNODC: Vienna, 2005), 67, <http://www.unodc.org/unodc/en/data-and-analysis/Studies-on-Drugs-and-Crime.html> (Accessed 26 November 2008).

130. Ibid.

131. Cf. Manuel Castells, *End of Millennium*, second edition, (Blackwell: Oxford, 2000), Vol. 3 of the *Information Age* trilogy, 82–118.

132. William Reno, *Corruption and State Politics in Sierra Leone*, (Cambridge University Press: Cambridge, 1995), 3. Interestingly, the expression "shadow state" was used long before, by Jean Suret-Canale, "La Guinée dans le système colonial," *Présence Africaine* 29 (1959–60), 97.

133. William Reno, *Corruption and State Politics*, 2.

134. Cf. Tekena Tamuno and Robin Horton, "The changing position of secret societies and cults in modern Nigeria," *African Notes* 5, 2 (1969), 36–62.

135. Manuel Castells, *End of Millennium*, 98; see also Bayart et al., *Criminalization of the State*, chapters 1 and 2.

136. "Chinese gangs in Africa for long haul," *Jane's Intelligence Digest*, 8 July 2008.

The Inland Empire 8

Nick Reding

As the weeks that I traveled around the Midwest, the Southeast, and California turned to months in the summer and fall of 2005, I was beginning to see meth in America as a function not just of farming and food industry trends in the 1980s and '90s but also of changes in the narcotics and pharmaceuticals industries in the same period. It would take a few more years of watching what happened in Oelwein, and in the United States at large, before I completely understood what I was seeing. That, for instance, as economies had dwindled throughout the Great Plains and the Midwest, they had aligned a certain way in Southern California, and that the electrical current sweeping between these two increasingly unrelated American places, the coast and the middle, would presage what came to be called the "meth epidemic" thirty years later. So, too, would it take a while to see that the changes that linked Long Beach and Los Angeles with Oelwein were in fact changes tied to the emergence of the global economy. And that meth, if it is a metaphor for anything, is a metaphor for the cataclysmic fault lines formed by globalization.

Back in 2005, these things were just coming into focus as I went to Ottumwa, a town in southeast Iowa. It was in Ottumwa that the Midwest's principal meth wiring had been installed, and to which the drug's early advancement into Oelwein could be traced. If Oelwein was shaping up to be the face of meth in modern America, and an indicator of life in modern, rural America in general, then in Ottumwa there was a picture of Oelwein's skeletal forebears. And eventually a picture of Oelwein's future, though that part of the story was yet to evolve.

Like Oelwein, Ottumwa had for most of its history been a very prosperous place. Also like Oelwein, Ottumwa was a kind of economic outpost, a wealthy waypoint on the trade routes running between St. Louis, Chicago, and Omaha. Thanks to the Des Moines River, which runs right through the middle of Ottumwa, industry and transportation came quickly to the area once it was settled by a land rush in 1843. In 1850, John Morrell and Co. opened a flagship, state-of-the-art meat-processing plant in the center of town. By 1888, there were 10,500 miles of railroad track in Wapello County. Fifty-seven passenger trains on seven lines, the Burlington Railroad being the most famous, crossed the county every day. By the turn of the twentieth century, factories in Ottumwa made everything from boxcar loaders to cigars, and corn huskers to violins. By 1950, Ottumwa was home not only to over fifty thousand people but also to the largest air force base in the Midwest. Almost half the working-age men in town were in the employ of Hormel (the modern incarnation of John Morrell's packing plant) or John Deere, the farm-equipment manufacturer, where workers could hope, at a minimum, to maintain a lower-middle-class existence.

By 1980, though, Ottumwa's fortunes had, like Oelwein's, begun to decline. The story was much the same. The railroad's demise was followed by the closing of the air force base and then, in 1987, by the sale of Hormel to Excel Meat Solutions, a subsidiary of Cargill. Along with layoffs, wages, as they did a few years later at Oelwein's Iowa Ham plant, fell by two thirds. Like the shrinking workforce, the population of Ottumwa itself dried up like a prairie pothole in a drought, falling by an astounding 50 percent in just twenty-five years. Soon the town, starved of tax revenue and disposable income, was verging on bankruptcy. And, as had happened in Oelwein, methamphetamine moved into the new economic gap. The difference was that Ottumwa, more than any other place, defined the development of the modern American meth business in the Midwest. Meth from Ottumwa first helped to create, and then to sustain, the market not just in Oelwein but also in towns all over Iowa, Missouri, Nebraska, Kansas, and the Dakotas.

How this happened depended on several trends and events that merged seamlessly into one another: Emigration routes from the Midwest to California as working-class men and women headed to the coast in search of employment; immigration routes into the heartland as increasing numbers of Mexicans worked against the human tide in order to take low-wage jobs at meat-packing plants; the rise of industrial meth production; the increased lobbying power of pharmaceutical companies; and finally, government apathy, if not disregard, for the very drug war that at the time had been newly declared by First Lady Nancy Reagan.

At the center of it all, back in Ottumwa, stood a woman named Lori Arnold. It was she who was able to weave together these various political, sociological, and chemical threads into the Midwest's first and last bona fide crank empire, the official moniker for which was the Stockdall Organization, so named for

Lori's second husband, Floyd Stockdall. Lori's contribution to what at the time was not yet referred to as a "drug epidemic" was that she essentially wrote meth's genetic code in the Midwest. With her, the very concept of industrialized meth in places like Iowa was born, and it flourished in relative anonymity for the next ten years. The irony is that, while Lori worked, the Drug Enforcement Administration fruitlessly lobbied for laws that, had they passed, would have prevented Lori from ever going into business.

Lori Kaye Arnold is Ottumwa, Iowa's most famous daughter. Ottumwa's most famous son is Lori's brother, the comedian Tom Arnold, who is perhaps better known as the ex-husband of Roseanne Barr. Lori is forty-five years old, with shoulder-length light-brown hair and a longish, blunt nose, like a skinning knife. With Tom, she shares a toothy, crocodilian smile and the low center of gravity and powerful legs of a middleweight wrestler. Since 2005, I have corresponded with Lori, who's in federal prison — coincidentally, at the medium-security women's work camp in Greenville, Illinois, just a few hundred yards from where I met Sean and James during November 2004.

One of seven step- and half-siblings, Lori was born and raised in Ottumwa in a family that she describes as studiously normal and benign. Despite this, Lori dropped out of high school as a freshman and began living in an Ottumwa rooming house where, in the evenings, there was a running poker game. The landlady was also a madame. In exchange for room and board, Lori and her young cohorts could either agree to sleep with the men who played cards or deliver illegally prescribed methedrine pills, an early form of pharmaceutical meth, to the landlady's clients. Lori chose the latter; thus her career (along with her legend) was born.

Lori kept herself housed by delivering and selling "brown and clears," as pharmaceutical meth was called during the 1970s, when it was prescribed by the millions as a weight-loss aid and anti-depression drug. The landlady got most of Lori's profits, though, and to make ends meet, Lori still had to work six days a week at a local bar. (In Iowa minors can serve alcohol despite being legally unable to buy it.) By fifteen, Lori was married. By sixteen, she was divorced and was attending high school once again. By seventeen, she had dropped out for good; her peers, she says, seemed to her like children. By eighteen, she was married to Floyd Stockdall, who had come to Ottumwa from Des Moines in order to retire, at the ripe old age of thirty-seven, as the president of the Grim Reapers motorcycle gang.

Lori and Floyd moved into a cabin along the Des Moines River outside Ottumwa, where their only child, Josh, was born. Left alone to raise a son while Floyd pursued his retirement hobbies of drinking, playing pool, and selling cocaine, nineteen-year-old Lori became suicidally depressed. The bar, she now realized, had been her lifeline. In addition to the money she made, the people there were her people, the only family of which Lori ever felt a true part.

Without the bikers and the factory workers with whom she had all but grown up, Lori felt horribly lost and alone; her life had become an interminable slog. Worse yet, Floyd was an alcoholic, and beat her whenever he drank.

Then one day Floyd's brother stopped by the cabin. He, too, was a Grim Reaper, and he had with him some methamphetamine, a.k.a. biker dope, which had been illegally synthesized at a lab in Southern California. This was 1984, and the Reapers were just beginning to sell meth whenever they could get it from Long Beach. There, according to DEA, former Hells Angels had gone into business with maverick pharmaceutical company chemists in order to produce saleable quantities of highly pure, powdered methamphetamine. Lori's brother-in-law cut her two lines on the kitchen table inside her run-down shack on the Des Moines River on a sunny, clear Saturday afternoon. Of the experience, Lori, who was no stranger to narcotics, says simply that she had never felt so good in all her life. The singularity of that feeling is what would soon connect Ottumwa to a nascent California drug empire. In doing so, a major piece of the meth-epidemic puzzle would fall into place.

The first day Lori got high, she went to the bar. She says she'd been given a little meth to sell because Floyd's brother wanted to see what kind of a market Ottumwa might prove to be. Lori gave away half the meth, knowing intuitively that this would help hook her customers. The other half quickly sold out. In the process, she made fifty dollars. What she found, though, was worth millions, for Lori Arnold knew almost immediately that dealing meth was what she'd been born to do. It was the answer not just to her prayers, but to Ottumwa's, which for three long years had been pummeled by the farm crisis into a barely recognizable version of its former proud self. Thanks to meth, says Lori, the workers worked and played harder, and she became rich. Within a month, Lori was selling so much Long Beach crank in Ottumwa that she went around her brother-in-law and dealt directly with the middleman in Des Moines. A month after that, she was buying quarter pounds of meth for $2,500 and selling them for $10,000. Unsatisfied with the profit margin, she began dealing directly with the supplier in Long Beach, dispatching Floyd to California once every ten days with instructions to return from the 3,700-mile round-trip with as much meth as he could fit in the trunk of the Corvette Lori had bought him. Lori, meantime, stashed money in the wall of her cabin. Only six months after she had met Floyd's brother, the wall held $50,000 — nearly twice the median yearly income in Ottumwa today.

By the late 1980s, people like Jeffrey William Hayes and Steve Jelinek of Oelwein were buying massive amounts of dope from Lori and establishing their own meth franchises in Iowa, Illinois, Missouri, and Kansas by selling to the likes of Roland Jarvis, who, yet to start making his own meth, would take whatever he could get in order to work extra shifts at Iowa Ham. Lori, in turn, was dealing directly with what she calls the Mexican Mafia, a somewhat loose group of traffickers who manufactured large amounts of that era's most powerful dope: P2P. Made predominantly in Long Beach and Orange County, California, in large, clandestine laboratories, this stronger form of meth was more addictive, cheaper, and easier to produce than any other form of the drug available at the time. As such, it increased Lori's already burgeoning sales manifold.

The so-called Mexican Mafia with whom Lori dealt was built on the vision of two brothers, Jesus and Luis Amezcua, who'd been born in Mexico and lived in San Diego. For years, according to DEA, the Amezcuas had been nothing more than middling cocaine dealers. Until, that is, they perceived the convergence of two seemingly unrelated events. One was that, aided by former pharmaceutical engineers, the Amezcuas could access an enormous, completely legal, and unmonitored supply of the necessary ingredients to make P2P: Ephedrine and phenyl-2-propanone. The Amezcuas' second insight was that they could move large quantities of the drug throughout California and the West, thanks to the increasing numbers of Mexican immigrants who picked fruit in the Central Valley, cleaned homes in Tucson, Arizona, or built roads in Idaho. Furthermore, the brothers could access the Midwest via the ballooning population of Midwesterners who had been chased off their farms, all the way to Southern California.

During the 1980s, large numbers of people from the Corn Belt left in what sociologists call out-migration. Within the space of just a few years, many Iowa towns, Ottumwa and Oelwein included, lost from 10 to 25 percent of their residents, many of whom headed for the booming labor markets of Los Angeles and San Diego. Family and social connections became business connections as Iowan, Kansan, Dakotan, and Nebraskan laborers in Orange County, eager to get rich, sent loads of the Amezcuas' meth back home. Or, like Jeffrey William Hayes in Oelwein and Lori Arnold in Ottumwa, either drove out to get it themselves or sent someone in their stead.

Throughout its hundred-year history, meth has been perhaps the only example of a widely consumed illegal narcotic that might be called vocational, as opposed to recreational. The market for meth in America is nearly as old as industrialization. Poor and working-class Americans had been consuming the drug since the 1930s, whether it was marketed as Benzedrine, Methedrine, or Obedrin, for the simple reason that meth makes you feel good and permits you to work hard. Thanks to the Amezcuas and Lori Arnold, these same people no longer needed to rely on expensive prescriptions and were able to get a stronger form of meth at a much better price — this at a time when the drug's effects were arguably more useful than ever. That's to say that as meth's purity rose, its price dropped. So too did meth become much more widely available at exactly the moment that rural economies collapsed and people left. Under those circumstances, says Clay Hallberg, those who remained felt they needed the drug most.

By 1987, if you wanted meth and you lived in southern Iowa, or northern Missouri, you went to the bar that Lori Arnold now owned, the Wild Side.

There, the increasingly beleaguered Ottumwa police, whose numbers were shrinking alongside county and city tax revenues, had little chance of interrupting Lori's exorbitantly profitable crank business. At that point, says Lori, in addition to Floyd, she had a dozen runners going back and forth to Long Beach to buy meth from multiple so-called superlabs, which could produce up to twenty pounds of meth every thirty-six hours — an astounding amount of crank in those days. Because the cars that Lori's runners used were a drain on her profits (imagine the mileage accrued by driving nearly four thousand miles every ten days, month after month), Lori bought a car dealership. That way, she could have access to as many vehicles as she needed; she could also have her runners trade the cars and their tags with car dealers in any state along the way, thereby making themselves harder to follow. Then, to house her employees and further launder the money she was making, Lori bought fourteen houses in Ottumwa.

This was just the beginning of the means by which Lori, who had not made it past tenth grade, laundered her drug money at the same time that she moved to fill new markets around the region. In 1989, she bought fifty-two racehorses — and hired the dozen or so grooms, trainers, veterinarians, and jockeys it took to maintain them — along with a 144-acre horse farm from which to run her ever-multiplying, synergistic empires. People from Kentucky to the Dakotas and from Indiana to Colorado race, breed, buy, trade, and sell horses, making it the perfect cover for a narcotics distribution business. Lori's runners, tooling along in their duallies, a couple of geldings munching hay in the horse trailer, the wheel wells packed tight with crank, became the down-home *Dukes of Hazzard* version of coke-laden speedboats making the run from Eleuthera to Key Biscayne.

Lori's true stroke of genius, though, was to build under a series of military tents hidden in the wooded hills of her horse farm what for almost two decades would be the only meth superlab ever known to be in production outside the state of California. By then, she was in such good graces with the Amezcua brothers, the California "Kings of Crank," that they let her borrow a chemist, whom Lori flew to Iowa to teach her associates how to make meth in ten-pound batches every forty-eight hours: A state-of-the-art, up-to-the-minute operation. The effect was remarkable, for up until now, Lori had controlled sales of meth in Iowa and other parts of the Midwest while still having to rely on the Amezcuas for her product. Once Lori opened her own superlab, she was in control of the entire value chain: Manufacture, distribution, and retail. And while she still bought meth from the Amezcuas, principally to maintain good relations, Lori had no real competition to speak of. In just the two years between 1987 and 1989, an unassuming high school dropout from little Ottumwa, Iowa, had succeeded in cornering part of what was becoming one of the world's most lucrative narcotics markets. What's more amazing is how close she came to never getting started.

According to several former agents, back in 1987, there was deep institutional ambivalence within the Drug Enforcement Administration (DEA) toward methamphetamine. Meth was seen as a biker drug, strictly falling under the purview of losers who didn't have enough financial sense to put together a large-scale operation. These were the Reagan eighties, and as tastes ran for big, deregulated corporate successes, so ran America's taste for drugs. Cocaine was king. As such, DEA, whose job is to curb the excesses of the period as they are embodied by America's choice in narcotics, wasn't interested in anything aside from the Cali and Medellín cartels, drug-trafficking organizations run like multinational corporations capable of exceeding their host nation's GDP. Who could have imagined the business being built by two lowly coke-dealer brothers in the part of L.A. called the Inland Empire, or that this business would be connected with a kind of narcotic principate in Ottumwa, Iowa?

Only one person, it turns out: Gene Haislip, the deputy assistant administrator in DEA's Office of Compliance and Regulatory Affairs. Haislip knew that large amounts of ephedrine, which was imported in bulk to make nasal decongestants, were being redirected to the Amezcua organization with no oversight. Ephedrine processing took place in only nine factories around the world, all of them in India, China, Germany, and Czech Republic. To Haislip, the narrow processing window posed a perfect opportunity to siphon off the meth trade; all that was required was the cooperation of those nine factories, along with the pharmaceutical companies that depended on the ephedrine made in them. What Haislip proposed in 1985, two years before Lori Arnold went into large-scale meth production, was a federal law allowing DEA to monitor all ephedrine imports into the United States.

According to a 2004 investigative article written by Steve Suo in Portland's *Oregonian* newspaper, Haislip got the idea based on his earlier work on the illicit US trade in Quaaludes, a legal sleeping pill widely available on the black market. The manufacture of Quaaludes depended on the synthesis of another legal drug, methaqualone, which was predominately produced in Germany, Austria, and China. What Haislip noticed was that an enormous proportion of the methaqualone from these nations was being shipped to Colombia. There, the Cali and Medellín cartels were making it into an illegal form of Quaalude, which they sold in tandem with cocaine in the same market — one as an upper, one as a downer — in the same way that meth markets today are often saturated with Oxycontin, a prescription painkiller that smooths out the impending "tweak" of a meth high. In 1982, Haislip visited the nations whose factories made methaqualone and asked for their help in monitoring its sale. Congress then banned the use of prescription Quaaludes, which were manufactured by only one American company. By 1984, according to DEA's annual narcotics threat assessment, Quaaludes no longer constituted a significant danger to the illicit US drug market. With meth, Haislip simply hoped to keep organizations like the Amezcuas (and to a lesser extent, people like Lori Arnold) from legally procuring ephedrine without hurting the production and sale of cold medicine of licit companies like Warner-Lambert, the makers of Sudafed. Haislip's idea took the form of language inserted into the Controlled Substances Act, which would be debated by Congress in the fall of 1986.

What's important to understand is that, despite the fact that Haislip's job was to write legislation, DEA is not a political entity. According to the cliché, one of which most DEA agents seem proud, the administration occupies a place that is all but outside the law. While FBI agents stereotypically tail potential bad guys in their sedans, and CIA agents listen to phone conversations, DEA agents are supposedly assassinating major narco-figures in the world's more inhospitable environments. Whether or not this is a fantasy is unclear. What it suggests is an institutional frustration regarding the governmental process: It's easier to shoot people in other places than to write legislation here, which must then be tailored to the concerns of members of Congress and the lobbyists who influence them.

DEA's proposals are subject to long, withering debates and years of compromise. And that is where the administration, if not actually a political entity, is a highly politicized one. Back in 1986, even as Nancy Reagan gave her famous "just say no" speech, Haislip had to bow to pressure from Democrats and Republicans alike not to raise the ire of pharmaceutical lobbyists, whose job, in part, is to comb through legislative bills looking for anything that could potentially upset their clients' sales. That's how Haislip's bill, according to the *Oregonian* article, came to the attention of Allan Rexinger, who was in the employ of a trade group called the Proprietary Association on behalf of Warner-Lambert. Rexinger didn't like what he saw.

For several weeks during 1986, according to Rexinger, he worked to change the language of Haislip's bill in a way that would exempt Warner-Lambert from the potential bane of federal importation oversight. When DEA and Haislip continued to resist his pleas, said Rexinger, he had no choice but to get the White House involved by making a phone call to, as he proudly told Suo in 2004, "the highest levels of the United States government."

By the time Attorney General Edwin Meese III presented Haislip's bill to Congress in April 1987, five years had passed since Haislip had initially imagined nipping meth production in the bud. Meantime, the Amezcua cartel had spread throughout California and the Desert West, and had linked up with Lori Arnold's Stockdall Organization in Iowa, which by now was well on its way to producing its own industrially manufactured P2P meth. The language in Haislip's bill proposing oversight of ephedrine had been drastically altered as well, allowing for the drug to be imported in pill form with no federal regulations whatsoever. All that meth manufacturers had to do in order to continue making the drug would be legally to buy pill-form ephedrine in bulk and crush it into powder — a small, added inconvenience. What Haislip had imagined as an early answer to a still-embryonic drug threat instead became both a mandate and a road map for meth's expansion.

In 1987, the year that Cargill cut wages at its Ottumwa meatpacking plant from $18 an hour to $5.60 with no benefits, Lori Arnold sold a pound of pure, uncut crank for $32,000. This meant that with the very first ten pounds produced at her superlab, she had paid off the $100,000 initial investment in equipment and chemicals and had cleared a profit of nearly a quarter of a million dollars, or over a century's worth of median wages for an Ottumwa adult that year. Meanwhile, she was still buying ten pure pounds at a time of Mexican Mafia dope from California, at $10,000 a pound, which she then sold for three times the price, again making nearly a quarter of a million dollars every time one of her runners returned from the West Coast.

Where crank's personality converges with its mathematics is this: No one with whom I spoke, and this includes varsity-level addicts like Roland Jarvis, can physically handle snorting, smoking, or shooting 98 percent pure methamphetamine. So while Lori only sold her product uncut, each pound, once it was distributed, equated to three or four pounds of ingestible crank, and probably more, given that each dealer along the line was likely to continue cutting it — with bleach, laundry detergent, or baking soda. Seen that way, Lori's lab wasn't producing ten pounds every forty-eight hours; it was producing the eventual equivalent of thirty to forty pounds. (By that stretch, the biggest labs in the Central Valley of California today would be producing the so-called street equivalent of up to five hundred pounds a day, while an Indonesian megalab would make five thousand pounds of saleable meth each week.) In one month alone during Lori's prime, that's somewhere on the order of a quarter ton of meth being distributed in the relatively under-populated environs of the central Midwest. Add to that the dozen or so big loads she was getting from California each month, and it's easy to see how Lori was, by her own admission, involved in one manner or another with "thousands of people" and making "hundreds of thousands of dollars monthly." When pushed for an answer, Lori admits that she has no idea how much she made, in pounds or dollars.

When Lori first got into meth, a gram would last her an entire weekend. By 1991, Lori was snorting up to three grams a day. She remembers not sleeping for weeks at a time. She wore, she says, a lot of hats. Multiple-business owner, mother, drug baron: Without the meth, she could never have done it all. She was, she says, one of the main employers in Ottumwa, and a benevolent one, at that. She donated plenty of money to the local police and to the county sheriff. She planned to open a day care center and video game arcade next to the Wild Side, so local kids would have somewhere to go while their parents were in the bar. Together, Lori and meth were an antidote to the small-town sense of isolation, the collective sense of depression and low morale that had settled on

Ottumwa since most farms went belly-up, the railroad closed, and the boys at the meatpacking plant lost their jobs.

If you ask her, Lori Arnold will say she did more for the state of Iowa than all the politicians put together, who let the place go to hell overnight. People were proud of her, she says, and they should have been: She gave them back the life that the government and the corporations took away. If there was ever a problem with meth, says Lori, it wasn't with the clean dope she sold. Her dope wouldn't do anything freaky to you. It was the rot-gut the batchers cooked up that made people crazy. And it was always Lori's pleasure to put those people out of business — it was her civic duty to keep the likes of Roland Jarvis from selling too much crap-batch, getting people paranoid and blathering on about black helicopters and heads in trees. In Lori's reality, she was a businesswoman, not a drug dealer in what she calls "the classic sense." She's right, insofar as she had an unprecedented vertical monopoly, which she claims to have run at least in part to assuage the detrimental effects of the very monopolies like Cargill and Iowa Beef Packers that were born in that same era of deregulation. Add to this that Lori's rise required putting home cooks — the Iowa Hams of the meth world, if you will — out of business, and the self-styled Robin Hood of crank begins to look awfully corporate. At a deeper strata of irony, consider that Lori almost single-handedly ushered into the Midwest the next generation of the meth epidemic, which would be controlled by five Mexican drug-trafficking organizations that today enjoy the same kind of market control of meth that Cargill enjoys with respect to the food industry.

Perhaps inevitably, like Roland Jarvis, the kind of small-time tweaker for whom she had the utmost disdain, Lori did see a helicopter, though in her case it was real. It hovered over her house one day in 1990 while agents from the Bureau of Alcohol, Tobacco, and Firearms (ATF) took photos of her meth lab in the woods. Later that day, Lori was zooming around town in her green Jaguar Sovereign doing errands when she got the call from a stable boy that things were getting a little weird out at the farm. There were cars parked along the country roads, said the boy, and men with binoculars trained on the place. That night, Lori says, the feds sent in an army: ATF, FBI, DEA-you name it. By morning, she was in the local jail, telling jokes to the agents who stood guard. After all, says Lori, if you don't have a sense of humor, what do you have left?

Six months later, Lori Arnold's crank empire fell apart when she was convicted in federal court in the Southern District of Iowa of one count of continuing a criminal enterprise; two counts of money laundering; one count of carrying and using a firearm in conjunction with drug trafficking; and multiple counts of possession, distribution, and manufacture of methamphetamine. Floyd Stockdall was tried separately and sentenced to fifteen years in Leavenworth prison, where he died of a heart attack two months before he would have been paroled. Lori got ten years in the federal penitentiary in Alderson, West Virginia, and was released after serving eight, on July 2,

1999. Her son and only child, Josh, was fifteen years old; Lori had been gone for half his life. By then, the meth business in the Midwest had mutated into something Lori couldn't believe, though she was quick to comprehend that it was a new, much more fully developed phenomenon than that which she'd created along with the Amezcuas. And once Lori identified a spot for herself in the new order, she did the thing she'd been doing all her life: She went right back into business.

RESOURCES

The Illicit Abalone Trade in South Africa

9

Jonny Steinberg

There are five species of abalone endemic to South Africa, but only one, *Haliotis midae*, is of any commercial value. Known in South Africa as perlemoen (from the Dutch *Paarlemoer*, meaning mother-of-pearl), it was endemic to several hundred kilometers of South African coastline stretching from Table Bay to the Eastern Cape before overexploitation threatened it with extinction.[1] It is a large marine snail with a shell length of up to 230mm that lives in shallow water and takes seven to nine years to mature. It is believed to live for 30 years or longer.[2]

The story of its overexploitation is an extraordinary one. The meat of perlemoen has always been highly valued in East Asia, and South Africans were aware of its commercial value throughout the second half of the twentieth century. Unrestricted commercial harvesting began in South Africa in 1949. By the mid-1960s, about 2,800 tons of abalone were being taken from the sea annually. In a bid to stem overexploitation and protect the resource, seasonal quotas were introduced in 1970. The first annual quota (or Total Allowable Catch) was 700 tons, and decreased marginally and incrementally over the following two-and-a-half decades; by 1995, the annual quota was 615 tons.[3]

It is common knowledge that poaching is as old as the quota itself, but it is also common knowledge that levels of poaching remained negligible — or at very least containable — for the first two decades after the quota's introduction. All of this changed dramatically during South Africa's transition to democracy. Poaching began to escalate in the early 1990s. By the late 1990s it had become a highly organized, multi-million dollar illicit industry, controlled by street gangs on the shoreline and by transnational criminal enterprises on the trade routes to East Asia.[4] Despite increasing investments in shoreline patrolling and enforcement, the initiation of several large and well-resourced organized crime investigative projects, and countless plans to reorganize the control of South Africa's borders, it appears that the illegal industry has been able to harvest and export South African abalone at will. By 2002, more abalone was being confiscated by the enforcement authorities per year than were harvested by the commercial fishery.[5] The illegally harvested catch has escalated annually since then. Enforcement authorities believe that if the 2004–2005 season is as bad as the previous one, commercial fishery will be unsustainable by 2006.[6]

It has thus taken the illicit industry little more than a decade to bring wild perlemoen to the brink of commercial extinction.[7] The trajectory is nothing short of spectacular: In a remarkably short space of time, an endemic marine species has been taken out of the water, smuggled across South Africa's borders and transported across the ocean, all under the nose of a hapless enforcement regime.

The publication of this paper thus comes very late in the day. It is, in part, a post-mortem of failed efforts; in part, a description of brave, last-ditch attempts to turn the situation around. According to a very narrow reading of its brief, it would restrict itself to discussing how abalone has been smuggled over land, sea and air borders. Such a narrow reading would miss the point. It makes far more sense to follow the industry's value chain from the water's edge to the ports of East Asia, and to describe the enforcement interventions made at various points along the chain. The lessons to be learnt obviously have implications beyond the confines of the illicit abalone trade, and are generally relevant to the age-old debate about the relationship between law enforcement and transnational illicit trade.

The Rise of the Illicit Market

The birth and rapid growth of the illicit perlemoen trade in the 1990s can be accounted for by four factors. Each should be seen as crucial, in other words, as a necessary condition. The first was the weakening of the rand against the US dollar that began in the early 1990s and continued steadily for the following decade. The second factor was the pre-existing presence in South Africa of a large and highly efficient Chinese organized crime network. In other words, illicit trade routes between South Africa and East Asia were already firmly established. The third factor is the immense difficulty South Africa has had, and continues to have, in devising and executing an efficient border control function. Fourth, and with little doubt the most interesting and important, is the mutation in the socio-political identities of the colored fishing communities on the abalone-rich shoreline during South Africa's transition to democracy;

it was, above all, the evolution of a distinctive political consciousness that animated the taking of the perlemoen stock from the water.

The Weakening of the Rand and the Role of Bartering in the Illicit Economy

In December 1992 the South African currency dropped to three units to the US dollar for the first time. In March 1996 the rand hit four to the dollar, dropping to five in March 1997, six in July 1998, seven in May 2000, finally hitting thirteen in December 2001.[8] This nine-year period was, to say the least, a good time for those looking to export high value commodities traded in dollars. In the late 1990s, the South African intelligence community believed that South African abalone was being sold for more than US$65 per kilogram on the Chinese black market.[9] Hundreds of kilograms of perlemoen are harvested from the water, smuggled and exported cheaply by the ton. All of these costs — poaching, concealing and shipping — are paid in rands. It was already a lucrative commodity to trade when the rand was three to the dollar; by the late 1990s, it was a proverbial gold mine.[10]

The only factor that may have caused illicit capital to hesitate before investing in the perlemoen trade was risk. In the early 1990s, risk was rightly regarded as minimal. Chinese organized crime had been present in South Africa for more than a decade, and yet had barely been detected by the South African authorities.[11]

Indeed, abalone was by no means the only illicit export to surge in the 1990s. The declining rand saw dramatic increases in the export of a range of Southern African contraband. The most pronounced export increase was probably in cannabis. In the late 1980s, the export market for Southern African cannabis was so small that it barely registered in the records of European police agencies. Most players were small-time white businessmen who, as one of the investigators interviewed for this paper put it, "wanted to earn a bit extra to buy a boat for his house at the Vaal River." By 1998, much of the regional cannabis trade had been taken over by West African organized crime, and the British authorities reported that South Africa was the single largest cannabis exporter to the UK.[12] The export industry had grown from almost nothing to market leader in the space of a decade. Wholesaling at about £1,000 per compressed kilogram in London and Glasgow, those who exported it from South Africa were making a killing. Not only were their costs in rands, they were minimal. The cannabis itself was bought for next to nothing from peasant producers. The primary cost entailed shipping it in bulk from Southern African ports, disguised as rooibos tea, dried basil and whatever else a fertile imagination could invent.

If a weakening currency is good for licit exporters, it reaps even greater returns for astute contraband traders. This is because, in contrast to legitimate exporters, contraband traders barter. Bartering has played a central role in the international criminal economy for as long as there has been global trade. There is a wonderful fictional account of the role of bartering in the illicit markets of early twentieth century Europe in Joseph Roth's novel, *The Radetzky March*. Describing the traders in a fictional town on the eastern border of the Habsburg empire, Roth writes:

> They had no shops, no names, no credit. But they did possess a miraculous instinct for any and all secret sources of money. They dealt in feathers for feather beds, in horsehair, in tobacco, in silver ingots, in jewels, in Chinese tea, in southern fruit, in fields and woodlands. Some of them even dealt in live human beings. They sent deserters from the Russian army to the United States and young peasant girls to Brazil and Argentina. Their hands were gifted in striking gold from gravel like sparks from flint.[13]

Indeed, the most important institution in the illicit economy is the bazaar. As Ted Leggett describes it: "International brokers service a network of supplies and demands at once . . . Cash is taken from countries with hard currency, and commodities are shuffled between all the rest."[14] An intelligent trader based in a weak currency zone uses the barter economy to have his cake and eat it. He exports high value, dollar-denominated commodities from his weak currency zone (like cannabis or abalone) and trades them for high value commodities, which he imports. He thus makes mileage from his weak currency when he exports, and skirts it when he imports.

In South Africa, the price of cocaine, heroin and club drugs remained stable throughout the 1990s, despite the rapid decline in the value of the rand. The likelihood is that these drugs were being paid for in high value cannabis rather than low value rands. Indeed, the price of imported drugs in South Africa was so low during the 1990s that they could be re-exported at a profit.[15] Those exporting cannabis and importing cocaine and heroin had locked themselves into a virtuous circle.

The same virtuous circle was quick to emerge in the abalone market. In the mid 1990s, some of the major traders in the Western Cape's gang-based drug market descended on abalone-rich fishing villages such as Hawston and Kleinmont and took control of sizeable portions of the abalone market. At the same time, security agencies became aware that vast quantities of the chemical precursors of methaqualone, the drug of choice in the ghettos of the Cape Flats, were being smuggling into South Africa from East Asia. By the late 1990s, it was clear that methaqualone had been bartered for abalone for quite some time.

Nobody knows for certain quite what proportion of the illicit abalone catch is bartered for methaqualone, but anecdotal evidence suggests that it is quite considerable. On several occasions over the past six years, multi-ton methaqualone seizures have been linked to businessmen and women at the centre of the abalone trade. At the time of writing (January 2005) it appears that Chinese organized crime remains keenly interested in supplying the Cape Flats drug market. For the first time in two-and-a-half decades, methaqualone's market dominance on the Cape Flats is being threatened by a rival synthetic drug — crystal methamphetamine (its colloquial name is tik). In December 2004, four Chinese nationals — three of whom are known by security agencies to have a long involvement in the abalone trade — were arrested on the premises of a crystal methamphetamine factory in the Western Cape.[16]

Abalone was thus quick to take its place at the centre of the Western Cape's illicit economy. Chinese businesses bartered cheaply acquired chemical precursors for high value abalone, while Western Cape drug lords bartered cheaply acquired abalone for high value drugs. Those drug lords who gained control of significant volumes of abalone captured a monopoly over low-priced methaqualone. The result is that every serious player in the drug industry had to get his hands on abalone in order to stay in business. As an investigator with a colorful turn of phrase put it when interviewed for this project: "In the late 1990s, the traffic jams on the road to Betty's Bay were something to see. Every second car was packed with soldiers from the Flats. Everybody was making a beeline for the coast."

The Pre-existing Presence in Chinese Organized crime

Later, when this paper discusses the efficacy of various law enforcement initiatives, a more detailed account will be provided of the structure of Chinese organized crime in South Africa and its relation to the much-abused term "Triads." For the moment it is sufficient to note that Chinese organized crime had a considerable presence in South Africa for at least a decade before abalone poaching escalated in the early 1990s. Until 1991, this presence went almost undetected. The term "organized crime" was not in the lexicon of apartheid criminal investigators. When a crime was detected, the docket was allocated to a detective to investigate. The idea of gathering intelligence on, and investigating, criminal organizations rather than individual crimes was foreign to criminal investigation in South Africa. Such work was left to the security branch, whose task was to infiltrate and disrupt anti-apartheid organizations.

The police discovered Chinese organized crime the moment they established the institutions capable of detecting it. In 1991, the police formed an Organized Crime Intelligence Unit followed shortly by the establishment of provincial organized crime units. By 1993, these new agencies had discovered the existence in South Africa of two Hong Kong-based triads — 14K and Wo Shing Wo — and a criminal organization of Taiwanese nationals called the Table Mountain Gang. The networks of the two Hong Kong-based triads extended throughout the country, from every harbor city to Johannesburg and Pretoria. Their key players were all entrepreneurs who traded a mixture of licit and illicit commodities between South Africa and Hong Kong.[17]

Counterfactual scenarios are, of course, impossible to test conclusively and it is difficult to say just how much slower the abalone trade would have taken off if these networks had not had a presence in South Africa. Nonetheless, it must count for a great deal that the infrastructure, contacts and networks of illicit trade between South Africa and East Asia were firmly established by the early 1990s. Contraband traders specialize in trade routes rather than commodities; a single trade route can host an infinite array of commodities over time, and several commodities at the same time. At present, for instance, illicit trade routes between South Africa and China carry abalone, counterfeit goods ranging from clothes to electronics to cigarettes, the precursors of at least two synthetic drugs, guns, human beings and possibly diamonds. What goes into the mix depends, in part, on the margins of return and the risk surrounding any particular commodity at a given time. In the early 1990s, the margins on South African perlemoen were rising, while risk was negligible.

Borders

Strictly speaking, it is not possible to say precisely how abalone is smuggled across South African borders, for the simple reason that our commercial ports are not monitored sufficiently to enable an accurate audit. At South African seaports, for instance, exports are not searched for contraband unless the border control authorities receive information about a particular consignment.[18] It is thus not impossible that large consignments of abalone leave South Africa's commercial ports undetected.

Having said that, what anecdotal and quantitative information we do have suggests strongly that the bulk of South African abalone is not smuggled through seaports but across uncontrolled and commercial land borders and on unlogged air flights. Once it crosses the border into neighboring states, it is in juridical territory in which there is no law against transporting or shipping South African abalone without a permit. It is exported from sea and airports across Southern Africa.

There are no specific figures to verify this account, but there is a great deal of anecdotal evidence and some strong quantitative evidence. In a recently published paper, the organization TRAFFIC cites records of the Census and Statistic Department of Hong Kong which show that 200,000kg of frozen, shucked perlemoen and over 100,000kg of dried perlemoen were imported from Mozambique, Namibia, Tanzania, Swaziland and Zimbabwe to Hong Kong between the beginning of January 2002 and the end of June 2003. As the authors of the TRAFFIC paper point out, perlemoen is endemic to none of these countries with the exception of Namibia. "It is almost certain," the authors conclude, "that all this perlemoen was illegally harvested in South Africa, smuggled into the other African countries, and then re-exported to Hong Kong."[19]

The figures are truly astounding. When dried, perlemoen shrinks to one-tenth of its original size.[20] A hundred tons of dried produce is thus equivalent to 1,000 tons of fresh abalone. The Total Annual Catch in the 2002–2003 period was less than 350 tons. This means that, over a period of two seasons at most, considerably more South African perlemoen was entering Hong Kong from Southern African ports than the entire legally harvested quota.

These figures about the various trade routes are supported by the anecdotal evidence of all 12 investigators from six different security agencies interviewed for this study. Investigators from different agencies disagree about a great deal in regard to abalone smuggling. But in regard to modes of smuggling, they are largely in agreement. The majority of the contraband is smuggled across land borders or on light aircraft. Very little is exported directly out of South African commercial ports. Two investigators in particular had, between them, been responsible for monitoring the controlled delivery of 14 batches of dried abalone over a six-year period. Of these 14 batches, four left South Africa across unmonitored land borders, three across commercial land borders, five in light aircraft and only two through commercial ports.

According to investigators, the risk of transporting abalone in light aircraft is minimal. As one investigator put it:

> There are several dozen private airfields in the northern provinces of South Africa. If you are going to fly at an altitude below radar detection, you do not even have to log a flight plan. All you need to do is log the fact that you are taking off. You can fly across a remote section of the border at low altitude with more or less 100% assurance that nobody is going to report your movement to the authorities.

At present, the SAPS is compiling a national database of every private airstrip in the country. Each is to be classified according to its risk, and each will be monitored accordingly. Depending on their geographical location, high-risk airstrips will be policed either by personnel at local police stations or by border police stationed at nearby commercial ports. The initiative is, of course, a good one, but its planners worry that those assigned to the labor-intensive tasks of policing airstrips will not "own" the initiative, and may relegate it to the lower rungs of their hierarchy of tasks.

Until recently, it has also been possible to smuggle abalone from international airports at little risk. Until 2002, border control personnel at Lanseria, Polokwane and Nelspruit airports worked during the day and not at night. Moving contraband out of these airports in the early hours of the morning incurred minimal risk. Even at a large commercial airport like Johannesburg International Airport (JIA), investigators suspect that unscheduled flights leaving JIA late at night dip below radar, collect a consignment of contraband from an airstrip, and then continue with their logged flight plans.

And yet, even if current enforcement operations do increase the risk of using private airstrips and commercial airports, other more or less risk-free modes of smuggling remain available. South Africa has struggled to patrol its vast northern land borders over the past decade. In 1998, an overstretched SAPS handed the task over to the SANDF, which also found itself with insufficient staff and resources. At the time of writing, the task of patrolling land borders is being handed back to the SAPS, and a significant investment of personnel and resources is being ploughed into the project. It is far too early to tell whether the arrangement is going to make life significantly more difficult for abalone smugglers. All investigators interviewed for this project agree that until now, at any rate, smugglers have been able to move abalone across land borders at will.

In the event that movement across land borders and from airstrips does become more difficult, smugglers will be forced to place greater reliance on South Africa's commercial ports, which have, it appears, in large part been avoided until now for fear of greater detection. There is, however, some evidence that large consignments of perlemoen have been moving through South African commercial ports undetected. In late 2004, for instance, Hong Kong customs agents contacted the South African authorities to inform them that consignments from Johannesburg International Airport, collectively weighing more than a ton, had been detected.

In conclusion, it should be pointed out that those whose primary work and vocational passion is to combat abalone smuggling have been extremely frustrated by their encounters with South African border control. As is described at length in other papers in this series, border control since 1994 has been a difficult arena, one in which several agencies have struggled to co-ordinate their respective mandates. As the various government departments involved in border control have muddled through the difficult question of how to co-ordinate their priorities, it appears that nobody in the border control environment really "took ownership" of the issue of abalone smuggling. While border control officials were certainly trained to detect abalone and were diligent in updating and distributing smuggling modus operandi, it is probably safe to say that the South African border control function has never been in a position to conduct the sort of intensive, abalone-dedicated work that might have made a difference.

Dried Abalone

Abalone can be dried, preserved for months or years, and then rehydrated and returned to its natural state. This is crucial to the smuggling process for several reasons. First, live or frozen abalone has a pungent and distinctive smell and is thus difficult to transport or ship undetected. Dried abalone can also be disguised as another product, particularly when border and law enforcement officials have not been trained to recognize it. Second, dried abalone can be preserved indefinitely, which means that it can be gathered over long periods and shipped in bulk. Finally, dried abalone shrinks to about a tenth of its original mass, making it possible to store and ship very large consignments.

The drying process is an art, one not always practiced particularly well in South Africa. In China, a natural, sun-drying process, which takes up to two months to complete, has been passed down from generation to generation. In South Africa, the sun-drying process is seldom, if ever practiced, and the skill and quality of dryers fluctuates a great deal. Typically, the abalone is shucked, simmered in a preservative chemical, hung on racks in a room heated to 38°C, and left there to dry over a three-week period. Investigators have recently found abalone ovens heated to 70°C, which speeds up the process to between four and five days. Abalone that has been dried and rehydrated unskillfully can fetch as little as a quarter of the price of sun-dried abalone.

Over the years, investigators have found drying factories in a jagged line stretching from Cape Town all the way to the northern reaches of Limpopo. They have been found in Bloemfontein, Swaziland, on the East and West Rand of Johannesburg, in Midrand, Pretoria, Hammanskraal and Musina. In the early 1990s, most of the drying premises found consisted of cupboards or pantries. Today, the typical factory is far larger. Entire houses and commercial premises are turned into makeshift drying facilities. In 2003, several tons of drying abalone were seized from commercial premises in Swaziland.

Poachers and Fishing Communities

The weakening rand, the presence of Chinese organized crime and porous borders alone do not account for the speed with which the wild perlemoen stock has been taken from the water. These factors would have counted for very little were it not possible for poachers to harvest abalone en masse over a sustained period of time under the noses of the inhabitants of the villages and towns that dot the abalone-rich coastline.

For several generations, the relationship between the coastal colored communities and the sea has been a deeply political one. While I was gathering oral testimony about Western Cape history on the Cape Flats in 2003, in the course of an entirely unrelated project, the question of the relationship between racial domination and access to the water rolled off the tongues of one interviewee after another, entirely unsolicited. Here, for example, is the testimony of a woman called Gadija Tommy, who grew up in the False Bay town of the Strand in the late 1940s and early 1950s:

> My father was a fisherman. He sold his fish from pushcarts, wandering up and down the streets all day with fresh fish. There were no jobs. It was the beginning of apartheid. Coloreds one side, Europeans the other side. So my father and my uncle sold fish because there was nothing else. At that time the fish was free for everyone. Crayfish, fish, perlemoen. You could go into the sea and get it. Then they stopped you from going into the sea. It was no longer allowed. After that, there was nothing. My uncle and my father sat at home and drank.[21]

By the early 1990s, such narratives had become an integral part of the folklore and collective memory of the Western Cape's coastal communities. The transition to democracy carried with it a universal expectation that access to the sea ought to open up quickly and dramatically. To make the politics of the moment more complicated, many members of coastal colored communities were deeply suspicious of the recently unbanned ANC. Come South Africa's first democratic election in April 1994, the colored working class would vote overwhelmingly for the ruling party of the apartheid era, the National Party, in the hope that it would provide a bulwark against their fears of an African majority government.

It was a potent combination: On the one hand the expectation that democracy ought to be coupled with the speedy implementation of a just fishing regime; on the other, a deeply held suspicion that the new government would betray the colored working class. This cocktail of expectations and fears could not have been more propitious for abalone poaching. The resource was lying there in the sea and growing more lucrative by the day. Given the politics of the moment, a great many people who had lived their lives on the coastline believed that they were entitled to it, and to a share of the benefits that accrued from harvesting it.

If one drives through Hawston, Kleinmond or Hermanus's colored township today one sees garish double-storey face brick houses standing anomalously among the tiny matchbox houses of the coastal working class. Abalone money has quite literally changed the physical landscape. No systematic, quantitative study has been done on the impact of abalone poaching on the social economy of coastal towns and villages; but anecdotal evidence suggests that while it has made a few people very rich, its benefits have been dispersed across a wide spectrum of poor households. On a field trip to Hawston in late-2002, the following story, which appears to have become legend in the town, was repeatedly told to me by several interviewees. "By 1996, 1997, the schools were half empty. The kids could earn more in a week helping the poachers than their teachers earned in a month. So who wanted to go to school?"[22]

Indeed, by the mid-1990s, poaching was highly organized, and could boast of an elaborate array of functions, primarily marshaled to avoid detection. People drawn from the ranks of professionals, the unemployed and school children found lucrative employment on the fringes of the illegal industry. As a Hawston resident told an environmental criminologist in 1995:

> . . . there are those who are involved by giving the poachers the permission to hire something of theirs. There are those who help some of the poachers who don't have cars . . . There are those who are involved by . . . carrying for the poachers . . . . And there are those who are involved because their children are involved in poaching. They can't squeal, they can't go out and tell the police. You see, everyone is so involved . . . a parent of a child, a driver, a diver. It is a money-making business.[23]

The story is not quite as simple as that, however. It is not simply a question of entire communities, motivated by a collective sense of political injustice, deciding en masse to pillage the sea in order to make money. In a survey conducted among 42 Hawston residents in 1995 — when abalone poaching in that town was close to its peak — 80% of respondents stated that the poaching of marine resources was wrong, citing the damage done to marine resources.[24] Residents' relation to poaching has obviously always been a complex one. Nonetheless, the fact remains that at a time when socio-political factors increased coastal communities' levels of tolerance toward poaching, the illegal harvesting of abalone became an extremely lucrative activity and a livelihood for many coastal households.

Whether the speedy implementation of a more equitable fishing regime in the mid-1990s would have curtailed abalone poaching is a moot point; another counterfactual scenario that is impossible to demonstrate. Perhaps the gap between the returns on illicit and legal harvesting was always too great, and any regulatory regime would have struggled.

Notes

1. R. Tarr, *Perlemoen: The South African Abalone*, <http://www.environment.gov.za>, 2003, viewed in January 2005.

2. T. Hecht, "Behavioural thermoregulation of the abalone Haliotis Midae and the implications for intensive culture," *Aquaculture* 126 (1994): 171–181; R. Tarr, "Abalone," in A. Payne and R. Crawford (eds.) *Oceans of Life off Southern Africa*, (Cape Town: Vlaeberg, 1989); A. Willock, M. Bergener and A. Sancho *First Choice or Fallback? An examination of issues relating to the application of Appendix III of CITES to marine species*, TRAFFIC International, (2004).

3. R. Tarr, *Perlemoen, the South African abalone.*

4. See, *inter alia*, M. Hauck and N.A. Sweijd, "A case study of abalone poaching in South

Africa and its impact on fisheries management," *ICES Journal of Marine Science*, 56 (1999): 1024–1032; M. Hauck, *Crime, conservation and community development: Ecological criminology and the case study of abalone poaching*, Masters thesis, University of Cape Town, (1997).

5. R. Tarr, *Perlemoen, the South African abalone*.

6. Author's interview with Marcel Kroese, deputy director of monitoring and surveillance, Marine and Coastal Management, January 2005.

    To make matters worse, South Africa's stock of wild abalone simultaneously came under threat from a natural predator. Baby abalone take shelter from predators under the spines of sea urchins, enabling them to survive in areas where there is little natural shelter. In the early 1990s, for reasons marine scientists have yet to determine, a large population of Cape rock lobsters moved into the inshore coastal region between Hermanus and Hangklip, virtually destroying the sea urchin population in the area, and thus depriving baby abalone of a primary source of protection. Scientists believe that illegal harvesting would have taken far longer to decimate the perlemoen population in the absence of the rock lobster migration. See R. Tarr, *Perlemoen, the South African abalone*.

7. I say "wild" perlemoen because perlemoen farming is growing apace. At the time of writing there are 11 perlemoen farms in South Africa, which, combined, are responsible for exporting more abalone than the wild harvest.

8. See <www.reservebank.co.za>.

9. This information was gleaned from an interview with a law enforcement official. During the course of the research I interviewed people from several security agencies who had been involved in investigating the abalone trade: The SAPS Endangered Species Unit, the SAPS Organised Crime Unit, SAPS Crime Intelligence, the Justice Department's Directorate of Special Operations, the National Intelligence Agency and the South African Secret Service. Their names are not published because they prefer to remain anonymous.

10. Every law enforcement official interviewed for this study was asked to calculate prices and profit margins at every point in the value chain. Everybody offered different figures, leading to the inevitable conclusion that law enforcers simply do not know. One is thus left with the trite but undeniably correct statement that trading in contraband abalone is very lucrative!

11. P. Gastrow, *Triad Societies and Chinese Organised Crime in South Africa*, Pretoria, Institute for Security Studies, Paper 48, (2001).

12. <www.homeoffice.gov.uk>.

13. J. Roth, *The Radetzky March* trans. Joachim Neugroschel, (New York: Overlook, 2002), 192 (first published as *Radetzkymarsch*, Berlin, 1932).

14. T. Leggett, *Rainbow Vice: The drugs and sex industries in the new South Africa*, (London: Zed, 2001), 36.

15. T. Leggett, *Rainbow Vice*, p 36.

16. See, *inter alia*, "Tik case: Focus on immigration," 21/01/2005 at <http://www.news24.com/News24/South_Africa/News/0,,2-7-1442_1650562,00.html>.

17. P. Gastrow, *Triad Societies and Chinese Organised Crime in South Africa*.

18. With the exception, in recent times, of cargo bound for the United States. Under the recently implemented Container Security Initiative (CSI), American border control officials risk-profile every US-bound cargo container at the point of origin. The CSI is a counter-terrorism initiative and aims to prevent the smuggling of nuclear, chemical and biological weapons. It has been operational at South African ports since mid-2004.

19. Willock et al., *First Choice or Fallback?*, 30.

20. Author's interview with Angus MacKenzie, chief oceanographic technician, abalone research: Inshore resources, Marine and Coastal Management, January 2005.
21. Author's interview with Gadija Tommy, Heideveld, Cape Town, 12 June 2003.
22. Author's interview with Hawston resident, 22 November 2002.
23. M. Hauck, *Crime, conservation and community development*, 112.
24. Ibid, pp 115–116.

Toxic Exports: Despite Global Treaty, Hazardous Waste Trade Continues

10

Jennifer Clapp

In the middle of the night on August 19, 2006, hundreds of tons of toxic oil sludge were secretly dumped at numerous locations throughout the city of Abidjan in the Ivory Coast. This waste, containing lethal substances, including hydrogen sulphide, phenols, and caustic soda, was brought to West Africa from Europe by ship operators seeking to illegally dispose of the waste in order to save on the cost associated with disposing of it properly.[1] The toxic sludge originated on the Trafigura, a Panamanian ship chartered by a Swiss-based oil and metals trading transnational corporation. The operators of the ship originally tried to offload the toxic oil sludge in Amsterdam, but after they were informed that it would cost over US$300,000 to dispose of it there, it ended up being dumped surreptitiously in Abidjan.[2] 17 people died immediately from exposure to the waste, and some 30,000 people sustained serious injuries associated with their exposure to it. Over 30,000 Ivoirians launched a civil lawsuit in London against the company. A settlement was paid out in 2009, though the firm continues to deny any wrongdoing, insisting that the waste was not harmful.[3]

This story illustrates the extent to which the management of toxic waste has become an increasingly global business. The worldwide generation of hazardous waste is currently around 440 million tons, of which an estimated 10 percent makes its way across international boundaries.[4] A variety of industries generate toxic wastes, ranging from chemicals to electronics and from plastics to metal plating. These toxic wastes have adverse affects on the natural environment and have been linked with various health problems, including respiratory diseases as well as immune and reproductive disorders. These environmental and health concerns make decisions about where to dispose of toxic waste highly contentious politically, especially when transboundary issues are involved.

Hazardous materials are nonetheless transported with relative ease from one country to another, albeit subject to certain rules. The international trade in hazardous wastes is governed by various national and international regulations, such as the Basel Convention, which purport to deal with wastes in an environmentally sound manner. Although the purpose of global regulations is to prevent adverse environmental outcomes, the existing agreements nonetheless contain several key weaknesses or "cracks" that allow the trade to continue, often in ways that fall short of environmental standards.

The Rise of the Waste Trade and the Emergence of Global Rules to Govern It

Prior to the late 1980s, there was little regulation at either the national or the international level to control the transboundary trade in toxic wastes. The bulk of the hazardous waste trade flowed between rich countries, and thrived on regulatory differences between countries.[5] However, it is estimated that at least twenty percent of these wastes also made their way to poorer, developing countries, where costs were lower and environmental regulations weaker.[6] A number of high profile cases of hazardous waste exports from firms in industrialized to developing countries in the 1980s and the early 1990s brought international attention to this issue. Wastes were shipped from countries with high disposal costs and strict regulations to countries with low disposal costs and weak regulations. Because most poor countries did not have the equivalent capacity to dispose of wastes in an environmentally sound manner, concern mounted over the trade in wastes between rich and poor countries.[7] Toxic wastes sent to poor countries were often disposed of in ways that led to adverse and harmful environmental effects. For example, the toxic waste originating from an Italian firm dumped in a Nigerian farmer's field and the toxic fly ash from a Philadelphia waste broker that wound up littering the beaches of Guinea and Haiti in the 1980s were early cases demonstrating the health and environmental impacts of careless disposal.[8] This is in stark contrast to the way toxic wastes are stored in rich industrialized countries, where storage and disposal facilities have to meet high safety and environmental standards.

By the late 1980s, many developing countries were outraged by what they viewed as negligent dumping practices by the industrialized world under the guise of trade. This provided the impetus for the development of strong international, regional, and national regulations to control these particular trade flows. At the international level, the Basel Convention on the Transboundary Movement of Hazardous Wastes and their Disposal seeks to regulate the trade of toxic wastes and, in particular, aims to protect developing countries from unwanted toxic waste imports. The Basel Convention was adopted in 1989 and came into legal force in 1992 after being ratified by 20 countries. The convention establishes that parties should reduce their exports of toxic wastes to a minimum and that wastes should only be traded internationally if the exporting state does not have the capacity to dispose of them in an environmentally sound manner or if the wastes constitute "raw materials" (i.e., they are to be "recycled") to be used by the importing countries. The convention also requires parties to refrain from exporting wastes to states that have banned such imports. Additionally, it stipulates that parties should refrain from trade in hazardous wastes with non-parties, unless a bilateral or regional agreement with equivalent or more stringent regulations exists. In the case of hazardous waste trade between parties, the convention requires that states from which exports of toxic wastes originate give prior notification to states where the wastes are to be shipped, and receive the importing country's written consent before the exporter can send the shipment. In this way, parties have the right to refuse imports of toxic waste if they so choose.

At the national level, a number of countries have passed laws regarding waste trade. Many developing countries have banned the importation of toxic wastes, and some industrialized countries have banned their exportation to developing countries. In addition, there are a number of regional waste trade agreements that place an outright ban on the trade in wastes between rich and poor countries. These include the 1991 Bamako Convention, which covers sub-Saharan Africa and prohibits the import of toxic waste to the region; the 1995 Waigani Convention, banning the import of toxic wastes into the South Pacific region; the 1996 Izmir Protocol, which prohibits the trade in toxic waste between OECD and non-OECD countries in the Mediterranean region; and finally, a European Union regulation, passed in 1997, banning the export of hazardous waste to non-OECD countries.[9]

The adoption of these national and international rules that sought to control the transnational trade in toxic waste resulted in a significant reduction in exports of toxic waste for disposal in developing countries by the early 1990s. At the same time, however, a new problem emerged. It soon became apparent that instead of exporting wastes for *disposal*, waste exporters shifted their business toward the export of toxic wastes to developing countries for *recycling*. There was, in effect, a loophole in the rules that allowed waste transfer to continue — legally — under the auspices of recycling. While recycling may imply environmentally sound waste management, in many cases, particularly in developing countries, it has resulted in detrimental environmental outcomes. A large proportion of toxic wastes destined for recycling operations in the developing world are not, in fact, recyclable. In addition, the process of recovering useful elements from these wastes often leaves hazardous by-products that must then be disposed of.[10] For example, throughout the 1990s the UK exported spent mercury to South Africa for recycling; poor waste management, however, claimed a number of lives and resulted in severe soil and water contamination.[11] Several Southeast Asian and Latin American countries faced similar environmental and health effects as of result of recycling imported lead-acid batteries, used plastic, and scrap metals.[12]

Attempts to close this recycling loophole in the Basel Convention became the subject of a heated debate over the course of the mid-1990s. Poor countries and environmental NGOs argued for a ban on this type of trade between rich and poor countries, while most rich countries and the global recycling lobby argued against it. Painstaking negotiations finally yielded an amendment to the convention, the Basel Ban Amendment. The Amendment explicitly prohibited trade between the rich, industrialized countries (those listed in Annex VII) and developing countries of waste destined for recycling operations.[13] Though the amendment was adopted in 1995, it has not yet come into legal force. This amendment, which has come be known as the Basel Ban, required ratification by three-fourths of the parties that adopted it (82 countries were present when it was adopted) in order to come into force. The number of required ratifications was presumed by many to be 62. However, when the 62nd ratification was deposited with the Basel Secretariat in 2006, it emerged that the amendment requires ratification by three-fourths of the parties at the time it was adopted. Under this rule, as of March 2008, the Ban Amendment was still 18 ratifications short of coming into force.[14]

In addition to the fact that the Basel Ban Amendment is not yet in force, there are several additional weaknesses in the existing waste trade regime. Although the volume of waste trade to poor countries has decreased substantially since the mid-1990s, its continuation in several forms is still significant enough to raise concern.[15] One of the difficulties is getting key players to commit to the existing rules and abide by them, which underscores the frailty of the convention's enforcement mechanism. Another cause for concern is the uncertainty regarding the legality of several forms of waste trade that have emerged over the past decade: The export of decommissioned ships for "shipbreaking" and the export of electronic wastes for recycling in developing countries. Finally, quite apart from the regulatory regime dealing with trade flows in the strict sense, there remains the possibility that an increasing share of the world's toxic wastes will shift toward developing countries as a result of waste generating industries relocating from their home bases in the industrialized world to more attractive investment locations in poorer countries. Unless rules are also put into place to govern foreign direct investment in "toxic" industries, hazardous wastes may still wind up in other countries via this alternate route.

The Difficulty of Getting Key Players to Abide by the Rules

Though the national and international rules controlling the trade in wastes have become stronger over the years, getting key players to first commit to and then abide by these rules has been difficult in practice. A major problem is that not all countries that are important participants in the global waste trade are parties to the Basel Convention. As of November 2009, some 20 years after its adoption, the convention has 172 parties, which is an impressive participation rate. However, this does not include the United States, which is a major player in the generation and trade in toxic waste. Several attempts have been made in the United States to pass legislation enabling ratification of the Basel Convention, but these have been unsuccessful. The US government argues that its own laws are compatible with the regulations stipulated in the convention, and as such that its failure to ratify the treaty does not result in greater trade in hazardous waste. However, as will be discussed below, the US is a major source of continued trade in hazardous waste in the form of electronic waste and toxic ships.

In addition to the difficulty of getting key generators of toxic waste to sign onto the agreement, it has taken much longer to garner the necessary ratifications for the Amendment than it took for the original convention to enter into force, which leaves the question of export of toxic waste for recycling purposes in a legal limbo. Until the Basel Ban Amendment becomes legally binding, the parties are powerless to close the "recycling" loophole because of the ambiguity about its legality. A group of countries, referred to as JUSCANZ, including Japan, the US, Canada, Australia and New Zealand, have argued strongly against the need for the Basel Ban Amendment, which has not helped in terms of garnering the needed number of ratifications for it to come into force.

In the meantime, rich to poor country exports of waste for recycling has continued, albeit in smaller quantities than was the case during the mid-1980s. The United States, for example, as a non-party to the Basel Convention, has continued to export toxic waste to developing countries. In the late 1990s, for example, a US chemical firm, HoltraChem Manufacturing, attempted to export spent mercury waste from its Maine plant to India. HoltraChem used mercury to produce chlorine and other chemicals for use in the paper industry.

When the company's Maine plant closed in September 2000, it left behind 260,000 pounds of mercury waste. HoltraChem announced that it would sell the waste to a broker who planned to ship it to India, already the largest recipient of mercury exports from the United States.[16] News of this planned shipment sparked a huge controversy in both the United States and India. The US government claimed that the spent mercury was a metal with trade value, not merely waste, exempting it from regulations on waste exports. In the end though, the Indian government refused the shipment, which was returned to the United States.[17]

Quite apart from the difficulties of increasing the number of parties to the Basel Convention, the existing regulatory regime suffers from poor enforcement. Indeed, even countries that have ratified the Basel Convention have been known to violate the terms of the agreement. In 1999, a Japanese firm shipped 2,700 metric tons of waste for disposal to the Philippines. Labeled as paper for recycling, the shipment was in fact a mix of hazardous medical and industrial wastes unsuitable for recycling.[18] Once the shipment was revealed, the Japanese government took the wastes back. Another example is India, which despite its status as a party to the Basel Convention, continues to import hazardous wastes for recycling purposes. In fact, between March 1998 and March 1999 the country imported more than 100,000 metric tons of toxic wastes, including used batteries, zinc ash and residue, copper cables potentially coated with PVC, and toxic metal.[19] These wastes came from both rich countries and other developing countries. Although India is a party to the Basel Convention and has national laws banning the import of toxic waste, it has not yet ratified the Basel Ban Amendment, and its laws allow certain hazardous wastes to be imported for recycling.

Such cases have continued, even amongst countries that are parties to agreements seeking to curb the waste trade. The illegal dumping of toxic waste in Ivory Coast in 2006 is a prime example. The Ivory Coast is a signatory to the Bamako Convention, which should have signaled that it was not open for waste imports in the first place. Both Panama and Switzerland are parties to the Basel Convention and have ratified the Basel Ban Amendment, such that the waste should never have been exported to Ivory Coast in the first place. But because the operation was carried out illegally, under the cover of night and in deception, it was virtually impossible to have been able to prevent it.

Recycling Loophole Widens: The Trade in E-Waste and Toxic Ships

Two major, additional challenges to the Basel Convention have emerged over the past decade that relate directly to the problem of recycling of toxic waste in developing countries. Although wastes destined for recycling operations are technically covered by the treaty, they can easily escape the rules of the convention when they are shipped under the guise of 'reuse' or are not declared to be waste (or in the case of ships, out of commission) until they reach their destination. Because of these loopholes, it is difficult for exporters and importers to enforce the rules of the convention.

One challenge in this respect is the export of ships containing toxic materials to developing countries for scrapping or breaking. Since the mid-1990s, there have been a number of ships exported from industrial countries to scrap yards in developing countries, most commonly India and Bangladesh, for decommissioning. These ships often contain highly toxic materials such as polychlorinated biphenyls (PCBs) and asbestos. In developing countries, ships are commonly dismantled in dangerous and environmentally unsound conditions. Because the ships are technically in use when exported and often not designated as waste material until on the high seas or until they reach their final destination, they have frequently escaped control under the rules of the Basel Convention.[20] Environmental NGOs such as the Basel Action Network (BAN) and Greenpeace have launched campaigns to halt this practice by exposing the failure of exporting states to enforce the Basel Convention when toxic ships are exported from their ports.

There has recently been some success with the efforts to raise awareness about the problems associated with toxic ship breaking, as was seen with the 2006 decision of the French government to halt the export of the ship, the *Clemenceau*, which had been destined for scrapping in India. But other attempts have continued. In 2008 a US cruise ship containing PCBs, asbestos, and radioactive materials, the former *SS Independence* (which had been renamed several times) was exported for breaking, contravening regulations of the US government regarding the export of toxic substances. When the US Environmental Protection Agency sought to enforce its regulations, the firm that owned the ship changed its application to say that the ship was not destined for breaking, but was rather being sold for re-use. The ship lingered in the Middle East for over a year before it attempted to land at the Alang Shipyard in India in late 2009. The Indian government refused to accept the ship after ascertaining that was operating under falsified documents.[21]

The export of electronic waste (e-waste), including discarded computers, mobile phones and other electronic equipment, has also been on the rise since the late 1990s and has continued unabated since that time. E-waste, which contains numerous toxic components, including heavy metals and polyvinyl chloride (PVC), has been one of the fastest growing waste streams in industrial countries in the past decade. The growth in this type of waste is not surprising given the extent of technological change and innovation, particularly with mobile units which people in industrialized countries upgrade at a particularly rapid pace. It has emerged in recent years that much of this waste has been exported to developing countries in Asia and Africa, without being subjected to the Basel Convention rules on notification and consent and despite bans in those countries on the import of toxic waste.[22] Often these wastes are exported under the pretense of reuse, when in practice they are mined for parts or simply land-filled outright. The conditions under which these e-wastes are recycled and disposed in these locations are typically very dangerous and environmentally unsound. Environmental groups have conducted extensive research into the cases of China and Nigeria, where they found extremely disturbing practices of recycling and disposal, which resulted in toxic contamination of water, air and soil.[23]

Several factors have contributed to the continued export of e-waste to developing countries, including the fact that it can escape control when it is exported for reuse even though the majority is broken and beyond repair, and the lack of knowledge of the hazardous nature of second-hand electronic components on the part of customs officials. Environmental groups such as BAN have called for pre-testing of second-hand electronics before shipment to determine whether they are suitable for reuse or simply hazardous wastes, which would then be bound by the rules of the Basel Convention. Despite the awareness raised by these groups regarding the export of e-waste to developing counties, the practice has unfortunately continued.

Foreign Investment in Toxic Waste Generating Industries Opens a Further Loophole

Sadly, other avenues for exporting toxic wastes to developing countries also exist. It has become increasingly apparent that the developing world's share of toxic waste generation, especially in the manufacturing sector, is growing.[24] If regulations become tighter on the transnational trade in wastes, this may lead to increased investment in toxic industries in countries with more lenient waste disposal regulations. The end result is the same: More toxic waste is disposed of in countries with weaker environmental regulations. This phenomenon is already a problem, though the extent to which it is significant is subject to debate.[25] Some argue that while in theory such pollution havens are a possibility, in practice they have been more elusive. But in the case of toxic wastes, there does appear to be a clear movement of some of the hazardous waste-generating industries to relocate in order to take advantage of less stringent environmental regulations in other countries.[26]

Regardless of their motivations for relocating, many firms do take advantage of more lenient regulations where possible. For example, during the 1970s a number of Japanese-based hazardous waste-generating industries relocated to other Asian countries.[27] More recently, the *maquiladora* zone in Mexico represents a fairly obvious example of the migration of toxic waste-generating industries to a developing nation, successfully transferring wastes to other countries via investment rather than trade. These industrial factories are US-owned plants located just across the Mexican border. Originally set up to produce goods, such as garments, for export to the United States, an increasing number of industries that produce large amounts of toxic wastes have been converging there over the past two decades. These include plants in the electronics, chemicals, and furniture sectors.[28] By the early 1990s, the vast majority of *maquiladoras* along the US-Mexican border were generators of toxic waste, and at the same time the total number of these firms increased substantially.[29]

Technically, this increase in toxic wastes Mexico had to contend with should not have had an adverse effect on the local environment. In addition to Mexican law, the 1983 La Paz agreement between Mexico and the United States requires the return to the United States of any toxic waste generated by the *maquiladoras*. But in the early 1990s, less than three percent of the firms producing hazardous waste were returning it to the United States.[30] Both the United States and Mexico admitted at that time to not knowing the amount of toxic waste generated in the *maquiladora* zone.[31] After the adoption of NAFTA in 1994, improved monitoring systems were put in place to track the waste. Some improvements have occurred; figures show that the return of hazardous wastes to the United States has risen to 25–30 percent.[32] At the same time, accurate figures on toxic waste generation along the border are widely recognized to be elusive, and there are continuing reports of illegal waste dumping along the border.[33] NAFTA is one of the more progressive trade agreements in terms of acknowledging pollution havens as a possibility, and it even attempts to prevent them from occurring by asking treaty parties to refrain from relocating toxic industries in order to take advantage of lenient environmental regulations in host countries. However, enforcement of this provision has proven difficult, as evidenced by the continuing relocation of toxic waste-generating industries to Mexico.

Many environmental activists fear that, in the absence of global rules aimed at controlling foreign direct investment in toxic waste industries, more "*maquiladora* zones*" will emerge in other parts of the developing world.[34] Some see this as a process that is already underway. For example, multinational corporations (MNCs) in the chemicals industry relocated much of their production to Asia, the Pacific Rim, and Latin America over the course of the 1990s, as demand fell in the West and rose in newly industrializing countries.[35] Instead of exporting to these regions, MNCs in the chemicals industry reasoned that it would be easier to set up shop closer to their markets. In addition to saving on labor and transportation costs, these firms have in some cases also acknowledged that environmental cost factors have played a role. Bayer, for example, has admitted that stringent environmental regulations in Europe have been a main contributor to the movement of their production facilities to Asia.[36]

In addition, there have also been growing concerns about double standards practiced by the chemicals industry, whereby in their home country MNCs are more stringent with their operations than in developing countries.[37] The December 1984 accident in Bhopal stands out as a clear case of the dangers of double standards in the industry. In this case, Union Carbide followed vastly different environmental, health and safety standards in its India plant compared to standards in its US plant, even though both plants produced the same chemicals.[38] The Bhopal case appears not to be an isolated incident. For example, according to one U.N. study, over half of the MNCs surveyed in the Asia-Pacific region followed standards that were lower than those to which they adhered in developed countries.[39]

The Way Ahead

As long as waste disposal regulations differ among countries and the global regulatory framework for international trade in toxic wastes has serious flaws, large quantities of hazardous wastes will continue to be precariously managed, damaging the environment and human health, and transboundary waste movements will persist. Policy efforts must therefore be made on several fronts.

First, there must be a firm commitment by all countries to adopt and implement the rules set out in the Basel Convention, including the ratification and implementation of the Basel Ban Amendment. It is imperative that all countries not only adopt but also abide by these agreements in order to prevent future incidents of waste exports to developing countries that are ill equipped to handle them. Moreover, there is also a pressing need to recognize that the Basel Convention and the Basel Ban Amendment do not in themselves, even when properly implemented, end the risks associated with the trade in hazardous wastes.

Second, it is also essential that measures be taken to reduce the overall generation of toxic wastes. Governments, rich and poor alike, must enact tighter regulations on firms regarding emissions controls and waste management, and must promote policies to encourage the creation and adoption of clean production technology. While this may be unpopular amongst governments and firms because of the costs involved, it is a vital step. A major survey of MNCs has shown that the primary motivator for firms to improve their environmental practice is government regulation.[40] Although regulations are a strong motivator, over the past decade governments have preferred to rely instead on voluntary measures by firms to promote cleaner production. While such measures might encourage firm participation precisely because they are involved in setting the voluntary standards, in practice such measures have typically been less stringent than government-based regulation.[41]

Finally, rules governing foreign direct investment in "toxic" industries need to be strengthened. A binding global agreement governing the environmental practices of transnational corporations could go some way toward ensuring that stronger rules are implemented. Such an agreement could include performance-based criteria with respect to hazardous waste management and clean production. A first step might be an agreement requiring transnational firms to abide by their home country's environmental regulations when host country regulations are not equally stringent. In addition, a requirement to publicly disclose information with respect to hazardous waste generation and its export should also be considered. These measures would help prevent MNCs from taking advantage of regulatory differences between countries. Unless a more comprehensive approach is embraced, the remaining cracks in the international regulatory regime will continue to allow the international trade in toxic wastes to thrive.

Notes

1. Meirion Jones and Liz MacKean, "Dirty Tricks and Toxic Waste in Ivory Coast," *BBC Newsnight*, May 13, 2009. http://news.bbc.co.uk/2/hi/programmes/newsnight/8048626.stm
2. Lydia Polgreen and Marlise Simons, "Global Sludge Ends in Tragedy for Ivory Coast," *New York Times*, October 2, 2006; Debora MacKenzie, "Toxic Waste Mystery in Ivory Coast Deepens," *New Scientist*, September 15, 2006.
3. Trafigura Reaches a Global Settlement: http://www.guardian.co.uk/world/2009/sep/16/trafigura-toxic-dump-global-settlement; Trader Trafigura Says Settled Ivorian Waste Case: http://www.reuters.com/article/latestCrisis/idUSLK593911.
4. The figure for total waste generation is from the preface to the 1999 version of the Basel Convention. The estimate for the amount of wastes traded is from Christoph Hilz, *The International Toxic Waste Trade*, (New York: Van Nostrand Reinhold, 1992), 20. These are only estimates, and the precise amounts of toxic waste generated and traded internationally are not known because of discrepancies in the definitions of waste and in the diverging criteria for reporting the trade in those wastes.
5. For a discussion of the trade in toxic waste among OECD countries, see Kate O'Neill, *Waste Trading Among Rich Nations*, (Cambridge, MA: MIT Press, 2000).

6. Jonathan Krueger, *International Trade and the Basel Convention*, (London: RIIA, 1999), 14; Hilz, *The International Toxic Waste Trade*, 20–21.

7. The term "rich" refers here primarily to the industrialized countries of the Organization for Economic Cooperation and Development (OECD); the term "poor" on the other hand, refers primarily to those developing countries and Eastern European countries that are not members of the OECD.

8. For a full discussion of these and other dumping incidents in the developing world, see Jennifer Clapp, *Toxic Exports: The Transfer of Hazardous Wastes from Rich to Poor Countries*, (Ithaca: Cornell University Press, 2001), 32–38.

9. For further details on these regional agreements, see the Basel Action Network website: http://www.ban.org.

10. Jim Puckett. "Disposing of the Waste Trade: Closing the Recycling Loophole," *The Ecologist* 24 (1994): 2, 53–58.

11. For a complete discussion of spent mercury exports to South Africa, see F. Kockott, *Wasted Lives: Mercury Waste Recycling at Thor Chemicals*. (Amsterdam: Greenpeace International and Earthlife Africa, 1994).

12. These cases were publicized by NGOs. See, for example, Madeline Cobbing, *Lead, Astray: The Poisonous Lead Battery Waste Trade*, (Amsterdam: Greenpeace International, 1994); Bill Moyers and CIR, *Global Dumping Ground*. (Cambridge: Lutterworth Press, 1994), 52–61; and Greenpeace, *The Waste Invasion of Asia*. (Sydney: Australia: Greenpeace, 1994), 20–22.

13. Annex VII includes member states of the EU and the OECD, and Liechtenstein.

14. See Basel Action Network, Basel Convention Ban Amendment — Entry into Force Country Analysis. June 2008. Posted at: http://www.ban.org/Library/BanRatPartiesCOP9_CountryAnalysis.pdf.

15. The Basel Action Network (BAN) maintains a website that tracks waste transfers from rich to poor countries: http://www.ban.org.

16. Susan Young, "Fed Refuse HoltraChem Mercury, Company May Send Chemical to India," *Bangor Daily News*, 17 November 2000; Danielle Knight, "Outcry over US Toxic Chemical Shipment to India," *Inter Press Service*, 11 December 2000.

17. Danielle Knight, "Controversy Around Mercury Shipment from US to India," *Inter Press Service*, 25 January 2001; Susan Young, "New Home for Mercury Hard to Find," *Bangor Daily News*, 28 March 2001.

18. "Illegal Dumping," *Mainichi Daily News* (Niigata, Japan), 13 January 2000.

19. Greenpeace International, "Toxic Waste — Poisons from the Industrialized World," http://www.ban.org

20. Judit Kanthak, *Ships for Scrap: Steel and Toxic Wastes for Asia*, (Hamburg: Greenpeace, 1999).

21. See Basel Action Network, "Indian Government Blocks US Toxic Ship," November 9, 2009, at: http://www.ban.org/ban_news/2009/091109_indian_government_blocks_toxic_us_ship.html and *BBC US*, Toxic Ship Banned in India, November 10, 2009, at http://news.bbc.co.uk/2/hi/8351957.stm.

22. See Alastair Iles, "Mapping Environmental Justice in Technology Flows: Computer Waste Impacts in Asia," *Global Environmental Politics*, 4, 4 (2004): 76–107; Henrik Selin and Stacy VanDeveer, "Raising Global Standards: Hazardous Substances and E-Waste Management in the European Union," *Environment*, 48, 10 (2006): 7–18.

23. Basel Action Network, "The Digital Dump: Exporting Re-Use and Abuse to Africa," 2005, posted at: http://www.ban.org/Library/TheDigitalDump.pdf and Basel Action Network,

"Exporting Harm: The High-Tech Trashing of Asia," 2002, posted at: http://www.ban.org/E-waste/technotrashfinalcomp.pdf.

24. Patrick Low, "The International Location of Polluting Industries and the Harmonization of Environmental Standards," in H. Munoz and R. Rosenberg (eds.) *Difficult Liaison: Trade and the Environment in the Americas*, (London: Transaction Publishers, 1993), 25.

25. See Eric Neumayer, "Pollution Havens: An Analysis of Policy Options for Dealing With an Elusive Phenomenon," *Journal of Environment and Development*, 10, 2 (2001), 147–177.

26. H. Jeffrey Leonard, *Pollution and the Struggle for the World Product: Multinational Corporations, Environment and International Comparative Advantage*, (Cambridge: Cambridge University Press, 1988), 232; see also Jennifer Clapp, *Toxic Exports*.

27. Hans Maull, "Japan's Global Environmental Policies," *The Pacific Review*, 4, 3 (1991), 254–62; Derek Hall, "Dying Geese: Japan and the International Political Ecology of Southeast Asia" (paper presented at the annual meeting of the International Studies Association, Toronto, Canada, March 1997).

28. Edward Williams, "The Maquiladora Industry and Environmental Degradation in the United States-Mexico Borderlands," *St. Mary's Law Journal*, 27, 4 (1996), 777–779.

29. Leslie Sklair, *Assembling for Development*, (San Diego: University of California, Center for US-Mexican Studies, 1993), 79–80.

30. Leslie Sklair, L. *Assembling for Development*, 253–4; Diane Perry et al.. "Bi-national Management of Hazardous Waste: The Maquiladora Industry at the U.S.-Mexico Border," *Environmental Management* 14, 4 (1990), 442.

31. John Harbison and Taunya McLarty, "A Move Away from the Moral Arbitrariness of Maquila and NAFTA-Related Toxic Harms," *UCLA Journal of Environmental Law and Policy*, 14, 1 (1995–1996), 6.

32. Cyrus Reed, "Hazardous Waste Management on the Border: Problems with Practices and Oversight Continue," *Borderlines* 6:5 (1998). http://www.us-mex.org/borderlines/1998/bl46/bl46haz.html (May 23, 2001). See also HAZTRAKS at http://www.epa.gov/earth1r6/6en/h/haztraks/haztraks.htm.

33. Enrique Medina, "Overview of Transboundary Pollution Issues Along the Mexico-U.S. Border," in Thomas La Point, Fred Price, and Edward Little, (eds.) *Environmental Toxicology and Risk Assessment: Fourth Volume*, (West Conshohocken, PA: American Society for Testing and Materials, 1996), 9.

34. Jennifer Clapp, *Toxic Exports*, 113–120.

35. P. Abrahams, "The Dye is Cast by Growth and Costs," *Financial Times*, 31 May 1994; Andrew Wood, "Asia-Pacific: Rising Star on the Chemical Stage," *Chemical Week* (February 15, 1995), 36.

36. P. Abrahams, "The Dye is Cast by Growth and Costs," *Financial Times*, 31 May 1994.

37. Birtha Bergsto and Sylvi Endresen. "From North to South: A Locational Shift in Industrial Pollution?" FIL Working Paper no. 6, in Bersto et al., (eds.) *Industrial Pollution in the South*, (Oslo: FIL, 1995), 19.

38. Thomas Gladwin, "A Case Study of the Bhopal Tragedy," in C. Pearson, (ed.) *Multinational Corporations, the Environment, and the Third World*, (Durham, NC: Duke University Press, 1987).

39. ESCAP/UNCTC, *Environmental Aspects of Transnational Corporation Activities in Pollution-Intensive Industries in Selected Asian and Pacific Developing Countries*, (Bangkok: UN/ESCAP, 1990), 61.

40. UNCTAD, "Programme on TNCs," *Environmental Management in Transnational Corporations:*

Report on the Benchmark Corporate Environmental Survey, (New York: United Nations, 1993), 38.

41. See, for example, Peter Utting and Jennifer Clapp. *Corporate Accountability and Sustainable Development*, (Delhi: Oxford University Press, 2008).

11 The Stolen Forests: Inside the Covert War on Illegal Logging

Raffi Khatchadourian

The town of Suifenhe, a former Russian imperial outpost on the Trans-Siberian Railway, has belonged to China since the nineteen-forties, and occupies a broad valley in northern Manchuria. From a distance, its homes and factories appear to cling to a rail yard, with tracks fanning out into a vast latticework of iron as they emerge from the Russian border. Suifenhe is a place of singular purpose. Nearly every train from Russia brings in just one commodity: Wood — oak, ash, linden, and other high-value species. There is also poplar, aspen, and larch, and occasionally great trunks of Korean pine, a species that was logged by the Soviets until there was almost none left to cut down. In a year, more than five billion pounds of wood cross over from Primorski Krai, the neighboring province in the Russian Far East. Hundreds of railcars enter Suifenhe every day, many loaded beyond capacity with logs. The wood is shuttled between mills by hand, often six men to a log. Other workers, many of whom are migrants from elsewhere in China, operate cranes to empty the rail carriages, and at sundown they bring the machinery to rest, with beams pointing upward, like arms outstretched, waiting for the rush of timber that will arrive the following day.

On a warm afternoon last May, an environmental activist named Alexander von Bismarck and a man whom I will call Wu De entered Suifenhe by taxi. They had brought with them surveillance equipment; they were working for a nonprofit group called the Environmental Investigation Agency, which tries to uncover how plants, wildlife, and industrial chemicals are smuggled. Von Bismarck is the organization's executive director, and one of the world's leading experts on timber smuggling. He is thirty-six years old, trim and tall, with fiery red hair, but he possesses a quiet bearing that allows him to recede in a crowd. (Most people know him as Sascha, but a few friends call him RoboCop, because once, while in the tropics, he insisted on jogging in hundred-degree heat.) Wu is from Southeast Asia, but he is fluent in Mandarin Chinese. Both men had prepared false identities, as employees of Axion Trading — one of several companies created by E.I.A. as fronts.

Chances are good that if an item sold in the United States was recently made in China using oak or ash, the wood was imported from Russia through Suifenhe. Because as much as half of the hardwood from Primorski Krai is harvested in violation of Russian law — either by large companies working with corrupt provincial officials or by gangs of men in remote villages — it is likely that any given piece of wood in the city has been logged illegally. This wide-scale theft empowers mafias, robs the Russian government of revenue, and assists in the destruction of one of the most precious ecosystems in the Northern Hemisphere. Lawmakers in the province have called for "emergency measures" to stem the flow of illegal wood, and Russia's Minister of Natural Resources has said that in the region "there has emerged an entire criminal branch connected with the preparation, storage, transportation, and selling of stolen timber."

When von Bismarck and Wu arrived in Suifenhe, they saw traces of this immense crime — a destructive black market merging into the global economy. This is what they had come to investigate.

John le Carré once described a spy as a "silent spectator," someone who builds himself a persona from "all the odd bits of his life that are left over after he has given the rest away." When constructing his aliases, von Bismarck often draws upon his personal history. (He has asked me not to explain which bits, so as not to ruin his cover.) As the great-great-grandnephew of Otto von Bismarck, the Iron Chancellor, he can trace his genealogy back at least seven hundred years. He is the grandson of Klaus von Bismarck, a German military officer who fought during the Second World War but was a staunch anti-Nazi who later became president of the Goethe-Institut. Sascha's father, Gottfried, is a business executive and engineer who helped equip West German submarines with sonar. His mother, Kai Maristed, is an American novelist — a daughter of James Abegglen, who served in the Pacific as a marine and later became a specialist on Japanese business culture and a vice-president of the Boston Consulting Group. Sascha was born in Munich, but his parents divorced soon afterward, and, following a difficult custody battle, he split his youth between Germany and the United States. He said, "There was this sort of existence of going back and forth between two poles, two very different worlds, and arriving in this other camp, and loving both sides, and speaking to both sides, and becoming very aware of the hurt on both sides."

Von Bismarck developed a quiet manner and an unwavering earnestness. He entered Harvard in 1990, with an interest in biology, but he was restless and repeatedly took time off. He tried his hand at competitive horse jumping and thought that the Olympics might be a realistic goal. He assisted in a study of aquatic life in Lake Victoria. He joined the Marines, hoping to become involved in military intelligence, but left after two years. When he first learned about E.I.A., in 1995, from an article in a German newspaper, he immediately flew to its main office, in London, for an interview, again ready to suspend college. (He graduated from Harvard in 2002.) "The office was like a newsroom," he recalled. "Everyone was running around and screaming and taking calls." At the time, E.I.A. was a little more than ten years old. Its founders — Allan Thornton, an environmentalist from Canada; Dave Currey, a photographer from the United Kingdom; and Jennifer Lonsdale, a former cook — had ties to Greenpeace, and were influenced by its aggressiveness, but felt lost in its size. Thornton had considered calling their organization the Conservation Investigation Agency, he told me, but ruled it out because the initials "would be a never-ending joke." Still, E.I.A. is sometimes mistaken for a government agency, "which is normally not to our advantage," von Bismarck said. "Once, while going up a river in the Mosquito Coast, we tried to radio a pilot to tell him who we were: E.I.A. He told us that listening in on those calls were drug smugglers, and he was certain they thought we were American agents trying to stop the cocaine coming through. We had even seen cocaine floating in the lagoons."

Not long after he joined the organization, von Bismarck began working on campaigns designed to curtail deforestation. Currently, a third of the world's landmass is forested, which may seem substantial but represents a stark historical decline. During the past ten thousand years, the planet's original forest cover has decreased by nearly half. While Rome grew, Horace wrote of the farmer who "subdues his woodland with flames and plow." In medieval China, the poet Mencius described "bald" landscapes — a reference to forests cleared for fuel and grazing. In Europe and North America, deforestation occurred at a rapid pace centuries ago, but no cycle of forest loss has been as dramatic as that of the modern era. Much of the world's forest cover has been destroyed in the past two centuries — since 1990 the planet lost nearly half a million square miles of forest, an area twice the size of France. Michael Williams, an emeritus professor of geography at Oxford and the author of "Deforesting the Earth," refers to the period of deforestation following the Second World War as "the great onslaught."

A fifth of the world's wood comes from countries that have serious problems enforcing their timber laws, and most of those countries are also experiencing the fastest rates of deforestation. Until a decade ago, many governments were reluctant to acknowledge illegal logging, largely because it was made possible by the corruption of their own officials. As early as the nineteen eighties, the Philippines had lost the vast majority of its primary forests and billions of dollars to illegal loggers. Papua New Guinea, during roughly the same period, experienced such catastrophic forest loss that it commissioned independent auditors to assess why it was happening; they determined that logging companies were "roaming the countryside with the self-assurance of robber barons; bribing politicians and leaders, creating social disharmony and ignoring laws in order to gain access to, rip out, and export the last remnants of the province's valuable timber." In 1998, the Brazilian government announced that most of the country's logging operations were being conducted beyond the ambit of the law.

E.I.A. began to focus on illegal logging after receiving a plea for help from scientists working in the jungles of Southeast Asia. In 1999, Biruté Mary Galdikas, a leading expert on orangutans and an acolyte of Louis Leakey, told Thornton that men with chain saws were cutting into protected Indonesian forests where she had been conducting her research. "It turned out that someone had just illegally redrawn the boundary of the park so that the local timber baron could have access to the trees," Thornton said. Indonesia is home to more endangered species than any other place in the world, and logging was conducted in a state of near total anarchy. By the late nineteen-nineties, the government estimated that as much as seventy per cent of the country's total timber harvest was illegal, and the World Bank calculated that Indonesia was losing three and a half billion dollars annually because of it. In a series of undercover investigations, E.I.A. and an Indonesian group called Telapak discovered that many loggers were targeting a tree called ramin, which had great strength, was easy to stain, and could be sliced into thin pieces. Ramin turned up in the West in countless cheap items: Paintbrushes, two-dollar pool cues, dowels. Even after Indonesia banned the export of ramin, in 2001, the wood was still smuggled out of the country in large volumes.

Von Bismarck's first undercover job, he told me, was "following the ramin trail." By temperament and upbringing, he seemed well suited for clandestine operations. He once told me that his favorite book, which he had read in the fourth grade, was "All the King's Men." When I asked him why, he said, "In terms of how the world works, you have people interacting in a very sensible way, and in some cases it added up to corruption, and in some cases it added up to good things. The book presents a very complicated system, a muddled world, but also a very human world." Von Bismarck's family life was also complicated and muddled and very human, of course, and Gottfried, his father, told me that "as a result, I think, he has developed a great ability to integrate conflicting parties." Occasionally, I heard von Bismarck speak empathetically about the very people he was trying to catch — "poor guys doing really hard work, destroying the natural resources of their own area, and getting arrested."

In 2003, von Bismarck picked up the trail in Singapore, where he went undercover and met with a trafficker who boasted that profits from black-market ramin were "better than drug smuggling." In Malaysia, he met with associates of an underworld figure known as the Ramin King, who described how the wood was given false Malaysian paperwork to obscure its origins. In Taiwan, he secretly filmed a baby-crib manufacturer named Jim Lee, who made products that were sold at J. C. Penney, and who said that he was shipping thousands of cribs made with ramin to Wal-Mart, "even though it is smuggled." Von Bismarck presented this information to Taiwanese officials, who raided Lee's facilities and barred half of his stock from export. (Lee now maintains that his wood was legal.) Von Bismarck also contacted J. C. Penney and Wal-Mart — both took steps to remove items made of ramin from their stores — and notified American authorities, who put imports from Lee's factory on a watch list. A former customs officer told me, "He gave us the same kind of information that we would have expected from another agent. It was amazing to us that there was somebody out there who could keep track of that sort of thing." This year, some of von Bismarck's undercover footage — of a manufacturer in Shanghai who allegedly sold illicit ramin to American companies — helped bring about a US federal indictment.

Lee had told von Bismarck that furniture manufacturers were leaving Taiwan in large numbers for mainland China, and after his workplace was raided he opened a factory there, too. While more and more manufacturers were moving to China, the forest products industry there was dramatically changing. In 1998, the Yangtze River watershed flooded, killing more than three thousand people and causing more than thirty billion dollars in damage. At the time, some Communist Party officials believed that the flood was exacerbated by soil erosion — the result of "over quota" cutting of trees — and the government banned logging throughout much of the country. In order to meet its immense demand for raw materials, China began to buy unprecedented quantities of wood from abroad; it is now the largest importer of logs and also the largest exporter of finished wood products. China began to act the way many developed countries in North America and Europe do: It had destroyed much of its primary forests, gained from doing so, and was now protecting the trees it had left by buying wood indiscriminately, often from "high risk" countries, like Indonesia. The year of the flood, China started importing large volumes of wood from Russia, which has more forest than any country in the world and was in a state of political and economic anarchy. The greatest traffic in illicit wood is now thought to be from Russia to China.

All investigations must begin with a plan, and von Bismarck had begun devising his operation in Manchuria months earlier, from an office in a small brick house near Dupont Circle, in Washington, D.C. The workspace is crammed into three small rooms. There are maps on the walls, reports piled on shelves, and a computer workstation to edit undercover video footage. Eight E.I.A. campaigners, and sometimes a dog, spend most of their daytime hours there, and some late nights, too. Their annual budget is nine hundred thousand dollars, an improvement from the organization's earliest form of financing: Credit cards. The most popular word in the office is probably "leverage," because E.I.A. tends to use its undercover information to pressure governments and companies to change their behavior.

Von Bismarck had not been to northern China before, nor was he very familiar with Russian timber, but he knew that he wanted to frame his investigation around an American retailer that was enmeshed in the trade, and that he could leverage. He chose Wal-Mart. A tenth of China's exports to the United States are sold by Wal-Mart; if the company were a sovereign nation, it would be China's eighth-largest trading partner. "We knew that American demand for wood was causing forest destruction," he told me. "If we could get the biggest company in the country to take note, then we thought we could make a difference." He intended to chart the wood's journey from the Russian forest to suburban store shelves through the complicated network of Wal-Mart's Chinese suppliers — whose identities the company takes care to obscure. When he was done, he planned to show the company what he had discovered or release his findings to the media.

The first step was a physical audit of every wood product that Wal-Mart sold, to try to determine its precise origin. This was done in two stores by a twenty-eight-year-old E.I.A. campaigner named David Groves. "I probably put in four eight-hour days in each store," Groves told me. "I would get there around ten in the morning and not leave until six. I ate what was in a Wal-Mart. I sustained myself on a laughable amount of cheeseburgers." Evidently, one can walk into a Wal-Mart, systematically turn boxes on end, and take notes without interference from employees. "I actually got a lot more customers asking me stuff than Wal-Mart staff," Groves told me. The size of the task became apparent early on. Groves began by including paper in his inventory, but soon became overwhelmed. "I was like, 'That is completely undoable,'" he said. He confined his audit to wood, and ultimately collected data on more than nine hundred products, which von Bismarck used as a blueprint for his trip. Groves also studied two cities in China's far north that serve as the main gateways for the trade in wood: Manzhouli, near Siberia; and Suifenhe.

In the nineteen-eighties, Suifenhe became a test city for what Party officials called "socialism with Chinese characteristics" — the gradual and controlled opening of Chinese markets. Russians would come to the city with furs or old military-issue goods and exchange them for Chinese-made products. The practice became known as *dao bao*, or "changing bags." Largely because of its proximity to Russia and its distance from the central government, Suifenhe developed an energetic and violent shadow economy. Some Chinese "entrepreneurs" smuggled opium and ephedrine, which was widely available in China but forbidden in Russia. Local mobsters flourished, and reached out to their Russian counterparts. At times, they clashed. Marc Mooney, an American timber trader who recently tried to conduct business in Suifenhe, told me, "I've heard stories of Chinese men going on the other side of the border and just disappearing." Occasionally, they were discovered: An entrepreneur who had travelled to Russia to buy trucks ended up floating off the coast of Vladivostok with bullet wounds in his head; two others were found fatally shot in a car that had been parked in a Russian forest.

The timber industry in Suifenhe is largely centered on "primary processing," the most rudimentary type of production — cutting logs into sawn wood, for instance, which is then shipped to other cities in China for more refined manufacturing. Von Bismarck wanted to start at the base of the Wal-Mart chain — the suppliers to the suppliers — and the most logical target was the Shanglian Group. It belongs to Sun Laijun, who grew up in Harbin, the provincial capital, but began going to Suifenhe in 1991, in search of opportunity. "The first thing I did when I arrived in Suifenhe was to look for a Russian translator," he recalled in an interview with CCTV. One of his first big barter deals involved swapping twenty railway cars of urea, a chemical used in fertilizers, for apples. In 1998, when China's logging ban was enacted, he formed Suifenhe Longjiang Shanglian Import and Export Company, and became heavily involved in the timber trade. Longjiang Shanglian now imports one out of every ten logs that enter China from Russia.

The company has been the focus of a number of environmental investigations, and has grown suspicious of strangers. When von Bismarck and Wu, in their guise as representatives of Axion Trading, tried to arrange a meeting with Sun, a receptionist told them that he was in Russia and directed their inquiries to another executive, who asked right away if they belonged to an environmental group. "What groups?" Wu asked, and the executive said, "If you don't know what that is, then you're O.K." A meeting was set up with Longjiang Shanglian's manager, Sun Laijun's brother Laiyong, the following afternoon. "To a certain extent, you have to consider security," Wu later told me. "They own half of Suifenhe, probably, and, from what we know about the timber traders all around the world — some of them can be real nasty."

"Let's go," von Bismarck told Wu, and they headed into Longjiang Shanglian's headquarters, a gray building that towers over the city's factories. Both men were wired with hidden video and audio equipment. After presenting themselves to a security guard, they went to the third-floor office of Sun Laiyong, who was surrounded by a coterie of senior managers. "The whole rail yard, stretching all the way to the mountainside, belongs to our family," Sun Laiyong said. The men talked about the company's operations in Russia, where it bought nearly all its wood. About forty minutes into the meeting, Wu attempted to steer the discussion toward illegality. He asked about problems that the company faced, and Sun Laiyong said, "There are transportation costs, customs fees, mafia protection money —"

"Mafia protection money?" Wu asked.

"Mafia protection money, and other miscellaneous costs. Russia is very —"

One of the managers interrupted. "Even the police is like the mafia," he said.

Sun Laiyong continued, "Doing business in timber, you'll have to pay protection money to them."

"So when you go to Russia —"

"*We* don't want to go there!" Sun Laiyong said. "We send others there instead." He claimed that Chinese businesses were able to muscle out Japanese companies, which for decades have had a presence in the Russian Far East, because the business climate was "dark," and often required payments made by the suitcase. "Small Japanese companies can't buy any timber in Russia," Sun Laiyong said. "They buy it here." He gestured to von Bismarck, and said, "He will not be able to buy any timber in Russia. We bring cash there and pay up front. Cash trade. Anything happens."

"Millions of dollars in cash?" Wu asked.

"Yes."

Wu asked what kinds of mafia groups Longjiang Shanglian dealt with. "All kinds," Sun Laiyong said. He described a contract murder he had heard about that took place in 2001, during a struggle to control Nakhodka, one of Russia's largest ports, on the Pacific. "The manager didn't want to sell it, and a few days later he was killed," he said. Sun Laiyong mentioned the mayor of Vladivostok, a crime boss known as Winnie the Pooh, who was convicted on corruption charges. "Vladivostok's mayor was caught," Sun Laiyong said. "But he was the head of the mafia."

After the meeting, von Bismarck and Wu got into a car and reviewed the encounter. They had obtained evidence that Longjiang Shanglian's operations were enmeshed with corruption in Russia, and that Sun Laiyong regarded bribery as a mundane expense, but they had failed to learn how it affected the company's supply. "When it came to the actual logging, he said, 'Oh, yes, we have all the proper documents. Otherwise, how can you log?'" Wu said. "So, as soon as he said that, he kind of shut the door on me."

Wu leaned back. "Ach, I'm disappointed," he said.

"Yeah?" von Bismarck said.

"I should think that I did really poorly."

"Don't say that," von Bismarck told him, and the two men sat in silence as the car rumbled across the uneven pavement, toward their hotel.

Sun Laiyong's references to organized crime pointed to one of the most disturbing aspects of the illegal timber trade: The violence that supports it. Last December, the body of a Russian banker with close ties to the timber industry was found at the bottom of his swimming pool, near Moscow. A bag had been pulled over his head, and his arms had been tied to his ankles. In a sloppy attempt at a cover-up, a suicide note had been left at the scene, prompting a law-enforcement official to say, "He's not Harry Houdini." I heard of a similar "suicide" not far from Vladivostok earlier this year: an activist working with the World Wildlife Fund was found at a remote hunting cabin, fatally shot, an unconvincing note by his side. This type of violence can be found elsewhere.

Earlier this year, in Peru, a community leader who tried to report a shipment of stolen timber was shot to death in a government office. Three years ago, in Brazil, a missionary and community organizer from Ohio, Sister Dorothy Stang, was murdered in the state of Pará, where a third of the Brazilian Amazon's deforestation is occurring and where she had made enemies of loggers.

In 2001, experts with the United Nations in the Democratic Republic of Congo coined a phrase, "conflict timber," to describe how logging had become interwoven with the fighting there. The term is apt for a number of other places. In Burma, stolen timber helps support the junta and the rebels. In Cambodia, it helped fund the Khmer Rouge, one of the most brutal rebel factions in history. Charles Taylor, the former President of Liberia, distributed logging concessions to warlords and a member of the Ukrainian mafia, and the Oriental Timber Company — known in Liberia as Only Taylor Chops — conducted arms deals on his behalf. The violence tied to Taylor's logging operations reached unprecedented levels, and in 2003 the U.N. Security Council imposed sanctions on all Liberian timber. (China, the largest importer of Liberian timber, tried to block the sanctions.) Shortly afterward, Taylor's regime collapsed. An American official told me that the US intelligence community "absolutely put the fall of Taylor on the timber sanctions."

When von Bismarck discusses this type of violence, there is emotion in his voice. He once told me that he looked up to his grandfather Klaus, who had written in his memoirs of defying an order to execute captured Soviets during the war: It "contravened everything I had been taught and was incompatible with my conscience." When Hitler's regime collapsed, Klaus joined Allied programs designed to erase the Nazi legacy. Martín Escobari, von Bismarck's Harvard roommate, told me, "This is something that clearly had an impact on Sascha. He is very proud of his grandfather, who had been part of the reconstruction of Germany, making up for very evil stuff. Sascha's family comes from a long history of military service. I think he has also tried to make up for previous wrongs."

Not long ago, von Bismarck testified in Congress about timber smuggling and about activists who had been attacked in countries where he had gone undercover. "We're not talking about fuzzy technicalities," he told me. "We're talking about people getting killed, and poor people's livelihood stolen." Some of the people had worked with E.I.A., such as a reporter in Indonesia who had been attacked by thugs carrying machetes. At the hearing, he said, "We are the unwitting financiers of this crime."

Von Bismarck often argues that illegal logging is as much a problem of global demand as it is of supply — which isn't necessarily obvious. Today, the worldwide sales of forest products are worth about a trillion dollars annually, but more wood is used locally, for fuel, than is traded for industrial purposes; in Africa, nearly ninety per cent of all wood harvested is for energy. Moreover, many developed countries import raw timber from places that do not have substantial illegal-logging problems. But wood can be chopped, sliced, and pulverized in countless ways, by any number of middlemen, and large quantities of stolen timber end up in the West as finished products. The United States is the world's largest consumer of finished wood items. In a year, every American uses the equivalent of seventy-two cubic feet of wood. Despite advances in recycling and technology, the per-capita consumption of wood in the United States has risen since the mid-nineteen-sixties.

It is rising elsewhere, too. Wood consumption in China is about fifteen times lower than it is in the United States. For centuries, the Chinese have made paper from bamboo, rice straw, and other non-wood fibers, but the central government recently decided to push the country's papermaking industry away from those raw materials, because the quality was poor, and the process polluted too much water. The authorities closed down thousands of factories, and, between 1980 and 2002, the proportion of non-wood fiber used in Chinese papermaking fell by half. Meanwhile, the over-all amount of paper consumed increased. If it ever grows to the level of American consumption, then China alone would end up using double the planet's current paper production — if that level of demand could ever be met. In India, too, the use of paper is expected to double by 2015. Improving standards of living, combined with population growth, have created a twofold pressure on forests: More people are demanding wood, and people are demanding more of it.

No one has attempted to calculate what it would cost to restrict all wood products to sustainable forests and plantations. Murray Gell-Mann, the Nobel Prize-winning physicist, once defined sustainability as "living on nature's income rather than its capital." As a planet, then, if we are consuming the world's forest capital — and deforestation suggests that we are — everything we use that is derived from wood is undervalued. Von Bismarck told me that an economy that structurally undervalues wood is bound to accept illegal timber without much resistance, because the excess black-market supply only reinforces the misconception that wood is cheap and the supply nearly inexhaustible. (According to one estimate, there is enough illicit timber traded worldwide to depress global prices for wood by as much as sixteen per cent.) The notion is reinforced by the murkiness of the timber economy. Very few companies take the trouble to discover where the wood in their products originates. To do so would be expensive, and consumers don't demand it of them. Indifference has become the norm.

From the docks and tall buildings of Dandong, one can see, across the Yalu River, a North Korean metropolis called Sinuiju, enveloped by smog. On the Chinese side of the border, Dandong is surrounded by hills covered in chestnut trees. The city is home to a firm called Dandong Maisafu, China's largest exporter of toilet seats. The company sends its entire stock to Wal-Mart. Many of its toilet seats are made from oak, and von Bismarck was trying to find out where the wood came from.

An unexpected discovery by David Groves brought von Bismarck and Wu to Dandong. Groves had been combing through an enormous customs database called PIERS, which, every day, gathers more than twenty-five thousand bills of lading from around the world. Looking into PIERS is a bit like looking into the Matrix: There are thousands upon thousands of rows of numbers — tracking codes, shipping codes, container I.D.s. Wal-Mart generally chooses to remove its shipments from the publicly available version of PIERS, but, by chance, the company left on the record forty thousand entries on wood imports from China — including Russian oak toilet seats from a company called Dandong Anmin. When von Bismarck and Wu visited Anmin, they were told that it was no longer dealing with Wal-Mart. (Later, they learned that Anmin was selling some of its products, through a middleman, on Amazon.com.) A senior manager at Anmin referred them to Dandong Maisafu, which was run by one of the owner's relatives.

As the investigation progressed, von Bismarck found that this type of reshuffle was common. "We had been given the gift of this data," he told me, referring to the PIERS information. "But then we found there was an added challenge: the turnover in Wal-Mart suppliers. It was the 'Wal-Mart phenomenon' that we were bumping into, the phenomenon of leveraging suppliers by dumping them at a high frequency." He and Wu would encounter factory owners who had just shipped Wal-Mart goods made with Russian wood but could or would no longer settle for Wal-Mart's price. "That made our investigation difficult, but it also made it difficult for Wal-Mart to get reliable wood," he said. "It created incentives for suppliers to get bad wood."

Von Bismarck and Wu called the offices of Dandong Maisafu, again posing as commodities traders, and met with Chunshou Zhuo, a garrulous, potbellied man in his late fifties, who wore a plaid shirt, jeans, and a trucker's cap. Zhuo said that he owned Maisafu with his daughter, and that they entered the toilet-seat business about eight years ago. His company made two million dollars a month, and exported furniture made from oak and other species to Wal-Mart. When Wu asked where the oak came from, Zhuo said that it was Chinese — "from here, in the mountains" — but Wu learned from a Maisafu floor manager that some of the toilet seats were made from Russian timber. Zhuo's daughter later confirmed that the company used Russian hardwood for about a fifth of its products.

That afternoon, von Bismarck and Wu visited Dalian Huafeng, one of the largest furniture manufacturers in China. From the PIERS data, von Bismarck learned that Huafeng manufactured cribs for an American company called Simplicity for Children, which was, in turn, a Wal-Mart supplier. Huafeng, it turned out, was buying wood from Longjiang Shanglian — the importer in Suifenhe that paid protection money in Russia. Slowly, the pieces of Wal-Mart's wood-supply chain began to come together.

Von Bismarck asked a Huafeng manager, "Big clients like Wal-Mart, they don't ask where the wood is from?"

"No, no, never," she said. "Never."

While there are international treaties designed to protect the oceans and the planet's biodiversity, and to address climate change and the ozone layer, there are no corresponding agreements on how best to manage the planet's trees. This has not been for lack of trying. In 1992, at the Rio Earth Summit, such a convention was proposed and debated, but the talks faltered on the question of who should bear the cost of keeping the planet's forests intact — the countries that consume so much of the world's wood or those who own it? No one could agree. It did not help that more than eighty per cent of the world's forests are under state control, and that governments tend to regard them as sovereign resources.

The only treaty that governs the global trade in forest products is the Convention on International Trade in Endangered Species — what one American official described to me as a kind of "emergency room" for rare plant and animal species at the threshold of extinction. When von Bismarck was investigating ramin, which is protected by the convention, law-enforcement agents could, in theory, confiscate shipments of goods made from the wood if they did not have the proper permits. (No commercially traded Russian timber has this level of protection.) In practice, the system does not always work very well. Von Bismarck once tipped off the authorities about undocumented ramin headed to a crib company called Baby Trilogy, in Lubbock, Texas. The owners, friends of the Bush family, enlisted the office of Senator John Cornyn, of Texas, to help get the shipment released, and it was. (They say that they did not understand the law, and that this was their last shipment of ramin.) Several years ago, a study found that large volumes of mahogany — the only other commercially significant tree protected by the convention — were entering the United States without permits.

During the past several years, von Bismarck and his colleagues have been campaigning for a new way to control timber imports: An amendment to a curious law called the Lacey Act, which, for more than a century, has been a cornerstone of nature protection in America. John F. Lacey, a Civil War veteran and congressman, introduced the legislation in 1900, banning the interstate trade of illegally hunted game. Over time, the Lacey Act was expanded to cover the international trade of wildlife.

John Lacey was a passionate advocate for forests, but, for reasons that are unclear, the law that bears his name fell short of protecting plants the way it did animals. Von Bismarck told me that in 2005 he began "bouncing from Hill office to Hill office, looking for a champion to move forward an amendment" that would expand the act. A congressional aide told him that he would have to get the support of timber-industry associations, but to do that he had to overcome decades of antagonism. "To say there was animosity is an understatement," the aide told me. A member of the Hardwood Federation, which is made up mostly of family-owned businesses, said, "The industry is, really, full of very conservative, rural, property-rights-oriented Republicans, who have been deeply suspicious that the environmentalist community's only interest was to put them out of business." Illegal logging is not only a foreign phenomenon: In the nineteen-nineties, it was estimated that a hundred million dollars' worth of trees were stolen from public lands every year. Von Bismarck was asking the timber industry to lobby for tougher regulation of its own business.

As it happened, a number of American companies believed that they were being hurt by illegal wood — "especially coming out of China, the numbers made no sense to us," said Harry Demorest, who was then a board member of the Hardwood Federation and the C.E.O. of Columbia Forest Products. "We knew what the market price was for logs, and the products were being sold at less than cost." Another industry group, the American Forest and Paper Association, estimated that the trade in stolen wood was costing the domestic forest-products industry a billion dollars annually. Both groups — along with some large retailers — eventually agreed to support the amendment. (The Bush Administration declined to do so.) It was sponsored in the Senate and in the House by two Democratic legislators from Oregon, Senator Ron Wyden and Representative Earl Blumenauer, but much of the bill's fine-tuning occurred in conferences off the Hill.

Following months of negotiation, an amendment took shape: It would prohibit taking any plant or plant product out of any country in violation of its natural-resource laws. There would be no "innocent owner" defense, which meant that importers who claimed not to know they had bought illegal wood, or items made from it, would still be subject to penalties. This provision generated strong opposition from some industry groups, but it was central to the bill's design. "The idea is that you want to stop illegal plants from being in the market, the same way you don't want illegal art in the market — it can be seized wherever it is found," von Bismarck told me. But the bill's greatest strength was also its greatest weakness: While it used the American legal system to reinforce the laws of other countries, forestry codes in some countries are so vague and contradictory that they are hard to follow, even for loggers with good intentions, and even more difficult for American judges to interpret. When I asked von Bismarck about this, he told me, "We want to get to a point where the rules matter, then we want to fight to have them be the right rules."

Just before the amendment was up for a vote in the House, lobbyists from Monsanto and a trade group called the Biotechnology Industry Organization, or BIO, suddenly expressed their unease about it. "It was late in the game," von Bismarck told me. "Everybody was saying, 'Oh, my God, they're going to kill this thing.'" It turned out that BIO and Monsanto had only one major request: To be exempted from the law. At a meeting convened in the Capitol to discuss their concerns, Jen Daulby, Monsanto's representative, argued that the amendment would prevent companies from using genetic samples it acquired overseas. She said that foreign laws could be unreasonable. A timber lobbyist who was there recalled, "It looked pretty bad. We all thought the same thing: Did they just say that they wanted to take plants out regardless of whether the particular country wants them to?"

Daulby told me she was concerned that Monsanto "would be violating the Lacey Act" if the amendment covered all plants and plant products, and that the bill would "prohibit the research materials that were coming back." She said these things on a conference call with two other Monsanto officials listening in, and only a bit later, after a reminder from the company's press officer, did she add, "As Brad mentioned, we are following other countries' laws, but having a bill in the United States that endorses those is a totally different thing."

Ultimately, the biotech industry obtained its exemption. Von Bismarck told me, "They are arguably stealing the intellectual property of poor countries, and there exists the whole debate about that, which is an interesting debate, because they will try to claim the high ground and say, 'We all happily benefit from some of those medicines.'" But the bill's supporters did not want to risk getting the amendment killed over an exemption that, as Monsanto pointed out, was unrelated to the timber trade. Still, von Bismarck said, when the biotech lobbyists joined in, "it was a big, eye-opening moment in terms of how government works."

Von Bismarck decided to publish the results of the Wal-Mart investigation in December, in a report that drew upon eight undercover meetings in China and upon Groves's research. It stated that two hundred thousand cribs made from high-risk Russian poplar and birch were being sold to Wal-Mart by Simplicity for Children, and noted that "at least thirty-one thousand trees reach Wal-Mart each year in the form of solid wood toilet seats made in Dandong." Von Bismarck compared Wal-Mart's fastidiousness about pricing with "the company's inattention to the legality of its raw materials," and noted that "Wal-Mart's customers currently risk financing criminal timber syndicates."

Simplicity for Children denied using illegal Russian wood. Wal-Mart's response was surprisingly less confrontational. The company told von Bismarck that it had already been examining its supply chain, and had just created a new position — senior manager for strategic sourcing — to oversee its forest products. During a conference call with several E.I.A. campaigners, Tom Flynn, who had been assigned to the position, said that his job had been created in part because of the report.

Flynn is a soft-spoken man with a disarming nature. "I've been with Wal-Mart for just about four years," he told me. "My background — and you'll find this a little peculiar — is in the apparel industry, denim sourcing. When I was first approached about this job, I said, 'You know, I don't have a Ph.D. in forestry,' and they told me, 'Well, that's not what we are looking for.'" He added, "Fifteen or twenty years ago, people were never checking their factories in the apparel world. You go back to the days of articles about children being chained to machines, and the industry basically said, 'This is not acceptable.'" Flynn said that he had begun pretty much the way David Groves had, by grabbing a legal pad and walking through a nearby Wal-Mart. "I got to the fourth page, and I gave up," he said. Instead, he worked with what he called a "risk assessment" team to build a database of every wood-based product in Wal-Mart's inventory, and identify the ones he should worry about. Flynn was explaining this by speakerphone, with a Wal-Mart press officer listening in; she, too, conceded that the company had "a learning curve in all of this."

In July, Wal-Mart signed an agreement with the World Wildlife Fund to eliminate illegal wood from its furniture within six years, and to work together on Flynn's risk assessment. "It is a very important signal, but it will only be as important as its follow-through," von Bismarck said. The company had good reason to act quickly. Its announcement followed the passage into law of the Lacey Act amendment, and similar legislation had already been introduced in the British Parliament and was being considered by the European Union. Wal-Mart began advising its suppliers to meet with attorneys about the new law.

Earlier this year, von Bismarck travelled to the Russian Far East to document the timber theft at its source. He flew to Vladivostok and met with Denis Smirnov, the forestry director of the World Wildlife Fund's branch office in the Russian Far East. Smirnov is thirty-eight, and has been living in Vladivostok since 2002, but he was born in Leningrad, and at times demonstrates the haughtiness of an urbanite in one of Russia's most remote provinces. ("In my nightmares, I did not imagine that I would spend my life on illegal logging," he said.) The two men planned to drive through the winter night, to see if they could catch gangs of illegal loggers deep in the taiga the following morning. In daylight, they feared, scouts might see them.

By seven in the evening, the sky had turned dark, and von Bismarck and Smirnov were heading north on the M-60, a two-lane highway running along the Ussuri River, which divides the Russian frontier from northern China. For long stretches, the road was paved, but in places it was completely caked over with snow. Elsewhere, the pavement had crumbled away entirely, leaving behind raw, frozen earth. A few Chinese-made tractor-trailers heading north left clouds of white powdery snow in their wake.

Smirnov drove. He had picked up a special officer from a regional police unit devoted to fighting "economic crimes." The officer, a taciturn man in his early twenties, who wanted to be known only as Vladimir, sat in the passenger seat. He was dressed in camouflage, but over his uniform he wore a puffy black jacket. "He is not yet corrupt," Smirnov said. "It's not ordinary for a policeman." Small, impoverished villages drifted by in the darkness. In the taiga many homes used wood stoves for heating and for cooking. Smirnov drove past timber depots with enormous stockpiles of logs headed for China, but soon they, too, disappeared.

Not far from a logging town called Dalnerechensk — an area where Longjiang

Shanglian acquires some of its timber — Smirnov described how loggers had once sabotaged his car. "For me, it is painful to see this wilderness disappear — and it is useless, actually, because nobody is profiting from the disappearance," he said. "It could be justified if our country, our people, would get some real profit from this harvesting. I think the head of these gangs, they are only thinking about their pockets. They are not thinking about the future, and the people who are living here. These guys can move to — I don't know where, Hawaii or the Bahamas. But other people have no such opportunities."

Sometime after midnight, he drove into a labyrinth of narrow forest trails. Wherever a trail forked, loggers had hung bottles or boxes on branches as markers. Roughly half of the trails crossed frozen bogs, impassable in spring and summer. The car finally stopped in a clearing, and Smirnov, von Bismarck, and Vladimir spent the rest of the night there. For a time, they kept the engine running, but eventually turned it off. Frost formed on the insides of the windows. In the morning, Smirnov drove down snow-covered trails, and soon found one with fresh treads. It led to a pile of cut linden in the snow, and von Bismarck filmed the scene. There were shavings near the logs. He listened for the sound of chain saws, but the forest was quiet.

The search continued fruitlessly until mid-afternoon, when someone saw a flash of color behind a row of trees. In the distance, several men were standing near a pile of logs that was worth several thousand dollars. Vladimir and von Bismarck made their way through the woods to them. It is difficult to describe the sense of uncertainty that precedes a confrontation among strangers who are so far removed from civilization. At the turn of the last century, an imperial Russian geographer wrote, "In the Ussurian taiga, one must expect at times to meet with a wild beast, but the most dangerous meeting of all is with a man." As Vladimir drew near, he removed a handgun from a holster and transferred it to his jacket pocket. Von Bismarck saw this. "I was still worried about them being armed," he told me later. "I did have some kind of sense that Vladimir knew what he was doing, but he was very young."

Vladimir approached the men, but, as they spoke, another logger about fifty feet away powered up a chain saw and cut into a tree. It must have been the final cut, because the tree came crashing into a blanket of snow. "So a tree fell down, and, for me, when you hear a tree falling it is like the Holy Grail," von Bismarck said. "Because when we are trying to catch these guys, I mean, just the visual of an illegal logger in action, actually cutting down a tree — we have really only gotten it once, in Indonesia, and we have used that image a lot." The logger was dressed in an outfit made from thick pieces of beige felt or wool. With one foot, he stabilized the felled tree, and with a bright-orange chain saw he began to sever it into logs. Vladimir approached him. "The logger looked up and his face went numb, and then you could see him making a kind of fight-or-flight decision," von Bismarck recalled. For an instant, nothing happened, and then the logger began to run. Vladimir yelled, in Russian, "Where are you going?"

The man kept running, and Vladimir raised his gun over his head and fired a shot, but the man did not slow down. Vladimir was now running, too, through the snow, which was knee deep in places, and von Bismarck, with his camera, was not far behind, attempting to photograph the arrest. The chase seemed to move in slow motion. In winter, when the vegetation is brittle and devoid of leaves, there are not many places to hide in a forest. Still, the logger, middle-aged and visibly out of shape, ran with startling alacrity. In one hand, he was carrying his chain saw. Twigs snapped against his body. "Where are you going?" Vladimir yelled again as he drew nearer, and for a moment the uncertainty of real violence hung in the air. Von Bismarck plunged into the snow after the men; the cold air pinched his lungs as he ran — he later said that he felt as if his chest had been submerged in ice water. "I was eager to stay right with Vladimir, right over his shoulder, to get the shot," he said. The logger continued running, so Vladimir fired his gun into the air again, and an instant later he grabbed the logger by the arm, and the chase came to an abrupt end.

Blood Oil 12

Sebastian Junger

On June 23, 2005, a group of high-ranking government officials were convened in a ballroom of the Four Seasons Hotel in Washington, D.C., to respond to a simulated crisis in the global oil supply. The event was called "Oil ShockWave," and it was organized by public-interest groups concerned with energy policy and national security. Among those seated beneath a wall-size map of the world were two former heads of the C.I.A., the president of the Council on Foreign Relations, and a member of the Joint Chiefs of Staff. The scenario they were handed was this:

> Civil conflict breaks out in northern Nigeria — an area rife with Islamic militancy and religious violence — and the Nigerian Army is forced to intervene. The situation deteriorates, and international oil companies decide to end operations in the oil-rich Niger River delta, resulting in a loss of 800,000 barrels a day on the world market. Since Nigerian oil is classified as "light sweet crude," meaning that it requires very little refining, this makes it a particularly painful loss to the American market. Concurrently, in this scenario, a cold wave sweeping across the Northern Hemisphere boosts global demand by 800,000 barrels a day. Because global oil production is already functioning at close to maximum capacity (around 84 million barrels a day), small disruptions in supply shudder through the system very quickly. A net deficit of almost two million barrels a day is a significant shock to the market, and the price of a barrel of oil rapidly goes to more than $80.

The United States could absorb $80 oil almost indefinitely — people would drive less, for example, so demand would decline — but the country would find itself in an extremely vulnerable position. Not only does the American economy rely on access to vast amounts of cheap oil, but the American military — heavily mechanized and tactically dependent on air power — literally runs on oil. Eighty-dollar oil would mean that there was virtually no cushion in the world market and that any other disruption — a terrorist attack in Saudi Arabia, for example — would spike prices through the roof.

According to the Oil ShockWave panel, near-simultaneous terrorist attacks on oil infrastructure around the world could easily send prices to $120 a barrel, and those prices, if sustained for more than a few weeks, would cascade disastrously through the American economy.

Gasoline and heating oil would rise to nearly $5 a gallon, which would force the median American family to spend 16 percent of its income on gas and oil — more than double the current amount. Transportation costs would rise to the point where many freight companies would have to raise prices dramatically, cancel services, or declare bankruptcy. Fewer goods would be transported to fewer buyers — who would have less money anyway — so the economy would start to slow down. A slow economy would, in turn, force yet more industries to lay off workers or shut their doors. All this could easily trigger a recession.

The last two major recessions in this country were triggered by a spike in oil prices, and a crisis in Nigeria — America's fifth-largest oil supplier — could well be the next great triggering event. "The economic and national security risks of our dependence on oil — and especially on foreign oil — have reached unprecedented levels," former C.I.A. director Robert Gates (now secretary of defense) warned in his introduction to the Oil ShockWave–study report. "To protect ourselves, we must transcend the narrow interests that have historically stood in the way of a coherent oil security strategy."

In January 2006, less than seven months after the first Oil ShockWave conference — almost as if they'd been given walk-on parts in the simulation — several boatloads of heavily armed Ijaw militants overran a Shell oil facility in the Niger delta and seized four Western oil workers. The militants called themselves the Movement for the Emancipation of the Niger Delta and said they were protesting the environmental devastation caused by the oil industry, as well as the appalling conditions in which most delta inhabitants live. There are no schools, medical clinics, or social services in most delta villages. There is no clean drinking water in delta villages. There are almost no paying jobs in delta villages. People eke out a living by fishing while, all around them, oil wells owned by foreign companies pump billions of dollars' worth of oil a year. It was time, according to MEND, for this injustice to stop.

The immediate effect of the attack was a roughly 250,000-barrel-a-day drop in Nigerian oil production and a temporary bump in world oil prices. MEND released the hostages a few weeks later, but the problems were far from over.

MEND's demands included the release of two Ijaw leaders who were being held in prison, $1.5 billion in restitution for damage to the delicate delta environment, a 50 percent claim on all oil pumped out of the creeks, and development aid to the desperately poor villages of the delta. MEND threatened that, if these demands were not met — which they weren't — it would wage war on the foreign oil companies in Nigeria.

"Leave our land while you can or die in it," a MEND spokesman warned in an e-mail statement after the attack. "Our aim is to totally destroy the capacity of the Nigerian government to export oil."

Because Nigerian oil is so vital to the American economy, President Bush's State Department declared in 2002 that — along with all other African oil imports — it was to be considered a "strategic national interest." That essentially meant that the president could send in the US military to protect our access to it. After the first MEND attack, events in the Niger delta unfolded almost as if they had been scripted by alarmist Pentagon planners. In mid-February, MEND struck again, seizing a barge operated by the American oil-services company Willbros and grabbing nine more hostages. Elsewhere on the same day, other MEND fighters blew up an oil pipeline, a gas pipeline, and a tanker-loading terminal, forcing Shell to suspend 477,000 barrels a day in exports. The nine hostages were released after a reportedly huge ransom was paid, but oil prices on the world market again started to climb. MEND had shown that 20 guys in speedboats could affect oil prices around the world.

The problem was one of scale. The Nigerian military — as poorly equipped as it is — can protect any piece of oil infrastructure it wants by simply putting enough men on it. But Shell has more than 3,720 miles of oil and gas pipelines in the creeks, as well as 90 oil fields and 73 flow stations, and there is no way to guard them all. And moving the entire industry offshore isn't a good option, either. Not only is deepwater drilling very expensive, but there are still immense oil and gas reserves under the Niger delta that have not yet been exploited. And — as it turns out — the deepwater rigs aren't immune to attack anyway. In early June, militants shocked industry experts by overrunning a rig 40 miles out at sea. Offshore oil platforms generally sit 40 or 50 feet above water level, but their legs are crisscrossed with brackets and struts that are not difficult to climb. After firing warning shots, dozens of militants scampered up the legs and ladders to the main platform, rounded up eight foreign oil workers — including an American — and forced them at gunpoint into their boats. They were back in the creeks within hours.

The militants are also capable of striking in the cities. In January of last year, about 30 militants ran their speedboats straight into the Port Harcourt compound of the Italian oil company Agip, killed eight Nigerian soldiers, robbed the bank, and made their getaway. In May, a man on a motorbike shot an American oil executive to death while he sat in Port Harcourt traffic in his chauffeured car. In August, members of another militant group walked into a popular bar named Goodfellas and abducted four Western oil workers. By the end of September, militants had kidnapped — and released for ransom — more than 50 oil workers, and onshore Nigerian oil production had been cut by 25 percent, or about 600,000 barrels a day. That represented a loss of nearly a billion dollars a month to the Nigerian government.

In early October, two separate attacks in the creeks reportedly killed at least 27 Nigerian soldiers and sank or captured two navy gunboats. In response, militants claimed, Nigerian helicopters strafed and then torched an Ijaw village named Elem Tombia. No one was killed, but it was a clear escalation of the conflict. By mid-October, the Niger River delta was on the brink of all-out war.

Into the Delta

The Ijaw village was just a scattering of huts along a meager break in the mangrove, and when our boatman spotted it he slowed and circled and ran his boat up onto the shore. Dugouts had been pulled onto a narrow sand beach, and cook fires smoked unenthusiastically through the thatched roofs of the huts. Behind us, a miles-wide tributary of the Niger River unloaded a continent's worth of freshwater into the Gulf of Guinea. Village children gathered to study our arrival, and a local man saw us and walked away to tell someone that a boatful of strangers had just arrived.

After a few minutes a young man came and motioned for us to follow him, and we stepped carefully through the village and took seats on a wooden bench outside a thatched hut. It was very hot. Somewhere a transistor radio was playing Western music. The huts were sided with rough-milled planks and thatched with palm fronds, and inside women cooked on small fires. Malaria is rampant in these villages, as are cholera, typhoid, and dysentery, and almost none of the communities have safe drinking water. The people survive — barely — off local fish stocks that have been decimated by pollution from oil wells. After a while we heard gunshots, and then a group of young men came walking out of the forest and gathered around us. "Don't be scared," one of them said. "Feel free."

An American photographer named Mike Kamber and I had come to this village to meet MEND, but things had already acquired that unmistakable feeling of not going according to plan. One of the young men had a bottle of Chelsea gin with him, and he shook a splash onto the ground as a blessing and then poured himself a shot. The bottle proceeded like that around the little group. After the gin was finished they told us to follow them, and we were led back into the center of the village and told to sit in some white plastic chairs that had been set out for us. A joint was passed around. More Chelsea gin was brought out. Eventually the village chief took a seat at a small table under a mango tree and asked what we were doing in his village. It wasn't an unfriendly question, but neither was it an invitation to feel right at home. Young men with guns started to drift into the area and position themselves around the group. I stood up and explained that Mike and I were journalists and that we wanted to document the impact of oil drilling in the area, and that a MEND contact had directed us to this village for a meeting.

The truth was a little more complicated. The official MEND spokesman is a mysterious online entity known as Jomo Gbomo, who trades sharply articulate e-mails with foreign journalists who arrive in the delta to cover the oil wars. No one seems to know Jomo's real name or even where he lives; according to *The Wall Street Journal*, his Yahoo account carries an electronic code that may indicate his e-mails are sent from a computer in South Africa. Jomo is the person whom visiting journalists turn to for permission to go into the creeks, and he has refused every single request. A few days after getting the bad news from Jomo, though, Mike and I met with an Ijaw priest named President Owei, who also has contacts with MEND. Owei said that he could arrange a meeting for us if we wanted; all we had to do was hire a boat. By noon the next day we were gripping the mahogany thwarts of a 25-foot open speedboat, slamming southward at full throttle.

Throughout most of the delta there is a weak cell-phone signal, and MEND has run its entire military campaign using a flicker of reception and $3 phones. We were later told that, as word of our arrival spread, Ijaws in South Africa began calling to warn that we might be spies, and others, in the United States, were looking us up online to figure out who we were. The first sign of trouble was when one of the village boys got in our boat and drove it away into the creeks so that we couldn't leave. Another hour went by, and dusk started to creep in through the mangrove. Finally we heard the sound of a powerful outboard motor, and then a boatload of gunmen roared past the village, plowed a couple of angry circles into the narrow creek, and came into the landing at what looked like full throttle. The women in the village fled. MEND had arrived.

They climbed out of the boat with their weapons propped upright on their hips and their faces immobile and expressionless. They didn't bother to look at us and we hardly dared look at them. They carried heavy belt-fed Czech machine guns with the ammunition draped across their bare chests like deadly-looking snakes, and some wore plaid skirts called "Georges," and others wore shorts or cast-off camouflage. One was naked except for his ammunition and a pair of dirty white briefs. They had painted their faces with white chalk to signify purity, and they had tied amulets around their arms and necks and foreheads for protection from bullets. Some had stuck leaves in their clothing so the enemy would see trees rather than men. One of them had painted the Star of David on his stomach to signify the lost tribe of Israel. They were a collection of walking nightmares, everything that is terrifying to the human psyche, and when confronted with them, Nigerian soldiers have been known to just drop their weapons and run.

Their leader was a slender boy wrapped in a red turban and white robe who was helped out of the boat almost like a child. Leaders are often chosen by the Ijaw god of war, Egbesu, and leadership can change daily. Egbesu sometimes communicates his desires by appearing in the dreams or visions of one of his followers and instructing him to be leader for that day. If the man tells the truth about Egbesu, others follow him without question; if he lies about it, Egbesu might kill him. The followers of Egbesu refrain from sex during time of war, and fast to increase their powers. Those powers, I was told, include the ability to drink battery acid without harm. "The spirit enters them when they go into battle," one anthropologist who had lived in Nigeria for years told me. "They don't have the same fears as you and I."

Mike and I were told to rise and we stood there like penitent schoolboys while the young leader approached. He handed his rifle to one of the other militants without bothering to look at us and said, "Which one of you is Sebastian?"

"I am," I said. The boy handed me a cell phone and walked away.

It was Jomo. "I told you that you couldn't go out into the creeks," Jomo said. I started to try to explain, but he cut me off. "What is the spelling of your last name?" he asked. I told him. "Don't worry," he said. "Everything's going to be all right." I handed the phone to the leader and walked back to where Mike stood. A few minutes later, one of the militants strode up to me and pointed his finger at my face. He was short but extremely strong and was covered in white war paint.

"You," he said matter-of-factly. "I am going to kill you."

Half an hour later, Jomo told the MEND leader to release us, and we were in our speedboat headed back to town.

Poverty and Corruption

As is often the case in Africa, many of Nigeria's problems come as much from wealth as from poverty. African countries that happen to have valuable resources — oil in Angola and Nigeria, diamonds in Congo and Sierra Leone — are among the poorest and most violent on the continent. Economists refer to this phenomenon as the "resource curse." The resource curse holds that underdeveloped countries with great natural wealth fail to diversify their industry or to invest in education, which leads to long-term economic decline. The per capita gross national product of OPEC countries, for example, has been in steady decline for the past 30 years, whereas the per capita G.N.P. of non-oil-producing countries in the developing world has steadily risen.

According to the World Bank, most of Nigeria's oil wealth gets siphoned off by 1 percent of the population, condemning more than half of the country to subsist on less than a dollar a day. By that standard, it is one of the poorest countries in the world. Since independence in 1960, it is estimated that between $300 and $400 billion of oil revenue has been stolen or misspent by corrupt government officials — an amount of money approaching all the Western aid received by Africa in those years. Former president Sani Abacha and his inner circle stole at least $2 billion. In a recent crackdown on corruption, the president of the Nigerian senate had to resign after accusations that he had solicited a bribe in exchange for pushing through an inflated education budget (which presumably would then have been plundered by others). A former inspector general of the national police, after being accused of stealing between $52 and $140 million, was recently sentenced to six months in prison for a lesser charge. And two Nigerian admirals were put on trial for trying to sell stolen oil to an international crime syndicate.

The list of wrongdoing continues almost without end. With top government officials so brazenly violating the social contract, everyone downstream inevitably follows suit. The Nigerian constitution stipulates that just under 50 percent of national oil revenue must be distributed to state and local governments, and that an additional 13 percent must go to the nine oil-producing states of the Niger delta. Last year that amounted to almost $6 billion for the nine delta states — plenty, it would seem, to take care of basic social services. The problem, however, is that the money goes to the governors' offices and then simply disappears. A financial-crimes commission was recently formed to investigate all of the country's 36 governors, and it wound up accusing all but 5 of corruption. The most apparently egregious case was that of Diepreye Alamieyeseigha, who was accused of embezzling hundreds of millions of dollars while he was governor of Bayelsa State. He fled to England, was arrested for money-laundering, jumped bail, and slipped back into Nigeria dressed as a woman. (The English authorities had taken his passport.) When asked how he managed to make the trip, he said he had no idea. "All the glory goes to God," he explained. He is now in custody awaiting trial.

"It's going to be tough," human-rights activist Oronto Douglas said when I asked him about reforming Nigerian politics. "Nobody who has privilege surrenders it easily. The struggle is to get people to give up power who got it illegally."

The problem isn't purely a Nigerian one, either. Oil companies have long been thought to pay for the allegiance of local youth gangs, and Jomo claims that Agip offered to pay MEND $40 million in exchange for "repairs" to the company's pipelines. (An Agip spokesman strongly denies any payment to or contact with MEND.) The American corporation Halliburton has admitted that its then subsidiary KBR paid $2.4 million in bribes to the Nigerian government and is under investigation for its role in earlier bribes totaling $180 million. And House representative William Jefferson, of Louisiana, is being investigated by the F.B.I. for allegedly accepting bribes from the vice president of Nigeria, Atiku Abubakar. These were said to be in exchange for help steering lucrative business contracts to Africa. (Jefferson has denied any wrongdoing, despite the fact that the F.B.I. found $90,000 in cash in his freezer.)

Because of this corruption, most of Nigerian society has been starved of money and is effectively cannibalizing itself. Between Port Harcourt and the delta city of Warri there are 20 or 30 police checkpoints — some within sight of one another — where drivers simply hand cash out the window in order to pass. I was told that when police arrive at the scene of a bad car accident they won't call for medical help until the injured and dying have paid them off. There are car accidents all the time — I saw two fatal accidents on as many drives across the delta — because the roads have not had major repairs since the early 1980s. Even expressways have collapsed, turning a drive that once took several hours into a terrifying ordeal that can last days.

Every sector of society has been left to fend for itself. The airline industry, for example, is so slack in its maintenance that it has seen three catastrophic plane crashes in the past 16 months, which together have killed more than 300 people. The airport at Port Harcourt was shut down in 2005 after an incoming Air France flight plowed into a herd of cows that had wandered onto the runway; it still has not reopened. Tens of millions of people live in urban slums without water or sanitation, restaurants have to hire guards with AK-47s to protect the diners, and the levels of chaos and street violence rival that of many countries at war. A dead man lay on the street near my hotel for two days before someone finally came to take him away. Even during Liberia's darkest days of civil war, the dead were usually gathered up and buried faster than that.

When Nigerians are asked about these problems, few can offer more than anger and despair — or the promise of violence. A typical Nigerian reaction came from President Owei, the Ijaw priest who tried to help with our first trip into the creeks. Owei is the head of an organization that promotes Ijaw rights and protects their communities in the delta. At first, my questions just provoked a torrent of indignation. "The people of the Niger delta don't need theory — they need practical things," he declared. "We need to be made to feel like human beings. There is an economic blockade of the Niger delta — they don't want money to flow here. With the wealth that Nigeria has, the whole nation should have roads and free education."

Owei lives in the great, seething slum of Bundu-Waterside, on the outskirts of Port Harcourt. Bundu-Waterside is a community built literally atop garbage and mud. High tide and raw sewage continually threaten to rise up over the thresholds of its thousands of plank-and-corrugated-iron shacks. People are packed into Bundu-Waterside with such desperate ingenuity that almost every human activity — cooking, fighting, eating, sleeping, defecating — seems to be observable from almost anywhere at any given moment. When I met with Owei, he and several of his assistants were seated on a wooden bench beneath a canopy of corrugated iron that serves as an open-air community center. Young boys swam in the tidal muck while, a few feet away, other young boys squatted to relieve themselves. Every 20 minutes or so, an oil-company helicopter thumped past on its way to one of the offshore rigs.

"The Niger-delta people are the new world power," Owei informed me solemnly. "I don't have a bulletproof vest, but I can drink acid. Can you drink acid? I can drink acid. We are a world power. We are waiting. We want to live in peace because God is peaceful, but the rest of the world is building armaments while they wait for Jesus. I don't know."

A History of Violence

On November 10, 1995, an Ogoni author named Ken Saro-Wiwa and eight other anti-Shell activists were hanged by the Abacha government on trumped-up charges of incitement to murder. Saro-Wiwa had been a driving force in the formation of a group called the Movement for the Survival of the Ogoni People — MOSOP — which had taken a stand against environmental damage caused by the oil industry and the uncompensated appropriation of Ogoni land for oil drilling. Ignored by the Nigerian government, MOSOP petitioned Shell and the other oil companies directly. They wanted $10 billion in accumulated royalties and environmental-damage compensation, and a greater say in future oil exploration. Again ignored, Saro-Wiwa organized mass protests that managed to shut down virtually all oil production in Ogoniland. It was a severe blow not only to the oil industry but also to the system of corruption and patronage it had spawned, and the Nigerian military reacted with predictable brutality.

"Shell operations still impossible unless ruthless military operations are undertaken," the commander of the Rivers State Internal Security Task Force wrote to his superior on May 12, 1994. The memo went on to suggest "wasting operations during MOSOP and other gatherings, making constant military presence justifiable." (The memorandum was leaked to the press, though its authenticity was questioned by Shell.) Nine days later, the military moved into Ogoniland in force. They razed 30 villages, arrested hundreds of protesters, and killed an estimated 2,000 people. Four Ogoni chiefs were murdered during the chaos — possibly by government sympathizers — and the military used their deaths as a pretext to arrest the top MOSOP leaders. Saro-Wiwa was subjected to a sham trial and condemned to death. Before he was hanged, Saro-Wiwa's last words were "Lord take my soul, but the struggle continues."

Indeed it did.

The next major outbreak of violence occurred in 1998, when several Ijaw groups tried to duplicate MOSOP's strategies by declaring Ijaw territory off limits to the Nigerian military and demanding a stop to all oil extraction. Their rebellion was called Operation Climate Change. Within days, the Nigerian military saturated the delta and Bayelsa State with up to 15,000 soldiers and commenced a series of attacks that resulted in dozens — if not hundreds — of civilian deaths. Ijaw militants retaliated by shutting off and destroying oil wellheads in their area, and over the next several years an armed militancy evolved that the government was unable to contain. Fighting also broke out between different armed factions — many of which were hired by politicians to intimidate local rivals — and in 2004 an Ijaw leader named Mujahid Dokubu-Asari retreated into the creeks to wage "all-out war" against the government and the oil companies. His statement helped drive New York oil-futures prices above $50 for the first time ever.

Asari was a convert to Islam and had briefly worried US authorities by expressing his admiration for Osama bin Laden. His overriding concern, however, was control of the oil resources of the Niger delta. One form of control, according to Asari, was simply stealing back the oil that he believes has been stolen from the Ijaw. In Nigeria, stealing oil is called "bunkering," and it is huge business; by some estimates, 10 percent of the oil exported from Nigeria every year — several billion dollars' worth — is actually bunkered.

The safest way to bunker oil is essentially to bribe people into letting you steal it. Vastly more dangerous, and common, is tapping crude directly out of the pipelines themselves. Light sweet crude is extremely volatile, so metal-on-metal contact can touch off a massive explosion. Bunkerers start by building a temporary enclosure around a small section of underwater pipe, pumping the water out and then drilling a hole into the steel casing that contains the crude. They then fit the hole with a short pipe and valve and let the creek water back in so that the apparatus is underwater, and therefore hidden from oil-company inspectors. Crude moves through the pipeline under a pressure of 600 pounds per square inch, and with such pressure it takes only a few hours to fill up a 1,000-metric-ton barge. The barge is then moved offshore to a transport ship — an operation that is vastly simplified by renting the Nigerian military.

"Most of the soldiers are paid 15,000 naira [around $100] a month, so you go to the military man and say, 'I want to make you richer,'" a bunkerer in Warri told me. He had just worked all night moving bunkered oil; the work had probably netted his boss upwards of a hundred thousand dollars. "You say, 'This pipe will bring money; every night you will work here.' Then they will guard you. We give them five months' salary in a single night. Every time they bring in new people, we make new friends."

This man claimed that the federal government could easily stop bunkering if it wanted to, but local officials are making so much money off it that they would revolt. Ideally, he'd like to get out of the business. "There's so much risk in bunkering — fire risk, water risk, ambush risk. What I want to do is work for the oil companies as a production supervisor," he said. "I'm just bunkering until I get a job. There are plenty of people here with degrees in petroleum engineering who can't get jobs. They're offered positions by the bunkerers, so of course they take them."

Bunkering would not be possible without guns — militant groups are constantly fighting one another over access — and of course those guns are bought with oil money. The most impressive weapons I saw were Czech-made Rachot UK-68s that were new and well oiled and looked like they had just been unpacked from their crates. Rachots are highly portable general-purpose machine guns that can also be mounted on tripods for use against aircraft; they are not the sort of secondhand weapons commonly found floating around West African war zones. Someone brought those in with a special purpose in mind. "Their supplies seem to be unending," an arms expert named Dr. Sofiri Joab-Peterside told me in his office, in Port Harcourt. "The police have to count the rounds that they use — they don't have more than 10 or 15 each. The militants have belt-fed guns that can sustain action for 20 minutes. That, too, is a problem."

According to another contact of mine — a man who freely associates with the militants — the most recent arms shipment was 300 Russian-made AK-47s, built in 1969 but never used, that came from Moscow via London. He also said that in early October a South African businessman unloaded a ship full of weapons in the creeks in exchange for bunkered oil, which he then sold on the international market. Nigerian soldiers who have recently returned from peacekeeping missions in Liberia and Sierra Leone are known to sell their guns, he told me, as are soldiers currently stationed in the delta. There are even rumors of floating weapons bazaars — freighters filled with guns — anchored off the Nigerian coast. All you have to do is pull up in your boat with cash.

However violent and dysfunctional it may seem, the convergence of bunkered oil, smuggled weapons, and illegal payoffs has worked fairly well within the broader violence and dysfunction of Nigeria. The original concerns of activists such as Saro-Wiwa were environmental degradation of the delta from oil spills, and the extreme poverty and backwardness of the villages. Two and a half million barrels of crude spilled or leaked into the delicate riverine environment between 1986 and 1996, resulting in wholesale devastation of the fish stocks that most villagers rely on. Flaring of excess natural gas has produced a blighting acid rain in the mangrove swamps, and freshwater even around wells that have been capped for years is still so polluted with hydrocarbons that it cannot be drunk safely. But people still do.

The costs of fully protecting the delicate delta ecology are almost incalculable. Once the militants participate in illegalities, however, the Nigerian government can dismiss the entire movement. "I recently directed the Nigerian security services to arrest and prosecute persons responsible for kidnapping . . . under whatever guise the criminals and terrorists carry out these dangerous acts," President Olusegun Obasanjo declared in August 2006. Further complicating the issue is that much of the oil pollution in the creeks is from sloppy bunkering operations — which villagers then use as a basis for further claims of environmental damage to the delta. Shell recently appealed a decision by the Nigerian courts that ordered it to pay $1.5 billion to the Ijaw people in compensation for environmental damage to the delta. Under the current system, everyone involved in the oil business — from corrupt government officials to military commanders to the militants themselves — makes vastly more money than he would in a transparent economy. And the bunkered oil isn't lost to the market; it simply becomes an additional tax borne by the oil companies for doing business in Nigeria.

The brutal functionality of this system started to break down in January 2006, when MEND arrived on the scene. MEND was not simply another bunkering cartel; it renewed the grievances first voiced by Saro-Wiwa and began to seriously disrupt the flow of oil from the creeks. "We are not communists or even revolutionaries," Jomo commented by e-mail to a journalist. "We're just extremely bitter men."

The formation of MEND seems to have been triggered by Asari's arrest in September 2005. Asari had threatened to "dismember" Nigeria, which smelled enough like treason for the Obasanjo government to finally go after him. The first MEND attack came four months later and was soon followed by e-mails from Jomo demanding the release of both Asari and Diepreye Alamieyeseigha, the Bayelsa state governor charged with corruption. (Alamieyseigha is Ijaw and was closely connected to Asari.) The first four oil workers kidnapped by MEND were lectured for 19 days on the poverty and environmental degradation of the delta. More than ransom money, the militants said they wanted all foreigners to leave their territory. In other words, they wanted control of their oil.

A former hostage whom I talked to (who did not want to be identified by name) reported essentially the same experience. He was a contract pilot for Shell who was taken from a landing platform in 2000 and held for two weeks. He was never physically abused or threatened, though he did worry that he might eventually get malaria and die. "Their grievances are legitimate," this man told me. "It's just that those who do the kidnapping don't necessarily do it for the community. There's no water in these communities, no education, no medical facilities whatsoever. To be out in the swamp without any electricity or drinking water — of course they're upset."

We were sitting at an open-air bar inside the Shell compound near Warri. It was early evening, and bats flitted through floodlights that illuminated a tennis court. On the other side of the compound's chain-link fence was a local village that had been plunged into darkness. "The host community here," the man went on, waving at the ramshackle houses, "they are without electricity for days sometimes. This is obscene. They are looking through the fence at golf courses and tennis courts where the floodlights are on at midnight. Why not throw them an electric line? I mentioned it to someone at Shell. I said, 'Why not? You've got the turbines! Let there be light!' He said, 'If we do that, they'll all want that.'"

After his release, this man was repatriated to his home country and immediately came down with malaria. While he was recovering, he received a letter from the lead militant of the group that had kidnapped him. It was directed to his wife and children, and it even had a return address. "I apologize for kidnapping your husband and father," the letter read. "I did it because of Shell. I am born again and I will not do it again. I should be forgiven."

"They used light plastic speedboats with 75-horsepower engines," the man said. "They take the top off the engine to get more cooling. They know exactly what they're doing. The army will never have a chance."

Combustion Chamber

This is why oil is so valuable: One tank of gas from a typical S.U.V. has the energy equivalent of more than 60,000 man-hours of work — roughly 100 men working around the clock for nearly a month. That is the power that the American consumer can access for about $60 at the gasoline pump. If gasoline were a person, we would be paying 10 cents an hour for his labor. Easily accessible reserves are running dry, though, which means that the industry must develop increasingly ingenious — and costly — techniques for getting at the oil. Deepwater drilling, for example, now happens so far offshore that rigs can no longer be anchored to the seabed; they must be held in place by an array of propellers, each the size of a two-car garage. The cost of deepwater drilling is close to twice that in shallow water.

As a result, oil is one of the few commodities with virtually no surplus production; just about every drop of oil that gets pumped gets used. The world currently goes through 84 million barrels a day, a figure that is expected to rise to almost 120 million barrels in the next 25 years. As that happens, oil will become more and more expensive to extract. When oil was first exploited, in 1859, the energy equivalent of one barrel of oil was required to pump 50 barrels of oil out of the ground. Now that ratio is one-to-five. Thus far, nearly half of the proven, exploitable oil reserves in the world have been used up. Barring the discovery of new reserves or new drilling technology, some experts predict the world will run out of oil by 2040.

Added to these technological problems is the fact that — as if by some divine prank — most of the world's oil reserves happen to be in politically unstable parts of the world. (The alternative theory is that oil exploitation tends to destabilize underdeveloped countries.) Because of the financial risks involved, oil reserves in politically stable countries have more value, per barrel, than oil in politically unstable countries. As we speak, the value of Nigerian oil — as a function of the capital investment that must be risked to produce it — is in steady decline.

That is MEND's trump card. It has several times threatened to shut down all Nigerian oil production, but it's possible MEND doesn't quite dare, because of the chance it will provoke a military retaliation it wouldn't survive. By the same token, the Nigerian military has threatened to sweep the delta with overwhelming force, but it doesn't know whether that might force MEND to carry out one devastating counterstrike — taking out the Bonny Island Liquefied Natural Gas facility with a shoulder-fired rocket, for example. An act of sabotage on this scale could drive Shell and the other oil companies from Nigeria for good, completely wiping out the national economy. One major company, Willbros, has already discontinued operations in Nigeria because of the security threat.

On the world stage, as well, MEND's political power depends on its ability to cause economic pain in other countries. Some industry experts contend that new market mechanisms and the availability of US petroleum reserves would mitigate the effects of even a complete shut-in of Nigerian oil. "Look at Katrina," one oil analyst at the Department of Energy told me. "There was a spike in oil prices for a couple of weeks, but then demand shifts and there is a little bit of conservation. Two years ago we were at $28 a barrel and now we are in the mid-50s. Short-term market predictions are a fool's game."

The Oil ShockWave panel wasn't so sure. It found that a complete shut-in that coincided with another event — a terrorist attack in the Persian Gulf or even an exceptionally harsh winter, for example — could trigger a major recession. Furthermore, there seemed to be no good options for dealing with it. Opening up the US Strategic Petroleum Reserve — some 700 million barrels of oil in underground salt caverns along the Gulf Coast — would lower oil prices for the whole world without providing a long-term solution. Begging Saudi Arabia for more oil could compromise the United States politically and damage our long-term interests in the region. And sending the US military into the Niger delta would be politically risky and possibly unfeasible, given American commitments in Afghanistan and Iraq.

That did not stop the US government from authorizing a joint training exercise with the Nigerian military in 2004. It was reported to have been focused on "water combat."

Two weeks after our first trip to the creeks, Jomo told me by e-mail that he would arrange for MEND to take us into its camp. It was deep in the mangrove swamps, and he said that no journalist had ever been there. Allegedly, the only foreigners who have ever seen the MEND camps were hostages.

We hired a boat at the Port Harcourt waterfront and headed south into the creeks, hoping not to run into any Nigerian gunboats. We had the feeling that the authorities knew what we were up to, and it seemed like an encounter that would end badly. We passed a few fishing villages and a flow station and two gas flares, and then we swung into the broad expanse of Cawthorne Channel. Twenty miles to the east, wobbling in the heat shimmer, was the Bonny Island L.N.G. facility. The rumor in Port Harcourt was that MEND was planning to blow it up. A wind had come up, and we banged our way southward into a hard chop and finally swerved into one of the nameless creeks and ran our boat into the village where we'd been two weeks earlier.

Calls went out, and half an hour later a boatful of militants dressed raggedly in old Western clothes pulled into the landing, and we climbed on board. We continued south for a while, almost to open ocean, then plunged back into the mangrove up a creek that got narrower and narrower until we had to duck to avoid getting hit by branches. We passed under a talisman strung between two trees, and minutes later we were at the camp. Every tree, it seemed, had a man behind it with a gun pointed at our heads.

Mike and I stepped out onto land and were immediately blessed by a man who dipped a handful of leaves into what might have been palm wine and splashed us twice. No one blesses someone before killing him, I thought. The camp was a rough wood barracks hidden in the trees with a few nylon tents scattered around. There was a small generator and a satellite hookup for television. There were two Egbesu shrines, unremarkable little thatched enclosures with inexplicable things tied to them. The men had stocking masks on their faces with leaves sticking out of the eye slits, and they watched our every move through the slits, though they had stopped pointing their guns at us. Some of the militants couldn't have been 15 years old. They carried old British guns from the colonial days and ugly little submachine guns with the clips sticking out to the side — and the big belt-fed Rachot machine guns that Nigerian soldiers were so scared of. We walked through the camp rubber-kneed and weak, or at least I did. Their leader was named Brutus and he sat on a wooden bench in a clearing. He motioned me to take a seat next to him, and I opened my notebook and sat down. His men surrounded us in a semicircle with guns cocked at all angles.

"I have been instructed by Jomo to answer any question you have," he said. "And to let you take any pictures you want. The Nigerian government has been marginalizing the people who have the resources of this country. We are deprived of our rights. This time around we don't even want to wait for them to attack. When the order is given we can go ahead and crumble whoever we can crumble, because we don't die; we live by the grace of God. If one man remains, that man can win the cause — that is my own belief."

I had heard this before — that the delta was bracing for a wave of attacks. The attacks were rumored to include coordinated car bombings, assassinations, and hostage-taking. I asked Brutus what was going to happen next. "The first phase was just a test run for the equipment," he assured me. "Soon the real violence will come up and will be let loose. We are waiting for the orders from above and we won't waste an hour. . . . This is modern-day slavery. They have killed so many people in the struggle. The government will attack us, but we are very ready for them. We are just waiting for orders from above. Then we will move." (On December 18, two explosions were reported at Shell and Agip facilities in the delta. MEND claimed responsibility for the attacks.)

Brutus looked at me through the eyeholes of his mask. "When the Nigerian man moves," he said, "nothing can stop him."

NEW ORGANIZATIONS IV

Inside the Global Hacker Service Economy   13

Scott Berinato

By 2003, online banking was not yet ubiquitous but everyone could see that, eventually, it would be. Everyone includes Internet criminals, who by then had already built software capable of surreptitiously grabbing personal information from online forms, like the ones used for online banking. The first of these so-called form-grabbing Trojans was called Berbew.

Berbew's creator is believed to be a VXer, or malware developer, named Smash, who rose to prominence by co-founding the IAACA — International Association for the Advancement of Criminal Activity — after the Feds busted up ShadowCrew, Smash's previous hacking group.

Berbew was wildly effective. Lance James, a researcher with Secure Science Corp., believes it operated undetected for as long as nine months and grabbed as much as 113GB of data — millions of personal credentials.

Inside an Identity Theft Site

A sophisticated new breed of online criminals is making it easier than ever for the bad guys to engage in identity theft and other cybercrime.

Like all exploits, Berbew was eventually detected and contained, but, as is customary with malware, strands of Berbew's form-grabbing code were stitched into new Trojans that had adapted to defenses. The process is not unlike horticulturalists' grafting pieces of one plant onto another in order to create hardier mums.

Thus, Berbew code reappeared in the Trojan A311-Death, and A311-Death in turn begat a pervasive lineage of malware called the Haxdoor family, authored by Corpse, who many believe was part of a well-known, successful hacking group called the HangUp Team, based in the port city of Archangelsk, Russia, where the Dvina River empties into the White Sea, near the Arctic Circle.

By 2006, online banking was ubiquitous and form-grabbers had been refined into remarkably efficient, multi-purpose bots. Corpse himself was peddling a sophisticated Haxdoor derivative called Nuclear Grabber for as much as $3,200 per copy. Nordea Bank in Sweden lost 8 million kronor ($1.1 million) because of it.

But by last October, despite his success, Corpse decided that it was time to lay low. A message appeared on a discussion board at pinch3.net, a site that sold yet another Haxdoor relative called Pinch.

"Corpse does cease development spyware? news not new, but many do not know" reads a post by "sash" translated using Babelfish. It then quotes Corpse: "I declare about the official curtailment of my activity of that connected with troyanami [trojans]."

This past January, a reporter for *Computer Sweden* chatted with Corpse, pretending to be a potential customer. Corpse tried to sell him Nuclear Grabber for $3,000 and crowed that banks sweep 99 percent of online fraud cases under the rug. After *Computerworld Australia* published the chat, Corpse disappeared. He hasn't been heard from since.

But his form-grabbing code resurfaced, when a friend of Don Jackson asked Jackson to look at a file he found on his computer, as a favor.

That file led Jackson behind the curtain to find hacking with a level of sophistication he'd never seen before.

January: Discovery

Don Jackson is a security researcher for SecureWorks, one of dozens of boutique security firms that have emerged to deal with the inherently insecure, crime-ridden, ungovernable Internet. Jackson's company and others like it usually sell security products, but their real value is in the research they do. With law enforcement overtaxed by and under-trained for electronic crime, these firms have become a primary source of intelligence on underground Internet activity and VXers' latest innovations.

Seems like an expensive hobby for a small company but the expense associated with the hardcore intel and technically arduous research is more than paid for by its value as a marketing tool. Being the first to market, even when your product is bad news about security, wins press attention and, it's hoped, customers. As such, the little security startups stock up on researchers like Jackson who have a working, or sometimes intimate, knowledge of the criminal hacker underground. All day, every day, security researchers at these small companies are dissecting malware that they discover, chatting with bad guys and poking around their domains.

Still, neither the sheer number of firms and jobs like Jackson's created in the past five years, nor the fact that larger companies like Verizon, Symantec, IBM, and BT are acquiring those companies, are signs that the good guys are catching up. It's more a sign of how much money can be made trying to catch up. Internet crime is profitable for everyone, except of course its victims.

Jackson's friend was a victim, but of what he wasn't sure. All he could say was that several of his online accounts had been hijacked and that a scan of his computer turned up a conspicuous executable, or exe, file, one that wasn't detected as malware, but wasn't recognized as something legitimate either. The friend asked Jackson if, as a favor, he'd take a look.

Jackson obliged and discovered that the file had been on the system since December 13, 2006, almost a month. If it turned out to be something new and malicious, then Jackson had discovered a 0-day exploit. It would be a publicity boon for SecureWorks.

Jackson downloaded the exe to a lab computer. "Generally, the exe is not all that exciting to researchers who see hundreds of samples each month," says Jackson. "There are some exceptions." This was not an exception. Jackson found a derivative of Corpse's Haxdoor form grabber, just a new cultivar of an old species, albeit a reasonably well-crafted one. Like several form grabbers before it, this one intercepted form data before it was SSL-encrypted, meaning that the little glowing lock in the corner of the browser, the one that online merchants will tell you ensures you that you're on a safe page, meant nothing of the sort.

Jackson named his discovery after the transliteration of a Russian word he found inside the source code: Pesdato. Later, when he learned what that word meant in Padonki, a kind of Russian hacker slang, he changed its name, instead choosing the moniker of a cartoon character that he made up in grade school: Gozi.

The process of fully deconstructing Gozi took Jackson three days. On the third day, as he pored over the source code, Jackson noticed that the sample on his lab computer was communicating with an IP address that he thought was owned by the Russian Business Network. RBN is a notorious service provider out of St. Petersburg, Russia that Jackson and others say is an ISP with a reputation for accommodating spam and other malware outfits. Normally, Jackson thought, bots would be stealthier about communicating with RBN. Maybe this was a mistake. Curious, he decided to poke his head in and look around on the RBN server that Gozi was talking to.

And what he found stunned him. As he sailed off through the servers and in and out of files and almost over a database to where Gozi's home base was, Jackson found a full-fledged e-commerce operation. It was slick and accessible, with comprehensive product offerings and a strong customer focus. Jackson, no one really, had ever seen anything like it. So business-like. So fully conceived. So professional.

It was early February by the time he found a 3.3 GB file containing more than 10,000 online credentials taken from 5,200 machines — a stash he estimated could fetch $2 million on the black market. He called the FBI as he prepared to go undercover to learn more. If he had known at the time what pesdato, that Padonki slang word meant, he might have uttered it under his breath when he realized what he had stumbled on to.

Jackson had stumbled on to the next phase of Internet crime. Gozi was significant not because the Gozi Trojan was innovative or hard to detect. It wasn't. It was in many ways no different than its four-year old ancestor Berbew. No, Gozi was significant, Jackson thought, because it wasn't really a product at all. It was a service.

The Golden Age

Gozi represents the shift taking place in Internet crime, from software-based attacks to a service-based economy. Electronic crime has evolved, from an episodic problem, like bank robberies carried out by small gangs, to a chronic one, like drug trafficking run by syndicates.

Already every month, Lance James' company Secure Science discovers 3 million compromised login credentials — for banks, for online email accounts, anything requiring a username and password on the Internet — and intercepts 250,000 stolen credit cards. On an average week, Secure Science monitors 30–40GB of freshly stolen data, "and that's just our company," says James.

Given that, you think you'd have heard more about Gozi, or about this chronic condition in general. But you haven't. Beyond the research community, Gozi and the other Trojans stealing all this data have been largely ignored. A half-dozen CSOs and CISOs contacted for this story, including some representing banks and online merchants, had either never heard of Gozi or vaguely recalled the name and not much else. And why would they? Gozi made it through a news cycle and it was reported without context, with a tally of the known damage, like a traffic accident. And yet, Gozi wasn't that at all. It was an idea, a business model.

Even after it fell out of the news, and despite the fact that Don Jackson and the FBI believed they knew how it worked, and who was running it, the Gozi Trojan continued to adapt to defenses, infect machines and grab personal information.

"Do you have a credit card? They've got it," states another researcher who used to write malware for a hacking group and who now works intelligence on the Internet underground and could only speak anonymously to protect his cover. "I'm not exaggerating. Your numbers will be compromised four or five times, even if they're not used yet."

"I take for granted everything I do on the Internet is public and everything in my wallet is owned," adds Chris Hoff, the security strategist at Crossbeam and former CISO of Westcorp, a $25 billion financial services company. "But what do I do? Do I pay for everything in cash like my dad? I defy you to do that. I was at a hotel recently and I couldn't get a bottle of water without swiping my credit card. And I was thirsty! What was I gonna do?"

That's the thing about this wave of Internet crime. Everyone has apparently decided that it's an unavoidable cost of doing business online, a risk they're willing to take, and that whatever's being lost to crime online is acceptable loss. Banks, merchants, consumers, they're thirsty! What are they gonna do?

The cops lack resources and jurisdiction. And in some cases, security companies are literally shifting their strategies away from trying to secure machines connected to the Internet; they're giving up because they don't believe it can be done.

It's a conspiracy of apathy. For the criminals, this is great news. They stand blinking into the dawn of a golden age of criminal enterprise. Like Barbary Pirates in the 18th century, and like Colombian drug cartels in the 1970s, malicious hackers will run amok, unfettered, unafraid and perhaps even protected. Only they won't use muskets or mules. They'll use malicious code to run syndicates that will be both less violent and more scalable than in the past.

Now is the criminal hacker's time. In Archangelsk, Russia, it is the HangUp Team's time.

February: Access

What Don Jackson found when he followed Gozi back to the RBN server was called 76service.com. The home page was pretty and simple, just a stylized login box. But how this service worked wasn't yet clear, so Jackson went undercover. On carders forums, the online hangouts for people who run credit card rackets, he found some members who knew about Gozi and 76service. He recognized their avatars — online personas usually marked by a picture that gets posted with their comments on discussion boards — as ones that belonged to members of the HangUp Team. "It confirmed to me they were involved," Jackson says, "but how still wasn't clear. For all I knew, they just sold the bot to someone."

In response to requests he posted, one of these HangUp Team members e-mailed Jackson at an anonymous safe-mail.com account. The e-mail told Jackson to log on to a specific IRC chat room with a specific name at a specific time. Jackson, using a machine configured to hide its location, did so.

The room was virtually crowded. "I get there, and there's lots of conversation. Lots of Russian that's flying by me," Jackson says. Everyone spoke freely.

Jackson did not sense any fear of law enforcement, or curious researchers, snooping. In fact, Jackson thinks that a kind of show bidding was taking place. The channel moderator was offering preview accounts to 76service such that the users could tour the site. The hope was they'd come back saying Pesdato! and offer a good price for access.

Jackson asked if he could take a test run, too. If he seemed nervous and unpracticed about doing business here, it was because he was. "The moderator says, 'You don't speak Russian. Where are you from?' I say, 'The UK.' He says, 'Only people we know get test runs.'" A few others derided Jackson for his ignorance and, in so many words, told him to go away. And that was that.

Plan B: Jackson called on a friend who followed the HangUp Team closely, almost the way a CIA analyst builds up expertise. He figured this friend may know how to get access. It was a stab in the dark but remarkably it worked. One colleague knew all about 76service, which he said had been online for several months, and he lent Jackson login credentials to 76service.com.

The 76service Business Model

When Jackson logged in, the genius of 76service became immediately clear. 76service customers weren't paying for already-stolen credentials. Instead, 76service sold subscriptions or "projects" to Gozi-infected machines. Usually, projects were sold in 30-day increments because that's a billing cycle, enough time to guarantee that the person who owns the machine with Gozi on it will have logged in to manage their finances, entering data into forms that could be grabbed.

Subscribers could log in with their assigned user name and password any time during the 30-day project. They'd be met with a screen that told them which of their bots was currently active, and a side bar of management options. For example, they could pull down the latest drops — data deposits that the Gozi-infected machines they subscribed to sent to the servers, like the 3.3 GB one Jackson had found.

A project was like an investment portfolio. Individual Gozi-infected machines were like stocks and subscribers bought a group of them, betting they could gain enough personal information from their portfolio of infected machines to make a profit, mostly by turning around and selling credentials on the black market. (In some cases, subscribers would use a few of the credentials themselves.)

Some machines, like some stocks, would under perform and provide little private information. But others would land the subscriber a windfall of private data. The point was to subscribe to several infected machines to balance that risk, the way Wall Street fund managers invest in many stocks to offset losses in one company with gains in another.

Grabbing forms provides several advantages to both buyer and seller compared with the old model of pulling account numbers out of databases and selling them. For the seller, it's safer. He becomes a broker; a middle man. He barely handles stolen data. For the buyer, it's the added value of an identity compared to a credential. For example, a credit card number alone might be worth $5, but add the three- or four-digit security code associated with that card and the value triples. Add billing address, phone number, cardholder names and so forth which allow a buyer to create new lines of credit and the value can reach into the hundreds of dollars.

Grab the primary and secondary authentication forms used for financial services login in addition to all that, and you've hit the jackpot: A real person's full financial identity. Everything that person had entered into forms online would create an avatar that could be used in the real world to buy goods, apply for credit and passports, buy cell phones, open new bank accounts and manipulate old ones. A dossier like that would be one of the most valuable commodities available on the information black market.

That's why the subscription prices were steep. "Prices started at $1,000 per machine per project," says Jackson. With some tinkering and thanks to some loose database configuration, Jackson gained a view into other people's accounts. He mostly saw subscriptions that bought access to only a handful of machines, rarely more than a dozen.

The $1K figure was for "fresh bots" — new infections that hadn't been part of a project yet. Used bots that were coming off an expired project were available, but worth less (and thus, cost less) because of the increased likelihood that personal information gained from that machine had already been sold. Customers were urged to act quickly to get the freshest bots available.

This was another advantage for the seller. Providing the self-service interface freed up the sellers to create ancillary services. 76service was extremely customer-focused. "They were there to give you services that made it a good experience," Jackson says. You want us to clean up the reports for you? Sure, for a small fee. You want a report on all the credentials from one bank in your drop? Hundred bucks, please. For another $150 a month, we'll create secure remote drops for you. Alternative packaging and delivery options? We can do that. Nickel and dime. Nickel and dime.

March: Containment

SecureWorks researcher Don Jackson was focused on his technical analysis of form-grabbing software, but he continued correspondence with the source who gave him access to 76service.com. After several email exchanges with Jackson, the source decided that he could trust him enough to share what he knew about the people behind 76service. This is part of what he shared.

He told Jackson that the operation was run by just two people, known as 76 and Exoric. 76 was in Russia. Exoric seemed to be based out Mexico. 76 was a member of the HangUp Team who broke off to launch this service. He probably bought the Haxdoor form-grabbing code grafted onto Gozi from his old crew. He might have traded for it. He also probably had a relationship with the RBN from his HangUp Team days. The lack of manpower beyond the two of them might also explain some of the mistakes 76service made, such as the direct connection to RBN servers and the site configuration that allowed Jackson to view other people's projects. It appears 76 recruited Exoric for his server-side knowledge, whereas 76 was coding the actual Trojan.

Jackson was sharing all of this with a field agent from the local FBI office, who sent it up to agents in DC, who in turn coordinated with Russian authorities on an investigation, according to Jackson. (The FBI has refused to comment specifically on the case.) Meanwhile Jackson contacted Infraguard which in turn shared his findings with financial institutions. Jackson wrote an exhaustive technical report, one of the most detailed ever created, that covered both how Gozi worked and how the service did, too. After he published it, and his PR team spread the word, the press pounced: "Gozi Trojan leads to Russian Data Hoard."

Gozi had been known to be in the wild for at least three months. But Jackson also believed that the "Winter Edition" of 76service was by no means the first edition. He suspected that 76service had been operating undetected for perhaps as long as 9 months.

But by mid-March, the good guys seemed to be getting ahead of it. Anti-virus and anti-spyware vendors were adding Gozi signatures to their products to detect the bot. 76service servers had been sent on the run as the FBI and ISPs detected and blocked the IP addresses that Gozi connected to, forcing 76 and Exoric to move the site around constantly. Around March 12, the loose coalition of FBI, researchers, ISPs and others finally seemed to get the 76service shut down.

This spurred a fire sale of whatever data had been left unsold at 76service. Jackson says that after March 12, some banks saw hundreds of accounts opened each day that were traced back to Gozi-grabbed data. Some of those account holders managed to make several cash transfers up to $49,000. "They're playing with limits on fraud," says Jackson. That is, they know the banks won't flag 5 transfers under 50 grand, but will flag one $250,000 transfer. Jackson says many of these transfers were wired to, of all places, Belgium, though he didn't know if anyone had been caught picking up the cash there. Some other accounts were detected and blocked from activity before transfers were made. Jackson says the United States Secret Service was briefed. (The USSS declined to comment.) Gozi and 76service finally seemed to be contained.

But it hardly mattered. By this time, another form-grabbing Trojan had been discovered: Torpig.

Torpig

Torpig's technical architecture and its service were nearly identical to Gozi and 76service, including links to RBN servers. But Torpig was engineered to target bank forms specifically — excluding less useful (read: Valuable) credentials like email logins or logins for newspaper sites. Torpig shipped with a database of financial Web sites' URLs and, when it recognized one of these URLs in the browser's address bar, it woke up and added a redirect command to the URL.

Jackson says that intelligence suggested that the criminals had set up real accounts at the banks on Torpig's hit list and then captured their own legitimate transaction traffic to see what "normal" transactions looked like at each bank. This way, they could tailor each bank's redirect command to mimic a normal transaction, so that filters wouldn't register anomalous activity. Jackson called it "Gozi on steroids." It has proven much more problematic to researchers, banks and law enforcement. Shutting it down has been far more difficult than taking out Gozi, too, because Torpig communicated with a network of servers. Gozi had only connected to the one RBN server.

That is, until March 21, when 76service was discovered back online, running off of a new server in Hong Kong. By March 27, Jackson had confirmed that it used a new variant of Gozi, undetected by filters. It was the "spring edition."

Distributed Pain/Concentrated Gain

The HangUp Team's online art gallery is populated with a disturbing mishmash of images and messages like "Fraud 4ever" and "In Fraud We Trust" (One picture, for example, combines a picture of Hitler, a Cannibas leaf and the head of Eugene Kaspersky, who owns a Russian-based anti-virus company, on a platter.) And yes, pictures of its members often include what have come to be hackneyed criminal hacker clichés, with members posing with their cash, for example.

But do not mistake this culture for incompetence. HangUp Team is one a number of highly successful businesses that some researchers claim earn their members millions of dollars per month. "As a security professional you don't want to say you're impressed by them," says "John" (not his real name), the security professional at a large bank who agreed to talk only if he could remain anonymous, because he didn't have permission from his bank to speak. "But they're better run and managed than many organizations. They're properly funded, they have a clear goal, they're performance driven, focused on a single mission. It's like an MBA case study of success."

There are two key tenets underscoring that success: Distributed pain with concentrated gain, and distributed risk.

The more important of these is distributed pain with concentrated gain.

The massive size of the market that Internet criminals prey on allows them to spread losses across hundreds or thousands of victims. "If you take $10 off of 10,000 credit cards, you've made $100,000 that no one victim either recognized or felt enough to care," says Jim Maloney, a former CSO at Amazon.com who now runs his own security consulting firm. "Then scale that up to five different banks' credit cards." Each bank loses roughly $20,000. "The gain is concentrated for this one hacker group, but the penalty to each bank is still written off as acceptable loss.

"Then go to law enforcement. Unless they hear from many victims and can aggregate the problem as one big one, so that the resources required to chase it down are justified, they won't, they can't chase it down."

And if they did decide to open an investigation, who do they go after? That's the distributed risk element. Groups like the HangUp Team, and 76 himself, deal in access to credentials. 76, for example, barely handles stolen data. He also contracts out the distribution of his malware. And he sells to people who themselves don't commit fraud with the credentials but usually turn around and sell them to still others who actually commit the final fraud by turning stolen information into money and goods.

That's several links in a supply chain all sharing the risk (It's instructive to note that, according to several researchers, one of the biggest frustrations for groups like HangUp Team recently has been "newbies" to the credentials market who buy a credit card and immediately rack up tens of thousands of dollars in luxury goods on that card — essentially concentrating the pain and raising a red flag that can threaten to put the good guys on the scent. It's reminiscent of the movie Goodfellas, when, after the Lufthansa heist, Robert DeNiro's character nervously castigates his crew for bringing attention to themselves by showing up at a Christmas party with new cars and furs.)

The Internet criminals' model perfectly mirrors the drug cartel model, which relies on a stratified market that spreads the risk out to pushers, distributors, mules, manufacturers, and all the money flows up, to the cartel. Disrupting the middle men — and that's what HangUp Team is becoming — doesn't solve the problem. Other middle men will simply arise to fill the void, much the way Smash started the IAACA to fill the void left by ShadowCrew when it was taken down.

"Information is currency, that's the radical change," says Chris Rouland, CTO and IBM Distinguished Engineer with IBM's Internet Security Systems group. "These guys don't need to steal from anyone. They've moved themselves way up the value chain."

April: The iFrame Problem

In early April, the Spring Edition 76service server in Hong Kong was taken down. Filters added the new Gozi variant to their lists of detected malware. On the run again, 76 and Exoric would fold up their tent and modify Gozi to be undetectable again while they found a new place to set up shop. And when they did, the steps would start again, the two sides entwined in an endless, uneasy foxtrot.

Jackson continued to help where he could, but much of this was out of his hands. He had since immersed himself in another facet of 76service — its distribution mechanism.

No matter how inspired the idea of a subscription to infected machines was, or how cleverly engineered the bot that infected those machines was, 76's and Exoric's success with 76service, surprisingly, relied on something they didn't develop themselves, but rather contracted out: Distribution, for which they used iFrames, a browser feature that allows Web sites to deliver content from a remote Web site within a frame on a page. Think of stock quotes origination from one site streamed into a small box on another site. (For more about iFrames, see Death by iFrame.) 76 and Exoric used iFrames to infect computers — but in April they had contracted this part of the work out to another service, iFramebiz.com.

Jackson found a partial list of sites hosting the iFrames used exclusively for Gozi. Jackson sampled 5,848 pages, only a portion of the infected pages on his partial list (meaning 76 and Exoric probably paid tens of thousands of dollars for iFrame infections). Some of the iFramed sites on his list were offline. Some had been cleaned up. But 2,079 of them, more than a third of the sample, still had the code online, ready to deliver new, undetectable versions of Gozi as soon as they were ready. A month later, when Jackson took attendance again, 98 percent of the 2,079 were still hosting the iFrame.

Even if Gozi was gone for good, the iFramers would be happy to resell access to these iFrames to the next malware developer.

Transferred Risk

As much as the HangUp Team has relied on distributed pain for its success, financial institutions have relied on transferred risk to keep the Internet crime problem from becoming a consumer cause and damaging their businesses. So far, it has been cheaper to follow regulations enough to pass audits and then pay for the fraud rather than implement more serious security. "If you look at the volume of loss versus revenue, it's not horribly bad yet," says Chris Hoff, with a nod to the criminal hacker's strategy of distributed pain. "The banks say, 'Regulations say I need to do these seven things, so I do them and let's hope the technology to defend against this catches up.'"

"John" the security executive at the bank, one of the only security professionals from financial services who agreed to speak for this story, says "If you audited a financial institution, you wouldn't find many out of compliance. From a legal perspective, banks can spin that around and say there's nothing else we could do."

The banks know how much data Lance James at Secure Science is monitoring; some of them are his clients. The researcher with expertise on the HangUp Team calls consumers' ability to transfer funds online "the dumbest thing I've ever seen. You can't walk into the branch of a bank with a mask on and no ID and make a transfer. So why is it okay online?"

And yet banks push online banking to customers with one hand while the other hand pushes problems like Gozi away, into acceptable loss budgets and insurance — transferred risk. As long as consumers don't raise a fuss, and thus far they haven't in any meaningful way, the banks have little to fear from their strategies.

But perhaps the only reason consumers don't raise a fuss is because the banks have both overstated the safety and security of online banking and downplayed negative events around it, like the existence of Gozi and 76service.

So did the banks create a false sense of security or did consumers drive them not to address it through their apathy? The banks themselves might argue that they are acting responsibly. It's hard to tell since most decline to talk about the problem. Bill Nelson is president of the Financial Services Information Sharing and Analysis Center, or FS-ISAC, a group for bank security executives where they can safely share intelligence and other information. Membership in the FS-ISAC has increased from 68 in 2004 to 2,200 this year. "That's not a lack of interest," says Nelson.

Nelson was the closest person to bank security executives who would speak on the record. He bristled at the notion that banks are carelessly pushing services they can't secure. "It's being misinterpreted that banks don't care about security. They spend millions of dollars on this. These are good, quality people," Nelson says.

If anything, say Nelson and others, blaming banks is precisely backwards. If you want to point fingers look at their customers, who've created the demand for the product in the first place. "It's kind of ridiculous to think you wouldn't, as a bank, use the Internet as a transport," notes Hoff. "If you're not offering some form of online banking, you're going to wither away and go out of business."

Eric Johnson, an economist at Dartmouth who recently published a study on malware on peer-to-peer networks says, "Customers are the banks' worst enemies here. Customers are exposing lots of material that creates an environment for identity theft."

Indeed, many malware problems are intimately connected to insecure PCs and finicky consumers who, even if they say otherwise, value convenience over security. As one CISO at a bank put it — anonymously, of course, "Users are pretty dumb."

May: A Poor Re-emergence

The hackers known as 76 and Exoric weren't just the managers of 76service; they were also clients. Through his undercover work, SecureWorks researcher Don Jackson found that Exoric himself owned a project — a portfolio of trojan-infected machines — just like the ones the team sold. Only, since access was free to him, his was a much bigger project, with hundreds of bots focused exclusively on Gozi-infected machines in Mexico and Chile (.mx and .cl domains), and no 30-day expiration. For a while, Exoric also used his own storefront for the Latin and South American markets, called GucciService.

But by May the business was strained by the constant pursuit of researchers writing signatures to detect Gozi and law enforcement working with them to find and take down the 76service servers.

Early in the month, Jackson was able to say "Gozi isn't working. No one is going to the site." At this time, his personal site was also the victim of what he termed a poor DDoS attack that lasted 36 hours. Soon after that, when he visited 76service.com, he found it abandoned, with a simple message: "I choose shadow. Please, never come back again."

It seemed that, finally, it was over. But it wasn't, of course. In fact even before Jackson found 76service.com abandoned, a new Gozi variant was already at work, and it would be learned that it had been infecting machines since at least April 14. This latest Gozi bot was better than ever. It had added keystroke logging as an alternative to form grabbing. And recognizing that researchers were their primary adversaries, the new version added features to stymie detection and reverse engineering. "Every copy of Gozi has a unique infection ID," explains Jackson. "So when data comes into the server, it can check against the ID to make sure it's a valid infection. This new version also checked to see what your bot had sent before. Basically it could shut you off if you kept logging in without delivering good data, which is what researchers do." The new version also logged the bot's IP address so that it could be blocked from communicating with the server.

But there were problems. A programming glitch caused the service to create huge files of redundant information, interrupting service to customers while the duo tried to fix it. "That's why QA testing is so important," deadpans Jackson. They had only nabbed about 500MB of data off of 200 infected PCs when their new ISP, which Jackson says was based in Panama, took them offline again.

It was a poor reemergence. Lurking on a discussion board with a colleague who could translate Russian, Jackson found a post by someone named 57, a hacker thought to be part of the HangUp Team. 57 wrote that 76 broke off work with Exoric because the two were spending more time on the lam than they did running the service.

The FBI had wound down on the case, according to Jackson (though in an official statement given to CSO from the press office, the FBI says it welcomes any leads on information related to Gozi and 76service, which it termed "unique"). While they continued to monitor some accounts they knew were connected to 76service, Jackson didn't think it would progress beyond that. 76service was officially defunct. By early June, 76 and Exoric had dissolved their partnership.

But 57 also seemed to indicate that 76 was back with HangUp Team and busy rewriting the Gozi form grabber. The new architecture would allow 76 to hide the drop servers from prying eyes, making it harder to interrupt or shut services down.

Jackson predicted at the time that a new 76service would follow in kind. After all, 76service didn't fail because of the service model. It failed because of a lack of manpower to secure and manage the service. It couldn't scale. "I think they cobbled together Gozi and 76service to see what it could do," says Jackson. "They realize what they need to do next. They spotted weaknesses. Torpig was the next step; it was better. Now what's next?" With the help of the HangUp Team, a 76service-like site capable of enduring its own success, will return using some descendant of Gozi or Torpig.

The Radical New Strategy?

If users are, as one bank CISO said, dumb; and if banks can just write off their losses; and if the Internet is fundamentally insecure; and if vendors defenses can't keep up; and if law enforcement is overmatched; what happens next?

Don Jackson thinks that the banks will simply transfer more of the risk. "The banks are worried, but their answer is not to track these guys down or be more diligent about security," says Jackson, who says he remembers talking about this with bank security types at last year's Information Systems Security Association (ISSA) conference. "Their answer is to shift more responsibility on to their customers. They'll lower fraud limits, the amount of stolen funds they'll cover. They'll make it harder for consumers to prove they were defrauded — and easier to say it was the customer's fault. You'll have to prove that you kept your end of the deal by patching your system and so forth. Watch the terms of use for online banking. I think you'll see changes."

Like Jackson, Chris Rouland of IBM ISS believes the days of acceptable loss at the banks are numbered, but he has a hard time seeing a "blame the customer" strategy succeed. "These write-offs, this thing about putting it on consumers, it will end. It has to," he says.

Rouland says that he is rethinking security at a fundamental level, and many others in the industry are as well. "We're basically telling banks that client security is your problem, not [your customers'] problem. We're saying all the awareness in the world can not adequately secure client machines. Telling customers to secure themselves will not work. We believe that in order to fix the problem, you have to protect customers' customers. You have no choice."

Notice Rouland did not say you have to secure the client. He never says the banks must figure out a way to protect that machine. That's careful and deliberate, because Rouland doesn't believe that's what banks have to do. When it comes to security PCs, Rouland's advice is radical: Give up.

"In the next generation," he says, "we will all do business with infected end points," he says.

He was asked to repeat what he said, just to be sure. So he did: "Our strategy is we have to figure out how you do business with an infected computer. How do you secure a transaction with an infected machine? Whoever figures out how to do that first will win."

June: Disturbing Developments

By mid-June, Gozi was practically forgotten, and the new thing was MPACK. This one even had some veteran researchers muttering pesdato!

A typical Trojan like Gozi might rely on one exploit to try and open up a connection with the target PC. MPACK, on the other hand, is a briefcase full of exploits, a dozen or more of them. Mostly they're old exploits, but the idea is that if you try 15 different lock picks, one is bound to get you in. What's more, MPACK then reports back to its server which exploits worked where and stores that information in a database, an intelligence function used to effectively pack the briefcases with the most successful lock picks. The practice seems to have vastly increased the successful infection rate of PCs that visit sites delivering MPACK.

MPACK is actually sold with malware such that once the briefcase of exploits gets access, a Trojan — often Torpig — will be delivered to the PC. Other Trojans, like Apophis (which steals digital certificates) and even the old Nuclear Grabber that Corpse was hocking more than a year ago are also available in conjunction with MPACK. It costs hundreds to thousands of dollars.

Researchers still trying to penetrate this service say that MPACK is being sold by sash, likely the same as "sash" whom posted news of Corpse's semi-retirement on the Pinch3.net discussion board. (Sash sells Pinch, too.) Sash in turn seems to be working with Step57, a group likely run by 57, the HangUp Team coder who Jackson had found who posted the news of 76service's demise. All of these players have connections to the Russian Business Network, according to several researchers, including Jackson.

MPACK's multiple-exploit technique was used before in an exploit called WebAttacker. But MPACK is more effective because of iFrames. Disturbingly, the iFramers seem to have come up with some automated exploit kit capable of infecting a massive number of Web pages with illicit iFrames in a short period of time, "like a machine gun spraying holes in sites" says Lance James. The first round of iFrame injections created to deliver MPACK showed up, literally, overnight — more than 10,000 pages were infected, mostly on Italian sites. Since then, the process has repeated itself, moving country to country. Thousands of infections all at once.

Researchers are still trying to understand what allows the deployment of so many iFrames so quickly. Mostly they're reporting on rumors and theories. Using a virtual host to infect many sites is one working theory. But no one knows yet for sure how it's done. What they do know is iFraming is officially pandemic. "The iFramers are making a killing," Jackson says. "They don't get their hands dirty with the actual malware. They just break into a server with scripts. It's a good business to be in right now."

Fraud 4ever

"The thing about MPACK," says James, "this is the start of the whole thing." By this, he seems to mean that Golden Age of Internet Crime, that dawning era. "They're starting to think like architects instead of engineers." MPACK brings together the best iFrames, the best exploits and some state-of-the-art malware into a single package, all of which is being improved constantly, and sold with a focus on customer service. In marketing parlance, it's not a product, it's a solution.

Business is good. Internet criminals operate with de facto immunity. The pool of vulnerable computers to exploit remains massive. The target financial institutions still treat their crime as acceptable loss. Law enforcement is otherwise occupied. And technical defenses are mere market conditions to adapt to. For example, when some clever banks came up with a way to beat keylogging by having users use "virtual keyboards" on the screen, criminal hackers just developed Briz, code that captures the pixels around the cursor, the pictures of the characters being typed. Problem solved.

The criminals innovate. Some tactics will make the hair on your neck prickle. Rumors persist of a nasty Brazilian banking Trojan that can change banking account numbers, routing numbers, balance, and payment/transfer values by injecting HTML or even whole, cloned HTTP requests into an online banking session on the fly, such that the person banking would see false information that reflected their intentions and not the actual transfer. Chris Rouland of IBM has seen similar functionality in a bot called Grams.

Prg, another form-grabbing Trojan discovered last October, makes researchers awfully nervous. New variants emerge every couple of months and managed to steal tens of GB of data before being detected. Its encryption is strong and well-designed, its ability to hide itself with anti-forensics deft.

In June, Don Jackson found a new Prg variant. It shipped with a development kit which allows anyone who buys it to adapt the code on the fly in order to evade anti-virus and anti-spyware. On the server where he found it, he also found a staging area where new variants were already developed and waiting to be released as soon as the defenses recognized and blocked the current variant. He also found a couple of drops for two different groups who had bought Prg and distributed it through both iFrames and some good old-fashioned "click-on-this-link" emails. The drops comprised 10,000 account credentials, including second factors of authentication and answers to those security check questions like your mother's maiden name meant to layer extra security into the online banking process.

"There's a consumer side of me that says, Be cautious but life must go on. Someone somehow will take care of this," says Christopher Hoff. "And the security side of me wants to curl up in the fetal position and not go out."

After Jackson discovered the Prg variant, he learned of two more Gozi variants found in the wild. The EXE inside these versions is called 76.EXE, and is probably the product of 76's reunion with the HangUp Team. It's pesdato! It has vastly improved its server network and obfuscation techniques. It bounces traffic from country to country. It hides its drops well. In fact, Jackson's not sure what it even connects to. He's looking for the front end, the next 76service. He knows it's out there. But so far he can't find it.

14 Illicit Money: Can It Be Stopped?

Raymond Baker & Eva Joly

On May 4, the Obama administration announced a plan to crack down on offshore tax havens, which it said are costing the United States tens of billions of dollars each year. The President's proposals were primarily aimed at finding ways to increase revenue from wealthy companies and investors who use loopholes in the law and offshore subsidiaries to reduce their US taxes. But the administration is largely missing a far more devastating problem related to offshore finance: Money gained from criminal and other illicit sources. With the use of tax havens and other elements of an increasingly complex "shadow" financial network, vast sums of illegal money are being shifted throughout the global economy virtually undetected.

Illicit money is usually generated by one of three kinds of activities: Bribery and theft; organized crime; and corporate dealings such as tax evasion and false commercial transactions. Because they are largely invisible, flows of illicit money across borders are difficult to measure. The World Bank estimates that they range from $1 trillion to $1.6 trillion annually, of which about half — $500 billion to $800 billion — comes out of developing countries ranging from Equatorial Guinea to Kazakhstan to Peru.

Friedrich Schneider, an Austrian economist, suggests that money laundering on behalf of organized crime and other illegal sources in just twenty OECD countries amounts to some $600 billion per year. Global Financial Integrity, an organization in Washington, D.C., finds that illegal flows of money from developing countries to banks in Western countries may reach more than $1 trillion annually. While there are different ways to quantify the problem and obtaining reliable data is difficult, these estimates are within a surprisingly narrow range.[1] Taken together, they suggest that trillions of dollars of illicit money are flowing through international financial markets. Where is this money coming from?

Drug trafficking, racketeering, and terrorist financing are among the leading causes of money laundering, while in recent years the financial corruption of rogue political figures such as General Sani Abacha of Nigeria, Vladimiro Montesinos, the former intelligence chief of Peru, Pavlo Lazarenko, the former prime minister of Ukraine, and others has received much attention in the press. In fact, however, organized crime accounts for only about a third of illicit money flows, while money stolen by corrupt government officials amounts to just 3 percent. The most common way illicit money is moved across borders — accounting for some 60 to 65 percent of all illicit flows — is through international trade.

According to the World Trade Organization, the total annual global trade in goods and services before the current economic crisis was approaching $40 trillion;[2] but as much as $2 trillion of the total may be illicit money that has been illegally moved out of a country, or has been used to provide illegal kickbacks to corrupt executives or officials.

Russia has experienced what is probably the greatest theft of resources ever to occur in a short period of time, some $200 billion to $500 billion since the early 1990s. Almost all of this was accomplished by the deceptive under pricing of exports of oil, gas, diamonds, gold, tin, zinc, nickel, timber, and other resources. Oil was ostensibly sold abroad for as little as $10 a metric ton, with the balance of the real value paid into European and American bank accounts of Russian oligarchs. China has experienced a similar drain of financial assets, again accomplished through under pricing exports of, at first, consumer goods and now a widening range of technology products.

Of any major country Nigeria has probably had the highest percentage of its gross domestic product stolen — largely by corrupt officials — and deposited externally. Since the 1960s, up to $400 billion has been lost because of corruption, with $100 billion shifted out of the country. Of the population of about 150 million, some 100 million live on $1 to $2 a day. Unrest in the poverty-ridden Niger Delta is so severe that oil production has dropped from a peak of 2.6 million barrels a day in 2006 to 1.7 million today.

Venezuela's state-owned oil company, Petróleos de Venezuela S.A., has abused transfer pricing to shift enormous wealth abroad. Crude oil is under-priced and sold to Petróleos's twenty-three foreign refineries in the United States, Europe, and the Caribbean, which then sell gasoline and other products at normal prices; the profits are thereby largely kept outside the country, for the use of corrupt officials. Hugo Chávez recently appointed his sixth managing director as he attempts to wrest control of the company, which is the state's principal provider of revenue, while at the same time running a government as corrupt as its predecessors.

In these and other cases, a common strategy for hiding and moving large sums of money is falsified pricing in international trade. Prices are falsified in one of two ways. In the first, the invoice from the exporter is sent to an office in a tax haven where it is rewritten with an altered price. Then the new invoice is forwarded on to the importer. Alternatively, a false price may appear on the invoice sent directly by the exporter to the importer after they have agreed, usually verbally, to deposit a portion of the payment in a foreign account. Unlike invoices that are rewritten, this second form of mispricing is invisible in recorded international trade statistics but can be detected by comparing major and consistent deviations in pricing from normal world market prices. For example, research by Simon Pak and John Zdanowicz has shown systematic under pricing on invoices for US exports, including car seats exported to Belgium that were invoiced for $1.66 each; ATM machines exported to El Salvador for $35.95 each; and forklift trucks exported to Jamaica for $384.14 each. By this strategy, the US exporter drastically reduces its US tax burden, while presumably receiving much larger sums from the buyer that may then be hidden in offshore banks. Within multinational corporations, the practice of mispricing can also be used as a tax-avoidance strategy. Take the following simplified example: A company in country A makes photocopy machines that have a production cost of $1,000. The company establishes a dummy corporation in a tax haven that buys the copiers at cost for $1,000 apiece. Since the company has not made any profit on the sale, no taxes are owed. The dummy corporation in the tax haven then sells the copiers to another subsidiary in country C, at a price of $2,000 each. Now the company in country A is making a profit of $1,000 on each machine sold, but since the sales are through the offshore dummy corporation, the company pays only those marginal taxes that are charged in the tax haven. The subsidiary in country C may in turn sell the copiers on the open market for $1,500 each, allowing it to claim, for tax purposes, a $500 loss on the $2,000 purchase price. But since the company in country A owns all of the parties involved in the transaction, it is actually making a $500 profit on each sale.

The Global System of Illicit Finance

Falsified pricing and other money-laundering techniques have been facilitated by the rapid growth of tax havens and secrecy jurisdictions ranging from Monaco to the Cayman Islands. By welcoming disguised corporations, anonymous trust accounts, fake foundations, and other entities for hiding money, these offshore financial centers create the space in which many billions of dollars in unseen and unrecorded proceeds can be shifted across borders.

Minor parts of this system were in existence earlier, but the 1960s marked the takeoff point for two reasons. First, from the late 1950s through the end of the 1960s, forty-eight countries gained independence from colonial powers. Many leaders in these new countries, sometimes influenced by domestic instability and cold war politics, wanted to take money abroad; bankers in Western countries responded by devising creative strategies such as the use of secret accounts and false invoices for moving large sums across borders. Leaders including Mobutu Sese Seko in the Congo, Ferdinand Marcos in the Philippines, Suharto in Indonesia, and others made use of dozens of overseas banks competing for their millions of dollars of ill-gotten gains.

Second, during the 1960s a number of large corporations became multinational, establishing hundreds of locations across the globe, sometimes even moving corporate headquarters offshore. "Tax planning" — devising creative ways to reduce or avoid corporate taxes — became a normal practice.

Thus, decolonization and the growing international reach of corporations propelled the development of a whole system of offshore finance that was designed to avoid taxes and regulation. In the process, the system also obscures the origin and destination of the increasingly large sums of money passing through it.

Of course, some financial activities in tax havens are perfectly legal, and many individuals and corporations may use them simply to move funds offshore to reduce their tax exposure in their country of residence. But by enacting privacy laws and allowing corporations and individuals to be represented by trustees, many such havens permit companies and foundations established in their jurisdictions to mask the true identity of their owners. This enables all types of depositors to circumvent standard accounting and reporting requirements on transactions and profits simply by routing them through a tax haven. In recent years, the Swiss bank UBS created offshore accounts for thousands of US clients, violating US law in the process. The bank is paying a $780 million fine on the resulting criminal charge and is being forced to provide the names of 4,450 of its US clients in settlement of a civil action by the US.

Through the combination of low or no taxes, little or no financial reporting requirements, lax regulation, and well-defended secrecy, tax havens have grown to the point where they control an estimated $6 trillion in assets. Many now cater to particular market niches. The Isle of Jersey serves companies such as Bank of America and Morgan Stanley that are active in the London market, just as Panama, which is used by AIG and American Express, among other companies, serves the US market, and Vanuatu the Australian market. Mauritius is a channel for investments into India. Cyprus is a preferred center for Russian money laundering, and the British Virgin Islands have become especially favored by Chinese businesses shifting illicit capital in and out of their home country.

Providing the highest level of secrecy are Liechtenstein, Singapore, Dubai, and the Turks and Caicos Islands. Bermuda and Guernsey use favorable tax laws to draw in billions of dollars in reinsurance funds from firms such as

Scottish Re. The Cayman Islands, which hold nearly $2 trillion in foreign-owned cash and other liquid assets, are home to more than ten thousand "collective investment schemes" such as hedge funds.[3] Banks in Switzerland, London, and New York, among them Credit Suisse, Barclays, and Citigroup, serve very rich clients by directing transactions through more than twenty Caribbean tax havens.[4]

Economic Development

Through the 1990s and into the current decade, overseas development assistance to poor countries has totaled about $50 billion to $80 billion a year from all sources. But compare this amount to the World Bank's estimate of $500 billion to $800 billion of capital that is being sent illegally out of these same countries: For every $1 handed out across the top of the table, the West has been receiving back up to $10 under the table. This outflow of illicit money is the most damaging economic condition in the developing world. It drains hard currency reserves, increases inflation, reduces tax collection, widens income gaps, forestalls investment, stifles competition, and undercuts free trade. Until development experts account for total capital going into and coming out of recipient countries, aid will continue to be offset by a much larger counter-force of fleeing capital.

In recent years some human rights groups have begun to address flight capital and other forms of financial corruption as a human rights issue, among them Global Witness, Human Rights Watch, Christian Aid, Action Aid–UK, and the Open Society Institute. The environmental group Greenpeace's recent report "Conning the Congo" is an example, criticizing a Swiss-based logging group for "using an elaborate profit-laundering system designed to move income out of Africa and into offshore bank accounts."[5]

The international system of illicit finance has another serious consequence — its contribution to the shift of taxes away from large businesses, which can evade them, and onto everyday workers. This assures rising incomes for the wealthy and visibly stagnating incomes for the middle class, contributing to the dramatic increase in income disparity in rich and poor nations alike. Political analysts have largely ignored how a capitalist system increasingly operating outside the rule of law affects the ability to spread the rule of law. How can the US and other countries claim to extend democracy while they allow an international financial system to flourish that worsens the condition of poor people?

Consequences for Security

The growth of illicit finance comes at a heavy price not only to taxpayers in advanced nations and poor people in developing nations, but also to global security. For almost every kind of criminal organization, a major concern is transferring illegitimate gains into the legitimate financial system. Beginning in the late 1960s and 1970s, the Medellín and Cali cartels and other drug traffickers started making use of tax havens and countries that allowed them secrecy to launder their proceeds. In 1989 the G-7 authorized the establishment of a Financial Action Task Force in Paris to address this problem. Now, twenty years later, how effective has it been against the flagrant target, the drug trade? In fact, the supply of illegal drugs has not been curtailed and prices are largely stable, except in Europe where soaring demand has elevated traffickers' receipts. Meanwhile, over the past two decades, other kinds of racketeers — ranging from arms dealers to human traffickers — have begun using the same offshore financial mechanisms to launder tens of billions of dollars.

Many militant groups and terrorist organizations now use the same system of offshore finance. During the decade before the September 11 attacks an estimated $30 million to $50 million a year was passed to al Qaeda through fake foundations, disguised corporations, and bankers based in tax havens. Supporters of Hezbollah have engaged in cigarette smuggling in the United States and diamond smuggling in West Africa. Hamas is believed to be active in crime and money laundering in the tri-border region of Latin America where Brazil, Argentina, and Paraguay meet. In Iran, the Islamic Revolutionary Guard Corps is allegedly involved in smuggling oil, arms, electronics, and consumer goods, possibly amounting to $12 billion a year.[6]

The Saddam Hussein regime was especially adept at large-scale money laundering. During the decade after the Persian Gulf War, Saddam amassed some $10 billion via the Oil-for-Food program, smuggling, and kickbacks on trade transactions, which helped to purchase radar systems, combat helicopters, tanks, and other armaments. The Iraqi regime's lavish military spending helped persuade the United States, Britain, and others to believe that it had the capacity to acquire weapons of mass destruction. If it were not for Saddam's manipulation of illicit finance, Western forces might not be in Iraq today.

What Is to Be Done?

International efforts to address illicit financial flows are plainly inadequate. In many Western countries, tax laws have many loopholes and legislation against money laundering is poorly enforced. For example, the United States bars the incoming proceeds of drug trafficking as well as terrorist financing, bank fraud, and theft by foreign government officials; but it does not bar proceeds generated abroad from such activities as handling stolen property, counterfeiting, contraband, slave trading, human smuggling, trafficking in women, environmental crimes, and foreign tax evasion.

In April, the Manhattan district attorney's office filed charges against a Chinese defense company for using shell companies to channel the proceeds of armament deals with the Iranian military through New York banks, including Bank of America, JP Morgan Chase, and American Express Bank. Both the parent Chinese company and its Iranian client had been barred from doing business in the United States, but the source and destination of the illicit money was unknown to the banks in question. Indeed, US Treasury Department officials estimate that 99.9 percent of the money that US law prohibits from entering the country is accepted for deposit the first time it is presented to a US bank.

Can anything be done? The goal should be to curtail this activity, not to try to stop it, which would be impossible. Widespread support for a few select and straightforward steps would do much to contain illicit financial networks.

The European Union Savings Tax Directive is one example of such a step. Put into effect in 2005, it requires tax information to be automatically shared among twenty-four European countries, with Austria, Belgium, and Luxembourg planning to join over the next two years. Ten overseas territories associated with the UK and the Netherlands are also participating. Currently, the agreement requires disclosure to EU governments of payments to non-resident EU citizens of interest earned on deposits, corporate and government bonds, negotiable debt securities, and investment funds.

European leaders are now discussing extending this oversight to corporations, shell companies, trusts, and foundations, as well as requiring companies to report dividends, realized capital gains, income from pensions and insurance, and interest on other types of bonds. Annual reporting of such earnings will go a long way toward curtailing tax evasion by citizens and corporations in EU member states. Such automatic sharing of financial information should become a global standard.

The European Economic and Monetary Affairs Committee of the EU Parliament has also approved a proposal to require country-by-country reporting of profits by corporations within the EU. Corporations currently compile these figures for internal purposes but do not report such information to state regulators. Country-by-country accounting to such regulators for revenues, costs, and profits would therefore not be a burden to corporations but would be hugely beneficial to tax authorities and go far toward reducing the usefulness of tax havens.

Financial institutions should be required to know the beneficial owners of every entity with which they do business, going beyond nominees and trustees to the names of individuals or publicly quoted parent companies. The USA Patriot Act, signed into law shortly after the September 11 attacks, took such a step regarding foreign shell banks operating behind cloaks of secrecy. It prohibited any US financial institution from receiving money from a foreign shell bank and any foreign financial institution from transferring money to the US received from a foreign shell bank, and even banned wire transfers of such funds that momentarily passed through New York City correspondent banking accounts. In other words, with a stroke of the legislative pen, the threat posed by foreign shell banks was largely removed from the shadow financial system — which will now try to circumvent the new law.

Senator Charles Grassley of Iowa has also proposed a bill that would eliminate the loopholes in US anti-money-laundering laws by specifying simply that it is a felony offense to knowingly handle the proceeds of a crime, including tax evasion, whether committed in the United States or abroad. Senator Carl Levin of Michigan and other lawmakers have proposed a tax haven abuse act aimed at substantially curtailing tax evasion by US citizens and corporations. Key provisions of Senator Levin's bill are now being incorporated into a similar bill drafted by Senator Max Baucus, chairman of the Senate Finance Committee. At first somewhat behind Europe, momentum is now building in the United States to deal with these issues.

A simple step available to developing countries to curtail abusive transfer pricing, and recently recommended to Congo by the Washington-based organization Global Financial Integrity, is to require two signatures on commercial invoices. On the standardized invoice form, importers and exporters would each have to confirm that prices reflect world market norms, constitute no violations of anti-money-laundering laws anywhere, and contain no element of mispricing for the purpose of manipulating customs duties, VAT taxes, or income taxes in the exporting or importing countries or jurisdictions through which the transaction passes. If multinational corporations asked employees to sign patently false statements giving such assurances, they could potentially be held criminally liable under the laws of exporting or importing countries.

Countries with adequate banking sectors but severe transfer pricing problems, such as Russia, can require imports and exports above a certain value to be covered by confirmed, irrevocable letters of credit containing a provision that 100 percent of export proceeds must be remitted by the importer's bank to the exporter's bank. Such letters of credit can likewise require that banks verify prices on invoices, as is now required in the United States under standards set by the Federal Financial Institutions Examination Council.

The World Bank should declare the entire question of world financial movements to be a problem demanding immediate analysis and action. Cutting the flow of illicit flight capital out of poor countries by even 25 percent, a modest goal, would leave more money in poor countries than the total of overseas development assistance provided by rich-country donors. Far greater than a 25 percent reduction in such outflows is readily achievable, if the political will is there.

Recent scandals are widening the perception that illegal, hidden dealings are incurring huge costs to the global economy. Enron, WorldCom, and Parmalat; Liechtenstein and UBS involvement in tax evasion; Elf Aquitaine and alleged BAE Systems corruption; the financial forces behind today's severe banking crisis — these and many more cases confirm the destructive role played by a global financial system that permits trillions of dollars to evade accountability.

Yet the first two meetings of the G-20 left every element of the shadow financial system in place, albeit with promises that some regulatory improvements would be applied to tax havens, banks, and financial instruments. A containment strategy is emerging, but it is far from being adequately applied. The culture of financial opacity and corruption, if continued, will increase the misery of the poor and undermine the stability of nations throughout the world.

Notes

1. See "Stolen Asset Recovery (StAR) Initiative: Challenges, Opportunities, and Action Plan," (Washington, DC: World Bank, 2007); Friedrich Schneider, "Money Laundering and Financial Means of Organized Crime: Some Preliminary Empirical Findings," Johannes Kepler University of Linz working paper (July 2008), p. 24; and Dev Kar and Devon Cartwright-Smith, "Illicit Financial Flows from Developing Countries: 2002–2006" (Global Financial Integrity, 2009), pp. 21–22.
2. World Trade Organization data puts global exports and imports of goods and services at $33.8 trillion in 2007 and $39.1 trillion in 2008.
3. Cayman Islands Monetary Authority, "Regulatory Framework: Statistics" (June 2008), http://www.cimoney.com.ky/section/regulatoryframework/sub/default.aspx?section=PD&id=666.
4. Richard Murphy, "Tax Havens: Creating Turmoil," (Tax Justice Network UK, 2008), p. 24.
5. "Conning the Congo" (Greenpeace International, July 2008), p. 2.
6. Ali Alfoneh, "How Intertwined Are the Revolutionary Guards in Iran's Economy?," Middle Eastern Outlook, No. 3 (October 2007).

Weapons for Warlords: Arms Trafficking in the Gulf of Aden

15

Andrew Black

In the Hobbesian anarchy that has been the norm in Somalia since the late 1980s, the proliferation of weapons has been associated not only with the pursuit of political power but also with international terrorism and the protection and furtherance of economic objectives in the region. Somalia lies at the heart of regional arms trafficking networks that include governments and private traders in East Africa and the Arabian Peninsula. Developed over many years, this market relies on traditional trade routes, military supply lines and corruptible government actors to provide material support to clansmen, warlords, and militants who purchase or barter for small arms, such as Kalashnikov rifles, rocket propelled grenades (RPGs) and larger weapons systems, such as anti-aircraft guns and "technicals" (armored pick-up trucks with weapons mounted in the back). Currently sustained and developed primarily by a mix of opportunistic businessmen and foreign governments who are strengthening local proxies, the arms trade in and around Somalia serves as a reliable, highly adaptable, and readily accessible wellspring of material that feeds regional conflicts.

Collapsing Regimes and the Rise of Private Traffickers

The arms markets around the Gulf of Aden were developed as a byproduct of the Cold War, as the great powers sought to further their strategic objectives in the region. During the latter years of the Cold War, East Africa played an important role in the great power dynamic, with the United States and the Soviet Union propping up regional proxies such as the governments of Somalia, Ethiopia, and the People's Democratic Republic of Yemen (i.e., South Yemen). However, with the end of the Cold War and the collapse of the governments in Somalia and Ethiopia, official stocks of arms increasingly became available through regional markets. The fall of the communist Dergue regime in Ethiopia in 1987 and the Siad Barre dictatorship in Somalia in 1991 released a large amount of weapons, including tanks, into various East African markets. The region witnessed another influx of weapons later in the 1990s as governments and private vendors supplied the Ethiopian and Eritrean militaries in their war against one another.[1]

In the 1980s and 1990s, arms markets and influential parties in the region, particularly in Somalia, received weapons through the activities of private arms dealers and corporations operating in Somalia. These private vendors came to public attention in March 1994 with the murder in Somalia of Italian journalist Ilaria Alpi and her cameraman, Miran Hrovatin. The two were in Somalia investigating rumors of embezzled humanitarian aid and illicit arms trafficking from Italy to Somalia.[2] Another case involved a Polish company, Cenrex, which exported arms to Latvia, which were then shipped to Croatia and Somalia, two countries that were under U.N. arms embargos at the time.[3]

European businesses also supplied weapons to Somali clansmen and warlords as a means of obtaining permission for various activities such as illegal fishing or toxic waste disposal. One example involved an Italian firm that dumped toxic waste in Somalia after providing weapons and ammunition to powerful Somali clansmen.[4] Included in this network was Giancarlo Marocchino, a well-known Italian shipping businessman based in the port city of Karaan, who was arrested by U.N. troops in Mogadishu in 1993 for his suspected involvement in arms trafficking. Deals arranged by this Italian network and other brokers included arms shipments from Ravenna, La Spezia, and Leghorn in Italy, and the involvement of Italian Mafia, particularly the Calabrians.[5] Other publicized trafficking routes from this era include one running from Ireland to Somalia, via Cyprus and Lebanon.[6]

This history of arms traffic into and within the Horn of Africa not only provided the foundations for the regional arms trade — contributing a crucial influx of material and experienced traders — but it also exacerbated many of the drivers of the current conflict in Somalia. Moreover, the supply lines established in earlier decades, such as those outlined above, continue to feed the still vibrant Somali arms market.

The Somali Market Adapts to a New Era

In recent years, the development of a militant Islamist opposition to rival the U.N.-recognized Transitional Federal Government (TFG) has rejuvenated the flow of arms into Somalia from foreign governments and suppliers. Regional governments, led by Ethiopia and Eritrea, provided arms and financial support to their proxies on either side of the Somali conflict.

The Ethiopian military has provided broad and vital support to the TFG and friendly Somali clans, including material, training and troops even before the Ethiopian military invaded Somalia in late 2006. While the amount of support that Ethiopia has provided to date is difficult to verify, successive U.N. reports have pointed to substantial support from Addis Ababa to the TFG and authorities in Puntland and Somaliland.[7] As noted below, Ethiopian troops and associates in the TFG are a common and prolific source of weapons for the Somali arms markets.

On the other side of this dynamic, the government of Eritrea has been singled out by the U.N. as having provided significant material and financial support to Islamist groups. In late July 2006, two cargo shipments that landed at Mogadishu airport were suspected of bringing arms to the Islamic Courts Union (ICU). Though bearing Kazakh markings and rumored to be owned by or affiliated with Russian arms dealer Viktor Bout, the shipment is widely suspected to have been provided by Eritrea but may have originated in Yemen or Libya, according to a Western diplomat stationed in the region at the time. More recently, Omar Hashi Aden, the Security Minister of the TFG, claimed that three aircraft landed at an airstrip outside Mogadishu loaded with arms from Eritrea for Islamist insurgents.[8] Abdulkadir Haji Muhammad Dakane of the Asmara wing of the Alliance for the Re-Liberation of Somalia (ARS-Asmara) denied the allegation.[9]

While governments like Ethiopia and Eritrea have facilitated the supply of arms to local proxies, elements within Saudi Arabia, the United Arab Emirates, and Yemen have served as key sources of weapons and finances entering the Somali market.[10] Yemen in particular — where large arms markets have historically supported militants and intertribal conflict in the Arabian Peninsula and East Africa — is a well-documented source of weapons for vendors in Somalia selling to clansmen, warlords, and Islamists alike. Prior to the government's efforts to curtail domestic markets, major arms markets existed in the Jahanah,

Sa'dah, Al-Bayda, Al-Jawf, and Abyan provinces.[11] Despite Yemen's efforts to reduce the arms market, the U.N. noted that, "commercial imports, mainly from Yemen, remain the most consistent source of arms, ammunition and military material to Somalia."

Transport routes for arms entering Somalia are fluid and varied, following traditional trade routes across the Gulf of Aden and responding rapidly to new markets and government countermeasures. For example, an investigation by the Stockholm International Peace Research Institute (SIPRI) reported that aircraft used to transport humanitarian aid and peacekeeping support had also been used in transporting arms.[12] Alternatively, weapons from the Arabian Peninsula often enter Somali ports on dhows or are offloaded onto Somali vessels at sea. Indeed the U.N. has claimed that "maritime traffic from Yemen, across the Gulf of Aden, remains [Somalia's] largest single source of arms." Weapons trading from Yemeni dhows through remote natural ports are a part of the wider general trade (fuel, plastic-ware, cement, food, etc.) aimed at avoiding customs duties. Usually, several weapons traders arrange for their respective consignments to be transported on the same dhow to share transport costs. Popular ports include Heis, Maidh and Laasqoray in northern Somalia, Haradheere and Hobyo in the Mudug region, and Ceel Dheer in the Galgaduud region. Kismayo has also been a common port for arms from the Arabian Peninsula and East African sources, and other southern locations appear to be popular trans-shipment points for arms heading for the ethnic-Somali Ogaden National Liberation Front (ONLF) in eastern Ethiopia.

The Domestic Market in Somalia

Within Somalia, supply and trans-shipment points can be found from Somaliland to Kismayo, providing a complex milieu through which vendors can access the broad array of customers active in Somali markets. In the north, locations like Burao and Hargeisa in Somaliland are popular destinations for arms entering from the Arabian Peninsula. This region is dominated by traders in the Warsangeli sub-clan, who offer fishing rights to traffickers who supply the region with arms and more traditional commodities like cement and plastics. Notably, the Warsangeli clan controls Gaan in northern Somalia, close to the town of Laasqoray where Italian sailors were held by Somali pirates.[13] Warsangeli clansmen provide arms to vendors throughout Somalia as well as sell directly to Somali clansmen, warlords, and the ONLF in Ethiopia.

As already indicated, arms markets in Somalia are sustained by an assortment of sources including elements within the Transitional Federal Government, the African Union Mission in Somalia (AMISOM), the Ethiopian military and militant Islamist groups such as al-Shabaab. The U.N. estimates that up to eighty percent of the weapons circulating in the domestic arms market come from the TFG and Ethiopian forces alone. In its April 2008 report, the U.N. arms embargo monitoring group reported a process whereby the government and Ugandan peacekeeping forces, who entered the market through their Somali translators, resell seized arms caches through Somali middlemen into the domestic market and even directly to al-Shabaab.[14]

Indeed, furthering the argument that government and peacekeeping personnel are engaged in arms trading, several militant leaders have noted the corruptible role of government forces in the Somali arms markets. For example, Sheikh Mukhtar Robow Abu Mansur, the former spokesman for al-Shabaab, addressed the issue of TFG troops returning to southern Somalia after training in Ethiopia by declaring "We say to these troops: Do not imperil your lives, desert your duties. If you come to us, we will buy your arms and save your lives."[15] A year earlier, the ONLF chairman denied that his organization was receiving support from Eritrea, but instead admitted they were acquiring weapons in Somalia from sources that included the Ethiopian military.[16]

Traditionally, the principal access point to the Somali arms market was through the Bakaara Market in Mogadishu. However, since 2006, the market has devolved into a network of smaller markets due in part to pressure from the ICU and increasing insecurity in the Bakaara Market area of Mogadishu. The U.N. reports that a somewhat coordinated network of markets has emerged in and immediately surrounding Mogadishu, centered around sub-clan areas and buyers and located at Suuq Ba'ad, Karaan, Huriwa, Elasha, Medina, and Arjantin. Using revenues from smuggling, remittances from the diaspora, piracy revenues, and even funding from the Eritrean government, al-Shabaab and similar groups are able to readily obtain a broad array of weaponry, according to the U.N. The typical weapons available through these markets are small arms and crew-served infantry weapons, including Kalashnikov assault rifles, RPGs, mortars, anti-tank weapons, and surface to air missiles like the SA-7.

Efforts to Contain the Market

Governments around the Gulf of Aden have instituted a number of policies and accords to limit the regional flow of arms, in part as a means of containing the potential security implications of bleed-out from Somalia. Examples of these policies include the 1992 U.N. Arms Embargo, the 2004 Nairobi Protocol, and the ongoing development of Yemen's coast guard, supported by the US. While existing government efforts have had periodic successes — Yemen in particular has been lauded by the U.N. as having "reduced the volume of exports to Somalia and driven up arms prices in Somali markets" — these efforts have largely been uncoordinated, inconsistent, and ineffectual at reducing the flow of arms. Consequently, the impact on the Somali arms market has been marginal.

However, promising signs for the future may be seen in the potential for a new U.N. Arms Trade Treaty that is meant to standardize arms trade regulations and help coordinate government efforts. The recent growth of piracy and consequently the presence of multi-national naval forces patrolling the Gulf of Aden may contribute to reducing the flow of traffic between Yemen and Somalia. The potential for linkages between piracy and arms trafficking should encourage the international community to proactively reduce the flow of arms around the Horn of Africa as a means of stabilizing the region and safeguarding commercial maritime routes.[17]

The Path Forward

Nevertheless, the potential is remote for a coordinated and sustained international effort to control the flow of arms into Somalia and other regional markets. Built on the influx of material from the collapsed Barre and Dergue regimes in the late 1980s and sustained through the 1990s on arms imported by private European firms and Arab arms traders, the legacy of the Somali arms market is strong and durable. Over this period, regional supply networks and local markets have proven highly adaptable to fluid market dynamics, counter-proliferation efforts, and violent conflict. This capacity to adapt to changing circumstances will help to ensure the survival of these networks.

In the current era, the ability for local brokers to tap traditional sources and access official stocks and seized caches from government and peacekeeping forces ensures the continued availability of arms for militants in Somalia and surrounding conflict areas. This combination of factors means that in the near to medium term, the prospects for containment or elimination of this market are unlikely owing to the lack of regional capacity combined with the arms market's maturity, adaptability, and continued strong demand.

Notes

1. *Yemen Times*, March 15, 1999; March 21, 1999.
2. ANSA [Rome], January 20, 1998; September 30, 1998.
3. *Rzeczpospolita* [Warsaw], October 1, 1998.
4. *Famiglia Cristiana* [Milan], October 1, 2000.
5. *Corriere della Sera* [Milan], December 29, 2006.
6. *La Republica* [Rome], June 3, 1996.
7. For a complete list of the reports of the U.N. Monitoring Group on Somalia, please refer to: www.un.org/sc/committees/751/mongroup.shtml.
8. VOA, May 4.
9. Shabelle Media Network, May 5.
10. U.N. Monitoring Group on Somalia, April 2008.
11. *Elaph* [London], May 26, 2007, see also *Terrorism Monitor*, May 6, 2005.

12. Hugh Griffiths and Mark Bromley, "Air Transport and Destabilizing Commodity Flows," SIPRI Policy Paper no. 24, May 2009.

13. *Il Giornale*, April 16.

14. U.N. Monitoring Group on Somalia, April 2008.

15. *Hiiraan*, July 31, 2008.

16. *VOA News*, April 25, 2007.

17. *VOA News*, May 23, 2008.

Future Conflict: Criminal Insurgencies, Gangs and Intelligence

16

John P. Sullivan

Gangs dominate the intersection between crime and war. Traditionally viewed as criminal enterprises of varying degrees of sophistication and reach, some gangs have evolved into potentially more dangerous and destabilizing actors. In many areas across the world — especially in "criminal enclaves" or "lawless zones" where civil governance, traditional security structures, and community or social bonds have eroded — gangs thrive. This essay briefly examines the dynamics of crime and war in these contested regions. Specifically, it provides a framework for understanding "criminal insurgencies" where acute and endemic crime and gang violence challenge the solvency of state political control.

Criminal gangs come in many forms. They challenge the rule of law and employ violence to dominate local communities. In some cases they are expanding their reach and morphing into new warmaking entities capable of challenging the legitimacy and even the solvency of nation-states. This potential brings life to the prediction made by Martin van Creveld who noted, "In the future, war will not be waged by armies but by groups whom today we call terrorists, guerrillas, bandits and robbers, but who will undoubtedly hit upon more formal titles to describe themselves."[1]

Some advanced gangs — known as "third generation gangs" and/or *maras* — are waging "wars" and changing the dynamics of crime. In some extreme cases they are waging a *de facto* criminal insurgency. As Adam Elkus and I recently noted: "Criminal insurgency is haunting the police stations and barracks of North America. Powerful criminal networks increasingly challenge the state's monopoly on force, creating new threats to national security."[2] Mexico is currently challenged by extreme criminal violence,[3] but it is by no means the only state in the Americas suffering from criminal insurgency. Transnational criminal organizations ranging from the transnational street collective *Mara Salvatrucha* (MS-13) to the powerful Mexican drug cartels are steadily increasing in both power and reach. Even some American street gangs are evolving into 'third generation' gangs: Large, networked, transnational bodies that may yet develop true political consciousness.[4]

Criminal insurgency presents a challenge to national security analysts used to creating simulations and analytical models for terrorism and conventional military operations. Criminal insurgency is different from "regular" terrorism and insurgency because the criminal insurgents' sole political motive is to gain autonomous economic control over territory. They do so by hollowing out the state and creating criminal enclaves to maneuver.[5]

Global Gangs/Transnational Crime

These criminal gangs and their impact are no longer a localized criminal issue. Transnational gangs and crime have hemispheric and global potentials. Gangs are essentially a form of organized crime and in an age of globalization, transnational or global crime can change the nature of war and politics.

These potentials find their underpinnings in the virulence of transnational crime. Transnational crime has effectively become a threat to political, economic, environmental and social systems worldwide. This threat involves more than drug trafficking. In addition to the substantial illegal global drug trade and its attendant violence, transnational crime also embraces major fraud, corruption and manipulation of both political and financial systems. Canadian intelligence analyst Samuel Porteous describes this, explaining that transnational crime undermines civil society, political systems and state sovereignty by normalizing violence and legitimizing corruption. It also erodes society by distorting market mechanisms through the disruption of equitable commercial transactions, and degrades the environment by sidelining environmental regulation and safeguards. All these potentials have the cumulative effect of destabilizing nations and economies.[6]

Transnational gangs and criminals extend their reach and influence by co-opting individuals and organizations through bribery, coercion and intimidation to "facilitate, enhance, or protect"[7] their activities. As a consequence, these groups are emerging as a serious impediment to democratic governance and a free market economy. This danger is particularly evident in Mexico, Colombia, Nigeria, Russia and other parts of the former Soviet Union where corruption has become particularly insidious and pervasive. At sub-national levels, such corruption can also have profound effects. At a neighborhood level, political and operational corruption can diminish public safety, placing residents at risk to endemic violence and inter-gang conflict, essentially resulting in a "failed community." This is the virtual analog of a "failed state."[8]

Examining Cartel Evolution

Drug cartels are one type of organized criminal enterprise that have challenged states and created "lawless zones" or criminal enclaves. Examining cartel evolution can help illuminate the challenges to states and civil governance posed by criminal gangs and cartels. Robert J. Bunker and I looked at cartel evolution and related destabilizing potentials in our 1998 paper "Cartel Evolution: Potentials and Consequences."[9] In that paper, we identified three potential evolutionary phases. These are described below.

1st Phase Cartel (Aggressive Competitor)

The first phase cartel form originated in Colombia during the 1980s and arose as an outcome of increasing US cocaine demand. This type of cartel, characterized by the Medellín model, realized economies of scale not known to the individual cocaine entrepreneurs of the mid-1970s. This early cartel was an aggressive competitor to the Westphalian state because of its propensity for extreme violence and willingness to directly challenge the authority of the state.

2nd Phase Cartel (Subtle Co-Opter)

The second phase cartel form also originally developed in Colombia, but in this instance, is centered in the city of Cali. Unlike their Medellín counterparts, the Cali cartel was a shadowy organization devoid of an actual kingpin. Its organization is more distributed and network-like, rather than hierarchical. Many of its characteristics and activities were stealth-masked and dispersed, which yielded many operational capabilities not possessed by the first phase cartel form. Specifically, it possessed leadership clusters that are more difficult to identify and target with a decapitation attack. The Cali cartel was also more sophisticated in its criminal pursuits and far more likely to rely upon corruption, rather than violence or overt political gambits, to achieve its organizational ends. This cartel form has also spread to Mexico with the rise of the Mexican Federation, an alliance of the "big four" mafias based in Tijuana, Sonora, Juárez, and the Gulf. This dynamic is still evolving.

3rd Phase Cartel (Criminal State Successor)

Third phase cartels, if and when they emerge, have the potential to pose a significant challenge to the modern nation-state and its institutions. A Third Phase Cartel is a consequence of unremitting corruption and co-option of state institutions. While this "criminal state successor" has yet to emerge, warning signs of its eventual arrival are present in many states worldwide. Of current importance in the United States are the conditions favoring narco- or criminal-state evolution in Mexico. Indeed, the criminal insurgency in Mexico could prove to be the genesis of a true third phase cartel, as Mexican cartels battle among themselves and the state for dominance. Essentially, third phase cartels rule criminal enclaves, acting much like warlords.

Table 16.1 Phases of Cartel Evolution

1st Phase Cartel Aggressive Competitor	2nd Phase Cartel Subtle-Co-opter	3rd Phase Cartel Criminal State Successor
Medellin Model	Cali Model	Ciudad del Este/Netwarrior Model
Hierarchical Limited Transnational and Inter-enterprise Links Emerging Internetted Organization	Local (Domestic) Internetted Organization Emerging Transnational and Inter-enterprise Links	Global Internetted Organization Evolved Transnational and Inter-enterprise Links
Indiscriminate Violence	Symbolic Violence Corruption	Discriminate Violence Entrenched Corruption (Legitimized)
Criminal Use and Provision	Transitional (both criminal and mercenary) Use	Mercenary Use and Provision
Conventional Technology Use and Acquisition	Transitional Technology Use and Acquisition	Full Spectrum Technology Use, Acquisition and Targeting
Entrepreneurial Limited Economic Reach	Semi-Institutionalized Widening Economic Reach	Institutionalized Global Economic Reach Small
Small Scale Public Profiting	Regional Public Profiting	Mass Public Profiting
Limited "Product" Focus	Expanding "Product" Focus	Broad Range of Products/ Activities
Criminal Entity Emerging Netwarrior	Transitional Entity Nascent Netwarrior	New Warmaking Entity Evolved Netwarrior

Source: Robert J. Bunker and John P. Sullivan. "Cartel Evolution: Potentials and Consequences," *Transnational Organized Crime*, 4, 2 (1998).

Criminal Enclaves

The fullest development of a criminal enclave exists in the South American jungle at the intersection of three nations. Ciudad del Este, Paraguay is the center of this criminal near free state. Paraguay, Brazil and Argentina converge at this riverfront outpost. A jungle hub for the world's outlaws, a global village of outlaws, the triple border zone serves as a free enclave for significant criminal activity, including people who are dedicated to supporting and sustaining acts of terrorism. Denizens of the enclave include Lebanese gangsters and terrorists, drug smugglers, Nigerian gangsters and Asian mafias: Japanese Yakuza, Tai Chen (Cantonese mafia), Fuk Ching, the Big Circle Boys, and the Flying Dragons. This polyglot mix of thugs demonstrates the potential of criminal netwarriors to exploit the globalization of organized crime.[10]

The blurring of borders — a symbol of the post-modern, information age — is clearly demonstrated here, where the mafias exploit interconnected economies. With the ability to overwhelm governments weakened by corruption and jurisdictional obstacles, the mafias of Ciudad del Este and its Brazilian twin city of Foz do Iguacu demonstrate remarkable power and reach. Terrorism interlocks with organized crime in the enclave, a post-modern free city that is a haven to Middle Eastern terrorists, a hub for the global drug trade, a center of consumer product piracy, and base for gunrunners diverting small arms (from the US) to the violent and heavily armed drug gangs in the *favelas* of Rio de Janeiro and São Paulo.

The convergence of cartel evolution and manifestation of inter-netted criminal enterprises is so pronounced in this enclave, Robert Bunker and I call this third phase cartel the Ciudad del Este model.[11] The transnational criminal organizations here demonstrate the potential for criminal networks to challenge state sovereignty and gain local dominance. These networked "enclaves," or a third phase cartel embracing similar characteristics, could become a dominant actor within a network of transnational criminal organizations, and potentially gain legitimacy or at least political influence within the network of state actors. Mexico's current battle for the "plazas" may be an early manifestation of criminal enclave formation.

Transnational Gangs

Transnational gangs are another state challenger. They are a concern throughout the Western Hemisphere. Criminal street gangs have evolved to pose significant security and public safety threats in individual neighborhoods, metropolitan areas, nations, and across borders. Such gangs — widely known as *maras* — are no longer just street gangs. They have morphed across three generations through interactions with other gangs and transnational organized crime organizations (*e.g.*, narcotics cartels/drug trafficking organizations) into complex networked threats.[12]

Transnational *maras* have evolved into a transnational security concern throughout North and Central America. As a result of globalization, the influence of information and communications technology, and travel/migration patterns, gangs formerly confined to local neighborhoods have spread their reach across neighborhoods, cities and countries. In some cases, this reach is increasingly cross-border and transnational. Current transnational gang activity is a concern in several Central American states and Mexico (where they inter-operate with cartels).[13]

Transnational gangs can be defined as having one or more of the following characteristics: 1) criminally active and operational in more than one country; 2) criminal operations committed by gangsters in one country are planned, directed, and controlled by leadership in another country; 3) they are mobile and adapt to new areas of operations; and 4) their activities are sophisticated and transcend borders.[14] The gangs most frequently mentioned in this context are *Mara Salvatrucha* (MS-13) and Eighteenth Street (M-18), both originating in the *barrios* of Los Angeles. In order to understand the potential reach and consequences of transnational *maras*, it is useful to review third generation gang theory.

Street Gangs: Three Generations on the Road to Netwar

A close analysis of urban and transnational street gangs shows that some of these criminal enterprises have evolved through three generations — transitioning from traditional turf gangs, to market-oriented drug gangs, to a new generation that mixes political and mercenary elements.

The organizational framework for understanding contemporary gang evolution was first explored in a series of papers starting with the 1997 article "Third Generation Street Gangs: Turf, Cartels, and Netwarriors."[15] These concepts were expanded in another article with the same title, and the model further refined in the 2000 *Small Wars and Insurgencies* paper "Urban Gangs Evolving as Criminal Netwar Actors."[16] In these papers (and others), I observed that gangs could progress through three generations.

As gangs negotiate this generational shift, their voyage is influenced by three factors: *Politicization*, *internationalization*, and *sophistication*. This gang form — the "third generation" gang — entails many of the organizational and operational attributes found with net-based triads, cartels and terrorist entities. The characteristics of all three generations of gangs are summarized in Table 16.2.

Table 16.2 Characteristics of Street Gang Generations

	Politicization	
limited ◄————————————————————————►		*evolved*
	Internationalization	
local ◄————————————————————————►		*global*
1st Generation	2nd Generation	3rd Generation
turf gang	drug gang	mercenary gang
turf protection	market protection	power/financial acquisition
proto-netwarrior	emerging netwarrior	netwarrior
	Sophistication	
less sophisticated ◄————————————————————————►		*more sophisticated*

Source: John P. Sullivan, "Third Generation Street Gangs: Turf, Cartels, and Net Warriors," *Transnational Organized Crime*, 3, 3 (1997).

The three generations of gangs can be described as follows:

Turf: First Generation Gangs are traditional street gangs with a turf orientation. Operating at the lower end of extreme societal violence, they have loose leadership and focus their attention on turf protection and gang loyalty within their immediate environs (often a few blocks or a neighborhood). When they engage in criminal enterprise, it is largely opportunistic and local in scope. These turf gangs are limited in political scope and sophistication.

Market: Second Generation Gangs are engaged in business. They are entrepreneurial and drug-centered. They protect their markets and use violence to control their competition. They have a broader, market-focused, sometimes overtly political agenda and operate in a broader spatial or geographic area. Their operations sometimes involve multi-state and even international areas. Their tendency for centralized leadership and sophisticated operations for market protection places them in the center of the range of politicization, internationalization and sophistication.

Mercenary/Political: Third Generation Gangs have evolved political aims. They operate — or seek to operate — at the global end of the spectrum, using their sophistication to garner power, aid financial acquisition and engage in mercenary-type activities. To date, most third generation (3 GEN) gangs have been primarily mercenary in orientation; yet, in some cases they have sought to further their own political and social objectives.

A more detailed discussion of these three generations follows.

First Generation Gangs

Traditional street gangs are almost exclusively turf-oriented. They operate at the lower threshold of extreme societal violence, possess loose leadership and concentrate their attention on turf protection and gang loyalty within their immediate environs (often a few blocks, a cell-block, or a neighborhood). When they engage in criminal activity, it is largely opportunistic and individual in scope. Turf gangs are limited in political scope, and are unsophisticated in tactics, means, and outlook. When they engage in rivalry with competing gangs, it is localized. Despite their limited spatial influence, these gangs, due to their informal network-like attributes, can be viewed as proto-netwarriors. Local criminal organizations can evolve into armed bands of non-state soldiers should they gain in sophistication within failed communities with disintegrating social structure. While most gangs will stay firmly in the first generation, a few (*e.g.*, some "Crip" and "Blood" sets and some Hispanic gangs) span both the first and second (nascent organized crime groups with a drug focus).

Second Generation Gangs

Second generation gangs are essentially criminal businesses. They are entrepreneurial in outlook and generally drug-centered. They use violence to protect their markets and limit or control their competition. They seek a broader, market-focused, occasionally overt political agenda and often operate in a broader spatial or geographic area. Their operations sometimes involve multistate, cross-border, or international reach. They tend to embrace centralized leadership and conduct sophisticated operations for market protection. As such, they occupy the center of the range of politicization, internationalization and sophistication. Second generation gangs sometimes use violence as political interference to incapacitate enforcement efforts by police and security organs. Generally, this instrumental violence occurs in failed states, but clearly occurs when gangs dominate community life within "failed communities." Further evolution of these gangs is a danger when they link with and provide services to transnational criminal organizations or collaborate within narcotics trafficking and distribution networks and other criminal ventures. Because of their attributes, second generation gangs can be considered emerging netwarriors.

Third Generation Gangs

The overwhelming majority of street or prison gangs remain firmly in the first or second generations; however, a small number in the United States, Canada,

Central and South America, as well as South Africa have acquired third generation characteristics. Third generation gangs have evolved political aims, operate or seek to operate at the global end of the spectrum, and employ their sophistication to acquire power, money, and engage in mercenary or political activities. To date, these gangs have been primarily mercenary in orientation; yet, in some cases they seek political and social objectives. Examples of third generation gangs can be seen in Chicago, San Diego, Los Angeles, Brazil, South Africa, and throughout Central America.

These gangs have evolved from turf-based entities, to drug-oriented enterprises operating in up to 35 states, to complex organizations controlling entire housing projects, schools and blocks, that conduct overt political activity while actively seeking to infiltrate and co-opt local police and contract security forces. These activities demonstrate the often-subtle interaction of gangs and politics. This shift from simple market protection to power acquisition is characteristic of third generation activity.

Internationalization is the final indicator of gang evolution. Gangs in Los Angeles and San Diego have been notable in this regard, with Los Angeles gangs having outposts in Tijuana, Mexico, Nicaragua, El Salvador, and Belize, and San Diego gangs linking with Baja cartels. The mercenary foray of San Diego's 'Calle Treinta' ('30th St.'/'Logan Heights') gang into the bi-national orbit of the Arellano-Felix (Tijuana) cartel is notable for assassinations, drive-by shootings and other enforcement slayings. Because of their attributes, third generation gangs can be considered netwarriors. Networked organizational forms are a key factor contributing to the rise of non-state or criminal soldiers.[17]

Impact of Transnational 'Third Generation' Gangs (*Maras*)

Like their more sophisticated cartel counterparts, third generation gangs challenge state institutions in several ways. Naval Postgraduate School analyst Bruneau, paraphrased below, describes five (multi) national security threats or challenges associated with transnational *maras*:[18]

- They *strain government capacity* by overwhelming police and legal systems through sheer audacity, violence, and numbers.
- They *challenge the legitimacy of the state*, particularly in regions where the culture of democracy is challenged by corruption and reinforced by the inability of political systems to function well enough to provide public goods and services.
- They *act as surrogate or alternate governments*. For example in some regions

(*i.e.*, El Salvador and Guatemala) the "governments have all but given up in some areas of the capitals, and the *maras* extract taxes on individuals and businesses."

- They *dominate the informal economic sector*, establishing small businesses and using violence and coercion to unfairly compete with legitimate businesses while avoiding taxes and co-opting government regulators.
- They *infiltrate police and non-governmental organizations* to further their goals and in doing so demonstrate latent political aims.

These factors can be seen graphically in the battle for control of the drug trade in Mexico.

The Plazas of Conflict

Mexico's drug wars are fertile ground for seeking an understanding of criminal insurgency. Mexico and the cross-border region that embraces the frontier between Mexico and the United States are embroiled in a series of interlocking criminal insurgencies.[19] These criminal insurgencies result from the battles for dominance of the "plazas" or corridors for the lucrative transshipment of drugs into the United States. The cartels battle among themselves, the police and the military, enlisting the support of a variety of local and transnational gangs and criminal enterprises. Corrupt officials fuel the violence, communities are disrupted by constant onslaught of violence, and alternative social structures emerge. Prison gangs — like *Eme*, the Mexican Mafia — also play pivotal roles in the allocation of force and influence. Coping with these threats requires new operational and intelligence approaches.

Red teaming is one tool for understanding these "geosocial" dynamics. Looking at the influences, market imperatives, and factors that drive cartel and gang evolution, as well as the quest for dominance in the *plazas* helps place the violence encountered in criminal insurgency in context. In this analytical endeavor, red teaming is more than the tactical red cell penetration of vulnerable nodes. It is an adaptive exploration of the criminal enterprises and their interactions within the social and market dynamics of the *plazas*. This can be described as *analytical red teaming*.

Analytical red teaming looks at the network attributes of gangs and cartels in order to determine indicators for future activity. Which gangs or cartels are emerging in a particular area, what factors will extend their reach? Where are their new markets, what is the interaction between a specific gang or cartel? These intelligence questions can be explored through scenarios and analytical wargames. What factors are key market drivers? Where will new markets emerge? What counter-gang approaches will degrade criminal influences in failed communities? How can legitimate community political and social structures be marshaled to limit criminal reach and influence? By applying adaptive, analytical red teaming as an analytical tool, intelligence and law enforcement analysts can explore indicators of gang or cartel evolution, as well as potential courses of action to counter criminal insurgency.

Conclusion

Criminal organizations, particularly drug cartels and transnational gangs are becoming increasingly networked in terms of organization and influence. As these groups evolve, they challenge notions of the state and political organization. States are, at least in the current scheme of things, entities that possess a legitimate monopoly on the use of violence within a specified territory. Third phase cartels, criminal states or criminal enclaves are factors that challenge that monopoly, much the same as warlords within failed states.

As previously discussed, the current situation in Mexico may shed light on these processes. Mexico is consumed by a set of inter-locking, networked criminal insurgencies. Daily violence, kidnappings, assassinations of police and government officials, beheadings and armed assaults are the result of violent combat between drug cartels, gangs, and the police. The cartels vying for domination of the lucrative drug trade are seeking both market dominance and freedom from government interference. Tijuana, Ciudad Juárez, and other border towns are racked with violence. Increased deployments of both police and military forces are stymied in the face of corrupt officials who choose to side with the cartels.

The drug mafias have abandoned subtle co-option of the government to embrace active violence to secure safe havens to ply their trade. This *de facto* 'criminal insurgency' threatens the stability of the Mexican state. Not satisfied with their feudal outposts in the Mexican interior and along the US-Mexico frontier, the cartels are also starting to migrate north to the United States and Canada and south throughout Central America, and even to the Southern Cone, setting up business in Argentina, and across the South Atlantic to Africa. Money fuels global expansion, and transnational organized crime has learned it can thrive in the face of governmental crisis.

The cartels are joined by a variety of gangs in the quest to dominate the global criminal opportunity space. Third generation gangs — that is, gangs like *Mara Salvatrucha* (MS-13) that have transcended operating on localized turf with a simple market focus to operate across borders and challenge political structures — are both partners and foot soldiers for the dominant cartels. Gangs and cartels seek profit and are not driven by ideology. But the ungoverned, lawless zones they leave in their wake provide fertile ground for extremists and terrorists to exploit.

Understanding and anticipating these threats is essential to maintaining social control, stability and effective governance. Criminal insurgency requires a new set of skills and organizational capabilities. Intelligence can help craft the understanding needed to build these. The cartel evolution and third generation gang models discussed her are useful analytical frameworks for developing this understanding.

On the operational side, full spectrum policing — that is community policing, investigations, high intensity policing (for gangs and organized crime), public order/riot control, counterterrorism, and counterinsurgency — must be developed and deployed. This will require versatile formed units like Israel's Joint Operations Forces (JOF). These are essentially stability police units (*i.e.*, as gendarmerie/constabulary forces) such as an expeditionary police (EXPOL) or third force options.[20]

Finally, intelligence and operational art need to be closely integrated. A high degree of co-ordination and co-operation among government agencies and community groups at all levels of governance is needed.[21] This requires both police forces and intelligence services to co-operate across borders[22] to gain understanding and achieve the 'co-production' of intelligence necessary to counter transnational criminal threats.[23]

Notes

1. Martin van Creveld, *The Transformation of War*, (New York: The Free Press, 1991).
2. John P. Sullivan and Adam Elkus, "Red Teaming Criminal Insurgency," *Red Team Journal*, 30 January 2009 at http://redteamjournal.com/2009/01/red-teaming-criminal-insurgency-1/#more-711.
3. See John P. Sullivan and Adam Elkus, "State of Siege: Mexico's Criminal Insurgency," *Small Wars Journal*, August 2008.
4. See John P. Sullivan, "Transnational Gangs: The Impact of Third Generation Gangs in Central America," *Air & Space Power Journal* (Spanish Edition), Second Trimester 2008 at http://airpower.maxwell.af.mil.apjintrnational/apj-s/2008/2tri08/sullivan eng.htm for a discussion of recent developments related to transnational gangs.
5. "Hollow states" are defined by John Robb at his web blog *Global Guerrillas*; see http://global guerrillas.typepad.com for his many discussions on this topic.
6. Samuel D. Porteous, "The Threat from Transnational Crime: An Intelligence Perspective," Commentary No. 70, Canadian Security Intelligence Service, Winter 1996.
7. Phil Williams. "The Nature of Drug-Trafficking Networks." *Current History*, 97, 618 (1998): 154–159.
8. See John P. Sullivan and Keith Weston, "Afterward: Law Enforcement Response Strategies for Criminal-States and Criminal-Soldiers," in Robert J. Bunker (Ed.), *Criminal States and Criminal-Soldiers*, (London: Routledge, 2008), 287–300.
9. Robert J. Bunker and John P. Sullivan, "Cartel Evolution: Potentials and Consequences," *Transnational Organized Crime*, 4, 2 (1998): 55–74.
10. Ibid.
11. Ibid.

12. See John P. Sullivan, "Maras Morphing: Revisiting Third Generation Gangs," *Global Crime*, 7, 3–4 (2006): 487–504 for a detailed discussion of the current state of *maras* and third generation (3 GEN) gangs worldwide.

13. John P. Sullivan, "Transnational Gangs."

14. Cindy Franco, "The MS-13 and 18th Street Gangs: Emerging Transnational Gang Threats?" *CRS Report for Congress*, Washington, DC: Congressional Research Service (RL34233), 02 November 2007, p. 2.

15. John P. Sullivan, "Third Generation Street Gangs: Turf, Cartels, and Net Warriors," *Transnational Organized Crime*, 3, 3 (1997): 95–108

16. John P. Sullivan, "Urban Gangs Evolving as Criminal Netwar Actors," *Small Wars and Insurgencies*, 1, 1 (2000): 82–96.

17. See John P. Sullivan, "Gangs Hooligans, and Anarchists — The Vanguard of Netwar in the Streets," in John Arquilla and David Ronfeldt, *Networks and Netwars: The Future of Terror, Crime, and Militancy*, (Santa Monica: RAND, 2001), 99–128 for a discussion of the analysis underlying this section.

18. Thomas C. Bruneau, "The Maras and National Security in Central America," *Strategic Insights*, 4, 5 (2005), found at http://www.ccc.npps.navy.mil/si/2005/May/bruneauMay05.pdf.

19. John P. Sullivan and Adam Elkus, "Red Teaming Criminal Insurgency," John P. Sullivan and Adam Elkus, "State of Siege;" and John P. Sullivan, "Criminal Netwarriors in Mexico's Drug Wars," *GroupIntel*, 22 (2008) at http://www.groupintel.com/2008/12/22/criminal-netwarriors-in-mexico's-drug-wars/.

20. See John P. Sullivan, "The Missing Mission: Expeditionary Police for Peacekeeping and Transnational Stability," *Small Wars Journal*, (2008), http://smallwarsjournal.com/blog/2007/05/the-missing-mission-expedition/ and Doron Zimmerman, "On the Future of Counter-terrorism Force Development: The case for Third Force Options," unpublished paper presented to the Panel on Patterns of Conflict: Future Threat Analysis, International Studies association, *50th ISA Annual Convention*, NY, NY, 18 February 2009.

21. John P. Sullivan, "Forging Improved Government Agency Cooperation to Combat Violence, *National Strategy Forum Review*, 17, 4 (2008): 24–29.

22. See John P. Sullivan, "Global Terrorism and the Police," unpublished paper presented to the Panel on Bridging Divides in Counterterrorism Intelligence: Law Enforcement, Intelligence, and Non-Traditional Actors, International Studies Association, *49th Annual ISA Convention*, San Francisco, CA, USA, 29 March 2008.

23. See John P. Sullivan, "Terrorism Early Warning and Co-Production of Counterterrorism Intelligence," unpublished paper presented to Canadian Association for Security and Intelligence Studies, *CASIS 20th Anniversary Conference*, Montreal, Quebec, Canada, 21 October 2005, available at http://www.projectwhitehorse.com/pdfs/6.%20CASIS_Sullivan_paper1.pdf

Brave New War: The Next Stage of Terrorism and The End of Globalization

17

John Robb

The near future holds mind-bending promise for American business.[1] Globalization is prying open vast new markets. Technology is plowing ahead, fueling — and transforming — entire industries, creating services we never thought possible. Clever people worldwide are capitalizing every which way. But because globalization and technology are morally neutral forces, they can also drive change of a different sort. We saw this very clearly on September 11, 2001, and are seeing it now in Iraq and in conflicts around the world. In short, despite the aura of limitless possibility, our lives are evolving in ways we can control only if we recognize the new landscape. It's time to take an unblinking look.

We have entered the age of the faceless, agile enemy. From London to Madrid to Nigeria to Russia, stateless terrorist groups have emerged to score blow after blow against us. Driven by cultural fragmentation, schooled in the most sophisticated technologies, and fueled by transnational crime, these groups are forcing corporations and individuals to develop new ways of defending themselves.

The end result of this struggle will be a new, more resilient approach to national security, one built not around the state but around private citizens and companies. That new system will change how we live and work — for the better, in many ways — but the road getting there may seem long at times.

The conflict in Iraq has foreshadowed the future of global security in much the same way that the Spanish civil war prefigured World War II: It's become a testing ground, a dry run for something much larger. Unlike previous insurgencies, the one in Iraq comprises seventy-five to one hundred small, diverse, and autonomous groups of zealots, patriots, and criminals alike. These groups, of course, have access to many of the same tools we do — from satellite phones to engineering degrees — and they use them every bit as effectively. But their single most important asset is their organizational structure, an open-source community network — one that seems to me quite similar to what we see in the software industry. That's how they're able to continually stay one step ahead of us. It is an extremely innovative structure, sadly, and it results in decision-making cycles much shorter than those of the US military. Indeed, because the insurgents in Iraq lack a recognizable center of gravity — a leadership structure or an ideology — they are nearly immune to the application of conventional military force. Like Microsoft, the software superpower, the United States hasn't found its match in a Goliath competitor similar to itself, but in a loose, self-tuning network.

In Iraq, we've also witnessed the convergence of international crime and terrorism as they provide ample fuel and a global platform for these new enemies. Al-Qaeda's attack on Madrid, for example, was funded by the sale of the drug ecstasy. Moisés Naím, a former Venezuelan minister of trade and industry and the editor and publisher of the magazine *Foreign Policy*, documented this trend in his insightful book *Illicit: How Smugglers, Traffickers, and Copycats Are Hijacking the Global Economy*. Globalization has fostered the development of a huge criminal economy that boasts a technologically leveraged global supply chain (like Wal-Mart's) and can handle everything from human trafficking (eastern Europe) to illicit drugs (Asia and South America), pirated goods (Southeast Asia), arms (Central Asia), and money laundering (everywhere). Naím puts the value of that economy at between $2 and $3 trillion a year. He says it is expanding at *seven times* the rate of legitimate world trade.

This terrorist-criminal symbiosis becomes even more powerful when considered next to the most disturbing sign coming out of Iraq: The terrorists have developed the ability to fight nation-states strategically — without weapons of mass destruction. This new method is called *systems disruption*, a simple way of attacking the critical networks (electricity, oil, gas, water, communications, and transportation) that underpin modern life. Such disruptions are designed to erode the target state's legitimacy, to drive it to failure by keeping it from providing the services it must deliver in order to command the allegiance of its citizens. Over the past two years, attacks on the oil and electricity networks in Iraq have reduced and held delivery of these critical services below prewar levels, with a disastrous effect on the country, its people, and its economy.

The early examples of systems disruption in Iraq and elsewhere are ominous. If these techniques are even lightly applied to the fragile electrical and oil-gas systems in Russia, Saudi Arabia, or anywhere in the target-rich West, we could see a rapid onset of economic and political chaos unmatched since the advent of the blitzkrieg. (India's January arrest of militants with explosives in Hyderabad suggests that the country's high-tech industry could be a new target.) It's even worse when we consider the asymmetry of the economics involved: One small attack on an oil pipeline in southeast Iraq, conducted for an estimated $2,000, cost the Iraqi government more than $500 million in lost oil revenues. That is a return on investment of 25 million percent.

Now that the tipping point has been reached, the rise of global virtual states — with their thriving criminal economies, innovative networks, and hyper-efficient war craft — will rapidly undermine public confidence in our national security systems. In fact, this process has already begun. We've seen disruption of our oil supply in Iraq, Nigeria, Venezuela, and Colombia; the market's fear of more disruptions contributes mightily to the current high prices for oil. As these disruptions continue, the damage will spill over into the very structure of our society. Our profligate US Department of Defense, reeling from its inability to defend our borders on 9/11 or to pacify even a small country like Iraq, will increasingly be seen as obsolete.

Afghanistan's Entrepreneurs

Recognizing the proliferation of global guerrillas, states will become more and more likely to recruit them as temporary allies, usually for profit as much as for a cause. Fighting fire with fire is an irresistible tactic, and one we're likely to see much more of, as traditional warfare becomes unfeasible. In fact, we've already seen this in the Afghan war. Governments have always been eager to find proxies, but it has never been as easy as it is fast becoming.

Afghanistan's Taliban wasn't a government in the sense that we understand it. It was a loose association along feudal lines. Nonetheless, the senior clerics of the Taliban did exert power. One area of specific focus for the Taliban was the elimination of opium farming.

The remoteness of Afghanistan's valleys and the fierceness of its people made the country the perfect place for opium farming. In 1999, Afghanistan produced 75 percent of the world's supply. In 2000, however, Mohammed Omar, the Taliban's top cleric, banned the production of opium. This was followed by a fatwa that specified opium cultivation as contrary to the edicts of Islam. To enforce this edict, Taliban militias burned heroin labs and jailed farmers until they ceased growing opium. Over one thousand mullahs, farmers, and village elders were jailed in one province alone.

The effect was dramatic. By 2001, the vast majority of Afghanistan's opium crop had been eradicated. The only area left under cultivation in any meaningful way was the five percent of the territory under the control of the Western-supported Northern Alliance. In the words of Karim Rahimi, the United Nations drug control liaison in Jelalabad (during the Taliban's rule), "It is amazing, really, when you see the fields that last year were filled with poppies and this year there is wheat."[2]

What the Taliban didn't understand is that the ban on opium production had eliminated the support of a large number of Afghans. Overnight, billions of dollars in revenue that fueled the livelihood of over two million people were eliminated. Most important, it alienated the affections of powerful warlords-Afghanistan's guerrilla entrepreneurs.

When the United States decided to support the Northern Alliance before it attacked the Taliban in early 2002, US officials took action to ensure this disaffection. Direct payments from Central Intelligence Agency operatives and the potential of unfettered opium production under the Northern Alliance exerted a powerful influence on Afghanistan's guerilla entrepreneurs. This worked. The warlords didn't rise to support the Taliban or its al-Qaeda allies when the US attack began. As a result, the Taliban's few stalwart believers quickly fell in the face of carpet-bombing and direct pressure from the ground.

Less than two years later, the guerrilla entrepreneurs were back in business. Poppy production soared to new, unprecedented levels. By 2005, nearly 90 percent of the world's opium was being produced in Afghanistan. This production generated $2.5 billion a year or nearly half the country's gross domestic product (GDP).

A Modern Veneer on Ancient Mind-Sets

We who live in the real world are aware that literacy, mass communications, urbanization, the spread of engineering training, the internet and other developments have contributed to what social scientists call "social and political mobilization." The peoples of the world are not illiterate villagers anymore, as they largely were in the heyday of the British Raj. They aren't politically helpless and they won't put up with foreigners "policing" them, not for very long.

—Juan Cole, a historian of the Middle East and the author of the blog Informed Comment[3]

Rapid modernization (both economic integration and technological progress) has radically changed the structure, the capabilities, and the constituency of the terrorist groups we face today. The pools of talent that today's terrorist groups can draw on are substantially more educated, connected, and mobile than ever before in recorded history. There is ample evidence that this general improvement is reflected in the quality of terrorist recruits-poverty and a lack of education are not positively correlated with involvement in terrorism and may even be negatively correlated.[4] We aren't facing your father's uneducated, immobile, and poor rice paddy farmer.

But modernization hasn't changed the fundamental associations and interests that drive people. Modern technology has just been layered over already existing familial, tribal, ethnic, and national allegiances. It's just new means put to the same old ends.

In his paper "The New Warrior Class," Ralph Peters provides some insight into this. He defines the term *warrior* as "erratic primitives of shifting allegiance, habituated to violence, with no stake in civil order." He goes on to say:

> We have entered an age in which entire nations are subject to dispossession, starvation, rape, and murder on a scale approaching genocide-not at the hands of a conquering foreign power but under the guns of their neighbors. Paramilitary warriors — thugs whose talent for violence blossoms in civil war — defy legitimate governments and increasingly end up leading governments they have overturned. This is a new age of warlords, from Somalia to Myanmar/ Burma, from Afghanistan to Yugoslavia.[5]

He even provides a classification system for these warriors:

> **Underclass.** Losers with little education, no earning power, and no future.
> **Disrupted young males.** Young men and boys drawn into the warrior milieu because of the disruption of normal paths of development (school, work and so forth).
> **Believers.** Men who fight because of strong religious or patriotic beliefs or those who have suffered extreme personal loss.
> **Former military men.** Former soldiers who have not been reintegrated back into society.

According to Peters, the central paradox of the warrior culture is that these warriors continue conflict for their own gain — the spoils of war and the continuation of a way of life. Perversely, the continuation of violence prevents society from delivering the benefits necessary to rehabilitate them. The truth of who we are facing is somewhere in between Juan Cole's enlightened world that yearns to be free of Western domination and Peters's erratic warriors.

My conclusion is that globalization is quickly layering new skill sets on ancient mind-sets. Warriors, in our current context of global guerrillas, are not merely lazy and monosyllabic primitives as Peters implies. They are wired, educated, and globally mobile. They build complex supply chains, benefit from global money flows, travel globally, innovate with technology, and attack shrewdly. In a nutshell, they are modern. Despite this apparent modernity and an eager willingness to adopt technology, however, their value sets are often completely different from those we find acceptable in the West.

In short, these modern warriors fight for reasons we don't quite understand. Tribal loyalties, clan ties, religious reasons, and more are the basis of their moral cohesion as a group. These beliefs make it difficult, if not impossible, for them to fully integrate into the modern world.

Additionally, they do have a strong motivation to survive. This quest for survival, at any cost, has led them to push into areas that increase their chances of viability. Some have opted to create an alternative system, or proto-states, that conform to their values. We have seen this in Hezbollah and Hamas. Others, and this is the group that is on the rise, have opted to move with alacrity into transnational crime.

Guerrilla entrepreneurs, as I have described them in this chapter, are the central actors in this move toward sustainable nonstate entities. They provide innovation in warfare, leverage sources of moral cohesion to grow the group through fictive kinship, find new sources of income through integration with transnational criminality, and much more.

The Terrorist Social System

If these global guerrillas aim to hollow out the state or share power with it, wouldn't we see more terrorists hoping to take on government-like duties? Again, we already have. At the end of the twentieth century, the evolved form of the nonstate entity was the proto-state. Since the nation-state system was still fairly dominant, it makes sense that these new entities copied the old model and made it *their* own. These new terrorist social networks thrived in the vacuum created by failed states.

A good example of this is Hamas (which is serving as a model for Muqtada al-Sadr in Iraq). Since its founding in 1987, Hamas has proven to be a well-run counterweight to the late Yasser Arafat's corrupt Palestinian Authority (which in many ways is the Palestinian state). Hamas runs the following services:

- An extensive education network
- Distribution of food to the poor
- Youth camps and sports
- Elderly care
- Funding of scholarships and business development
- Religious services
- Public safety
- Health care

This network of social services provides Hamas with multiple benefits, including:

- Popular support that shelters the organization
- A plentiful supply of recruits for its terrorist mission

- Sources of external funding through charity organizations that support its social mission (much of which can be redirected to the terrorist mission) and funding through a small number of profitable businesses

The rise of terrorist social services indicates that the loose networks that power terrorist military organizations can also replicate the social responsibilities of nation-states.

As a challenger to the nation-state system, this capability speaks volumes. It has also yielded a form of success. Despite a decentralized, almost nonexistent command structure, Hamas won electoral control of Palestine in early 2006. Given the array of forces arranged against it, this assumption of power is likely to fail. It will be faced with the same weaknesses that made states vulnerable in the first place.

Transnational Crime

You can take their blood; then why not take their property?
—*Bakar Bashir, the spiritual head of Jemaah Islamiyah*[6]

The more robust, twenty-first-century model for survivability is based on the combination of guerrilla groups and transnational crime. Both have a similar set of goals — ineffectual governments to work around — and are quickly developing similar, twenty-first-century networks. Especially as proxy wars proliferate, the line between the two will blur.

One of the best sources for insight into the rapid growth of transnational crime is Naím's *Illicit*. Naím comes to the topic of transnational crime with immeasurable experience and insight. When his book came out, I was quick to send him a note of congratulations. For me, it was totally in sync with my work on global guerrillas. Interestingly, he responded that he had seen my op-ed in the *New York Times*[7] on open-source war and had intended to send me a similar note. We've shared quite a few e-mails since then, replete with the shorthand communication of two people who have come to many of the same unpopular conclusions.

In his book, Naím copiously documents how globalization and unrestricted interconnectivity have led to the rise of vast global smuggling networks. These networks live in the spaces between states. They are simultaneously everywhere and nowhere. They make money through an arbitrage (riskless trading that takes advantage of differences in prices for the same exact item in two locations) of the differences between the legal systems and the level of law enforcement of our isolated islands of sovereignty. To make this even easier, they use the vast profits of their operations to overwhelm underpaid government employees with floods of corruption. This allows them to take control of otherwise functional states. You would be surprised, Naín wrote in an e-mail to me, how little it costs to buy an entire government in most parts of the world. Of course, after seeing how little Jack Abramoff spent to corrupt the operation of the US government over the last decade, I am not at all surprised.

By all accounts, the amount of money involved is immense. In aggregate, these networks form a parallel "black" global supply chain, have a GDP of $1 to $3 trillion (some estimates have put this as high as 10 percent of the legal global economy), and are growing at seven times the rate of legal global trade. These networks supply the huge demand in the developed world for:

- Drugs (both recreational and pharmaceutical knockoffs)
- Undocumented workers (for corporations, home services, and the sex trade)
- Weapons (from small arms to rocket-propelled grenades, much of it from cold war arsenals)
- Intellectual property rip-offs (from digital content to brand-named consumer items)
- Money (laundered and unregulated financial flows)

Interestingly, these supply chains aren't run by the vertically integrated cartels and families of the twentieth century (those hierarchies are too vulnerable, slow, and unresponsive to be competitive in the current environment). Instead, they are undifferentiated structures (think Lego blocks) that are highly decentralized, horizontal, and fluid. Their specialization, to the extent that there is one, is in cross-border movement; therefore, they can handle all types of smuggling simultaneously (for example, putting both knockoffs of DVDs and drugs into the backpack of an illegal alien crossing the border). Finally, they are also very quick to adopt new technologies to improve the speed and coordination of their global networks.

Across the board, we are starting to see global guerrillas move into transnational crime. According to Drug Enforcement Administration statistics, nearly half of the forty-one groups on the US government's list of terrorist organizations are involved in drug trafficking — from the Taliban in Afghanistan, which provided protection for opium smuggling, to the guerrillas in Nigeria, who operate multibillion-dollar oil smuggling (bunkering) rings. This growth has been staggering. David Kaplan of *U.S. News & World Report* gets to the point:

> The terrorists behind the Madrid attacks were major drug dealers, with a network stretching from Morocco through Spain to Belgium and the Netherlands. Their ringleader, Jamal "El Chino" Ahmidan, was the brother of one of Morocco's top hashish traffickers. Ahmidan and his followers paid for their explosives by trading hashish and cash with a former miner. When police raided the home of one plotter, they seized 125,800 ecstasy tablets — one of the largest hauls in

Spanish history. In all, authorities recovered nearly $2 million in drugs and cash from the group. In contrast, the Madrid bombings, which killed 191 people cost only about $50,000 . . .

What is new is the scale of this toxic mix of jihad and dope. Moroccan terrorists used drug sales to fund not only the 2004 Madrid attack, but the 2003 attacks in Casablanca, killing 45, and attempted bombings of U.S. and British ships in Gibraltar in 2002. So large looms the North African connection that investigators believe jihadists have penetrated as much as a third of the $12.5 billion Moroccan hashish trade — the world's largest — a development worrisome not only for its big money but for its extensive smuggling routes through Europe.[8]

Notes

1. Robb, John, "Security: Power to the People," *Fast Company*, March 2006.
2. Gannon, Kathy, "U.N.: Taliban Virtually Wipes Out Opium Production in Afghanistan," Associated Press, February 16, 2001.
3. Cole, Juan. "Max Boot Is Out of This World," Antiwar.com, September 11, 2003, www.antiwar.com/cole/?articleid=966 (Accessed October 23, 2006).
4. Atran, Scott, "Genesis of Suicide Terrorism," *Science* 299, no. 5612 (March 7, 2003).
5. Peters, Ralph, "The New Warrior Class," *Parameters* (Summer 1994): 16–26, www.carlisle.army.mil/ (accessed October 23, 2006).
6. Kaplan, David E., "Paying for Terror," *U.S. News and World Report*, December 5, 2005.
7. Robb, John, "The Open-Source War," *New York Times*, October 17, 2005.
8. Kaplan, David E., "Paying for Terror," *U.S. News and World Report*, December 5, 2005.

Conclusion

Every conception of pathology must be based on prior knowledge of the corresponding normal state; but conversely, the scientific study of pathological cases becomes an indispensible phase in the overall search for laws of the normal state.[1]

—Georges Canguilhem

What Difference Does Deviant Globalization Make?

Deviant globalization matters to the future of the global political economy for three interconnected reasons. The first is the massive energy of innovation that exists within these processes. In a world desperately in need of innovative solutions to intractable social-political-economic-environmental problems, we can't afford to ignore what the entrepreneurs of deviant globalization have already figured out. The second is that these deviant entrepreneurs pose a fundamental challenge to the classical liberal view of statecraft, which sees state institutions as critical organizing and integrating mechanisms for economic and political development. Finally, the misunderstandings and mischaracterizations of those deviant, innovative energies, and the failure to appreciate their political consequences, is leading both governments and nongovernmental organizations to enact often dysfunctional policies that don't achieve their stated goals and sometimes make things worse. Calling these bad policy outcomes "unintended consequences" is no longer acceptable, for we are in a position to understand why they are happening — and to modify the consequences, if we use the right approaches.

The stories in this book capture the vast, if sometimes eccentric, innovation energies that deviant globalization taps. We all celebrate the extraordinary achievements of Sergey Brin and Larry Page, the Google entrepreneurs; but what about the Rodríguez Orejuela brothers of the Cali Cartel, whose competitive achievements during the 1980s against — as well as collaborative ventures with — the incumbents of Medellín were at least as impressive as Google's ongoing game with Microsoft?[2] Deviant entrepreneurs are some of the most audacious experimenters, risk-takers, and innovators in today's global economy. In their relentless search for competitive advantage, they engage in just about all of the activities that other entrepreneurs do — marketing, strategy, organizational design, product innovation, information management, financial analysis and so on. In many cases, they create enormous profits while extruding inefficiencies from huge markets. And they often go to extreme lengths to drive new business ventures to success, placing their economic livelihood and sometimes their lives at risk. Talk about "animal spirits" (Adam Smith) or "disruptive innovation" (Clayton Christensen) or "creative destruction" (Joseph Schumpeter) — it is all here. Just because these markets feature goods and services that may disgust us, does not mean we can't learn a great deal from deviant globalization's "success stories" and "best practices."[3]

As we said in the Introduction, the point of this book is not just to illustrate how deviant globalization is thriving alongside mainstream globalization; rather, it is to show how all of this ferment represents a new kind of geopolitical challenge. We promised that the wide-ranging examination of deviant globalization featured in this book would help us to reconsider the moral implications of the current global organization of wealth and power — as well as how to regulate and govern that global political economy. With this agenda very much in mind, we organize this conclusion around the following pragmatic discussions:

1. What conclusions can we draw about the relationship between deviant globalization, development, and human welfare?
2. What does deviant globalization do to nation-states and liberal hopes for the global political economy?
3. What can — or should — policy makers do about deviant globalization?

Challenging "Development"

Deviant globalization is in one sense easy to fit into existing and familiar narratives about development. As the stories in this book show, deviant globalization is, in many crucial respects, about unsavory things happening in the Global South, for the apparent benefit and pleasure of those in the Global North. Whether harvesting of organs, extra-legal extraction of commodities, deployment of weapons to insurgencies and rebels groups, or movement of laundered money into numbered Swiss bank accounts — these would all seem to indicate that deviant globalization represents yet another instance of the global rich oppressing the global poor. This classical view, shared by liberals and Marxists alike, holds that the sorts of illicit economies encompassed by deviant globalization represent a form of economic parasitism that diverts developmental energy, capital accumulation, human assets, and other valuable resources away from more "productive" uses; instead of providing a platform for self-sustained growth, such deviant markets appear merely to line the pockets of gangsters.

But the role of the deviant entrepreneur in the "development" of the Global South is more complicated than this view would suggest. Nations, institutions and NGOs from the Global North dedicate huge amounts of time and immense sums of money trying to help nations of the Global South modernize, diversify, and grow their economies. Liberal proponents of mainstream globalization view these efforts as a set of market-building steps toward delivering on the promise of capitalism. Marxist opponents criticize "development" practices for fostering dependency and, paradoxically, a permanent state of (at least relative) poverty. What both sides fail to appreciate is that many people living in poor nations in the Global South are already engaged in radical experiments in actual development through deviant globalization. Behind the backs of, and often despite, all those corporations and development NGOs as well as the World Bank and the International Monetary Fund, the poor are renting their bodies, selling their organs, stealing energy, stripping their natural environments of critical minerals and chemicals, manufacturing drugs, and accepting toxic waste not because they are evil, but in order to make a living. Thus, deviant globalization is a form of economic development.

Participating in the production side of deviant globalization — hopefully as an entrepreneur, but at least as a worker — is a survival strategy for those without easy access to legitimate, sustainable market opportunities, which is to say the poor, the uneducated, and those in locations with ineffective or corrupt institutional support for mainstream business.[4] People sell their organs, or become drug mules, or process toxic garbage, or offer sex to middle-aged foreigners because these jobs are often the fastest, best, easiest, and even in some cases the most sustainable way to make money. Even for the line workers in deviant industries, the money accumulated over a few years can often form a nest egg of capital to start more legitimate businesses.[5] To paraphrase John Lennon, deviant globalization is an important part of how development happens while the official development agencies "are busy making other plans."

To make the claim that deviant globalization is a form of development is not to deny the awfulness and oppressiveness of many deviant industries, or the significant social and environmental externalities that deviant globalization often imposes, or the fact that many of the participants in deviant globalization are coerced into their working roles. No doubt there are better and worse ways to improve one's lot in life, but it's rare that participating in deviant globalization is the worst available choice. Mining coal in China, for example, may be a more "legitimate" profession than pirating ships off of the coast of Somalia, but it is debatable whether the former is a better job than the latter. Most importantly, like them or not, both professions contribute to a kind of development.

Indeed, in many cases, states that host deviant industries recognize and embrace their developmental benefits. Consider the importance of sex tourism to the economies of countries such as Thailand, the Philippines, or Cuba. Except for sporadic crackdowns when international scrutiny grows too intense, these governments knowingly wink at sex tourism — it has been the foundation of much of their draw on the international tourism scene, and it is the source of very significant quantities of hard currency. In practice, sex tourism is a tacit part of their developmental strategy. Just as many countries are willing to tolerate physical pollution as a way to attract investment and jumpstart growth, so other countries are willing to tolerate what we might call social or moral pollution in order to achieve the same ends.[6]

Seen from this point of view, deviant industries are not just about crime; rather, they are wellsprings of innovation — disruption in the Christensen sense, creative destruction in the Schumpeterian sense — for political economies that need investment and growth and that have a hard time producing them via licit channels. At the same time, of course, the sort of innovation that deviant entrepreneurs produce is not a direct substitute for the kind of development proposed by metropolitan NGOs. Deviant development is different along several crucial dimensions:

- It is less transparent and operates according to more fluid rules of the game, for the deviant innovators are by definition less constrained — but it also creates new degrees of freedom
- It is less centered in formal organizations such as corporations, for deviant entrepreneurs don't organize in that way until and unless they have to — but it also enhances flexibility and adaptability
- It struggles to make, monitor, and enforce contracts — for even if the normal instruments of enforcement are weak in developing country settings, deviant entrepreneurs have even less access to them. This can get in the way of bargaining, increase transaction costs, and the like — but it also spurs the development of alternative means of deal making, monitoring, and enforcement
- Its success does not result in the long-term production of public goods, both because the deviant entrepreneurs are (for reasons of selection bias if nothing else) not public-minded sorts, and because the profits from deviant industries are rarely if ever taxed by the state, the classic provider of public goods — but what the state loses, local communities and organizations partly gain in the form of jobs and capital

Considering deviant globalization as a form of development challenges cherished views of the relationship between economic growth, transnational crime, and illicit behavior. Rather than representing a divergence from the liberal norm of licit growth in the formal economy, deviant globalization might better be conceived as a way for the globally excluded to find a space to be innovative, a space in which the rules of the game have not already been stacked against them. At the same time, this is not a subversively heroic Robin Hood morality tale. Today's deviant entrepreneurs are not proto-revolutionaries, aiming to remake society in an inclusive and collectively progressive fashion. Rather, they are opportunistic parasites whose public personae and brands are built around unbridled capitalist spirits — living fast, dying hard, and letting the rest of the world go to hell. The form of development they are enacting, in other words, is in many respects an ultra-libertarian one — one that tacitly rejects what liberal political economy defines as "the public good."

Challenging the State

Why does this matter? Even if one grants that state-led development has mostly failed (with a few very large but still exceptional exceptions) and been widely replaced, or at least back-filled, by illiberal forms of self-empowerment, does that matter for the larger geopolitical system? We have pointed several times to the argument that deviant globalization is just an annoying side effect of mainstream globalization, one that saps a small amount of blood from each of these mainstream processes as a kind of persistent tax, but which doesn't affect the larger functioning of the system. From this perspective, deviant globalization might be worth commenting on, but not worth taking all that seriously, compared to the big things that "really matter" in international politics.

We disagree. Our argument is that deviant

Back Story: The Tribulations of Modernist Development

When Communism died in the 1980s, what passed was not just the collectivist economic system and authoritarian politics of the Soviet Union and its satellites. Cremated along with the corpse of Communism was the broadly civic-minded conception of development as the central responsibility of the postcolonial state — a conception that had been largely shared by Communists and Liberals during the Cold War.[7] The disintegration of this statist, "modernist" conception of development was arguably the single most important intellectual event of the 1990s, one with huge implications for global economic policy making, not to mention the life choices available to people in the Global South.[8]

What emerged in the wake of this ideological collapse was the "Washington Consensus" — so-called because it represented the consensus of Neoliberal policy makers associated both with the Reagan-era US government and the technocrats at the International Monetary Fund, located just down the street from the White House in Washington, DC.[9] Pioneered as domestic policy in Margaret Thatcher's Great Britain and Ronald Reagan's United States, the program associated with the Washington Consensus soon became a model that London and Washington sought to export to the Global South and the post-Communist world.[10] Pointing to the undeniable corruption, inefficiency, and rent-seeking of most states in the Global South, the Neoliberals associated with the Washington Consensus demanded that aid recipients slash public bureaucracies and services, reduce dependence on foreign aid, dismantle trade barriers, and curtail the political power of organized labor. As Dani Rodrik has put it, "'Stabilize, privatize, and liberalize' became the mantra of a generation of technocrats who cut their teeth in the developing world and of the political leaders they counseled."[11] Such so-called structural adjustment programs left the states they were imposed on as *hollowed out shells of their former selves: the physical buildings and institutions of the state might remain in place, but the ambitions and capacities of the state shriveled.*[12]

This late– and post–Cold War hollowing out of states, particularly in the Global South, had two important results. First, it signaled to everyone in these countries that, "you are on your own." The end of the promise of building a public goods-providing state — or rather, the revelation that this promise had always been empty — unleashed a flood of survival entrepreneurship throughout the Global South, as well as in former Communist states. Some of these people of course entered legal industries; but many others chose to pursue faster profits in the deviantly globalized marketplaces of the

globalization has profound geopolitical implications because it is degrading state power, eroding state capacity, corroding state legitimacy, and, ultimately, undermining the foundations of mainstream globalization. More specifically, deviant globalization is creating a new type of political actor whose geopolitical importance will only grow in the coming decades. What makes these political actors unique is the fact that they thrive in weak-state environments, and their activities reinforce the conditions of this weakness. In his essay in this volume, John Robb refers to these new players as "global guerrillas."

Deviant entrepreneurs wield political power in three distinct ways. First, they have money. As we have seen, deviant entrepreneurs control huge, growing swathes of the global economy, operating most prominently in places where the state is hollowed or hollowing out. State corruption fueled by drug money on both sides of the US-Mexico border exemplifies this point. Second, many deviant entrepreneurs control and deploy a significant quota of violence — an occupational hazard for people working in extra-legal industries, who cannot count on the state to adjudicate their contractual disputes. This use of violence brings deviant entrepreneurs into primal conflict with one of the state's central sources of legitimacy, namely its monopoly (in principle) over the socially sanctioned use of force. Finally, and most controversially, these deviant entrepreneurs in some cases are also emerging as private providers of security, health care, and infrastructure — that is, precisely the kind of goods that functional states are supposed to provide to the public. Hezbollah in Lebanon, the MEND in Nigeria, the narco-traffickers in Mexico, the criminal syndicates in the *favelas* of Brazil — all are deviant entrepreneurs who not only have demonstrated that they can shut down their host states' basic functional capacity, thereby upsetting global markets half a world away, but who are also increasingly providing social services to local constituencies.

Deviant entrepreneurs generally do not start out as political actors, in the sense of actors who wish to control or usurp the state. In the first iteration, as we saw in the last section, deviant globalization represents a response to the failure of development and the hollowing out of the state. Once these deviant industries take off, however, they begin to take on a political life of their own. The state weakness that was a condition of deviant globalization's initial local emergence becomes something that the now empowered deviant entrepreneurs seek to perpetuate and even exacerbate. They siphon off money, loyalty, and sometimes territory; they increase corruption; and they undermine the rule of law. They also force well-functioning states in the global system to spend an inordinate amount of time, energy, and attention trying to control what comes in and out of their borders. Although deviant globalization may initially have flowered as a result of state hollowing out, as it develops, it becomes a positive feedback loop, in much the same way that many successful animal and plant species, as they invade a natural ecosystem, reshape their ecosystem in ways that improve their ability to exclude competitors.[15]

What's new in this dynamic is that many of these "political actors" only rarely develop an interest in actually taking control of the formal institutions of the state. Deviant entrepreneurs have developed market niches in which extractable returns are more profitable, and frankly easier, than anything they could get by "owning" enough of the state functions to extract rents from those instead. Organizations such as the First Command of the Capital in Brazil, the 'Ndrangheta in Italy, or the drug cartels in Mexico have no interest in taking over the states in which they operate. Why would they want that? This would only mean that they would be expected to provide a much broader and less selective menu of services to everyone, including ungrateful and low-profit clients, those so-called citizens. None of these organizations plan to declare sovereign independence and file for membership of the United Nations. What they want, simply, is to carve out

post–Cold War world or were lured into the role of foot soldiers in these flourishing deviant industries. From this perspective, deviant globalization represented "the economic strategy of the unemployed and the dispossessed . . . in a time of material contraction."[13]

The second and equally important impact of hollowed out states was the dismantling of the regulatory capacity in the Global South. These weak states lacked the institutions and the practical capacity to enforce the rules of international transactions, liberating the forces of both mainstream and deviant globalization.[14] In sum, the structurally adjusted states of the post–Cold War Global South no longer had either the ambition to provide their people with traditional, socially inclusive, and equitable development or the capacity to stop them from pursuing deviant alternatives of self-empowerment. In sum, the triumph of Neoliberalism was a critical (perhaps even essential) prerequisite for the rise of deviant globalization.

autonomous spaces where they can do their business without state intervention. This underscores a crucial point about deviant globalization: It does not thrive in truly "failed" states — that is, in places where the state has completely disappeared — but rather in weak but well-connected states, in which the deviant entrepreneur can establish a zone of autonomy while continuing to rely on the state for some of the vestigial services it continues to furnish.[16]

Alas, states and deviant entrepreneurs are unlikely to find a sustainable equilibrium. On the one hand, the more deviant industries grow, the more damage they do to the political legitimacy of the states within which the deviant entrepreneurs operate, thus undermining the capacity of the state to provide the infrastructure and services that the deviant entrepreneurs want to catch a free-ride on. On the other hand, the people living in the semi-autonomous zones controlled by deviant entrepreneurs increasingly recognize those entrepreneurs rather than the hollowed out state as the real source of local power and authority — if for no other reason than the recognition that if you can't beat them, you should join them. As these groups take over functions that would have been expected of the state, their stakeholders increasingly lose interest in the hollowed-out formal state institutions.[17] Thus, even though deviant entrepreneurs hardly want to kill their host state, they may end up precipitating a process whereby the state implodes catastrophically. Something like this took place in Colombia in the 1980s, in Zaire/Congo since the 1990s, and may be taking place in Mexico today.

Challenging Liberal Views of Globalization

The foregoing claims may be a tough pill for some cheerleaders of globalization to swallow.[18] It's not so much that they question the deleterious effects of globalization on the state; it's more that the most avid advocates of mainstream globalization don't judge those effects to be a problem on balance. In fact, they almost welcome them in their promotion of mainstream globalization, for weakening states that routinely promote national interests — such as excess taxation and trade restrictions — are a net positive for the global economy. The problem is that this argument makes sense only if one believes, first, in a zero-sum game between states and markets and, second, that what the state loses, globalization wins. It's an extreme position, hard to justify in historical terms, and blind to the important synergies between states and markets.

Even for more nuanced proponents of globalization — those who recognize the importance of public goods and the role that the state plays in regulating the excesses of the market — deviant globalization is something of a nightmare.

When deviant globalization comes to the fore, it calls into question sixty years of liberal economic development in the Global South and painfully replaces it with an version of unfettered economics and exploitation that causes dry rot in states. This is no longer a world in which states and markets find a tense but nonetheless functional balance of power. Rather, it is one in which the optimism that global economic integration will lift all boats is forced to confront the fact that deviant industries represent torpedoes aimed at these rising boats — torpedoes guided by deviant entrepreneurs who are as adaptable, ruthless, and consequential as their mainstream counterparts. Metropolitan observers and state leaders have failed to recognize that the existence of deviant globalization makes them less able to determine winners and losers in the global political economy. That loss of control is discomforting, but it is real. It is also a more nuanced and yet more challenging threat to conventional policy than the one that proponents of the "failed-states" language usually recognize. In other words, the problem is not simply that states are "failing" — a phrase that implies they can and want to get "fixed." Rather, it is that the synergy between weak states and strong deviant entrepreneurs creates — sometimes involving personal political connections at a very high level — a self-reinforcing dynamic that continually fortifies and extends the scope of deviant globalization.

All of this underscores the extent to which the liberalism that supports the idea of a wholly integrated global market is a fragile, contradiction-ridden ideology, especially when it attempts to encompass communities and institutions that aren't themselves imbued with liberal values. Deviant globalization is a product of this ideological and institutional stretch. And, paradoxically, these same illiberal groups in fact often participate in the global market from an ultra-liberal economic perspective. They are free-market entrepreneurs unburdened by the moral qualms and regulatory cuffs that confine the value-added processes of liberals in wealthier nations. It's really not a question of whether participants in mainstream globalization will let these deviant entrepreneurs into the tent. They're in. And because they're in, all of us face an important and challenging question: Is it really possible to be a global liberal in the early decades of the twenty-first century?

What Is to Be Done?

Many contemporary policy efforts that aim at stemming deviant globalization are dysfunctional — along a spectrum from simply ineffective to stunningly self-defeating. America's "war on drugs" is the poster child of the more extreme sort of failure. The US Government has been fighting this (declared) war now since the early 1970s, at an estimated cost so far of $2.5 trillion dollars.[19] Americans have rewritten criminal law, filled jails with convicts, deployed vast military capabilities abroad, revised the rules of city policing, and ruined millions of individual lives — and that is just the start. No one doubts who is losing this war. The vast costs to America's social and political fabric are hard to estimate but painfully visible. Even David Simon's extraordinary HBO series "The Wire" — a harrowing dramatization of these dynamics in Baltimore's school system, politics, port economy, and newspapers — probably understated the scale and scope of defeat. The biggest winners, of course, have been the narcotics supply chain entrepreneurs and their financiers.

Why is policymaking around deviant globalization generally so inept, and why hasn't it improved much with time? The answer is a mix of at least three reasons, in different proportions. First, policymakers are people who represent constituents, and along with them, they moralize. Public policy filtered through a sharply focused moral lens — no matter what the morality — tends to lack nuance and perspective when it confronts a diverse and highly adaptive world. When deviant entrepreneurs, their employees and associates, as well as their customers, become labeled "global criminals," or, more simply "bad actors," policy internalizes this moral logic. Governments then stop "managing" the problem; instead, they prohibit, target, capture, punish, strike, and kill. The shades of gray get lost in black and white. Ironically, that very logic empowers the adaptive advantages of deviant entrepreneurs who are not locked into those kinds of constraints and who recognize that every prohibition is a business opportunity if you look at it the right way.

Punish, strike, and kill policies fail because they focus on the sins of the actors, not the complex dynamics of the system in which the actors participate. By removing some subset of deviant entrepreneurs without at the same time addressing the underlying conditions that gave rise to and enabled them, policymakers create arbitrage opportunities and allow new actors to step into the roles of the old ones. We've learned this lesson before: Prohibition in the early part of the twentieth century is a case in point. Ironically, attempts to kill the deviant beast may only make it stronger, much like pouring partially effective antibiotics onto a rich microbiological ecology. On the one hand, we have a twisted form of adverse selection: Governments taking an aggressively prohibitionist approach are most likely to weed out the weaker players, clearing the field for the more clever, more ruthless deviant entrepreneurs. On the other hand, if governments are lucky, persistent, or powerful enough to take down some of the strongest deviant entrepreneurs, then they leave the second-tier players highly incentivized to evolve and innovate so as to avoid the mistakes of their predecessors. Adaptability is, after all, the hallmark of deviant globalization. There is no magical antibiotic or surgical solution. And we can't jail or kill 'them' all. That's a statement about the supply side, of course. But it's equally true of the demand side. Could any American government even contemplate locking up all its citizens who buy cocaine, are addicted to methamphetamines, collect the relics of endangered species, or dump their garbage (directly or indirectly) "elsewhere"?

The second reason policymaking regarding deviant globalization has often been misguided is that politicians, at least in democratic societies, are time-bound pragmatists who feel the need to show "progress." Voters certainly like it when elected officials and their appointees say that this is what they will do. The problem is that deviant entrepreneurs are in exactly the same situation vis-à-vis their constituencies but aren't constrained by votes and don't have to play by a codified set of rules. Instead, they show progress by generating more money in spite of what governments do. Putting up roadblocks, such as a long, technically sophisticated fence at the US-Mexican border, invites experimentation and risk-taking that leads to new and more effective smuggling routes for illegal immigrants, more powerful methamphetamines and, ultimately, surprisingly (but not unpredictably) destructive outcomes.[20] Likewise, introducing armored vehicles where insurgents in Iraq or Afghanistan routinely use IEDs has led — predictably — to more powerful and sophisticated IEDs.[21] Is that really a demonstration of progress? Policymakers who put selective pressure on deviant industries in order to show progress, without considering how the system will compensate and adapt, are almost sure to be surprised at just how much progress the deviant entrepreneurs will show in response.

The third reason for policymaking failures in the face of deviant globalization is that policymakers sometimes engage in denial. Isn't it sensible to just ignore deviant globalization and treat it as a small cost of doing global business? If the mainstream economy grows quickly enough, then perhaps deviant globalization will shrink in relative terms until it is nearly inconsequential. Unfortunately, this "growing pains" story is analytically flawed. There's no evidence to suggest that the global economy can "outgrow" the deviant globalization problem. In fact, the deviant markets are probably growing faster than mainstream globalization.[22] And deviant entrepreneurs find themselves enjoying windfalls, sometimes even monopoly profits, as a result of that growth. While there is probably some asymptote that limits the growth of deviant globalization, we have not seen it yet. And there is simply no reason to assume that growth of deviant industries will stop or even slow when they begin to crowd out or colonize mainstream markets. Witness cigarette smuggling in Eastern Europe after the end of Communism,[23] or the recent diversification of Mexican and Italian drug cartels into "legitimate" businesses.[24]

Well-meaning policymakers commonly mix bits of all three kinds of mistakes, as well as cycle between them, sometimes in frustration and sometimes in an effort to distinguish themselves from their political predecessors. That tends to make the situation worse from the government's perspective and better from the perspective of deviant entrepreneurs, for bad and especially inconsistent policy creates precisely the kind of legal, military, regulatory, and moral environment that the entrepreneurs can so profitably exploit.

Should governments throw in the towel and just let deviant globalization thrive? This is, ironically, sometimes a harder argument to confront directly, for there is more than a little countercultural, counterintuitive, almost nihilistic attractiveness to it. Not just ideologically charged libertarian activists but also others who have seen up close the extraordinary costs of the war on drugs, for example, can be forgiven for sometimes asking governments to simply stop doing harm.

But that's too stark a choice, both analytically and practically. It sets up a particularly dysfunctional debate, catching politicians between the pincers of "do nothing" and "declare war." Capable governments most of the time are not going to just give up; if the only palatable alternative is to declare war and make eradication the goal, that is what they will do. But, they will do it to no good end, as the chapters in this book so poignantly show.

It is our view that policymaking around deviant globalization needs to and can improve. The prerequisite is for policymakers to acknowledge — in an honest, decisive, and unapologetic fashion — that there is no perfect solution. The next step is to play for gains as you would in a strategic interdependence situation, an iterated game where the two sides can neither defeat nor control each other, but where each and every action they take affects the options that the other will have in the next round. In that context, there are real policy opportunities to curb the most pernicious of the deviant industries, to direct some of the deviant energy into less harmful channels, and to turn some of what deviant entrepreneurs know and are good at into goods that benefit a broader swathe of humanity and at lower cost. These are less ambitious but more realistic goals than eradication of deviant globalization.

There are five principles that can better guide policymakers. In putting forward these principles, we are not stealthily introducing the notion that the state is, should, or can be the ultimate arbiter of deviant globalization. In many instances, the state may not even get to be the first mover. Societies and individuals also have their own voices and options, which are separate, at least sometimes, from the state. But the state clearly does have a role, if only in making the laws that the deviant entrepreneurs will arbitrage. It is our view that in the iterated game of strategic interdependence currently underway, deviant entrepreneurs are outplaying states more frequently than the other way around. It is time to offer some advice to the less effective side:

Principle 1: State Policy Cannot Eliminate Deviant Globalization. So regulate it instead. Regulation is both a mindset and a to-do list. The mindset is a straightforward recognition of interdependence between those who regulate and those who are regulated. The to-do list is to learn from the vast experience in regulatory policy what can and can't be done efficiently, and at what cost. Here's a concrete example of a powerful regulatory principle that can work in an adapted fashion: "Make the polluters pay" in deviant globalization just as regulatory policy has tried to do in some legitimate industries. This would be an overall efficiency gain for globalization, in theory. It's efficient because deviant entrepreneurs and industries are not now bearing the full costs of the negative externalities they produce. And, thus, they are growing faster than they would in a market setting with fewer externalities. In practice, the effectiveness of regulation depends of course on the regulatory capacity of governments and the international community. In the short term, making polluters pay in one place incentivizes them to move their activities somewhere else where regulation is spottier — and some of them will do exactly that. But this regulatory move at least forces those players to move to a less attractive location where the costs of doing business are higher — and thus harms their business. It's worth noting that stated this way, the principle of regulating deviant globalization could appeal across the political spectrum of liberals and conservatives and pick up additional support from those who want environmental and climate regulation.

Principle 2: No State Can Impose Uniform Standards or Prices on "Moral Offensiveness." Peoples and cultures, certainly globally and often even within a particular state, are too diverse to make a single set of moral standards feasible. So let the advocates of different moral standards bargain with each other instead — and do so through institutional channels. What would that entail in practice? It would mean giving up the myth of universal moral opprobrium or shared repugnance, and acknowledging that the world is full of different views on these issues, held with varying intensities. It would mean negotiating trade-offs between what we can and cannot live with, in conjunction with the underlying trade-off functions that other states and societies hold differently but as strongly as we do. Bargaining becomes a reasonable second-best solution in that kind of setting, because enabling the players to bargain over what they want and how badly they want it promises at least to create focal points for policies that reflect the real desires and capabilities of the players in the game, not the desires or wishful thinking of political elites who don't have to live with the costs of what they choose. It also promises to deliver fewer surprises and "unintended consequences" — to all sides in the game.

Principle 3: Efficient and Fair Bargaining Requires Transparency about Costs, Benefits, and Preferences. So don't hide the deviant globalization story — from anyone. Don't hide it behind fantasy, weak analysis, or wishful thinking. And don't hide the reality from domestic political constituencies that insist that policymakers "fight evil" at all costs. Doing so may win a few votes in the next election. But it also creates new arbitrage opportunities and thus plays right into the hands of those willing and able to play the other side of the game. In order for policymakers to make good regulatory choices, their constituents need to understand that raising the price of, say, prostitution (by making it illegal) not only encourages sex trafficking and slavery, but also creates more abject conditions for the sex workers themselves. That's a choice a society might wish to make, but it should not make that choice (or the opposite choice for that matter) without a balanced scorecard that shows the real costs and benefits to everyone. The less transparency there is in the system, the more the bargaining table tilts in favor of the deviant entrepreneurs.

Principle 4: The Regulation of Deviant Globalization Should Err on the Side of Permissiveness. Don't try to regulate deviant industries into the ground. It doesn't work. Moreover, it's self-defeating, for deviant entrepreneurs will almost inevitably find an innovative way around regulatory controls, increasing their profits and power along the way. Regulation that errs on the side of permissiveness provides deviant entrepreneurs with space to operate, but forces them to curtail their worst excesses, and limits the negative political externalities associated with failed efforts at prohibition. It's the same logic that leads to warning labels on cigarettes, helmet laws for motorcyclists, and mandatory HIV testing for porn stars. This approach is especially important for the protection of the most unambiguously vulnerable individuals participating in deviant industries. While reasonable people will undoubtedly disagree about where to draw the line between those who should and should not be protected, we shouldn't let that irresolvable debate prevent our taking any action whatsoever, or tempt us to overreach into counterproductive prohibitionism.

Principle 5: The Global Political Economy Needs, Produces, and Rewards Rapid Innovation, Whether You Want It To or Not. So encourage mainstream innovation in sectors, places, and parts of the market where innovation by deviant entrepreneurs now flourishes. The point is to enable and accelerate innovation in legitimate spaces in order to crowd out the deviant sorts of innovation. That means creating alternative suppliers for the demand that deviant entrepreneurs now meet, and legitimate outlets for those deviant entrepreneurs' talents. Rather than demonize and criminalize them, encourage them to move into legal businesses, or legalize their current businesses. This will enhance efficiency, reduce exploitation, and curb negative externalities. Sometimes, radical innovation may be the best solution of all. It may be, for example, that the single best way to counter black markets for human organs is to accelerate funding for stem-cell research that could produce cloned organs and radically disrupt the deviant market.

There are also two "goals" that policymakers should not try to achieve, for they cannot do so, and trying to will at best waste resources and at worst be actively counterproductive:

Caution #1: Don't Try to "Turn back the Clock." Don't give in to anti-globalist pressures that have grown alongside both mainstream and deviant globalization. That is not to say that these pressures come from a completely irrational or reactionary place. There is a certain common sense in wanting to disconnect states, societies, and communities from global flows that include so much bad stuff. It's this "common sense" that sometimes binds together unusual coalitions of interests, such as when anti–organ-trade moralists find themselves aligned with labor unions opposed to outsourcing, who in turn form allies with extreme environmentalists who share goals with local culture protectionists who want YouTube blocked. These episodic coalitions will periodically burst onto the world stage and call for rolling back global integration, moving toward national autarky, restraining the excesses of markets, and returning to a long-lost ideal of culturally congenial, self-sufficient, public good–providing national states. It's a fantasy, and we shouldn't let it seduce us.

Caution #2: Don't Do Nothing. Don't ignore deviant globalization and hope for the best. For the Global North, the "best" (if that means outgrowing deviant globalization through the triumph of the mainstream) probably will not happen, as we have explained. And, for the Global South, the "best" (if that means relying on deviant globalization for development) is likely to contribute to state hollowing out and dysfunctionality. We need to change how we think and talk about deviant globalization and give it its due among the top ten global problems that require ingenious policy and collective action. We need to stop treating deviant industries as isolated criminal activities, for that prevents us from seeing its complex integration and force-multiplying innovation. We need to recognize, frankly, that we're all complicit — both the Global North and the South — in creating the conditions in which deviant supply meets deviant demand. The money, power, and violence generated by that dynamic are a political problem of the first order.

Ultimately, there are no policy solutions to deviant globalization. We have only choices between different sorts of imperfect outcomes. There are, however, analytic solutions. We have the ability to take a clear-eyed view of the actual choices posed by deviant globalization. We can analyze deviant globalization on its own terms. We can experiment, bargain, and regulate based on better, more analytically rigorous assumptions. We can adapt the same know-how that allows us to run mainsteam globalization — with its unfathomable complexity — to its deviant twin. Our final point is simply that many deviant industries can be regulated and managed, especially if we're willing to take account of the painful lessons we've learned from fighting deviant entrepreneurs in more traditional ways, such as through interdiction, criminalization, and war. Managing deviant globalization means learning to live with the reality of the ongoing demand for repugnant products and services, rather than pretending it isn't there, or trying quixotically to suppress it. It means playing a complex and strategically interdependent game, in which we have the tools to anticipate how deviant entrepreneurs will adapt to our management efforts. And it takes enormous political courage to admit that this is what we are doing.

We live in a fundamentally new reality, in which the professionalization, integration, and globalization of a wide set of deviant industries now touches the lives of almost everyone on the planet. Today, we can make informed choices that allow us to contain and live with deviant globalization in a way that minimizes its unpleasant impacts on politics, the state, and the human and natural ecologies of the planet. If we fail to seize this moment, our choices tomorrow are likely to be less pleasant.

Notes

1. Georges Canguilhem, *On the Normal and the Pathological*, translated by Carolyn R. Fawcett and Robert S. Cohen with an introduction by Michel Foucault (New York: Zone Books, 1989 [1966]).
2. Ron Chespesiuk, *Drug Lords: The Rise and Fall of the Cali Cartel* (New York: Milo Books, 2006).
3. Colin C. Williams, *The Hidden Enterprise Culture: Entrepreneurship in the Underground Economy* (Northhampton: Edward Elgar Publishing, 2006); Justin W. Webb, et al., "You Say Illegal, I Say Legitimate: Entrepreneurship in the Informal Economy," *Academy of Management Review* 34:3 (2009); Petter Gottschalk, *Entrepreneurship and Organised Crime: Entrepreneurs in Illegal Business* (London: Edward Elgar Publishers, 2009).
4. Sudhir Alladi Venkatesh, *Off the Books: The Underground Economy of the Urban Poor* (Cambridge: Harvard University Press, 2006)
5. Jeremy Seabrook, *Travels in the Skin Trade* (London: Pluto Press, 2001) and Rachel G. Sacks, "Commercial Sex and the Single Girl: Women's Empowerment through Economic Development in Thailand," *Development in Practice* 7:4 (1997) describe the way that Thai "bar girls" use savings from their days in prostitution to start sewing or hairdressing businesses back in their villages of origin. Another example is the way that rappers (legendarily) parlay profits from drug dealing into starting a recording company; see the obituary by Jon Pareles, "Eazy-E, 31, Performer Who Put Gangster Rap on the Charts," *New York Times*, 28 March 1995.
6. Ryan Bishop and Lillian S. Robinson, *Night Market: Sexual Cultures and the Thai Economic Miracle* (New York: Routledge, 1999); and Vidyamali Samarasinghe, "Female Labor in Sex Trafficking: A Darker Side of Globalization," in Lise Nelson and Joni Seager, eds., *A Companion to Feminist Geography* (London: Wiley, 2005).
7. Odd Arne Westad, *The Global Cold War: Third World Interventions and the Making of Our Times* (Cambridge: Cambridge University Press, 2006).
8. Peter J. Boettke, ed., *The Collapse of Development Planning* (New York: New York University Press, 1994) was symptomatic of development practitioners' loss of faith in state-led development planning. More historically-oriented critiques of so-called "high modernist" development schemes include James C. Scott, *Seeing Like a State: How Some Schemes to Improve the Human Condition Have Failed* (New Haven: Yale University Press, 1998) and Jan Nederveen Pieterse, *Development Theory* (London: SAGE, 2009).
9. John Williamson, "What Washington Means by Policy Reform," in John Williamson, ed., *Latin American Adjustment: How Much Has Happened?* (Washington: Institute for International Economics, 1990).
10. David Harvey, *A Brief History of Neoliberalism* (New York: Oxford University Press, 2007); Susan George, "A Short History of Neoliberalism," Paper presented at the Conference on Economic Sovereignty in a Globalising World, Bangkok, 24–26 March 1999.
11. Dani Rodrik, "Goodbye Washington Consensus, Hello Washington Confusion," *Journal of Economic Literature* 44:4 (2006).
12. Noel Thompson, "Hollowing Out the State: Public Choice Theory and the Critique of Keynesian Social Democracy," *Contemporary British History* 22:3 (2008). For two case studies of this process, see Teresa Caldiera, *City of Walls: Crime, Segregation and Citizenship in São Paulo* (Berkeley: University of California Press, 2000) and Colin Clarke, *Decolonizing the Colonial City: Urbanization and Stratification in Kingston, Jamaica* (New York: Oxford University Press, 2006).

13. Janet Roitman, *Fiscal Disobedience: An Anthropology of Economic Regulation in Central Africa* (Princeton: Princeton University Press, 2005), p. 94.

14. Guilhem Fabre, *Criminal Prosperity: Drug Trafficking, Money Laundering and Financial Crisis after the Cold War* (New York: Routledge, 2002).

15. John P. Sullivan and Robert J. Bunker, "Drug Cartels, Street Gangs, and Warlords," *Small Wars & Insurgencies* 13:2 (2002); Max G. Manwaring, "Street Gangs: The New Urban Insurgency," Strategic Studies Institute (2005); Enrique Desmond Arias, "The Dynamics of Criminal Governance: Networks and Social Order in Rio de Janeiro," *Journal of Latin American Studies* 38:2 (2006).

16. One critical misconception promoted by the liberal enthusiasts of globalization, most prominently by Thomas P. M. Barnett in *The Pentagon's New Map: War and Peace in the Twenty-First Century* (New York: Putnam, 2005), is that the cause of poverty and insecurity and ultimately state failure is "disconnectedness" from the world economy. In fact, all of the most seriously "failed" states — Congo, Somalia, Afghanistan — are deeply connected to the global economy, albeit in ways that are hard to see clearly from London, New York, or Washington. While it is true that they remain weakly connected to the *formal* and *legal* parts of the global economy, such places are in fact highly *deviantly* connected — via the illicit trade in minerals, via piracy, or via the global drug trade, and so on. The crucial issue, in other words, is not connectedness or disconnectedness, but rather what kind of connectedness. Everyone gets globalization; the only question is what kind.

17. Diane E. Davis, "Irregular armed forces, shifting patterns of commitment, and fragmented sovereignty in the developing world," *Theory and Society* 39:3–4 (2010). Although globalization is undermining national political institutions and identities, it is not necessarily producing a "global" political identity, as the utopian proponents of "cosmopolitics" have hoped, but rather driving people into more localized primary identities rooted in clan, sect, ethnicity, and gang.

18. Kenichi Ohmae, *The End of the Nation-State: The Rise of Regional Economies* (New York: Free Press, 1995) articulated the paradigmatic version of this "hyperglobalist" view from a neoliberal perspective. But hyperglobalism can also be celebrated from a Leftist, "cosmopolitan," perspective; see for example: Pheng Cheah and Bruce Robbins, eds., *Cosmopolitics: Thinking and Feeling beyond the Nation* (Minneapolis: University of Minnesota Press, 1999) and Daniele Archibugi, ed., *Debating Cosmopolitics* (London: Verso, 2003).

19. Claire Suddath, "The War on Drugs," *Time Magazine*, 25 March 2009.

20. Jerome H. Skolnick, "Rethinking the Drug Problem," *Daedalus* 121:3 (1992).

21. "Bombs away: Elaborate new devices designed to defeat makeshift explosives struggle to gain the upper hand in Iraq and Afghanistan," *The Economist*, 4 March 2010.

22. Moisés Naím, *Illicit: How Smugglers, Traffickers and Copycats are Hijacking the Global Economy* (New York: Doubleday, 2005).

23. Aida A. Hozic, "On the Tobacco Roads of Southeastern Europe," paper presented at the annual meeting of the International Studies Association, Le Centre Sheraton Hotel, Montreal, Quebec, Canada, 17 March 2004; see also Misha Glenny, *McMafia: Journey Through the Global Criminal Underworld* (New York: Vintage Books, 2008), pp. 25–26.

24. Roberto Saviano, *Gomorrah* (New York: Farrar, Straus and Giroux, 2007); and Alfredo Corchado, "Mexico's Zetas gang buys businesses along border in move to increase legitimacy," *Dallas Morning News*, 7 December 2009.

Bibliography

Emigration

"A Cargo of Exploitable Souls." *The Economist* 30 May 2002.

Andreas, Peter. "The Transformation of Migrant Smuggling Across the U.S.-Mexico Border." *Global Human Smuggling: Comparative Perspectives.* Ed. David Kyle and Rey Koslowski. New York: Johns Hopkins UP, 2001.

Bales, Kevin. *Disposable People: New Slavery in the Global Economy.* Berkeley, CA: University of California, 2004.

Barry, Brian, and Robert E. Goodin. *Free Movement: Ethical Issues in the Transnational Migration of People and of Money.* University Park, PA: Penn State, 1992.

Bowe, John. *Nobodies: Modern American Slave Labor and the Dark Side of the New Global Economy.* New York: Random House, 2007.

Chacon, Jennifer M. "Misery and Myopia: Understanding the Failures of U.S. Efforts to Stop Human Trafficking." *Fordham Law Review* 74 (2006).

Cohen, Robin. *Migration and Its Enemies: Global Capital, Migrant Labour and the Nation-state.* Grant Rapids: Ashgate, 2006.

Estabrook, Barry. "The Price of Tomatoes." *Gourmet* Mar. 2009.

Koser, Khalid. "Out of the Frying Pan and into the Fire: A Case Study of Illegality Amongst Asylum Seekers." *New Migration in Europe: Social Constructions and Social Realities.* Houndmills, Basingstoke, Hampshire: Macmillan, St. Martin's. 1998.

Kyle, David and John Dale. "Smuggling the State Back In: Agents of Human Smuggling Reconsidered." *Global Human Smuggling: Comparative Perspectives.* Ed. David Kyle and Rey Koslowski. New York: Johns Hopkins UP, 2001.

Lewis, Michael. "Commie Ball: A Journey to the End of A Revolution." *Vanity Fair* July 2008.

Liang, Zai and Wenzhen Ye. "From Fujian to New York: Understanding the New Chinese Immigration." *Global Human Smuggling: Comparative Perspectives.* Ed. David Kyle and Rey Koslowski. New York: Johns Hopkins UP, 2001.

Naím, Moisés. "Why is Slavery Booming in the 21st Century?" *Illicit: How Smugglers, Traffickers and Copycats are Hijacking the Global Economy.* New York: Doubleday, 2005. 86–108.

Shelley, Louise I. "The Rise and Diversification of Human Smuggling and Trafficking into the United States." *Transnational Threats Smuggling and Trafficking in Arms, Drugs, and Human Life.* Ed. Kimberley L. Thachuk. New York: Praeger Security International General Interest-Cloth, 2007. 194–210.

Skinner, E. Benjamin. *A Crime So Monstrous: Face-to-Face with Modern-Day Slavery.* New York: Free, 2008.

Vayrynen, Raimo. *Illegal Immigration, Human Trafficking and Organized Crime. World Institute for Development Economics Research.* United Nations University/UNHCR, Oct. 2003.

http://www.iom.int/
http://www.notforsalecampaign.org/

Sex

"The Sex Industry in Cambodia." *The Economist* 11 June 2009.

"Unwanted Visitors: The Law Catches Up With Travelling Paedophiles." *The Economist* 21 Aug. 2008.

Cole, Jeffrey. "Reducing the Damage: Dilemmas of Anti-Trafficking Efforts among Nigerian Prostitutes in Palermo." *Anthropologica* 48.2 (2006).

Finnegan, William. "The Countertraffickers: Rescuing the Victims of the Global Sex Trade." *The New Yorker* 5 May 2008.

Garland, Sarah. "This Woman was Forced into Slavery . . . in the U.S." *Marie Claire* May 2006.

Glenny, Misha. "Aliyah." *McMafia: A Journey Through the Criminal Underworld.* New York: Vintage, 2008. 104–110.

Hughes, Donna M. "The Natasha Trade: The Transnational Shadow Market of Trafficking in Women." *Journal of International Affairs* (Spring 2000).

Jones, Maggie. "Thailand's Brothel Busters." *Mother Jones* Nov. & Dec. 2003.

Kara, Siddharth. *Sex Trafficking Inside the Business of Modern Slavery.* New York: Columbia UP, 2009.

Landesman, Peter. "The Girls Next Door." *The New York Times Magazine* 25 Jan. 2004. Print.

Raymond, Janice G., and Donna M. Hughes. *Sex Trafficking of Women in the United States: International and Domestic Trends. National Institute of Justice.* 17 Apr. 2001. Web.

Skinner, E. Benjamin. "The New Slave Trade." *TIME* 18 Jan. 2010: 54–57.

Yen, Iris. "Of Vice and Men: A New Approach to Eradicating Sex Trafficking by reducing Male Demand through Educational Programs and Abolitionist Legislation." *Journal of Criminal Law & Criminology* 98.2 (2008).

Defense

"Flying Anything to Anybody: The Rise and Fall of Viktor Bout, Arms-Dealer Extraordinaire, Shows a Darker Side of Globalisation." *The Economist* 18 Dec. 2008.

"Small Weapons of Mass Destruction." *The Economist* 29 June 2006.

Bunker, Robert, ed. *Non-state Threats and Future Wars.* New York: Routledge, 2002.

Coll, Steve. "The Unthinkable: Can the United States be Made Safe from Nuclear Terrorism?" *The New Yorker* 12 Mar. 2007.

Cragin, Kim. *Arms trafficking and Colombia.* Santa Monica, CA: Prepared for the Defense Intelligence Agency [by] RAND National Defense Research Institute, 2003.

Duffield, Mark. *Global Governance and the New Wars The Merging of Development and Security.* New York: Zed, 2001.

Iklé, Fred Charles. *Annihilation from within the ultimate threat to nations.* New York: Columbia UP, 2006.

Keefe, Patrick Radden. "The Trafficker: The decades-long battle to catch an international arms broker." *The New Yorker* 8 Feb. 2010.

Landesman, Peter. "Arms and the Man: Profile of Victor Bout." *New York Times Magazine* 17 Aug. 2003.

Naím, Moisés. "Small Arms and Loose Nukes." *Illicit How Smugglers, Traffickers and Copycats are Hijacking the Global Economy*. New York: Doubleday, 2005. 38–64.

Shuster, Simon. "New Job for Ex-Soviet Pilots: Arms Trafficking." *TIME* 17 Dec. 2009.

Stohl, Rachel. "The Tangled Web of Illicit Arms Trafficking." *Center for American Progress*. 2004. Web.

http://globalguerrillas.typepad.com/

http://jamestown.org/programs/gta/terrorismmonitorgta/

http://www.controlarms.org/

http://www.smallarmssurvey.org/index.html

http://www.wired.com/dangerroom/

Pharma

"On the Trail of the Traffickers." *The Economist* 5 Mar. 2009.

"A World Awash in Heroin." *The Economist* 28 June 2007.

Dealey, Sam. "At War in the Fields of the Drug Lords." *GQ* Dec. 2006.

Dittrich, Luke. "Four Days on the Border." *Esquire* June 2008.

Gaynor, Tim, and Tiemoko Diallo. "Al Qaeda Linked to Rogue Aviation Network." *Reuters* 13 Jan. 2010.

Glenny, Misha. "March of Fear." *McMafia: A Journey Through the Criminal Underworld*. New York: Vintage, 2008. 240–263.

Guillermoprieto, Alma. "Days of the Dead: The New Narcocultura." *The New Yorker* 10 Nov. 2008.

Lacey, Marc. "From Cartel to Corporation: Drug Trade Economics." *The Economy and the Economics of Everyday Life — Economix Blog — NYTimes.com*. 7 Jan. 2010. Web.

Luhnow, David. "Saving Mexico." *The Wall Street Journal* 26 Dec. 2009.

Naím, Moisés. "No Business Like Drug Business." *Illicit: How Smugglers, Traffickers and Copycats are Hijacking the Global Economy*. New York: Doubleday, 2005. 65–85.

Orth, Maureen. "Afghanistan's Deadly Habit." *Vanity Fair* Mar. 2002.

Quinones, Sam. "The Heroin Road." *The Los Angeles Times* 14–16 Feb. 2010 (3 Part Series).

Syal, Rajeev. "Drug Money Saved Banks in Global Crisis, Claims UN Advisor." *The Guardian* 13 Dec. 2009.

Zackrison, James L. "Smuggling and the Caribbean: Tainting Paradise throughout History." *Transnational Threats Smuggling and Trafficking in Arms, Drugs, and Human Life*. Ed. Kimberley L. Thachuk. New York: Praeger Security International General Interest-Cloth, 2007. 177–93.

NGOs

Anderson, Jon Lee. "Gangland." *The New Yorker* 5 Oct. 2009.

Finnegan, William. "Silver or Lead." *The New Yorker* 31 May 2010.

Gettleman, Jeffrey. "The Pirates Have Seized the Ship." *GQ* Feb. 2009.

Goldberg, Jeffrey. "In the Party of God: Hezbollah Sets Up Operations in South America and the United States." *The New Yorker* 28 Oct. 2002.

Hagedorn, John M. *Gangs in the Global City: Alternatives to Traditional Criminology*. New York: University of Illinois, 2007.

Hagedorn, John. *World of Gangs: Armed Young Men and Gangsta Culture*. Minneapolis: University of Minnesota, 2008.

Kellner, Thomas. "Inside Mexico's Drug War." *World Policy Journal* 27.1 (2010): 29–37.

Lal, Rollie. "Japanese Trafficking and Smuggling." *Transnational Threats: Smuggling and Trafficking in Arms, Drugs, and Human Life*. Ed. Kimberley L. Thachuk. New York: Praeger Security International General Interest-Cloth, 2007. 143–49.

Langewiesche, William. "Letter from Sao Paulo: City of Fear." *Vanity Fair* Apr. 2007.

Manwaring, Max G. *Contemporary Challenge to State Sovereignty: Gangs and Other Illicit Transnational Criminal Organizations in Central America, El Salvador, Mexico, Jamaica, and Brazil*. Carlisle Barracks, PA: Strategic Studies Institute, US Army War College, 2007.

Naím, Moisés. "Citizens vs. Criminals." *Illicit: How Smugglers, Traffickers and Copycats are Hijacking the Global Economy*. New York: Doubleday, 2005. 199–216.

Orth, Maureen. "Inside Colombia's Hostage War." *Vanity Fair* Nov. 2008.

Papachristos, Andrew V. "Gang World." *Foreign Policy* 1 Mar. 2005.

Schneider, Barry, Jerrold M. Post, and Michael T. Kindt, eds. *The World's Most Threatening Terrorist Networks and Criminal Gangs*. New York: Palgrave-Macmillan, 2009.

Finance

Ahmed, Mohamad. "Somali Sea Gangs Lure Investors at Pirate Lair." *Reuters.com*. 1 Dec. 2009. Web.

Burrough, Bryan. "Pirate of the Caribbean." *The New Yorker* July 2009.

Kochan, Nick. *The Washing Machine: How Money Laundering and Terrorist Financing Soils Us*. New York: Texere, 2005.

Kroll, Andy. "Lawyers, Guns, and Money: How Big Banks, Sneaky Attorneys and a Host of Businessmen Funnel Dirty Cash Into the U.S." *Mother Jones* 3 Feb. 2010.

Lilley, Peter. *Dirty Dealing: The Untold Truth About Global Money Laundering, International Crime and Terrorism*. Philadelphia: Kogan Page, 2006.

Mathers, Chris. *Crime School Money Laundering: True Crime Meets the World of Business and Finance*. Buffalo, N.Y: Firefly, 2004.

Naím, Moisés. "The Money Washers." *Illicit: How Smugglers, Traffickers and Copycats are Hijacking the Global Economy*. New York: Doubleday, 2005. 131–156.

Naylor, R. T. "Treasure Island: Offshore Havens, Bank Secrecy, and Money Laundering." *Wages Of Crime: Black Markets, Illegal Finance, And The Underworld Economy*. New York: Cornell UP, 2005.

Reuter, Peter, and Edwin M. Truman. "Money Laundering: Methods and Markets (Chapter 3)." *Chasing Dirty Money: The Fight Against Money Laundering*. Washington, DC: Institute for International Economics, 2004.

Sharp, Heather. "Smuggling Fuels Gaza's Stalled Economy." *BBC News*. 31 Dec. 2009. Web.

Suter, Keith. "Money Laundering." *Contemporary Review* 280.1637 (2002).

Wechsler, William F. "Follow the Money." *Foreign Affairs* 80.4 (2001).

Wildlife

Bilger, Burkhard. "Swamp Things: Florida's Uninvited Predators." *The New Yorker* 20 Apr. 2009.

Christy, Bryan. "The Kingpin: An Expose of the World's Most Notorious Wildlife Dealer, His Special Government Friend, and His Ambitious New Plan." *National Geographic* Jan. 2010.

Crilly, Rob. "African Nations Clash Over Sales of Ivory." *The Christian Science Monitor*. 13 June 2007. Web.

Daniels, Alfonso. "Battling Siberia's Devastating Illegal Logging Trade." *BBC News*. 27 Nov. 2009. Web.

Davies, Ben. *Black Market: Inside the Endangered Species Trade in Asia*. San Rafael, CA: Earth Aware Eds., 2005.

Green, Alan. *Animal Underworld: Inside America's Black Market for Rare and Exotic Species*. New York: Public Affairs, 2006.

Jacobs, Andrew. "Tiger Farms in China Feed Thirst for Parts." *New York Times* 12 Feb. 2010.

Lovgren, Stefan. "Wildlife Smuggling Boom Plaguing L.A., Authorities Say." *National Geographic News*. 26 July 2007. Web

McMurray, Claudia Arne. "Wildlife Trafficking: U.S. Efforts to Tackle a Global Crisis." *Natural Resources & Environment* 23.3 (2009).

Naím, Moisés. "What Do Orangutans, Human Kidneys, Garbage, and Van Gogh Have in Common?" *Illicit How Smugglers, Traffickers and Copycats are Hijacking the Global Economy*. New York: Doubleday, 2005. 163–66.

Rufus, Anneli. "Endangered Species on the Grill: The Black Market in Illegal Meat Flourishes in the US." *AlterNet*. 15 Feb. 2010. Web.

Zimmerman, Mara. "The Black Market for Wildlife: Combating Transnational Organized Crime in the Illegal Wildlife Trade." *Vanderbilt Journal of Transnational Law* 36 (2003).

http://www.traffic.org/

High Tech

"Newly Nasty: Defences Against Cyberwarfare Are Still Rudimentary. That's Scary." *The Economist* 24 May 2007.

Barboza, David. "In China Underworld, Hacking for Fun and Profit." *The New York Times*. 1 Feb. 2010.

Brenner, Susan W. *Cyberthreats: The Emerging Fault Lines of the Nation State*. New York: Oxford UP, 2009.

Carr, Jeffrey. *Inside Cyber Warfare*. 2nd ed. Sebastopol, CA: O'Reilly Media, 2010.

Carvajal, Doreen. "The Evolution of CyberCrime, Inc." *The New York Times* 4 Apr. 2008.

Davies, Caroline. "Welcome to DarkMarket: Global One-stop Shop for Cybercrime and Banking Fraud." *The Guardian* [London] 14 Jan. 2010. Web.

Dixon, Robyn. "I Will Eat Your Dollars." *The Los Angeles Times* 20 Oct. 2005. Fallows, James.

Glenny, Misha. "Code Orange." *McMafia: A Journey Through the Criminal Underworld*. New York: Vintage, 2008. 264–284.

Jackman, Tom, and Jon Erickson, guests. "Hackers Have It Easy." *Talk of the Nation*. Host Neal Conan. NPR.org. 9 Sept. 2009. Web.

Ratliff, Evan. "The Zombie Hunters: On the Trail of Cyberextortionists." *The New Yorker* 10 Oct. 2005.

Wall, David S. *Cybercrime The Transformation of Crime in the Information Age*. Cambridge: Polity, 2007.

http://www.infowar-monitor.net/
http://www.wired.com/threatlevel/

Waste Disposal

Clayton, Jonathan. "Somalia's Secret Dumps of Toxic Waste Washed Ashore by Tsunami." *The Times* [London] 4 Mar. 2005.

Copeland, Brian R. "International Trade in Waste Products in the Presence of Illegal Disposal." *Economics of International Trade and the Environment.* Ed. Amitrajeet Arne Batabyal and Hamid Beladi. Boca Raton, Fla: Lewis, 2001.

Davis, Mike. "Slum Ecology." *Planet of Slums.* London: Verso, 2006. 121–150.

Granatstein, Solly, prod. "The Wasteland." *60 Minutes.* CBS. 30 Aug. 2009. Cbsnews.com. Web.

Johnson, Kimberly. "Toxic Dumping in Africa Elicits Calls for Better Controls." *National Geographic News.* 30 Oct. 2006.

Langewiesche, William. "Jungle Law." *Vanity Fair* May 2007.

Massari, Monica, and Paola Monzini. "Dirty Business in Italy: A Case-study of Illegal Trafficking in Hazardous Waste." *Global Crime* 6.3&4 (2004).

Naím, Moisés. "What Do Orangutans, Human Kidneys, Garbage, and Van Gogh Have in Common?" *Illicit: How Smugglers, Traffickers and Copycats are Hijacking the Global Economy.* New York: Doubleday, 2005. 167–169.

Quist-Arcton, Ofeibea. "Ivory Coast Tragedy Exposes Toxic Flow to Poor." *All Things Considered.* NPR. Npr.org, 20 Oct. 2006. Web.

Saviano, Roberto. "Land of Fires." *Gomorrah.* New York: Farrar, Straus and Giroux, 2007. 282–301.

White, Rob. "Toxic Cities: Globalizing the Problem of Waste." *Social Justice* 35.3 (2008). http://www.ban.org/

Medical

Cekola, James. "Outsourcing Drug Investigations to India." *Northwestern Journal of International Law and Business* 28.1 (2007).

Chopra, Anuj. "Harvesting Kidneys From the Poor for Rich Patients; The Thriving Black Market Trade in Human Organs." *U.S. News & World Report* 18 Feb. 2008.

Datta, Damayanti, and Sandeep Unnithan. "The Kidney Don's Crime File." *India Today* [New Delhi] 25 Feb. 2008.

Goodwin, Michele. *Black Markets The Supply and Demand of Body Parts.* New York: Cambridge UP, 2006.

Interlandi, Jeneen. "Not Just Urban Legend." *Newsweek* 19 Jan. 2009.

Lustgarten, Abrahm. "Drug Testing Goes Offshore." *Fortune* 8 Aug. 2005.

Moazam, Farhat, Riffat Moazam Zaman, and Aamir M. Jafarey. "Conversations with Kidney Vendors in Pakistan: An Ethnographic Study." *Hastings Center Report* 39.3 (2009).

Morgan, Nancy. "Human Organs: Another Chinese Import." *Human Events* 7 July 2000.

Naím, Moisés. "What Do Orangutans, Human Kidneys, Garbage, and Van Gogh Have in Common?" *Illicit: How Smugglers, Traffickers and Copycats are Hijacking the Global Economy.* New York: Doubleday, 2005. 157–63.

Rohter, Larry. "Tracking the Sale of a Kidney on a Path of Poverty and Hope." *The New York Times* 23 May 2004.

Rothman, David J. "The Shame of Medical Research." *The New York Review of Books* 30 Nov. 2000.

Rothman, Sheila M., and David J. Rothman. "The Organ Market." *The New York Review of Books* 23 Oct. 2003.

Scheper-Hughes, Nancy, and Loic J. D. Wacquant. *Commodifying Bodies*. London: Sage Publications, 2002.

Shimazono, Yosuke. "The State of the International Organ Trade." *Bulletin of the World Health Organization* 85.12 (2007).

Turner, Leigh. "Commercial Organ Transplantation in the Philippines." *Cambridge Quarterly of Healthcare Ethics* 18.2 (2009).

Trade in Counterfeit/Corrupt/Stolen Goods

Bate, Roger, and Rachel Nugent. "The Deadly World of Fake Drugs." *Foreign Policy* Sept. & Oct. 2008.

Browning, Frank, prod. "Stolen Fine Art: Organized Crime's New Commodity?" All Things Considered. *NPR.* 31 May 2007. Npr.org. Web.

Choate, Pat. *Hot Property: The Stealing of Ideas in an Age of Globalization*. New York: Knopf, 2005.

Faucon, Benoit. "No Cure for Fake Drugs: The Middle East Struggles with an Influx of Counterfeit Medicines." *The Wall Street Journal*. 16 Feb. 2010. Web.

MacFarquhar, Larissa. "Big Man." *The New Yorker* 19 Mar. 2007.

"Mind Games: Counterfeit Goods in China." *The Economist* 10 Nov. 2007.

Mueller, Tom. "Slippery Business: The Trade in Adulterated Olive Oil." *The New Yorker* 13 Aug. 2007.

Naím, Moisés. "The Global Trade in Stolen Ideas." *Illicit How Smugglers, Traffickers and Copycats are Hijacking the Global Economy*. New York: Doubleday, 2005. 109–130.

Samuels, David. "The Pink Panthers." *The New Yorker* 12 April 2010.

Thomas, Dana. "The Fake Trade." *Harper's Bazaar* Jan. 2008.

Von Lampe, Klaus. "The Cigarette Black Market in Germany and in the United Kingdom." *Journal of Financial Crime* 13.2 (2006).

Index

Page numbers in **bold** refer to illustrations.